PARSING TECHNIQUES
A Practical Guide

ELLIS HORWOOD SERIES IN COMPUTERS AND THEIR APPLICATIONS

Series Editor: IAN CHIVERS, Senior Analyst, The Computer Centre, King's College, London, and formerly Senior Programmer and Analyst, Imperial College of Science and Technology, University of London

Abramsky, S. & Hankin, C.J.	ABSTRACT INTERPRETATION OF DECLARATIVE LANGUAGES
Alexander, H.	FORMALLY-BASED TOOLS AND TECHNIQUES FOR HUMAN–COMPUTER DIALOGUES
Atherton, R.	STRUCTURED PROGRAMMING WITH BBC BASIC
Atherton, R.	STRUCTURED PROGRAMMING WITH COMAL
Baeza-Yates, R.A.	TEXT SEARCHING ALGORITHMS
Bailey, R.	FUNCTIONAL PROGRAMMING WITH HOPE
Barrett, R., Ramsay, A. & Sloman, A.	POP-11
Berztiss, A.	PROGRAMMING WITH GENERATORS
Bharath, R.	COMPUTERS AND GRAPH THEORY
Bishop, P.	FIFTH GENERATION COMPUTERS
Bullinger, H.-J. & Gunzenhauser, H.	SOFTWARE ERGONOMICS
Burns, A.	NEW INFORMATION TECHNOLOGY
Carberry, J.C.	COBOL
Carlini, U. & Villano, U.	TRANSPUTERS AND PARALLEL ARCHITECTURES
Chivers, I.D.	AN INTRODUCTION TO STANDARD PASCAL
Chivers, I.D.	MODULA 2
Chivers, I.D. & Sleighthome, J.	INTERACTIVE FORTRAN 77
Clark, M.W.	PC-PORTABLE FORTRAN
Clark, M.W.	TEX
Cockshott, W. P.	A COMPILER WRITER'S TOOLBOX: How to Implement Interactive Compilers for PCs with Turbo Pascal
Cockshott, W. P.	PS-ALGOL IMPLEMENTATIONS: Applications in Persistent Object-Oriented Programming
Colomb, R.	IMPLEMENTING PERSISTENT PROLOG
Cope, T.	COMPUTING USING BASIC
Curth, M.A. & Edelmann, H.	APL
Dahlstrand, I.	SOFTWARE PORTABILITY AND STANDARDS
Dongarra, J., Duff, I., Gaffney, P., & McKee, S.	VECTOR AND PARALLEL COMPUTING
Dunne, P.E.	COMPUTABILITY THEORY
Eastlake, J.J.	A STRUCTURED APPROACH TO COMPUTER STRATEGY
Eisenbach, S.	FUNCTIONAL PROGRAMMING
Ellis, D.	MEDICAL COMPUTING AND APPLICATIONS
Ennals, J.R.	ARTIFICIAL INTELLIGENCE
Ennals, J.R.	BEGINNING MICRO-PROLOG
Ennals, J.R., et al.	INFORMATION TECHNOLOGY AND EDUCATION
Filipič, B.	PROLOG USER'S HANDBOOK
Ford, N.	COMPUTER PROGRAMMING LANGUAGES
Grill, E.	RELATIONAL DATABASES
Grune, D. & Jacobs, C.J.H.	PARSING TECHNIQUES: A Practical Guide
Guariso, G. & Werthner, H.	ENVIRONMENTAL DECISION SUPPORT SYSTEMS
Harland, D.M.	CONCURRENCY AND PROGRAMMING LANGUAGES
Harland, D.M.	POLYMORPHIC PROGRAMMING LANGUAGES
Harland, D.M.	REKURSIV
Harris, D.J.	DEVELOPING DEDICATED DBASE SYSTEMS
Henshall, J. & Shaw, S.	OSI EXPLAINED, 2nd Edition
Hepburn, P.H.	FURTHER PROGRAMMING IN PROLOG
Hepburn, P.H.	PROGRAMMING IN MICRO-PROLOG MADE SIMPLE
Hill, I.D. & Meek, B.L.	PROGRAMMING LANGUAGE STANDARDISATION
Hirschheim, R., Smithson, S. & Whitehouse, D.	MICROCOMPUTERS AND THE HUMANITIES: Survey and Recommendations
Hutchins, W.J.	MACHINE TRANSLATION
Hutchison, D.	FUNDAMENTALS OF COMPUTER LOGIC
Hutchison, D. & Silvester, P.	COMPUTER LOGIC
Koopman, P.	STACK COMPUTERS
Kenning, M.-M. & Kenning, M.J.	COMPUTERS AND LANGUAGE LEARNING: Current Theory and Practice
Koskimies, K. & Paaki, J.	AUTOMATING LANGUAGE IMPLEMENTATION
Koster, C.H.A.	TOP-DOWN PROGRAMMING WITH ELAN
Last, R.	ARTIFICIAL INTELLIGENCE TECHNIQUES IN LANGUAGE LEARNING
Lester, C.	A PRACTICAL APPROACH TO DATA STRUCTURES
Lucas, R.	DATABASE APPLICATIONS USING PROLOG
Lucas, A.	DESKTOP PUBLISHING
Maddix, F.	HUMAN–COMPUTER INTERACTION: Theory and Practice
Maddix, F. & Morgan, G.	SYSTEMS SOFTWARE
Matthews, J.L.	FORTH
Millington, D.	SYSTEMS ANALYSIS AND DESIGN FOR COMPUTER APPLICATIONS
Moseley, L.G., Sharp, J.A. & Salenieks, P.	PASCAL IN PRACTICE
Moylan, P.	ASSEMBLY LANGUAGE FOR ENGINEERS
Narayanan, A. & Sharkey, N.E.	AN INTRODUCTION TO LISP
Parrington, N. & Roper, M.	UNDERSTANDING SOFTWARE TESTING
Paterson, A.	OFFICE SYSTEMS
Phillips, C. & Cornelius, B.J.	COMPUTATIONAL NUMERICAL METHODS

Series continued at back of book

PARSING TECHNIQUES
A Practical Guide

DICK GRUNE Ph.D.
CERIEL J. H. JACOBS M.Sc.
both of Department of Mathematics and Computer Science
Vrije Universeit, Amsterdam, The Netherlands

ELLIS HORWOOD
NEW YORK   LONDON   TORONTO   SYDNEY   TOKYO   SINGAPORE

First published in 1990 by
ELLIS HORWOOD LIMITED
Market Cross House, Cooper Street,
Chichester, West Sussex, PO19 1EB, England

A division of
Simon & Schuster International Group

Printed and bound in Great Britain
by Hartnolls, Bodmin, Cornwall

British Library Cataloguing in Publication Data

Grune, Dick
Parsing techniques: a practical guide. —
(Ellis Horwood series in computers and their
applications).
1. Natural language. Parsing
I. Title. II. Jacobs, Cereil J. H.
415
ISBN 0–13–651431–6

Library of Congress Cataloging-in-Publication Data available

Table of contents

Preface 11

1   **Introduction** 13
    1.1   Parsing as a craft 14
    1.2   The approach used 14
    1.3   Outline of the contents 15
    1.4   The annotated bibliography 15

2   **Grammars as a generating device** 16
    2.1   Languages as infinite sets 16
       2.1.1   Language 16
       2.1.2   Grammars 17
       2.1.3   Problems 18
       2.1.4   Describing a language through a finite recipe 22
    2.2   Formal grammars 24
       2.2.1   Generating sentences from a formal grammar 25
       2.2.2   The expressive power of formal grammars 27
    2.3   The Chomsky hierarchy of grammars and languages 28
       2.3.1   Type 1 grammars 28
       2.3.2   Type 2 grammars 32
       2.3.3   Type 3 grammars 37
       2.3.4   Type 4 grammars 40
    2.4   VW grammars 41
       2.4.1   The human inadequacy of CS and PS grammars 41
       2.4.2   VW grammars 42
       2.4.3   Infinite symbol sets 45
       2.4.4   BNF notation for VW grammars 45
       2.4.5   Affix grammars 46
    2.5   Actually generating sentences from a grammar 47
       2.5.1   The general case 47
       2.5.2   The CF case 49
    2.6   To shrink or not to shrink 51

2.7   A characterization of the limitations of CF and FS grammars 54
    2.7.1   The *uvwxy* theorem 54
    2.7.2   The *uvw* theorem 56
2.8   Hygiene in grammars 56
    2.8.1   Undefined non-terminals 56
    2.8.2   Unused non-terminals 57
    2.8.3   Non-productive non-terminals 57
    2.8.4   Loops 57
2.9   The semantic connection 57
    2.9.1   Attribute grammars 58
    2.9.2   Transduction grammars 59
2.10   A metaphorical comparison of grammar types 60

3   Introduction to parsing 62
3.1   Various kinds of ambiguity 62
3.2   Linearization of the parse tree 64
3.3   Two ways to parse a sentence 64
    3.3.1   Top-down parsing 65
    3.3.2   Bottom-up parsing 66
    3.3.3   Applicability 67
3.4   Non-deterministic automata 68
    3.4.1   Constructing the NDA 69
    3.4.2   Constructing the control mechanism 69
3.5   Recognition and parsing for Type 0 to Type 4 grammars 70
    3.5.1   Time requirements 70
    3.5.2   Type 0 and Type 1 grammars 70
    3.5.3   Type 2 grammars 72
    3.5.4   Type 3 grammars 73
    3.5.5   Type 4 grammars 74
3.6   An overview of parsing methods 74
    3.6.1   Directionality 74
    3.6.2   Search techniques 75
    3.6.3   General directional methods 76
    3.6.4   Linear methods 76
    3.6.5   Linear top-down and bottom-up methods 78
    3.6.6   Almost deterministic methods 79
    3.6.7   Left-corner parsing 79
    3.6.8   Conclusion 79

4   General non-directional methods 81
4.1   Unger's parsing method 82
    4.1.1   Unger's method without ε-rules or loops 82
    4.1.2   Unger's method with ε-rules 85
4.2   The CYK parsing method 88
    4.2.1   CYK recognition with general CF grammars 89
    4.2.2   CYK recognition with a grammar in Chomsky Normal Form 92
    4.2.3   Transforming a CF grammar into Chomsky Normal Form 94

4.2.4   The example revisited 99
4.2.5   CYK parsing with Chomsky Normal Form 99
4.2.6   Undoing the effect of the CNF transformation 101
4.2.7   A short retrospective of CYK 104
4.2.8   Chart parsing 105

5   **Regular grammars and finite-state automata** 106
5.1   Applications of regular grammars 106
5.1.1   CF parsing 106
5.1.2   Systems with finite memory 107
5.1.3   Pattern searching 108
5.2   Producing from a regular grammar 109
5.3   Parsing with a regular grammar 110
5.3.1   Replacing sets by states 111
5.3.2   Non-standard notation 113
5.3.3   DFA's from regular expressions 114
5.3.4   Fast text search using finite-state automata 116

6   **General directional top-down methods** 119
6.1   Imitating left-most productions 119
6.2   The pushdown automaton 121
6.3   Breadth-first top-down parsing 125
6.3.1   An example 125
6.3.2   A counterexample: left-recursion 127
6.4   Eliminating left-recursion 128
6.5   Depth-first (backtracking) parsers 130
6.6   Recursive descent 131
6.6.1   A naive approach 133
6.6.2   Exhaustive backtracking recursive descent 136
6.7   Definite Clause grammars 139

7   **General bottom-up parsing** 144
7.1   Parsing by searching 146
7.1.1   Depth-first (backtracking) parsing 146
7.1.2   Breadth-first (on-line) parsing 147
7.1.3   A combined representation 148
7.1.4   A slightly more realistic example 148
7.2   Top-down restricted breadth-first bottom-up parsing 149
7.2.1   The Earley parser without look-ahead 149
7.2.2   The relation between the Earley and CYK algorithms 155
7.2.3   Ambiguous sentences 156
7.2.4   Handling ε-rules 157
7.2.5   Prediction look-ahead 159
7.2.6   Reduction look-ahead 161

8   **Deterministic top-down methods** 164
8.1   Replacing search by table look-up 165

8.2   LL(1) grammars 168
        8.2.1   LL(1) grammars without ε-rules 168
        8.2.2   LL(1) grammars with ε-rules 170
        8.2.3   LL(1) versus strong-LL(1) 174
        8.2.4   Full LL(1) parsing 175
        8.2.5   Solving LL(1) conflicts 178
        8.2.6   LL(1) and recursive descent 180
8.3   LL(k) grammars 181
8.4   Extended LL(1) grammars 183

9   **Deterministic bottom-up parsing** 184
9.1   Simple handle-isolating techniques 185
        9.1.1   Fully parenthesized expressions 186
9.2   Precedence parsing 187
        9.2.1   Constructing the operator-precedence table 190
        9.2.2   Precedence functions 192
        9.2.3   Simple-precedence parsing 194
        9.2.4   Weak-precedence parsing 196
        9.2.5   Extended precedence and mixed-strategy precedence 197
        9.2.6   Actually finding the correct right-hand side 198
9.3   Bounded-context parsing 198
        9.3.1   Floyd productions 199
9.4   LR methods 200
        9.4.1   LR(0) 201
        9.4.2   LR(0) grammars 205
9.5   LR(1) 205
        9.5.1   LR(1) with ε-rules 210
        9.5.2   Some properties of LR(k) parsing 211
9.6   LALR(1) parsing 213
        9.6.1   Constructing the LALR(1) parsing tables 214
        9.6.2   LALR(1) with ε-rules 216
        9.6.3   Identifying LALR(1) conflicts 217
        9.6.4   SLR(1) 218
        9.6.5   Conflict resolvers 219
9.7   Further developments of LR methods 219
        9.7.1   Elimination of unit rules 220
        9.7.2   Regular right part grammars 220
        9.7.3   Improved LALR(1) table construction 220
        9.7.4   Incremental parsing 221
        9.7.5   Incremental parser generation 221
        9.7.6   LR-regular 221
        9.7.7   Recursive ascent 221
9.8   Tomita's parser 222
        9.8.1   Stack duplication 223
        9.8.2   Combining equal states 223
        9.8.3   Combining equal stack prefixes 226
        9.8.4   Discussion 226

9.9   Non-canonical parsers 227
9.10   LR(k) as an ambiguity test 228

10   Error handling 229
10.1   Detection versus recovery versus correction 229
10.2   Parsing techniques and error detection 230
         10.2.1 Error detection in non-directional parsing methods 230
         10.2.2 Error detection in finite-state automata 231
         10.2.3 Error detection in general directional top-down parsers 231
         10.2.4 Error detection in general directional bottom-up parsers 232
         10.2.5 Error detection in deterministic top-down parsers 232
         10.2.6 Error detection in deterministic bottom-up parsers 232
10.3   Recovering from errors 233
10.4   Global error handling 233
10.5   Ad hoc methods 237
         10.5.1 Error productions 237
         10.5.2 Empty table slots 237
         10.5.3 Error tokens 238
10.6   Regional error handling 238
         10.6.1 Backward/forward move 238
10.7   Local error handling 240
         10.7.1 Panic mode 240
         10.7.2 FOLLOW set error recovery 241
         10.7.3 Acceptable-sets derived from continuations 241
         10.7.4 Insertion-only error correction 244
         10.7.5 Locally least-cost error recovery 246
10.8   Suffix parsing 246

11   Comparative survey 249
11.1   Considerations 249
11.2   General parsers 250
         11.2.1 Unger 250
         11.2.2 Earley 250
         11.2.3 Tomita 250
         11.2.4 Notes 251
11.3   Linear-time parsers 251
         11.3.1 Requirements 251
         11.3.2 Strong-LL(1) versus LALR(1) 251
         11.3.3 Table size 252

12   A simple general context-free parser 253
12.1   Principles of the parser 253
12.2   The program 258
         12.2.1 Handling left recursion 260
12.3   Parsing in polynomial time 260

13   Annotated bibliography 264

13.1 Miscellaneous literature 265
13.2 Unrestricted PS and CS grammars 269
13.3 Van Wijngaarden grammars and affix grammars 271
13.4 General context-free parsers 273
13.5 LL parsing 279
13.6 LR parsing 282
13.7 Left-corner parsing 292
13.8 Precedence and bounded-context parsing 294
13.9 Finite-state automata 299
13.10 Natural language handling 300
13.11 Error handling 302
13.12 Transformations on grammars 310
13.13 General books on parsing 310
13.14 Some books on computer science 312

Author index 313

Index 317

Preface

Parsing (syntactic analysis) is one of the best understood branches of computer science. Parsers are already being used extensively in a number of disciplines: in computer science (for compiler construction, database interfaces, self-describing data-bases, artificial intelligence), in linguistics (for text analysis, corpora analysis, machine translation, textual analysis of biblical texts), in document preparation and conversion, in typesetting chemical formulae and in chromosome recognition, to name a few; they can be used (and perhaps are) in a far larger number of disciplines. It is therefore surprising that there is no book which collects the knowledge about parsing and explains it to the non-specialist. Part of the reason may be that parsing has a name for being "difficult". In discussing the Amsterdam Compiler Kit and in teaching compiler construction, it has, however, been our experience that seemingly difficult parsing techniques can be explained in simple terms, given the right approach. The present book is the result of these considerations.

This book does not address a strictly uniform audience. On the contrary, while writing this book, we have consistently tried to imagine giving a course on the subject to a diffuse mixture of students and faculty members of assorted faculties, sophisticated laymen, the avid readers of the science supplement of the large newspapers, etc. Such a course was never given; a diverse audience like that would be too uncoordinated to convene at regular intervals, which is why we wrote this book, to be read, studied, perused or consulted wherever or whenever desired.

Addressing such a varied audience has its own difficulties (and rewards). Although no explicit math was used, it could not be avoided that an amount of mathematical thinking should pervade this book. Technical terms pertaining to parsing have of course been explained in the book, but sometimes a term on the fringe of the subject has been used without definition. Any reader who has ever attended a lecture on a non-familiar subject knows the phenomenon. He skips the term, assumes it refers to something reasonable and hopes it will not recur too often. And then there will be passages where the reader will think we are elaborating the obvious (this paragraph may be one such place). The reader may find solace in the fact that he does not have to doodle his time away or stare out of the window until the lecturer progresses.

On the positive side, and that is the main purpose of this enterprise, we hope that by means of a book with this approach we can reach those who were dimly aware of the existence and perhaps of the usefulness of parsing but who thought it would forever be hidden behind phrases like:

$$\text{Let } \mathfrak{P} \text{ be a mapping } V_N \xrightarrow{\mathfrak{P}} 2^{(V_N \cup V_T)^*} \text{ and } \mathfrak{H} \text{ a homomorphism ...}$$

No knowledge of any particular programming language is required. The book contains two or three programs in Pascal, which serve as actualizations only and play a minor role in the explanation. What is required, though, is an understanding of algorithmic thinking, especially of recursion. Books like *Learning to program* by Howard Johnston (Prentice-Hall, 1985) or *Programming from first principles* by Richard Bornat (Prentice-Hall 1987) provide an adequate background (but supply more detail than required). Pascal was chosen because it is about the only programming language more or less widely available outside computer science environments.

The book features an extensive annotated bibliography. The user of the bibliography is expected to be more than casually interested in parsing and to possess already a reasonable knowledge of it, either through this book or otherwise. The bibliography as a list serves to open up the more accessible part of the literature on the subject to the reader; the annotations are in terse technical prose and we hope they will be useful as stepping stones to reading the actual articles.

On the subject of applications of parsers, this book is vague. Although we suggest a number of applications in Chapter 1, we lack the expertise to supply details. It is obvious that musical compositions possess a structure which can largely be described by a grammar and thus is amenable to parsing, but we shall have to leave it to the musicologists to implement the idea. It was less obvious to us that behaviour at corporate meetings proceeds according to a grammar, but we are told that this is so and that it is a subject of socio-psychological research.

Acknowledgements

We thank the people who helped us in writing this book. Marion de Krieger has retrieved innumerable books and copies of journal articles for us and without her effort the annotated bibliography would be much further from completeness. Ed Keizer has patiently restored peace between us and the pic|tbl|eqn|psfig|troff pipeline, on the many occasions when we abused, overloaded or just plainly misunderstood the latter. Leo van Moergestel has made the hardware do things for us that it would not do for the uninitiated. We also thank Erik Baalbergen and Frans Kaashoek for their critical remarks and contributions. The rose at the end of Chapter 2 is by Arwen Grune. Ilana and Lily Grune typed parts of the text on various occasions.

We thank the Faculteit Wiskunde en Informatica of the Vrije Universiteit for the use of the equipment.

In a wider sense, we extend our thanks to the hundreds of authors who have been so kind as to invent scores of clever and elegant algorithms and techniques for us to exhibit. We hope we have named them all in our bibliography.

Dick Grune
Ceriel J.H. Jacobs
Amstelveen/Amsterdam, July 1990

1

Introduction

Parsing is the process of structuring a linear representation in accordance with a given grammar. This definition has been kept abstract on purpose, to allow as wide an interpretation as possible. The "linear representation" may be a sentence, a computer program, a knitting pattern, a sequence of geological strata, a piece of music, actions in ritual behaviour, in short any linear sequence in which the preceding elements in some way restrict[†] the next element. For some of the examples the grammar is well-known, for some it is an object of research and for some our notion of a grammar is only just beginning to take shape.

For each grammar, there are generally an infinite number of linear representations ("sentences") that can be structured with it. That is, a finite-size grammar can supply structure to an infinite number of sentences. This is the main strength of the grammar paradigm and indeed the main source of the importance of grammars: they summarize succinctly the structure of an infinite number of objects of a certain class.

There are several reasons to perform this structuring process called parsing. One reason derives from the fact that the obtained structure helps us to process the object further. When we know that a certain segment of a sentence in German is the subject, that information helps in translating the sentence. Once the structure of a document has been brought to the surface, it can be converted more easily.

A second is related to the fact that the grammar in a sense represents our understanding of the observed sentences: the better a grammar we can give for the movements of bees, the deeper our understanding of them is.

A third lies in the completion of missing information that parsers, and especially error-repairing parsers, can provide. Given a reasonable grammar of the language, an error-repairing parser can suggest possible word classes for missing or unknown words on clay tablets.

[†] If there is no restriction, the sequence still has a grammar, but this grammar is trivial and uninformative.

1.1 PARSING AS A CRAFT

Parsing is no longer an arcane art; it has not been so since the early 70's when Aho, Ullman, Knuth and many others put various parsing techniques solidly on their theoretical feet. It need not be a mathematical discipline either; the inner workings of a parser can be visualized, understood and modified to fit the application, with not much more than cutting and pasting strings.

There is a considerable difference between a mathematician's view of the world and a computer-scientist's. To a mathematician all structures are static: they have always been and will always be; the only time dependence is that we just haven't discovered them all yet. The computer scientist is concerned with (and fascinated by) the continuous creation, combination, separation and destruction of structures: time is of the essence. In the hands of a mathematician, the Peano axioms create the integers without reference to time, but if a computer scientist uses them to implement integer addition, he finds they describe a very slow process, which is why he will be looking for a more efficient approach. In this respect the computer scientist has more in common with the physicist and the chemist; like these, he cannot do without a solid basis in several branches of applied mathematics, but, like these, he is willing (and often virtually obliged) to take on faith certain theorems handed to him by the mathematician. Without the rigor of mathematics all science would collapse, but not all inhabitants of a building need to know all the spars and girders that keep it upright. Factoring off certain detailed knowledge to specialists reduces the intellectual complexity of a task, which is one of the things computer science is about.

This is the vein in which this book is written: parsing for anybody who has parsing to do: the compiler writer, the linguist, the data-base interface writer, the geologist or musicologist who want to test grammatical descriptions of their respective objects of interest, and so on. We require a good ability to visualize, some programming experience and the willingness and patience to follow non-trivial examples; there is nothing better for understanding a kangaroo than seeing it jump. We treat, of course, the popular parsing techniques, but we will not shun some weird techniques that look as if they are of theoretical interest only: they often offer new insights and a reader might find an application for them.

1.2 THE APPROACH USED

This book addresses the reader at at least three different levels. The interested non-computer scientist can read the book as "the story of grammars and parsing"; he or she can skip the detailed explanations of the algorithms: each algorithm is first explained in general terms. The computer scientist will find much technical detail on a wide array of algorithms. To the expert we offer a systematic bibliography of over 400 entries, which is intended to cover all articles on parsing that have appeared in the readily available journals. Each entry is annotated, providing enough material for the reader to decide if the referred article is worth reading.

No ready-to-run algorithms have been given, except for the general context-free parser of Chapter 12. The formulation of a parsing algorithm with sufficient precision to enable a programmer to implement and run it without problems requires a considerable supporting mechanism that would be out of place in this book and in our experience does little to increase one's understanding of the process involved. The popular methods are given in algorithmic form in most books on compiler construction. The less widely used methods are almost always described in detail in the original publication, for which see Chapter 13.

1.3 OUTLINE OF THE CONTENTS

Since parsing is concerned with sentences and grammars and since grammars are themselves fairly complicated objects, ample attention is paid to them in Chapter 2. Chapter 3 discusses the principles behind parsing and gives a classification of parsing methods. In summary, parsing methods can be classified as top-down or bottom-up and as directional or non-directional; the directional methods can be further distinguished into deterministic and non-deterministic. This scheme dictates the contents of the next few chapters. In Chapter 4 we treat non-directional methods, including Unger and CYK. Chapter 5 forms an intermezzo with the treatment of finite-state automata, which are needed in the subsequent chapters. Chapters 5 through 9 are concerned with directional methods. Chapter 6 covers non-deterministic directional top-down parsers (recursive descent, Definite Clause Grammars), Chapter 7 non-deterministic directional bottom-up parsers (Earley). Deterministic methods are treated in Chapters 8 (top-down: LL in various forms) and 9 (bottom-up: LR, etc.). A combined deterministic/non-deterministic method (Tomita) is also described in Chapter 9. That completes the parsing methods per se.

Error handling for a selected number of methods is treated in Chapter 10. The comparative survey of parsing methods in Chapter 11 summarizes the properties of the popular and some less popular methods. Chapter 12 contains the full code in Pascal for a parser that will work for any context-free grammar, to lower the threshold for experimenting.

1.4 THE ANNOTATED BIBLIOGRAPHY

The annotated bibliography is presented in Chapter 13 and is an easily accessible supplement of the main body of the book. Rather than listing all publications in alphabetic order, it is divided into fourteen named sections, each concerned with a particular aspect of parsing; inside the sections, the publications are listed chronologically. An author index replaces the usual alphabetic list. The section name plus year of publication, placed in brackets, are used in the text to refer to an author's work. For instance, the annotated reference to Earley's publication of the Earley parser [CF 1970] can be found in the section CF at the position of the papers of 1970. Since the name of the first author is printed in bold letters, the actual reference is then easily located.

2

Grammars as a generating device

2.1 LANGUAGES AS INFINITE SETS

In computer science as in everyday parlance, a "grammar" serves to "describe" a "language". If taken on face value, this correspondence, however, is misleading, since the computer scientist and the naive speaker mean slightly different things by the three terms. To establish our terminology and to demarcate the universe of discourse, we shall examine the above terms, starting with the last one.

2.1.1 Language

To the larger part of mankind, language is first and foremost a means of communication, to be used almost unconsciously, certainly so in the heat of a debate. Communication is brought about by sending messages, through air vibrations or through written symbols. Upon a closer look the language messages ("utterances") fall apart into sentences, which are composed of words, which in turn consist of symbol sequences when written. Languages can differ on all these three levels of composition. The script can be slightly different, as between English and Irish, or very different, as between English and Chinese. Words tend to differ greatly and even in closely related languages people call *un cheval* or *ein Pferd*, that which is known to others as *a horse*. Differences in sentence structure are often underestimated; even the closely related Dutch often has an almost Shakespearean word order: "*Ik geloof je niet*", "*I believe you not*", and unrelated languages readily come up with constructions like the Hungarian "*Pénzem van*", "*Money-my is*", where the English say "*I have money*".

The computer scientist takes a very abstracted view of all this. Yes, a language has sentences, and these sentences possess structure; whether they communicate something or not is not his concern, but information may possibly be derived from their structure and then it is quite all right to call that information the *meaning* of the sentence. And yes, sentences consist of words, which he calls *tokens*, each possibly carrying a piece of information, which is its contribution to the meaning of the whole sentence. But no, words cannot be broken down any further. The computer scientist is not worried by this. With his love of telescoping solutions and multi-level techniques, he blithely claims that if words turn out to have structure after all, they are sentences in a different language, of which the letters are the tokens.

The practitioner of formal linguistics, henceforth called the formal-linguist (to distinguish him from the "formal linguist", the specification of whom is left to the imagination of the reader) again takes an abstracted view of this. A language is a "set" of sentences, and each sentence is a "sequence" of "symbols"; that is all there is: no meaning, no structure, either a sentence belongs to the language or it does not. The only property of a symbol is that it has an identity; in any language there are a certain number of different symbols, the *alphabet*, and that number must be finite. Just for convenience we write these symbols as $a,b,c \cdots$, but $\mathbb{C}, \twoheadrightarrow, \square, \cdots$ would do equally well, as long as there are enough symbols. The word *sequence* means that the symbols in each sentence are in a fixed order and we should not shuffle them. The word *set* means an unordered collection with all the duplicates removed; a set can be written down by writing the objects in it, surrounded by curly brackets. All this means that to the formal-linguist the following is a language: $\{a, b, ab, ba\}$, and so is $\{a, aa, aaa, aaaa, \cdots\}$ although the latter has notational problems that will be solved later. In accordance with the correspondence that the computer scientist sees between sentence/word and word/letter, the formal-linguist also calls a sentence a *word* and he says that "the word *ab* is in the language $\{a, b, ab, ba\}$".

Now let's consider the implications of these compact but powerful ideas.

To the computer scientist, a language is a probably infinitely large set of sentences, each composed of tokens in such a way that it has structure; the tokens and the structure cooperate to describe the semantics of the sentence, its "meaning" if you will. Both the structure and the semantics are new, that is, were not present in the formal model, and it is his responsibility to provide and manipulate them both. To a computer scientist 3+4*5 is a sentence in the language of "arithmetics on single digits" ("single digits" to avoid having an infinite number of symbols), its structure can be shown, for instance, by inserting parentheses: (3+(4*5)) and its semantics is probably 23.

To the linguist, whose view of languages, it has to be conceded, is much more normal than that of either of the above, a language is an infinite set of possibly interrelated sentences. Each sentence consists, in a structured fashion, of words which have a meaning in the real world. Structure and words together give the sentence a meaning, which it communicates. Words, again, possess structure and are composed of letters; the letters cooperate with some of the structure to give a meaning to the word. The heavy emphasis on semantics, the relation with the real world and the integration of the two levels sentence/word and word/letters are the domain of the linguist. "*The circle spins furiously*" is a sentence, "*The circle sleeps red*" is nonsense.

The formal-linguist holds his views of language because he wants to study the fundamental properties of languages in their naked beauty; the computer scientist holds his because he wants a clear, well-understood and unambiguous means of describing objects in the computer and of communication with the computer, a most exacting communication partner, quite unlike a human; and the linguist holds his view of language because it gives him a formal tight grip on a seemingly chaotic and perhaps infinitely complex object: natural language.

2.1.2 Grammars

Everyone who has studied a foreign language knows that a grammar is a book of rules and examples which describes and teaches the language. Good grammars make a careful distinction between the sentence/word level, which they often call *syntax* or *syntaxis*, and the word/letter level, which they call *grammar*. Syntax contains rules like "*pour que* is followed by the subjunctive, but *parce que* is not"; grammar contains rules like "the plural of an English noun is formed by appending an -*s*, except when the word ends in -*s*, -*sh*, -*o*, -*ch* or -*x*, in which case -*es* is appended, or when the word has an irregular plural."

We skip the computer scientist's view of a grammar for the moment and proceed immediately to the formal-linguist's one. His view is at the same time very abstract and quite similar to the above: a grammar is any exact, finite-size, complete description of the language, i.e., of the set of sentences. This is in fact the school grammar, with the fuzziness removed. Although it will be clear that this definition has full generality, it turns out that it is too general, and therefore relatively powerless. It includes descriptions like "the set of sentences that could have been written by Chaucer"; platonically speaking this defines a set, but we have no way of creating this set or testing whether a given sentence belongs to this language. This particular example, with its "could have been" does not worry the formal-linguist, but there are examples closer to his home that do. "The longest block of consecutive sevens in the decimal expansion of π" describes a language that has at most one word in it (and then that word will consist of sevens only), and as a definition it is exact, finite-size and complete. One bad thing with it, however, is that one cannot find this word; suppose one finds a block of one hundred sevens after billions and billions of digits, there is always a chance that further on there is an even longer block. And another bad thing is that one cannot even know if such a longest block exists at all. It is quite possible that, as one proceeds further and further up the decimal expansion of π, one would find longer and longer stretches of sevens, probably separated by ever-increasing gaps. A comprehensive theory of the decimal expansion of π might answer these questions, but no such theory exists.

For these and other reasons, the formal-linguists have abandoned their static, platonic view of a grammar for a more constructive one, that of the generative grammar: a *generative grammar* is an exact, fixed-size recipe for constructing the sentences in the language. This means that, following the recipe, it must be possible to construct each sentence of the language (in a finite number of actions) and no others. This does not mean that, given a sentence, the recipe tells us *how* to construct that particular sentence, only that it is possible to do so. Such recipes can have several forms, of which some are more convenient than others.

The computer scientist essentially subscribes to the same view, often with the additional requirement that the recipe should imply how a sentence can be constructed.

2.1.3 Problems
The above definition of a language as a possibly infinite set of sequences of symbols, and of a grammar as a finite recipe to generate these sentences, immediately gives rise to two embarrassing questions:
1.   How can finite recipes generate enough infinite sets of sentences?
2.   If a sentence is just a sequence and has no structure and if the meaning of a sentence derives, among other things, from its structure, how can we assess the meaning of a sentence?

These questions have long and complicated answers, but they do have answers. We shall first pay some attention to the first question and then devote the main body of this book to the second.

2.1.3.1 Infinite sets from finite descriptions
In fact there is nothing wrong with getting a single infinite set from a single finite description: "the set of all positive integers" is a very finite-size description of a definitely infinite-size set. Still, there is something disquieting about the idea, so we shall rephrase our question: "Can all languages be described by finite descriptions?". As the lead-up already suggests, the answer is "No", but the proof is far from trivial. It is, however, very interesting and famous, and it would be a shame not to present at least an outline of it here.

2.1.3.2 Descriptions can be enumerated
The proof is based on two observations and a trick. The first observation is that descriptions can be listed and given a number. This is done as follows. First, take all descriptions of size one, that is, those of only one letter long, and sort them alphabetically. This is the beginning of our list. Depending on what, exactly, we accept as a description, there may be zero descriptions of size one, or 27 (all letters + space), or 128 (all ASCII characters) or some such; this is immaterial to the discussion which follows.

Second, we take all descriptions of size two, sort them alphabetically to give the second chunk on the list, and so on for lengths 3, 4 and further. This assigns a position on the list to each and every description. Our description "the set of all positive integers", for instance, is of size 32, not counting the quotation marks. To find its position on the list, we have to calculate how many descriptions there are with less than 32 characters, say L. We then have to generate all descriptions of size 32, sort them and determine the position of our description in it, say P, and add the two numbers L and P. This will, of course, give a huge number[†] but it does ensure that the description is on the list, in a well-defined position; see Figure 2.1.

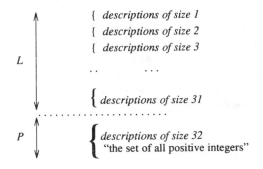

Figure 2.1 List of all descriptions of length 32 or less

Two things should be pointed out here. The first is that just listing all descriptions alphabetically, without reference to their lengths, would not do: there are already infinitely many descriptions starting with an "a" and no description starting with a higher

---

[†] Some (computer-assisted) calculations tell us that, under the ASCII-128 assumption, the number is 248 17168 89636 37891 49073 14874 06454 89259 38844 52556 26245 57755 89193 30291, or roughly $2.5*10^{67}$.

letter could get a number on the list. The second is that there is no need to actually do all this. It is just a thought experiment that allows us to examine and draw conclusion about the behaviour of a system in a situation which we cannot possibly examine physically.

Also, there will be many nonsensical descriptions on the list; it will turn out that this is immaterial to the argument. The important thing is that all meaningful descriptions are on the list, and the above argument ensures that.

2.1.3.3 Languages are infinite bit-strings

We know that words (sentences) in a language are composed of a finite set of symbols; this set is called quite reasonably *the alphabet*. We will assume that the symbols in the alphabet are ordered. Then the words in the language can be ordered too. We shall indicate the alphabet by Σ.

Now the simplest language that uses alphabet Σ is that which consists of all words that can be made by combining letters from the alphabet. For the alphabet $\Sigma=\{a, b\}$ we get the language { , a, b, aa, ab, ba, bb, aaa, $\cdots$ }. We shall call this language Σ^*, for reasons to be explained later; for the moment it is just a name.

The set notation Σ^* above started with " { , a,", a remarkable construction; the first word in the language is the *empty word*, the word consisting of zero *a*'s and zero *b*'s. There is no reason to exclude it, but, if written down, it may easily get lost, so we shall write it as ε (epsilon), regardless of the alphabet. So, $\Sigma^*= \{\varepsilon, a, b, aa, ab, ba, bb, aaa, \cdots\}$. In some natural languages, forms of the present tense of the verb "to be" are the empty word, giving rise to sentences of the form "I student"; Russian and Hebrew are examples of this.

Since the symbols in the alphabet Σ are ordered, we can list the words in the language Σ^*, using the same technique as in the previous section: First all words of size zero, sorted; then all words of size one, sorted; and so on. This is actually the order already used in our set notation for Σ^*.

The language Σ^* has the interesting property that all languages using alphabet Σ are subsets of it. That means that, given another possibly less trivial language over Σ, called L, we can go through the list of words in Σ^* and put ticks on all words that are in L. This will cover all words in L, since Σ^* contains any possible word over Σ.

Suppose our language L is "the set of all words that contain more *a*'s than *b*'s". $L=\{a, aa, aab, aba, baa, \cdots\}$. The beginning of our list, with ticks, will look as follows:

	ε
✔	a
	b
✔	aa
	ab
	ba
	bb
✔	aaa
✔	aab
✔	aba
	abb
✔	baa

>   *bab*
>   *bba*
>   *bbb*
>   ✔   *aaaa*
>
> ...   ...

Given the alphabet with its ordering, the list of blanks and ticks alone is entirely sufficient to identify and describe the language. For convenience we write the blank as a 0
and the tick as a 1 as if they were bits in a computer, and we can now write
L=0101000111010001 $\cdots$ (and Σ^*=1111111111111111 $\cdots$). It should be noted that
this is true for *any* language, be it a formal language like L, a programming language
like Pascal or a natural language like English. In English, the 1's in the bit-string will
be very scarce, since hardly any arbitrary sequence of words is a good English sentence
(and hardly any arbitrary sequence of letters is a good English word, depending on
whether we address the sentence/word level or the word/letter level).

2.1.3.4 Diagonalization
The previous section attaches the infinite bit-string 0101000111010001... to the
description "the set of all the words that contain more a's than b's". In the same vein
we can attach such bit-strings to all descriptions; some descriptions may not yield a
language, in which case we can attach an arbitrary infinite bit-string to it. Since all
descriptions can be put on a single numbered list, we get, for instance, the following
picture:

Description	*Language*
Description #1	000000100...
Description #2	110010001...
Description #3	011011010...
Description #4	110011010...
Description #5	100000011...
Description #6	111011011...
...	...

At the left we have all descriptions, at the right all languages they describe. We now
claim that many languages exist that are not on the list of languages above: the above
list is far from complete, although the list of descriptions is complete. We shall prove
this by using the diagonalization process ("Diagonalverfahren") of Cantor.

   Consider the language C=100110 $\cdots$, which has the property that its n-th bit is
unequal to the n-th bit of the language described by Description #n. The first bit of C is
a 1, because the first bit for Description #1 is a 0; the second bit of C is a 0, because the
second bit for Description #2 is a 1, and so on. C is made by walking the NW to SE
diagonal of the language field and copying the opposites of the bits we meet.

   The language C cannot be on the list! It cannot be on line 1, since its first bit
differs (is made to differ, one should say) from that on line 1, and in general it cannot
be on line n, since its n-th bit will differ from that on line n, by definition.

   So, in spite of the fact that we have exhaustively listed all possible finite descriptions, we have at least one language that has no description on the list. Moreover, any
broken diagonal yields such a language, where a diagonal is "broken" by replacing a

section of it as follows,

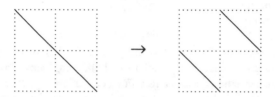

and so does any multiply-broken diagonal. In fact, for each language on the list, there are infinitely many languages not on it; this statement is, however, more graphical than it is exact, and we shall not prove it.

The diagonalization technique is described more formally in most books on theoretical computer science; see e.g., Rayward-Smith [Books 1983, pp. 5-6] or Hopcroft and Ullman [Books 1979, pp 6-9].

2.1.3.5 Conclusions
The above demonstration shows us several things. First, it shows the power of treating languages as formal objects. Although the above outline clearly needs considerable amplification and substantiation to qualify as a proof (for one thing it still has to be clarified why the above explanation, which defines the language C, is not itself on the list of descriptions), it allows us to obtain insight in properties not otherwise assessable.

Secondly, it shows that we can only describe a tiny subset (not even a fraction) of all possible languages: there is an infinity of languages out there, forever beyond our reach.

Thirdly, we have proved that, although there are infinitely many descriptions and infinitely many languages, these infinities are not equal to each other and that the latter is larger than the former. These infinities are called $\aleph_0$ and $\aleph_1$ by Cantor, and the above is just an adaptation of his proof that $\aleph_0 < \aleph_1$.

2.1.4 Describing a language through a finite recipe
A good way to build a set of objects is to start with a small object and to give rules how to add to it and construct new objects from it. "Two is an even number and the sum of two even numbers is again an even number" effectively generates the set of all even numbers. Formalists will add "...and no other numbers are even", but we'll skip that.

Suppose we want to generate the set of all enumerations of names, of the type "Tom, Dick and Harry", in which all names but the last two are separated by commas. We will not accept "Tom, Dick, Harry" nor "Tom and Dick and Harry", but we shall not object to duplicates: "Grubb, Grubb and Burrowes"[†] is all right. Although these are not complete sentences in normal English, we shall still call them *sentences* since that is what they are in our midget language of name enumerations. A simple-minded recipe would be:

     0.   Tom is a name, Dick is a name, Harry is a name;
     1.   a name is a sentence;

[†] *The Hobbit*, by J.R.R. Tolkien, Allen and Unwin, 1961, p. 311.

2.   a sentence followed by a comma and a name is again a sentence;
3.   before finishing, if the sentence ends in ", name", replace it by
        "and name".

Although this will work for a cooperative reader, there are several things wrong
with it. Clause 3 is especially wrought with trouble. For instance, the sentence does not
really end in ", name", it ends in ", Dick" or such, and "name" is just a symbol that
stands for a real name; such symbols cannot occur in a real sentence and must in the
end be replaced by a real name as given in clause 0. Likewise, the word "sentence" in
the recipe is a symbol that stands for all the actual sentences. So there are two kinds of
symbols involved here: real symbols, which occur in finished sentences, like "Tom",
"Dick", a comma and the word "and"; and there are intermediate symbols, like "sentence" and "name" that cannot occur in a finished sentence. The first kind corresponds
to the words or tokens explained above and the technical term for them is *terminal symbols* (or *terminals* for short) while the latter are called *non-terminals* (a singularly unin-
spired term). To distinguish them, we write terminals in small letters and start non-
terminals with a capital.

To stress the generative character of the recipe, we shall replace "X is a Y" by "Y
may be replaced by X": if "tom" is an instance of a Name, then everywhere we have a
Name we may narrow it down to "tom". This gives us:

0.   Name may be replaced by "tom"
        Name may be replaced by "dick"
        Name may be replaced by "harry"
1.   Sentence may be replaced by Name
2.   Sentence may be replaced by Sentence, Name
3.   ", Name" at the end of a Sentence must be replaced by "and Name"
        before Name is replaced by any of its replacements
4.   a sentence is finished only when it no longer contains non-terminals
5.   we start our replacement procedure with Sentence

Clause 0 through 3 describe replacements, but 4 and 5 are different. Clause 4 is not
specific to this grammar. It is valid generally and is one of the rules of the game.
Clause 5 tells us where to start generating. This name is quite naturally called the *start
symbol*, and it is required for every grammar.

Still clause 3 looks worrisome; most rules have "may be replaced", but this one
has "must be replaced", and it refers to the "end of a Sentence". The rest of the rules
work through replacement, but the problem remains how we can use replacement to
test for the end of a Sentence. This can be solved by adding an end-marker after it. And
if we make the end-marker a non-terminal which cannot be used anywhere except in
the required replacement from ", Name" to "and Name", we automatically enforce the
restriction that no sentence is finished unless the replacement test has taken place. For
brevity we write -> instead of "may be replaced by"; since terminal and non-terminal
symbols are now identified as technical objects we shall write them in a typewriter-like
typeface. The part before the -> is called the *left-hand side*, the part after it the *right-
hand side*. This results in the recipe in Figure 2.2.

This is a simple and relatively precise form for a recipe, and the rules are equally
straightforward: start with the start symbol, and keep replacing until there are no non-

```
     0.                Name     ->    tom
                       Name     ->    dick
                       Name     ->    harry
     1.          Sentence       ->    Name
                 Sentence       ->    List End
     2.              List       ->    Name
                     List       ->    List , Name
     3.      , Name End         ->    and Name
     4.      the start symbol is Sentence
```

Figure 2.2 A finite recipe for generating strings in the t, d & h language

terminals left.

2.2 FORMAL GRAMMARS

The above recipe form, based on replacement according to rules, is strong enough to serve as a basis for formal grammars. Similar forms, often called "rewriting systems", have a long history among mathematicians, but the specific form of Figure 2.2 was first studied extensively by Chomsky [Misc 1959]. His analysis has been the foundation for almost all research and progress in formal languages, parsers and a considerable part of compiler construction and linguistics.

   Since formal languages are a branch of mathematics, work in this field is done in a special notation which can be a hurdle to the uninitiated. To allow a small peep into the formal linguist's kitchen, we shall give the formal definition of a grammar and then explain why it describes a grammar like the one in Figure 2.2. The formalism used is indispensable for correctness proofs, etc., but not for understanding the principles; it is shown here only to give an impression and, perhaps, to bridge a gap.

   Definition 2.1: A *generative grammar* is a 4-tuple (V_N, V_T, R, S) such that (1) V_N and V_T are finite sets of symbols, (2) $V_N \cap V_T = \varnothing$, (3) R is a set of pairs (P, Q) such that (3a) $P \in (V_N \cup V_T)^+$ and (3b) $Q \in (V_N \cup V_T)^*$, and (4) $S \in V_N$.

   A *4-tuple* is just an object consisting of 4 identifiable parts; they are the non-terminals, the terminals, the rules and the start symbol, in that order; the above definition does not tell this, so this is for the teacher to explain. The set of non-terminals is named V_N and the set of terminals V_T. For our grammar we have:

V_N = {Name, Sentence, List, End}
V_T = {tom, dick, harry, ,, and}

(note the , in the set of terminal symbols).

   The intersection of V_N and V_T (2) must be empty, that is, the non-terminals and the terminals may not have a symbol in common, which is understandable.

   R is the set of all rules (3), and P and Q are the left-hand sides and right-hand sides, respectively. Each P must consist of sequences of one or more non-terminals and terminals and each Q must consist of sequences of zero or more non-terminals and terminals. For our grammar we have:

R = {(Name, tom), (Name, dick), (Name, harry),

(Sentence, Name), (Sentence, List End),
(List, Name), (List, List , Name), (, Name End, and Name)}

Note again the two different commas.
   The start symbol *S* must be an element of V_N, that is, it must be a non-terminal:

   S = Sentence

   This concludes our field trip into formal linguistics; the reader can be assured that there is lots and lots more. A good simple introduction is written by Révész [Books 1985].

2.2.1 Generating sentences from a formal grammar

The grammar in Figure 2.1 is what is known as a *phrase structure grammar* for our t,d&h language (often abbreviated to PS grammar). There is a more compact notation, in which several right-hand sides for one and the same left-hand side are grouped together and then separated by vertical bars, |. This bar belongs to the formalism, just as the arrow -> and can be read "or else". The right-hand sides separated by vertical bars are also called *alternatives*. In this more concise form our grammar becomes:

```
0.          Name    ->    tom | dick | harry
1.      Sentence_S  ->    Name | List End
2.          List    ->    Name | Name , List
3.    , Name End    ->    and Name
```

where the non-terminal with the subscript $_S$ is the start symbol. (The subscript $_S$ identifies the symbol, not the rule.)
   Now let's generate our initial example from this grammar, using replacement according to the above rules only. We obtain the following successive forms for Sentence:

Intermediate form	Rule used	Explanation
Sentence		the start symbol
List End	Sentence -> List End	rule 1
Name , List End	List -> Name , List	rule 2
Name , Name , List End	List -> Name , List	rule 2
Name , Name , Name End	List -> Name	rule 2
Name , Name and Name	, Name End -> and Name	rule 3
tom , dick and harry		rule 0, three times

The intermediate forms are called *sentential forms*; if a sentential form contains no non-terminals it is called a *sentence* and belongs to the generated language. The transitions from one line to the next are called *production steps* and the rules are often called *production rules*, for obvious reasons.
   The production process can be made more visual by drawing connective lines between corresponding symbols, as shown in Figure 2.3. Such a picture is called a *production graph* or *syntactic graph*, because it depicts the syntactic structure (with regard to the given grammar) of the final sentence. We see that the production graph normally

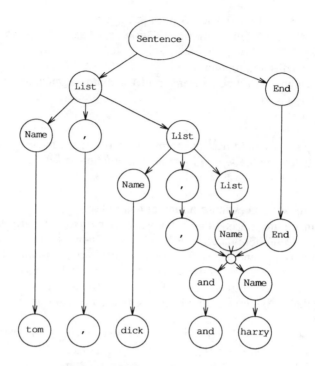

Figure 2.3 Production graph for a sentence

fans out downwards, but occasionally we may see starlike constructions, which result from rewriting a group of symbols.

It is patently impossible to have the grammar generate tom, dick, harry, since any attempt to produce more than one name will drag in an End and the only way to get rid of it again (and get rid of it we must, since it is a non-terminal) is to have it absorbed by rule 3, which will produce the and. We see, to our amazement, that we have succeeded in implementing the notion "must replace" in a system that only uses "may replace"; looking more closely, we see that we have split "must replace" into "may replace" and "must not be a non-terminal".

Apart from our standard example, the grammar will of course also produce many other sentences; examples are:

        harry and tom
        harry
        tom, tom, tom, and tom

and an infinity of others. A determined and foolhardy attempt to generate the incorrect form without the and will lead us to sentential forms like:

        tom, dick, harry End

which are not sentences and to which no production rule applies. Such forms are called *blind alleys*. Note that production rules may not be applied in the reverse direction.

2.2.2 The expressive power of formal grammars

The main property of a formal grammar is that it has production rules, which may be used for rewriting part of the sentential form (= sentence under construction) and a starting symbol which is the mother of all sentential forms. In the production rules we find non-terminals and terminals; finished sentences contain terminals only. That is about it: the rest is up to the creativity of the grammar writer and the sentence producer.

This is a framework of impressive frugality and the question immediately rises: Is it sufficient? Well, if it isn't, we don't have anything more expressive. Strange as it may sound, all other methods known to mankind for generating sets have been proved to be equivalent to or less powerful than a phrase structure grammar. One obvious method for generating a set is, of course, to write a program generating it, but it has been proved that any set that can be generated by a program can be generated by a phrase structure grammar. There are even more arcane methods, but all of them have been proved not to be more expressive. On the other hand there is no proof that no such stronger method can exist. But in view of the fact that many quite different methods all turn out to halt at the same barrier, it is highly unlikely[†] that a stronger method will ever be found. See, e.g. Révész [Books 1985, pp 100-102].

As a further example of the expressive power we shall give a grammar for the movements of a Manhattan turtle. A *Manhattan turtle* moves in a plane and can only move north, east, south or west in distances of one block. The grammar of Figure 2.4 produces all paths that return to their own starting point.

1.	Move$_S$	->	north Move south | east Move west | ε
2.	north east	->	east north
	north south	->	south north
	north west	->	west north
	east north	->	north east
	east south	->	south east
	east west	->	west east
	south north	->	north south
	south east	->	east south
	south west	->	west south
	west north	->	north west
	west east	->	east west
	west south	->	south west

Figure 2.4 Grammar for the movements of a Manhattan turtle

As to rule 2, it should be noted that some authors require at least one of the symbols in the left-hand side to be a non-terminal. This restriction can always be enforced by adding new non-terminals.

The simple round trip north east south west is produced as shown in Figure 2.5 (names abbreviated to their first letter). Note the empty alternative in rule 1

[†] Paul Vitány has pointed out that if scientists call something "highly unlikely" they are still generally not willing to bet a year's salary on it, double or quit.

(the ε), which results in the dying out of the third M in the above production graph.

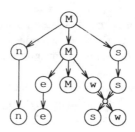

Figure 2.5 How the grammar of Figure 2.4 produces a round trip

2.3 THE CHOMSKY HIERARCHY OF GRAMMARS AND LANGUAGES

The grammars from Figures 2.1 and 2.2 are easy to understand and indeed some simple phrase structure grammars generate very complicated sets. The grammar for any given set is, however, usually far from simple. (We say "*The* grammar for a given set" although there can be, of course, infinitely many grammars for a set. By *the* grammar for a set, we mean any grammar that does the job and is not obviously overly complicated.) Theory says that if a set can be generated at all (for instance, by a program) it can be generated by a phrase structure grammar, but theory does not say that it will be easy to do so, or that the grammar will be understandable. In this context it is illustrative to try to write a grammar for those Manhattan turtle paths in which the turtle is never allowed to the west of its starting point. (Hint: use a special (non-terminal) marker for each block the turtle is located to the east of its starting point).

Apart from the intellectual problems phrase structure grammars pose, they also exhibit fundamental and practical problems. We shall see that no general parsing algorithm for them can exist, and all known special parsing algorithms are either very inefficient or very complex; see Section 3.5.2.

The desire to restrict the unmanageability of phrase structure grammars, while keeping as much of their generative powers as possible, has led to the *Chomsky hierarchy* of grammars. This hierarchy distinguishes four types of grammars, numbered from 0 to 3; it is useful to include a fifth type, called Type 4 here. Type 0 grammars are the (unrestricted) phrase structure grammars of which we have already seen examples. The other types originate from applying more and more restrictions to the allowed form of the rules in the grammar. Each of these restrictions has far-reaching consequences; the resulting grammars are gradually easier to understand and to manipulate, but are also gradually less powerful. Fortunately, these less powerful types are still very useful, actually more useful even than Type 0. We shall now consider each of the three remaining types in turn, followed by a trivial but useful fourth type.

2.3.1 Type 1 grammars

The characteristic property of a Type 0 grammar is that it may contain rules that transform an arbitrary (non-zero) number of symbols into an arbitrary (possibly zero) number of symbols. Example:

    , N E -> and N

in which three symbols are replaced by two. By restricting this freedom, we obtain
Type 1 grammars. Strangely enough there are two, intuitively completely different
definitions of Type 1 grammars, which can be proved to be equivalent.

A grammar is *Type 1 monotonic* if it contains no rules in which the left-hand side
consists of more symbols than the right-hand side. This forbids, for instance, the rule ,
N E -> and N.

A grammar is *Type 1 context-sensitive* if all of its rules are context-sensitive. A
rule is *context-sensitive* if actually only one (non-terminal) symbol in its left-hand side
gets replaced by other symbols, while we find the others back undamaged and in the
same order in the right-hand side. Example:

        Name Comma Name End -> Name and Name End

which tells that the rule

        Comma -> and

may be applied if the left context is Name and the right context is Name End. The contexts themselves are not affected. The replacement must be at least one symbol long;
this means that context-sensitive grammars are always monotonic; see Section 2.6.

Here is a monotonic grammar for our t,d&h example. In writing monotonic grammars one has to be careful never to produce more symbols than will be produced eventually. We avoid the need to delete the end-marker by incorporating it into the right-
most name.

$$
\begin{array}{rcl}
\text{Name} & \to & \text{tom | dick | harry} \\
\text{Sentence}_S & \to & \text{Name | List} \\
\text{List} & \to & \text{EndName | Name , List} \\
\text{, EndName} & \to & \text{and Name}
\end{array}
$$

where EndName is a single symbol.

And here is a context-sensitive grammar for it.

$$
\begin{array}{rcl}
\text{Name} & \to & \text{tom | dick | harry} \\
\text{Sentence}_S & \to & \text{Name | List} \\
\text{List} & \to & \text{EndName} \\
 & & \text{| Name Comma List} \\
\text{Comma EndName} & \to & \text{and EndName} \qquad \text{context is ... EndName} \\
\text{and EndName} & \to & \text{and Name} \qquad \text{context is and ...} \\
\text{Comma} & \to & \text{,}
\end{array}
$$

Note that we need an extra non-terminal Comma to be able to produce the terminal and
in the correct context.

Monotonic and context-sensitive grammars are equally powerful: for each
language that can be generated by a monotonic grammar a context-sensitive grammar
exists that generates the same language, and vice versa. They are less powerful than
the Type 0 grammars, that is, there are languages that can be generated by a Type 0
grammar but not by any Type 1. Strangely enough no simple examples of such

languages are known. Although the difference between Type 0 and Type 1 is fundamental and is not just a whim of Mr. Chomsky, grammars for which the difference
matters are too complicated to write down; only their existence can be proved (see e.g.,
Hopcroft and Ullman [Books 1979, pp. 183-184] or Révész [Books 1985, p. 98]).

  Of course any Type 1 grammar is also a Type 0 grammar, since the class of Type
1 grammars is obtained from the class of Type 0 grammars by applying restrictions.
But it would be confusing to call a Type 1 grammar a Type 0 grammar; it would be like
calling a cat a mammal: correct but not informative enough. A grammar is named after
the smallest class (that is, the highest type number) in which it will still fit.

  We saw that our t,d&h language, which was first generated by a Type 0 grammar,
could also be generated by a Type 1 grammar. We shall see that there is also a Type 2
and a Type 3 grammar for it, but no Type 4 grammar. We therefore say that the t,d&h
language is Type 3 language, after the most restricted (and simple and amenable) grammar for it. Some corollaries of this are: A Type n language can be generated by a Type
n grammar or anything stronger, but not by a weaker Type $n+1$ grammar; and: If a
language is generated by a Type n grammar, that does not necessarily mean that there is
no (weaker) Type $n+1$ grammar for it. The use of a Type 0 grammar for our t,d&h
language was a serious case of overkill, just for demonstration purposes.

  The standard example of a Type 1 language is the set of words that consist of
equal numbers of a's, b's and c's, in that order:

$$\underbrace{a\,a\ldots.a}_{n\text{ of them}}\quad\underbrace{b\,b\ldots.b}_{n\text{ of them}}\quad\underbrace{c\,c\ldots.c}_{n\text{ of them}}$$

2.3.1.1 Constructing a Type 1 grammar

For the sake of completeness and to show how one writes a Type 1 grammar if one is
clever enough, we shall now derive a grammar for this toy language. Starting with the
simplest case, we have the rule

  0.   S -> abc

Having got one instance of S, we may want to prepend more a's to the beginning; if we
want to remember how many there were, we shall have to append something to the end
as well at the same time, and that cannot be a b or a c. We shall use a yet unknown
symbol Q. The following rule pre- and postpends:

  1.   S -> abc | aSQ

If we apply this rule, for instance, three times, we get the sentential form

    aaabcQQ

Now, to get aaabbbccc from this, each Q must be worth one b and one c, as was to be
expected, but we cannot just write

    Q -> bc

because that would allow b's after the first c. The above rule would, however, be all right if it were allowed to do replacement only between a b and a c; there, the newly inserted bc will do no harm:

2.   bQc -> bbcc

Still, we cannot apply this rule since normally the Q's are to the right of the c; this can be remedied by allowing a Q to hop left over a c:

3.   cQ -> Qc

We can now finish our derivation:

aaabcQQ	(3 times rule 1)
aaabQcQ	(rule 3)
aaabbccQ	(rule 2)
aaabbcQc	(rule 3)
aaabbQcc	(rule 3)
aaabbbccc	(rule 2)

It should be noted that the above derivation only shows that the grammar will produce the right strings, and the reader will still have to convince himself that it will not generate other and incorrect strings.

$$S_S \quad \rightarrow \quad abc \mid aSQ$$
$$bQc \quad \rightarrow \quad bbcc$$
$$cQ \quad \rightarrow \quad Qc$$

Figure 2.6 Monotonic grammar for $a^n b^n c^n$

The grammar is summarized in Figure 2.6; since a derivation tree of $a^3 b^3 c^3$ is already rather unwieldy, a derivation tree for $a^2 b^2 c^2$ is given in Figure 2.7. The grammar is monotonic and therefore of Type 1; it can be proved that there is no Type 2 grammar for the language.

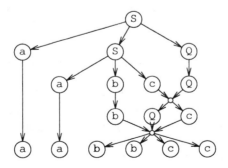

Figure 2.7 Derivation of $a^2 b^2 c^2$

Type 1 grammars are also called *context-sensitive grammars* (CS grammars); the latter name is often used even if the grammar is actually monotonic. There are no standard initials for monotonic, but MT may do.

2.3.2 Type 2 grammars

Type 2 grammars are called *context-free grammars* (CF grammars) and their relation to context-sensitive grammars is as direct as the name suggests. A context-free grammar is like a context-sensitive grammar, except that both the left and the right contexts are required to be absent (empty). As a result, the grammar may contain only rules that have a single non-terminal on their left-hand side. Sample grammar:

```
0.            Name    ->    tom | dick | harry
1.    Sentence_S      ->    Name | List and Name
2.            List    ->    Name , List | Name
```

Since there is always only one symbol on the left-hand side, each node in a production graph has the property that whatever it produces is independent of what its neighbours produce: the productive life of a non-terminal is independent of its context. Starlike forms as we saw in Figures 2.3, 2.5 or 2.7 cannot occur in a context-free production graph, which consequently has a pure tree-form and is called a *production tree*. An example is shown in Figure 2.8.

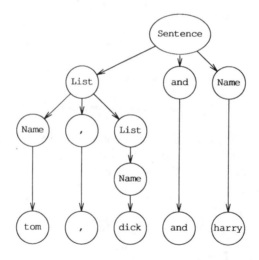

Figure 2.8 Production tree for a context-free grammar

Also, since there is only one symbol on the left-hand side, all right-hand sides for a given non-terminal can always be collected in one grammar rule (we have already done that in the above grammar) and then each grammar rule reads like a definition of the left-hand side:

☐   A Sentence is either a Name or a List followed by and followed by a Name.
☐   A List is either a Name followed by a , followed by a List, or it is a Name.
    In the actual world, many things are defined in terms of other things. Context-free

grammars are a very concise way to formulate such interrelationships. An almost trivial example is the composition of a book, as given in Figure 2.9.

```
              Book_S    ->    Preface ChapterSequence Conclusion
             Preface    ->    "PREFACE" ParagraphSequence
      ChapterSequence   ->    Chapter | Chapter ChapterSequence
             Chapter    ->    "CHAPTER" Number ParagraphSequence
    ParagraphSequence   ->    Paragraph | Paragraph ParagraphSequence
           Paragraph    ->    SentenceSequence
     SentenceSequence   ->    ...
                         ...
          Conclusion    ->    "CONCLUSION" ParagraphSequence
```

Figure 2.9 A simple (and incomplete!) grammar of a book

Of course, this is a context-free description of a book, so one can expect it to also generate a lot of good-looking nonsense like

```
PREFACE
qwertyuiop
CHAPTER V
asdfghjkl
zxcvbnm, .
CHAPTER II
qazwsxedcrfvtgb
yhnujmikolp
CONCLUSION
All cats say blert when walking through walls.
```

but at least the result has the right structure. The document preparation and text markup language SGML[†] uses this approach to control the basic structure of documents.

A shorter but less trivial example is the language of all elevator motions that return to the same point (a Manhattan turtle restricted to 5th Avenue would make the same movements)

```
      ZeroMotion_S   ->   up ZeroMotion down ZeroMotion
                      |    down ZeroMotion up ZeroMotion
                      |    ε
```

(in which we assume that the elevator shaft is infinitely long; they are, in Manhattan).

If we ignore enough detail we can also recognize an underlying context-free structure in the sentences of a natural language, for instance, English:

[†] David Barron, "Why use SGML?", *Electronic Publishing*, vol. 2, no. 1, p. 3-24, April 1989. Short introduction to *SGML* (Standard Generalized Markup Language) and comparison to other systems. Provides further references.

```
         Sentence_s   ->   Subject Verb Object
          Subject     ->   NounPhrase
           Object     ->   NounPhrase
       NounPhrase     ->   the QualifiedNoun
    QualifiedNoun     ->   Noun | Adjective QualifiedNoun
             Noun     ->   castle | caterpillar | cats
        Adjective     ->   well-read | white | wistful | ...
             Verb     ->   admires | bark | criticize | ...
```

which produces sentences like:

```
    the well-read cats criticize the wistful caterpillar
```

Since, however, no context is incorporated, it will equally well produce the incorrect

```
    the cats admires the white well-read castle
```

For keeping context we could use a phrase structure grammar (for a simpler language):

```
         Sentence_s   ->   Noun Number Verb
           Number     ->   Singular | Plural
    Noun Singular     ->   castle Singular | caterpillar Singular | ...
  Singular Verb       ->   Singular admires | ...
         Singular     ->   ε
      Noun Plural     ->   cats Plural | ...
     Plural Verb      ->   Plural bark | Plural criticize | ...
          Plural      ->   ε
```

where the markers Singular and Plural control the production of actual English words. Still this grammar allows the cats to bark.... For a better way to handle context, see the section on van Wijngaarden grammars (2.4.1).

The bulk of examples of CF grammars originate from programming languages. Sentences in these languages (that is, programs) have to be processed automatically (that is, by a compiler) and it was soon recognized (around 1958) that this is a lot easier if the language has a well-defined formal grammar. The syntaxes of almost all programming languages in use today are defined through a formal grammar.[†]

Some authors (for instance, Chomsky) and some parsing algorithms, require a CF grammar to be monotonic. The only way a CF rule can be non-monotonic is by having an empty right-hand side; such a rule is called an ε-*rule* and a grammar that contains no such rules is called ε-free. The requirement of being ε-free is not a real restriction, just a nuisance. Any CF grammar can be made ε-free be systematic substitution of the ε-rules (this process will be explained in detail in 4.2.3.1), but this in general does not improve the appearance of the grammar. The issue will be discussed further in Section

---

[†] COBOL and FORTRAN also have grammars but theirs are informal and descriptive, and were never intended to be generative.

2.6.

2.3.2.1 Backus-Naur Form

There are several different styles of notation for CF grammars for programming languages, each with endless variants; they are all functionally equivalent. We shall show two main styles here. The first is *Backus-Naur Form* (BNF) which was first used for defining ALGOL 60. Here is a sample:

```
<name>::=           tom | dick | harry
<sentence>S::=      <name> | <list> and <name>
<list>::=           <name>, <list> | <name>
```

This form's main properties are the use of angle brackets to enclose non-terminals and of ::= for "may produce". In some variants, the rules are terminated by a semicolon.

2.3.2.2 van Wijngaarden form

The second style is that of the CF van Wijngaarden grammars. Again a sample:

```
name:        tom symbol; dick symbol; harry symbol.
sentenceS:   name; list, and symbol, name.
list:        name, comma symbol, list; name.
```

The names of terminal symbols end in ...symbol; their representations are hardware-dependent and are not defined in the grammar. Rules are properly terminated (with a period). Punctuation is used more or less in the traditional way; for instance, the comma binds tighter than the semicolon. The punctuation can be read as follows:

:	"is defined as a(n)"
;	", or as a (n)"
,	"followed by a(n)"
.	", and as nothing else."

The second rule in the above grammar would be read as: "a sentence is defined as a name, or as a list followed by an and-symbol followed by a name, and as nothing else." Although this notation achieves its full power only when applied in the two-level van Wijngaarden grammars, it also has its merits on its own: it is formal and still quite readable.

2.3.2.3 Extended CF grammars

CF grammars are often made both more compact and more readable by introducing special short-hands for frequently used constructions. If we return to the Book grammar of Figure 2.9, we see that rules like:

```
SomethingSequence -> Something | Something SomethingSequence
```

occur repeatedly. In an *extended context-free grammar* (ECF grammar), we can write $Something^+$ meaning "one or more $Something$s" and we do not need to give a rule for $Something^+$; the rule

```
Something⁺ -> Something | Something Something⁺
```

is implicit. Likewise we can use `Something`* for "zero or more `Something`s" and `Something`$^?$ for "zero or one `Something`" (that is, "optionally a `Something`"). In these examples, the operators $^+$, * and $^?$ work on the preceding symbol; their range can be extended by using parentheses: `(Something ;)`$^?$ means "optionally a `Something`-followed-by-a-`;`". These facilities are very useful and allow the `Book` grammar to be written more efficiently (Figure 2.10). Some styles even allow constructions like `Something`$^+4$ meaning "one or more `Something`s with a maximum of 4" or `Something`$^+$, meaning "one or more `Something`s separated by commas"; this seems to be a case of overdoing a good thing.

$$
\begin{array}{rcl}
\text{Book}_\text{S} & -> & \text{Preface Chapter}^+ \text{ Conclusion} \\
\text{Preface} & -> & \text{"PREFACE" Paragraph}^+ \\
\text{Chapter} & -> & \text{"CHAPTER" Number Paragraph}^+ \\
\text{Paragraph} & -> & \text{Sentence}^+ \\
\text{Sentence} & -> & \text{...} \\
& \text{...} & \\
\text{Conclusion} & -> & \text{"CONCLUSION" Paragraph}^+
\end{array}
$$

Figure 2.10 An extended CF grammar of a book

The extensions of an ECF grammar do not increase its expressive powers: all implicit rules can be made explicit and then a normal CF grammar results. Their strength lies in their user-friendliness. The star in the notation X^* with the meaning "a sequence of zero or more X's" is called the *Kleene star*. If X is a set, X^* should be read as "a sequence of zero or more elements of X"; it is the same star that we saw in Σ^* in Section 2.1.3.3. Forms involving the repetition operators *, $^+$ or $^?$ and possibly the separators (and) are called *regular expressions*. ECF's, which have regular expressions for their right-hand sides, are for that reason sometimes called *regular right part grammars* (RRP grammars) which is more descriptive than "extended context free", but which is perceived to be a tongue twister by some.

There are two different schools of thought about the structural meaning of a regular right-hand side. One school maintains that a rule like:

$$
\text{Book} \quad -> \quad \text{Preface Chapter}^+ \text{ Conclusion}
$$

is an abbreviation of

$$
\begin{array}{rcl}
\text{Book} & -> & \text{Preface } \alpha \text{ Conclusion} \\
\alpha & -> & \text{Chapter | Chapter } \alpha
\end{array}
$$

as shown above. This is the "(right)recursive" interpretation; it has the advantage that it is easy to explain and that the transformation to "normal" CF is simple. Disadvantages are that the transformation entails anonymous rules (identified by α here) and that the lopsided parse tree for, for instance, a book of four chapters does not correspond to our idea of the structure of the book; see Figure 2.11.

The seconds school claims that

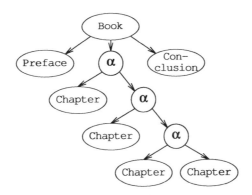

Figure 2.11 Parse tree for the (right)recursive interpretation

```
Book    ->    Preface Chapter⁺ Conclusion
```

is an abbreviation of

```
Book    ->    Preface Chapter Conclusion
        |     Preface Chapter Chapter Conclusion
        |     Preface Chapter Chapter Chapter Conclusion
        |     ...
...
```

This is the "iterative" interpretation; it has the advantage that it yields a beautiful parse tree (Figure 2.12), but the disadvantages that it involves an infinite number of production rules and that the nodes in the parse tree have a varying fan-out.

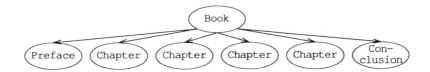

Figure 2.12 Parse tree for the iterative interpretation

Since the implementation of the iterative interpretation is far from trivial, most practical parser generators use the recursive interpretation in some form or another, whereas most research has been done on the iterative interpretation.

2.3.3 Type 3 grammars

The basic property of CF grammars is that they describe things that nest: an object may contain other objects in various places, which in turn may contain ... etc. When during the production process we have produced one of the objects, the right-hand side still "remembers" what has to come after it: in the English grammar, after having descended into the depth of the non-terminal Subject to produce something like the wistful cat, the right-hand side Subject Verb Object still remembers that a Verb must follow. While we are working on the Subject, the Verb and Object remain queued at the right in the sentential form, for instance,

        the wistful QualifiedNoun Verb Object

In the right-hand side

        up ZeroMotion down ZeroMotion

after having performed the up and an arbitrarily complicated ZeroMotion, the right-hand side still remembers that a down must follow.

The restriction to Type 3 disallows this recollection of things that came before: a right-hand side may only contain one non-terminal and it must come at the end. This means that there are only two kinds of rules:[†]

> A non-terminal produces zero or more terminals
> A non-terminal produces zero or more terminals followed by one non-terminal

The original Chomsky definition of Type 3 restricts the kinds of rules to

> A non-terminal produces one terminal
> A non-terminal produces one terminal followed by one non-terminal

Our definition is equivalent and more convenient, although the conversion to Chomsky Type 3 is not completely trivial.

Type 3 grammars are also called *regular grammars* (RE grammars) or *finite-state grammars* (FS grammars). Since regular grammars are used very often to describe the structure of text on the character level, it is customary for the terminal symbols of a regular grammar to be single characters. We shall therefore write t for Tom, d for Dick, h for Harry and & for and. Figure 2.13 shows a Type 3 grammar for our t,d&h language in this style.

$$
\begin{array}{rcl}
\text{Sentence}_S & \text{->} & \texttt{t | d | h | List} \\
\text{List} & \text{->} & \texttt{t ListTail | d ListTail | h ListTail} \\
\text{ListTail} & \text{->} & \texttt{, List | \&t | \&d | \&h}
\end{array}
$$

Figure 2.13 A Type 3 grammar for the t, d & h language

The production tree for a sentence from a Type 3 grammar degenerates into a chain of non-terminals that drop a sequence of terminals on their left. Figure 2.14 shows an example.

The deadly repetition exhibited by the above grammar is typical of regular grammars; a number of notational devices have been invented to abate this nuisance. The

---

[†] There is a natural in-between class, Type 2.5 so to say, in which only a single non-terminal is allowed in a right-hand side, but where it need not be at the end. This gives us the so-called *linear grammars*.

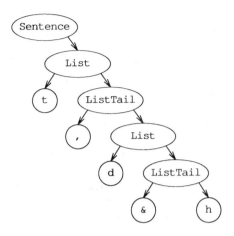

Figure 2.14 Production chain for a regular (Type 3) grammar

most common one is the use of square brackets to indicate "one out of a set of characters": [tdh] is an abbreviation for t|d|h:

$$
\begin{array}{lll}
S_S & -> & \text{[tdh] | L} \\
L & -> & \text{[tdh] T} \\
T & -> & \text{, L | \& [tdh]}
\end{array}
$$

which may look more cryptic at first but is actually much more convenient and in fact allows simplification of the grammar to

$$
\begin{array}{lll}
S_S & -> & \text{[tdh] | L} \\
L & -> & \text{[tdh] , L | [tdh] \& [tdh]}
\end{array}
$$

A second way is to allow macros, names for pieces of the grammar that are substituted properly into the grammar before it is used:

$$
\begin{array}{lll}
\text{Name} & -> & \text{t | d | h} \\
S_S & -> & \text{\$Name | L} \\
L & -> & \text{\$Name , L | \$Name \& \$Name}
\end{array}
$$

The popular parser generator for regular grammars *lex* (designed and written by Lesk and Schmidt [FS 1975]) features both facilities.

Note that if we adhere to the Chomsky definition of Type 3, our grammar will not get smaller than:

$$
\begin{array}{lll}
S_S & -> & \text{t | d | h | tM | dM | hM} \\
M & -> & \text{,N | \&P} \\
N & -> & \text{tM | dM | hM} \\
P & -> & \text{t | d | h}
\end{array}
$$

This form is evidently easier to process but less user-friendly than the *lex* version. We observe here that while the formal-linguist is interested in and helped by minimally sufficient means, the computer scientist values a form in which the concepts underlying the grammar ($Name, etc.) are easily expressed, at the expense of additional processing.

There are two interesting observations about regular grammars which we want to make here. First, when we use a RE grammar for generating a sentence, the sentential forms will only contain one non-terminal and this will always be at the end; that's where it all happens (using the grammar of Figure 2.13):

```
Sentence_S
List
t ListTail
t , List
t , d ListTail
t , d & h
```

The second observation is that all regular grammars can be reduced considerably in size by using the regular expression operators *, $^+$ and $^?$ introduced in Section 2.3.2 for "zero or more", "one or more" and "optionally one", respectively. Using these operators and (and) for grouping, we can simplify our grammar to:

$$S_S \quad \rightarrow \quad ((\text{ [tdh], })^* \text{ [tdh]} \&)^? \text{ [tdh]}$$

Here the parentheses serve to demarcate the operands of the * and $^?$ operators. Regular expressions exist for all Type 3 grammars. Note that the * and the $^+$ work on what precedes them; to distinguish them from the normal multiplication and addition operators, they are often printed higher than the level text in print, but in computer input they are in line with the rest.

2.3.4 Type 4 grammars

The last restriction we shall apply to what is allowed in a production rule is a pretty final one: no non-terminal is allowed in the right-hand side. This removes all the generative power from the mechanism, except for the choosing of alternatives. The start symbol has a (finite) list of alternatives from which we are allowed to choose; this is reflected in the name *finite-choice grammar* (FC grammar).

There is no FC grammar for our t,d&h language; if, however, we are willing to restrict ourselves to lists of names of a finite length (say, no more than a hundred), then there is one, since one could enumerate all combinations. For the obvious limit of three names, we get:

$$S_S \quad \rightarrow \quad \text{[tdh]} \mid \text{[tdh]} \& \text{[tdh]} \mid \text{[tdh]} , \text{[tdh]} \& \text{[tdh]}$$

for a total of $3+3*3+3*3*3=39$ production rules.

FC grammars are not part of the official Chomsky hierarchy, that is, they are not identified by Chomsky. They are nevertheless very useful and are often required as a tail-piece in some process or reasoning. The set of reserved words (keywords) in a programming language can be described by a FC grammar. Although not many grammars are FC in their entirety, some of the rules in many grammars are finite-choice. E.g., the first rule of our first grammar (Figure 2.2) was FC. Another example of a FC rule was the macro introduced in Section 2.3.3; we do not need the macro mechanism if we change

> zero or more terminals

in the definition of a regular grammar to

> zero or more terminals or FC non-terminals

In the end, the FC non-terminals will only introduce a finite number of terminals.

2.4 VW GRAMMARS

2.4.1 The human inadequacy of CS and PS grammars

In the preceding paragraphs we have witnessed the introduction of a hierarchy of grammar types:
- phrase structure,
- context-sensitive,
- context-free,
- regular and
- finite-choice.

Although each of the boundaries between the types is clear-cut, some boundaries are more important than others. Two boundaries specifically stand out: that between context-sensitive and context-free and that between regular (finite-state) and finite-choice; the significance of the latter is trivial, being the difference between productive and non-productive, but the former is profound.

The border between CS and CF is that between global correlation and local independence. Once a non-terminal has been produced in a sentential form in a CF grammar, its further development is independent of the rest of the sentential form; a non-terminal in a sentential form of a CS grammar has to look at its neighbours on the left and on the right, to see what production rules are allowed for it. The local production independence in CF grammars means that certain long-range correlations cannot be expressed by them. Such correlations are, however, often very interesting, since they embody fundamental properties of the input text, like the consistent use of variables in a program or the recurrence of a theme in a musical composition. When we describe such input through a CF grammar we cannot enforce the proper correlations; one (often-used) way out is to settle for the CF grammar, accept the parsing it produces and then check the proper correlations with a separate program. This is, however, quite unsatisfactory since it defeats the purpose of having a grammar, that is, having a concise and formal description of all the properties of the input.

The obvious solution would seem to be the use of a CS grammar to express the correlations (= the context-sensitivity) but here we run into another, non-fundamental but very practical problem: CS grammars *can* express the proper correlations but not in a way a human can understand. It is in this respect instructive to compare the CF grammars in Section 2.3.2 to the one CS grammar we have seen that really expresses a context-dependency, the grammar for $a^n b^n c^n$ in Figure 2.6. The grammar for the contents of a book (Figure 2.9) immediately suggests the form of the book, but the grammar of Figure 2.6 hardly suggests anything, even if we can still remember how it was constructed and how it works. This is not caused by the use of short names like Q: a version with more informative names (Figure 2.15) is still puzzling. Also, one would expect that, having constructed a grammar for $a^n b^n c^n$, making one for $a^n b^n c^n d^n$ would be straightforward. Such is not the case; a grammar for $a^n b^n c^n d^n$ is substantially more complicated (and even more opaque) than one for $a^n b^n c^n$ and requires rethinking of the problem.

$$
\begin{array}{rcl}
S_S & -> & a\ b\ c\ |\ a\ S\ bc\_pack \\
b\ bc\_pack\ c & -> & b\ b\ c\ c \\
c\ bc\_pack & -> & bc\_pack\ c
\end{array}
$$

Figure 2.15 Monotonic grammar for $a^n b^n c^n$ with more informative names

The cause of all this misery is that CS and PS grammars derive their power to enforce global relationships from "just slightly more than local dependency". Theoretically, just looking at the neighbours can be proved to be enough to express any global relation, but the enforcement of a long-range relation through this mechanism causes information to flow through the sentential form over long distances. In the production process of, for instance, $a^4 b^4 c^4$, we see several bc_packs wind their way through the sentential form, and in any serious CS grammar, many messengers run up and down the sentential form to convey information about developments in far-away places. However interesting this imagery may seem, it requires almost all rules to know something about almost all other rules; this makes the grammar absurdly complex.

Several grammar forms have been put forward to remedy this situation and make long-range relationships more easily expressible; among them are *indexed grammars* (Aho [PSCS 1968]), *recording grammars* (Barth [PSCS 1979]), *affix grammars* (Koster [VW 1971]) and *VW grammars* (van Wijngaarden [VW 1969]). The last are the most elegant and effective, and are explained below. Affix grammars are discussed briefly in 2.4.5.

2.4.2 VW grammars

It is not quite true that CF grammars cannot express long-range relations; they can only express a finite number of them. If we have a language the strings of which consist of a begin, a middle and an end and suppose there are three types of begins and ends, then the CF grammar of Figure 2.16 will enforce that the type of the end will properly match that of the begin.

$$
\begin{array}{rcl}
text_S & -> & begin1\ middle\ end1 \\
& | & begin2\ middle\ end2 \\
& | & begin3\ middle\ end3
\end{array}
$$

Figure 2.16 A long-range relation-enforcing CF grammar

We can think of (and) for begin1 and end1, [and] for begin2 and end2 and { and } for begin3 and end3; the CF grammar will then ensure that closing parentheses will match the corresponding open parentheses.

By making the CF grammar larger and larger, we can express more and more long-range relations; if we make it infinitely large, we can express any number of long-range relations and have achieved full context-sensitivity. Now we come to the fundamental idea behind VW grammars. The rules of the infinite-size CF grammar form an infinite set of strings, i.e., a language, which can in turn be described by a grammar. This explains the name "two-level grammar".

To introduce the concepts and techniques we shall give here an informal construction of a VW grammar for the above language $L = a^n b^n c^n$ for $n \geq 1$. We shall use the VW notation as explained in 2.3.2.2: the names of terminal symbols end in symbol and their representations are given separately; alternatives are separated by semicolons (;), members inside alternatives are separated by commas (which allows us to have spaces in the names of non-terminals) and a colon (:) is used instead of an arrow.

We could describe the language L through a context-free grammar if grammars of infinite size were allowed:

```
text_S:   a symbol, b symbol, c symbol;
          a symbol, a symbol,
              b symbol, b symbol,
              c symbol, c symbol;
          a symbol, a symbol, a symbol,
              b symbol, b symbol, b symbol,
              c symbol, c symbol, c symbol;
          ... ...
```

We shall now try to master this infinity by constructing a grammar which allows us to produce the above grammar for as far as needed. We first introduce an infinite number of names of non-terminals:

```
text_S:   ai, bi, ci;
          aii, bii, cii;
          aiii, biii, ciii;
          ... ...
```

together with three infinite groups of rules for these non-terminals:

```
ai:     a symbol.
aii:    a symbol, ai.
aiii:   a symbol, aii.
...        ...

bi:     b symbol.
bii:    b symbol, bi.
biii:   b symbol, bii.
...        ...
```

```
ci:     c symbol.
cii:    c symbol, ci.
ciii:   c symbol, cii.
...     ...
```

Here the i's count the number of a's, b's and c's. Next we introduce a special kind of name called a *metanotion*. Rather than being capable of producing (part of) a sentence in the language, it is capable of producing (part of) a name in a grammar rule. In our example we want to catch the repetitions of i's in a metanotion N, for which we give a context-free production rule (a *metarule*):

$$N ::\quad i ; i N .$$

Note that we use a slightly different notation for metarules: left-hand side and right-hand side are separated by a double colon (::) rather than by a single colon and members are separated by a blank ( ) rather than by a comma. The metanotion N produces i, ii, iii, etc., which are exactly the parts of the non-terminal names we need.

We can use the production rules of N to collapse the four infinite groups of rules into four *finite* rule templates called *hyper-rules*.

```
text_S:     a N, b N, c N.

a i:        a symbol.
a i N:      a symbol, a N.

b i:        b symbol.
b i N:      b symbol, b N.

c i:        c symbol.
c i N:      c symbol, c N.
```

Each original rule can be obtained from one of the hyper-rules by substituting a production of N from the metarules for each occurrence of N in that hyper-rule, provided that *the same production* of N is used consistently throughout. To distinguish them from normal names, these half-finished combinations of small letters and metanotions (like a N or b i N) are called *hypernotions*. Substituting, for instance, N=iii in the hyperrule

$$b \ i \ N: b \ symbol, b \ N.$$

yields the CF rule for the CF non-terminal biiii

$$biiii: b \ symbol, biii.$$

We can also use this technique to condense the finite parts of a grammar by having a metarule A for the symbols a, b and c. Again the rules of the game require that the metanotion A be replaced consistently. The final result is shown in Figure 2.17.

This grammar gives a clear indication of the language it describes: once the

```
N ::      i ; i N .
A ::      a ; b ; c .

text_S:   a N, b N, c N.
A i:      A symbol.
A i N:    A symbol, A N.
```

Figure 2.17 A VW grammar for the language $a^n b^n c^n$

"value" of the metanotion N is chosen, production is straightforward. It is now trivial to extend the grammar to $a^n b^n c^n d^n$. It is also clear how long-range relations are established without having confusing messengers in the sentential form: they are established *before* they become long-range, through consistent substitution of metanotions in simple right-hand sides. The "consistent substitution rule" for metanotions is essential to the two-level mechanism; without it, VW grammars would be equivalent to CF grammars (Meersman and Rozenberg [VW 1978]).

A very good and detailed explanation of VW grammars has been written by Craig Cleaveland and Uzgalis [VW 1977], who also show many applications. Sintzoff [VW 1967] has proved that VW grammars are as powerful as PS grammars, which also shows that adding a third level to the building cannot increase its powers. Van Wijngaarden [VW 1974] has shown that the metagrammar need only be regular (although simpler grammars may be possible if it is allowed to be CF).

2.4.3 Infinite symbol sets
In a sense, VW grammars are even more powerful than PS grammars: since the name of a symbol can be generated by the grammar, they can easily handle infinite symbol sets. Of course this just shifts the problem: there must be a (finite) mapping from symbol names to symbols somewhere. The VW grammar of Figure 2.18 generates sentences consisting of arbitrary numbers of equal-length stretches of equal symbols, for instance, $s_1 s_1 s_1 s_2 s_2 s_2$ or $s_1 s_1 s_2 s_2 s_2 s_3 s_3 s_4 s_4 s_5 s_5$, where s_n is the representation of i^n symbol. The minimum stretch length has been set to 2, to prevent the grammar from producing Σ^*.

```
N ::      n N; ε .
C ::      i; i C.

text_S:   N i tail.
N C tail: ε; N C, N C i tail.
N n C :   C symbol, N C.
C :       ε.
```

Figure 2.18 A grammar handling an infinite alphabet

2.4.4 BNF notation for VW grammars
There is a different notation for VW grammars, sometimes used in formal language theory (for instance, Greibach [VW 1974]), which derives from the BNF notation (see Section 2.3.2.1). A BNF form of our grammar from Figure 2.17 is given in Figure 2.19; hypernotions are demarcated by angle brackets and terminal symbols are represented

by themselves.

$$N \quad -> \quad i \mid i \ N$$
$$A \quad -> \quad a \mid b \mid c$$

$$<text>_S \quad -> \quad <aN> <bN> <cN>$$
$$<Ai> \quad -> \quad A$$
$$<AiN> \quad -> \quad A \ <AN>$$

Figure 2.19 The VW grammar of Figure 2.17 in BNF notation

2.4.5 Affix grammars

Like VW grammars, *affix grammars* establish long-range relations by duplicating information in an early stage; this information is, however, not part of the non-terminal name, but is passed as an independent parameter, an *affix*, which can, for instance, be an integer value. Normally these affixes are passed on to the members of a rule, until they are passed to a special kind of non-terminal, a *primitive predicate*. Rather than producing text, a primitive predicate contains a legality test. For a sentential form to be legal, all the legality tests in it have to succeed. The affix mechanism is equivalent to the VW metanotion mechanism, is slightly easier to handle while parsing and slightly more difficult to use when writing a grammar.

An affix grammar for $a^n b^n c^n$ is given in Figure 2.20. The first two lines are affix definitions for N, M, A and B. Affixes in grammar rules are traditionally preceded by a +. The names of the primitive predicates start with where. To produce abc, start with text + 1; this produces

```
list + 1 + a, list + 1 + b, list + 1 + c
```

The second member of this, for instance, produces

```
letter + b, where is decreased + 0 + 1, list + 0 + b
```

the first member of which produces

```
where is + b + b, b symbol.
```

All the primitive predicates in the above are fulfilled, which makes the final sentence legal. An attempt to let letter + b produce a symbol introduces the primitive predicate where is + a + b which fails, invalidating the sentential form.

Affix grammars are largely replaced by attribute grammars, which achieve roughly the same effect through similar but conceptually different means (see Section 2.9.1).

```
N, M::                   integer.
A, B::                   a; b; c.

text_S + N:              list + N + a, list + N + b, list + N + c.

list + N + A:            where is zero + N;
                         letter + A, where is decreased + M + N,
                                list + M + A.

letter + A:              where is + A + a, a symbol;
                         where is + A + b, b symbol;
                         where is + A + c, c symbol.

where is zero + N:       {N = 0}.

where is decreased
     + M + N:            {M = N - 1}.

where is + A + B:        {A = B}.
```

Figure 2.20 Affix grammar for $a^n b^n c^n$

2.5 ACTUALLY GENERATING SENTENCES FROM A GRAMMAR

2.5.1 The general case

Until now we have only produced single sentences from our grammars, in an ad hoc fashion, but the purpose of a grammar is to generate all its sentences. Fortunately there is a systematic way to do so. We shall use the $a^n b^n c^n$ grammar as an example. We start from the start symbol and systematically make all possible substitutions to generate all sentential forms; we just wait and see which ones evolve into sentences and when. Try this by hand for, say, 10 sentential forms. If we are not careful, we are apt to generate forms like aSQ, $aaSQQ$, $aaaSQQQ$,... only and we will never see a finished sentence. The reason is that we focus too much on a single sentential form; we have to give equal time to all of them. This can be done through the following algorithm, which keeps a queue (that is, a list to which we add at the end and remove from the beginning), of sentential forms.

Start with the start symbol as the only sentential form in the queue. Now continue doing the following:

☐ Consider the first sentential form in the queue.

☐ Scan it from left to right, looking for strings of symbols that match the left-hand side of a production rule.

☐ For each such string found, make enough copies of the sentential form, replace in each one the string that matched a left-hand side of a rule by a different alternative of that rule, and add them all to the end of the queue.

☐ If the original sentential form did not contain any non-terminals, write it down as a sentence in the grammar.

☐   Throw away the sentential form; it has been fully processed.

If no rule matched, and the sentential form was not a finished sentence, it was a blind alley; they are removed automatically by the above process and leave no trace.

The first couple of steps of this process for our $a^n b^n c^n$ grammar from Figure 2.6 are depicted in Figure 2.21. The queue runs to the right, with the first item on the left.

Step	Queue				Result
1	S				
2	abc	aSQ			abc
3	aSQ				
4	aabcQ	aaSQQ			
5	aaSQQ	aabQc			
6	aabQc	aaabcQQ	aaaSQQQ		
7	aaabcQQ	aaaSQQQ	aabbcc		
8	aaaSQQQ	aabbcc	aaabQcQ		
9	aabbcc	aaabQcQ	aaaabcQQQ	aaaaSQQQQ	aabbcc
10	aaabQcQ	aaaabcQQQ	aaaaSQQQQ		
11	aaaabcQQQ	aaaaSQQQQ	aaabbccQ	aaabQQc	
...	...				

Figure 2.21 The first couple of steps in producing for $a^n b^n c^n$

We see that we do not get a sentence for each time we turn the crank; in fact, in this case real sentences will get scarcer and scarcer. The reason is of course that as the process progresses, more and more side lines develop, which all require equal attention. Still, we can be certain that every sentence that can be produced, will in the end be produced: we leave no stone unturned. This way of doing things is called *breadth-first production*; computers are better at it than people.

It is tempting to think that it is unnecessary to replace *all* left-hand sides that we found in the top-most sentential form. Why not just replace the first one and wait for the resulting sentential form to come up again and then do the next one? This is wrong, however, since doing the first one may ruin the context for doing the second one. A simple example is the grammar

$$
\begin{array}{ccc}
S_S & \to & AC \\
A & \to & b \\
AC & \to & ac
\end{array}
$$

First doing A->b will lead to a blind alley and the grammar will produce nothing. Doing both possible substitutions will lead to the same blind alley, but then there will also be a second sentential form, ac. This is also an example of a grammar for which the queue will get empty after a (short) while.

If the grammar is context-free there is no context to ruin and it is quite safe to just replace the first match.

There are two remarks to be made here. First, it is not at all certain that we will indeed obtain a sentence for all our effort: it is quite possible that every new sentential form again contains non-terminals. We should like to know this in advance by examining the grammar, but it can be proven that it is in general impossible to do so. The formal-linguist says "It is undecidable whether a PS grammar produces the empty set", which means that there cannot be an algorithm that will for every PS grammar correctly tell if the grammar produces at least one sentence. This does not mean that we cannot prove for some given grammar that it generates nothing, if that is the case, only that the proof method used will not work for all grammars: we could have a program that correctly says Yes in finite time if the answer is Yes but that takes infinite time if the answer is No; in fact, our generating procedure above is such an algorithm that gives the correct Yes/No answer in infinite time (although we can have an algorithm that gives a Yes/Don't know answer in finite time). Although it is true that because of some deep theorem in formal linguistics we cannot always get exactly the answer we want, this does not prevent us from obtaining all kinds of useful information that gets close. We shall see that this is a recurring phenomenon. The computer scientist is aware of but not daunted by the impossibilities from formal linguistics.

The second remark is that when we do get sentences from the above production process, they may be produced in an unpredictable order. For non-monotonic grammars the sentential forms may grow for a while and then suddenly shrink again, perhaps to the empty string. Formal linguistics says that there cannot be an algorithm that for all PS grammars will produce their sentences in increasing (actually "non-decreasing") length.

The production of all sentences from a van Wijngaarden grammar poses a special problem in that there are effectively infinitely many left-hand sides to match with. For a technique to solve this problem, see Grune [VW 1984].

2.5.2 The CF case

When we generate sentences from a CF grammar, many things are a lot simpler. It can still happen that our grammar will never produce a sentence, but now we can test for that beforehand, as follows. First scan the grammar to find all non-terminals that have a right-hand side that contains terminals only or is empty. These non-terminals are guaranteed to produce something. Now scan again to find non-terminals that have a right-hand side that consists of only terminals and non-terminals that are guaranteed to produce something. This will give us new non-terminals that are guaranteed to produce something. Repeat this until we find no more new such non-terminals. If we have not met the start symbol this way, it will not produce anything.

Furthermore we have seen that if the grammar is CF, we can afford to just rewrite the left-most non-terminal every time (provided we rewrite it into all its alternatives). Of course we can also consistently rewrite the right-most non-terminal; both approaches are similar but different. Using the grammar

```
0.    N     ->    t | d | h
1.    S_S   ->    N | L & N
2.    L     ->    N , L | N
```

let us follow the adventures of the sentential form that will eventually result in $d, h \& h$. Although it will go several times up and down the production queue, we only depict here what changes are made to it. We show the sentential forms for left-most and right-most substitution, with the rules and alternatives involved; for instance, (1b) means rule 1 alternative b.

```
        S                                           S
   1b                                          1b
        L&N                                         L&N
   2a                                          0c
        N, L&N                                      L&h
   0b                                          2a
        d, L&N                                      N, L&h
   2b                                          2b
        d, N&N                                      N, N&h
   0c                                          0c
        d, h&N                                      N, h&h
   0c                                          0b
        d, h&h                                      d, h&h
```

The sequences of production rules used are not as similar as we would expect; of course, in grand total the same rules and alternatives are applied but the sequences are neither equal nor each other's mirror image, nor is there any other obvious relationship. Still both define the same production tree:

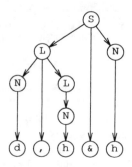

but if we number the non-terminals in it in the order they were rewritten, we would get different numberings:

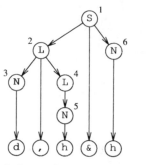

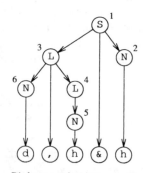

Left-most derivation order   *Right-most derivation order*

The sequence of production rules used in left-most rewriting is called the *left-most derivation* of a sentence. We do not have to indicate where each rule must be applied and need not even give its rule number; both are implicit in the left-most substitution. A *right-most derivation* is defined in the obvious way.

The production sequence S → L&N → N, L&N → d, L&N → d, N&N → d, h&N → d, h&h can be abbreviated to S $\overset{*}{\underset{l}{\to}}$ d, h&h. Likewise, the sequence S → L&N → L&h → N, L&h → N, N&h → N, h&h → d, h&h can be abbreviated to S $\overset{*}{\underset{r}{\to}}$ d, h&h. The fact that S produces d, h&h in any way is written as S $\overset{*}{\to}$ d, h&h.

The task of parsing is to reconstruct the parse tree (or graph) for a given input string, but some of the most efficient parsing techniques can be understood more easily if viewed as attempts to reconstruct a left- or right-most derivation of the input string; the parse tree then follows automatically. This is why the notion "[left|right]-most derivation" will occur frequently in this book (note the FC grammar used here).

2.6 TO SHRINK OR NOT TO SHRINK

In the previous paragraphs, we have sometimes been explicit as to the question if a right-hand side of a rule may be shorter than its left-hand side and sometimes we have been vague. Type 0 rules may definitely be of the shrinking variety, monotonic rules definitely may not, and Type 2 and 3 rules can shrink only by producing empty (ε), that much is sure.

The original Chomsky hierarchy [Misc 1959] was very firm on the subject: only Type 0 rules are allowed to make a sentential form shrink. Type 1 to 3 rules are all monotonic. Moreover, Type 1 rules have to be of the context-sensitive variety, which means that only one of the non-terminals in the left-hand side is actually allowed to be replaced (and then not by ε). This makes for a proper hierarchy in which each next class is a proper subset of its parent and in which all derivation graphs except for those of Type 0 grammars are actually derivation trees.

As an example consider the grammar for the language $a^n b^n c^n$ given in Figure 2.6:

1.	S$_S$	->	abc | aSQ
2.	bQc	->	bbcc
3.	cQ	->	Qc

which is monotonic but not context-sensitive in the strict sense. It can be made CS by expanding the offending rule 3 and introducing a non-terminal for c:

1.	S$_S$	->	abC | aSQ
2.	bQC	->	bbCC
3a.	CQ	->	CX
3b.	CX	->	QX
3c.	QX	->	QC
4.	C	->	c

Now the production graph of Figure 2.7 turns into a production tree:

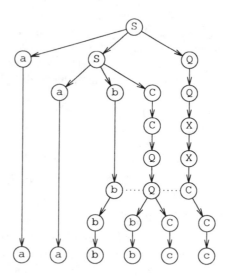

There is an additional reason for shunning ε-rules: they make both proofs and parsers more complicated. So the question arises why we should bother with ε-rules at all; the answer is that they are very convenient for the grammar writer and user.

If we have a language that is described by a CF grammar with ε-rules and we want to describe it by a grammar without ε-rules, then that grammar will almost always be more complicated. Suppose we have a system that can be fed bits of information, like: "Amsterdam is the capital of the Netherlands", "Truffles are expensive", and can then be asked a question. On a very superficial level we can define its input as:

$$\text{input}_S: \quad \text{zero-or-more-bits-of-info question}$$

or, in an extended notation

$$\text{input}_S: \quad \text{bit-of-info}^* \text{ question}$$

Since `zero-or-more-bits-of-info` will, among other strings, produce the empty string, at least one of the rules used in its grammar will be an ε-rule; the * in the extended notation already implies an ε-rule somewhere. Still, from the user's point of view, the above definition of input neatly fits the problem and is exactly what we want.

Any attempt to write an ε-free grammar for this input will end up defining a notion that comprises some of the later `bits-of-info` together with the `question` (since the `question` is the only non-empty part, it must occur in all rules involved!); but such a notion does not fit our problem at all and is an artifact:

$$\begin{array}{ll}\text{input}_S: & \text{question-preceded-by-info} \\ \text{question-preceded-by-info}: & \text{question} \\ & \text{| bit-of-info question-preceded-by-infc}\end{array}$$

As a grammar becomes more and more complicated, the requirement that it be ε-free becomes more and more a nuisance: the grammar is working against us, not for us.

This presents no problem from a theoretical point of view: any CF language can be described by an ε-free CF grammar and ε-rules are never needed. Better still, any grammar with ε-rules can be mechanically transformed into an ε-free grammar for the same language; we saw an example of such a transformation above and details of the algorithm are given in Section 4.2.3.1. But the price we pay is that of any grammar transformation: it is no longer our grammar and it reflects the original structure less well.

The bottom line is that the practitioner finds the ε-rule to be a useful tool, and it would be interesting to see if there exists a hierarchy of non-monotonic grammars alongside the usual Chomsky hierarchy. To a large extend there is: Type 2 and Type 3 grammars need not be monotonic (since they can always be made so if the need arises); it turns out that context-sensitive grammars with shrinking rules are equivalent to unrestricted Type 0 grammars; and monotonic grammars with ε-rules are also equivalent to Type 0 grammars. We can now draw the two hierarchies in one picture; see Figure 2.22.

		Chomsky (monotonic) hierarchy		non-monotonic hierarchy
global production effects	Type 0	unrestricted phrase structure grammars	monotonic grammars with ε-rules	unrestricted phrase structure grammars
	Type 1	context-sensitive grammars	monotonic grammars without ε-rules	context-sensitive grammars with non-monotonic rules
local production effects	Type 2	context-free ε-free grammars		context-free grammars
	Type 3	regular (ε-free) grammars		regular grammars regular expressions
no production	Type 4	finite-choice		

Figure 2.22 Summary of grammar hierarchies

Drawn lines separate grammar types with different power, broken lines separate conceptually different grammar types with the same power. We see that if we insist on non-monotonicity, the distinction between Type 0 and Type 1 disappears.

A special case arises if the language of a Type 1 to Type 3 grammar itself contains the empty string. This cannot be incorporated into the grammar in the monotonic hierarchy since the start symbol has already length 1 and no monotonic rule can make it shrink; the empty string has to be attached as a special property to the grammar. No such problem occurs in the non-monotonic hierarchy.

Many parsing methods will in principle work for ε-free grammars only: if something does not produce anything, you can't very well see if it's there. Often, however, the parsing method can be doctored so that it will be able to handle ε-rules.

2.7 A CHARACTERIZATION OF THE LIMITATIONS OF CF AND FS GRAMMARS

When one has been working for a while with CF grammars, one gradually gets the feeling that almost anything could be expressed in a CF grammar. That there are, however, serious limitations to what can be said by a CF grammar is shown by the famous *uvwxy* theorem, which is explained below.

2.7.1 The *uvwxy* theorem

When we have obtained a sentence from a CF grammar, we may look at each (terminal) symbol in it, and ask: How did it get here? Then, looking at the production tree, we see that it was produced as, say, the n-th member of the right-hand side of rule number m. The left-hand side of this rule, the parent of our symbol, was again produced as the p-th member of rule q, and so on, until we reach the start symbol. We can, in a sense, trace the *lineage* of the symbol in this way. If all rule/member pairs in the lineage of a symbol are different, we call the symbol *original*, and if all the symbols in a sentence are original, we call the sentence "original".

   Now there is only a finite number of ways for a given symbol to be original. This is easy to see as follows. All rule/member pairs in the lineage of an original symbol must be different, so the length of its lineage can never be more than the total number of different rule/member pairs in the grammar. There are only so many of these, which yields only a finite number of combinations of rule/member pairs of this length or shorter. In theory the number of original lineages of a symbol can be very large, but in practice it is very small: if there are more than, say, ten ways to produce a given symbol from a grammar by original lineage, your grammar will be very convoluted!

   This puts severe restrictions on original sentences. If a symbol occurs twice in an original sentence, both its lineages must be different: if they were the same, they would describe the same symbol in the same place. This means that there is a maximum length to original sentences: the sum of the numbers of original lineages of all symbols. For the average grammar of a programming language this length is in the order of some thousands of symbols, i.e., roughly the size of the grammar. So, since there is a longest original sentence, there can only be a finite number of original sentences, and we arrive at the surprising conclusion that any CF grammar produces a finite-size kernel of original sentences and (probably) an infinite number of unoriginal sentences!

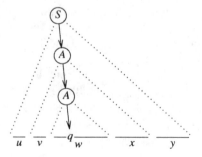

Figure 2.23 An unoriginal sentence: uvwxy

What do "unoriginal" sentences look like? This is where we come to the *uvwxy* theorem. An unoriginal sentence has the property that it contains at least one symbol in the lineage of which a repetition occurs. Suppose that symbol is a q and the repeated rule is A. We can then draw a picture similar to Figure 2.23, where w is the part produced by the most recent application of A, vwx the part produced by the other application of A and $uvwxy$ is the entire unoriginal sentence. Now we can immediately find another unoriginal sentence, by removing the smaller triangle headed by A and replacing it by a copy of the larger triangle headed by A; see Figure 2.24.

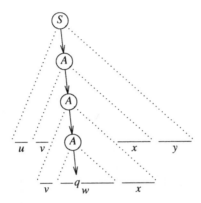

Figure 2.24 Another unoriginal sentence, uv^2wx^2y

This new tree produces the sentence $uvvwxxy$ and it is easy to see that we can, in this way, construct a complete family of sentences uv^nwx^ny for all $n \geq 0$; the w is nested in a number of v and x brackets, in an indifferent context of u and y.

The bottom line is that when we examine longer and longer sentences in a context-free language, the original sentences become exhausted and we meet only families of closely related sentences telescoping off into infinity. This is summarized in the *uvwxy* theorem: any sentence generated by a CF grammar, that is longer than the longest original sentence from that grammar, can be cut into five pieces u, v, w, x and y in such a way that uv^nwx^ny is a sentence from that grammar for all $n \geq 0$. The *uvwxy* theorem has several variants; it is also called the *pumping lemma for context-free languages*.

Two remarks must be made here. The first is that if a language keeps on being original in longer and longer sentences without reducing to families of nested sentences, there cannot be a CF grammar for it. We have already encountered the context-sensitive language $a^nb^nc^n$ and it is easy to see (but not quite so easy to prove!) that it does not decay into such nested sentences, as sentences get longer and longer. Consequently, there is no CF grammar for it.

The second is that the longest original sentence is a property of the grammar, not of the language. By making a more complicated grammar for a language we can increase the set of original sentences and push away the border beyond which we are forced to resort to nesting. If we make the grammar infinitely complicated, we can push the border to infinity and obtain a phrase structure language from it. How we can make a CF grammar infinitely complicated, is described in the Section on two-level grammars, 2.4.

2.7.2 The *uvw* theorem

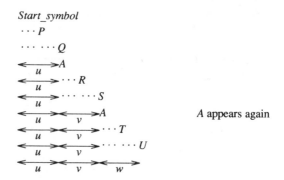

Figure 2.25 Repeated occurrence of A may result in repeated occurrence of v

A simpler form of the *uvwxy* theorem applies to regular (Type 3) languages. We have seen that the sentential forms occurring in the production process for a FS grammar all contain only one non-terminal, which occurs at the end. During the production of a very long sentence, one or more non-terminals must occur two or more times, since there are only a finite number of non-terminals. Figure 2.25 shows what we see, when we list the sentential forms one by one; the substring *v* has been produced from one occurrence of *A* to the next, *u* is a sequence that allows us to reach *A*, and *w* is a sequence that allows us to terminate the production process. It will be clear that, starting from the second *A*, we could have followed the same path as from the first *A*, and thus have produced *uvvw*. This leads us to the *uvw* theorem, or the *pumping lemma for regular languages*: any sufficiently long string from a regular language can be cut into three pieces *u*, *v* and *w*, so that $uv^n w$ is a string in the language for all $n \geq 0$.

2.8 HYGIENE IN GRAMMARS

Although the only requirement for a CF grammar is that there is exactly one non-terminal in the left-hand sides of all its rules, such a general grammar can suffer from a (small) number of ailments.

2.8.1 Undefined non-terminals

The right-hand sides of some rules may contain non-terminals for which no production rule is given. Remarkably, this does not seriously affect the sentence generation process described in 2.5.2: if a sentential form containing an undefined non-terminal turns up for processing in a left-most production process, there will be no match, and the sentential form is a blind alley and will be discarded. The rule with the right-hand side containing the undefined non-terminal will never have issue and can indeed be removed from the grammar. (If we do this, we may of course remove the last definition of another non-terminal, which will then in turn become undefined, etc.)

From a theoretical point of view there is nothing wrong with an undefined non-terminal, but if a user-specified grammar contains one, there is almost certainly an error, and any grammar-processing program should mark such an occurrence as an error.

2.8.2 Unused non-terminals
If a non-terminal never occurs in the right-hand side of any rule, its defining rules will never be used. Again this is no problem, but almost certainly implies an error somewhere.

This error is actually harder to detect than it looks. Just searching all right-hand sides is not good enough: imagine a rule $X \rightarrow aX$ where X does not occur elsewhere in the grammar. Then X occurs in a right-hand side, yet it will never be used. An algorithm to determine the set of unused non-terminals is given in Section 4.2.3.4.

2.8.3 Non-productive non-terminals
Suppose X has as its only rule $X \rightarrow aX$ and suppose X can be reached from the start symbol. Now X will still not contribute anything to the sentences of the language of the grammar, since once X is introduced, there is no way to get rid of X: any non-terminals that does not in itself produce a sublanguage is non-productive and its rules can be removed. Note that such removal will make the non-terminal undefined. An algorithm to determine if a non-terminal generates anything at all is given in 4.2.3.3.

To clean up a grammar, it is necessary to first remove the non-productive non-terminals, then the undefined ones and then the unused ones. These three groups together are called *useless non-terminals*.

2.8.4 Loops
The above definition makes "non-useless" all rules that can be involved in the production of a sentence, but there still is a class of rules that are not really useful: rules of the form $A \rightarrow A$. Such rules are called *loops*: loops can also be indirect: $A \rightarrow B$, $B \rightarrow C$, $C \rightarrow A$. A loop can legitimately occur in the production of a sentence, but if it does there is also a production of that sentence without the loop. Loops don't contribute to the language and any sentence the production of which involves a loop is *infinitely ambiguous*, meaning that there are infinitely many production trees for it. Algorithms for loop detection are given in Section 4.1.2.

Different parsers react differently to grammars with loops. Some (most of the general parsers) faithfully attempt to construct an infinite number of parse trees, some (for instance, the CYK parser) collapse the loop as described above and some (most deterministic parsers) reject the grammar. The problem is aggravated by the fact that loops can be concealed by ε-rules: a loop may only become visible when certain non-terminals produce ε.

2.9 THE SEMANTIC CONNECTION
Sometimes parsing serves only to check the correctness of a string; that the string conforms to a given grammar may be all we want to know, for instance because it confirms our hypothesis that certain observed patterns are indeed correctly described by the grammar we have designed for it. Often, however, we want to go further: we know that the string conveys a meaning, its semantics, and this semantics is directly related to the structure of the production tree of the string. (If it is not, we have the wrong grammar!)

Attaching semantics to a grammar is done in a very simple and effective way: to each rule in the grammar, a *semantic clause* is attached that relates the semantics of the members of the right-hand side of the rule to the semantics of the entire rule (in which case the semantic information flows from the leaves of the tree upwards to the start symbol) or the other way around (in which case the semantic information flows down-wards from the start symbol to the leaves) or both ways (in which case the semantic information may have to flow up and down for a while until a stable situation is reached). Semantic information flowing down is called *inherited*: each rule inherits it from its parent in the tree; semantic information flowing up is called *derived*: each rule derives it from its children.

There are many ways to express semantic clauses; since our subject is parsing and syntax rather than semantics, we will briefly describe only two often-used and well-studied techniques: attribute grammars and transduction grammars. We shall explain both using the same simple example, the language of sums of one-digit numbers; the semantics of a sentence in this language is the value of the sum. The language is generated by the grammar of Figure 2.26.

$$\begin{array}{rcl} \text{Sum}_\text{S} & \text{->} & \text{Digit} \\ \text{Sum} & \text{->} & \text{Sum + Digit} \\ \text{Digit} & \text{->} & \text{0 | 1 | ... | 9} \end{array}$$

Figure 2.26 A grammar for sums of one-digit numbers

One of its sentences is, for instance, 3+5+1; its semantics is 9.

2.9.1 Attribute grammars

The semantic clauses in an attribute grammar assume that each node in the production tree has room for one or more *attributes*, which are just values (numbers, strings or anything else) sitting in nodes in production trees. For simplicity we restrict ourselves to attribute grammars with only one attribute per node. The semantic clause of a rule in such a grammar contains some formulas which calculate the attributes of some of the non-terminals in that rule (=nodes in the production tree) from other non-terminals in that rule.

If the semantic clause of a rule R calculates the attribute of the left-hand side of R, that attribute is *derived*; if it calculates an attribute of one of the non-terminals in the right-hand side of R, say T, then that attribute is *inherited* by T. Inherited attributes are also called "synthesized attributes". The attribute grammar for our example is:

$$\begin{array}{llcll} 1. & \text{Sum}_\text{S} & \text{->} & \text{Digit} & \{A_0:=A_1\} \\ 2. & \text{Sum} & \text{->} & \text{Sum + Digit} & \{A_0:=A_1+A_3\} \\ 3a. & \text{Digit} & \text{->} & 0 & \{A_0:=0\} \\ & \cdots & \cdots & & \\ 3j. & \text{Digit} & \text{->} & 9 & \{A_0:=9\} \end{array}$$

The semantic clauses are given between curly brackets. A_0 is the (derived) attribute of the left-hand side, $A_1 \cdots A_n$ are the attributes of the members of the right-hand side. Traditionally, terminal symbols in a right-hand side are also counted in determining the index of A, although they do not (normally) carry attributes; the *Digit* in rule 2 is in position 3 and its attribute is A_3. Most systems for handling attribute grammars have less repetitive ways to express rule 3a through 3j.

The initial parse tree for 3+5+1 is given in Figure 2.27. First only the attributes for the leaves are known, but as soon as all attributes in a right-hand side of a

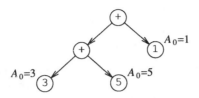

Figure 2.27 Initial stage of the attributed parse tree

production rule are known, we can use its semantic clause to calculate the attribute of its left-hand side. This way the attribute values (semantics) percolate up the tree, finally reach the start symbol and provide as with the semantics of the whole sentence, as shown in Figure 2.28. Attribute grammars are a very powerful method of handling the semantics of a language.

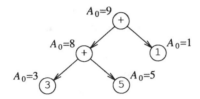

Figure 2.28 Fully attributed parse tree

2.9.2 Transduction grammars

Transduction grammars define the semantics of a string (the "input string") as another string, the "output string" or "translation", rather than as the final attribute of the start symbol. This method is less powerful but much simpler than using attributes and often sufficient. The semantic clause in a rule just contains the string that should be output for the corresponding node. We assume that the string for a node is output just after the strings for all its children. Other variants are possible and in fact usual. We can now write a transduction grammar which translates a sum of digits into instructions to calculate the value of the sum.

```
1.     Sum_s   ->    Digit            {"make it the result"}
2.     Sum     ->    Sum + Digit      {"add to the previous result"}
3a.    Digit   ->    0                {"take a 0"}
       ...           ...
3j.    Digit   ->    9                {"take a 9"}
```

This transduction grammar translates 3+5+1 into:

> take a 3
> make it the result
> take a 5
> add it to the previous result
> take a 1
> add it to the previous result

which is indeed what 3+5+1 "means".

2.10 A METAPHORICAL COMPARISON OF GRAMMAR TYPES

Text books claim that "Type n grammars are more powerful than Type $n+1$ grammars, for $n=0,1,2$", and one often reads statements like "A regular (Type 3) grammar is not powerful enough to match parentheses". It is interesting to see what kind of power is meant. Naively, one might think that it is the power to generate larger and larger sets, but this is clearly incorrect: the largest possible set of strings, Σ^*, is easily generated by the straightforward Type 3 grammar:

$$S_S \quad \text{->} \quad [\Sigma] \; S \; | \; \epsilon$$

where $[\Sigma]$ is an abbreviation for the symbols in the language. It is just when we want to restrict this set, that we need more powerful grammars. More powerful grammars can define more complicated boundaries between correct and incorrect sentences. Some boundaries are so fine that they cannot be described by any grammar (that is, by any generative process).

This idea has been depicted metaphorically in Figure 2.29, in which a rose is approximated by increasingly finer outlines. In this metaphor, the rose corresponds to the language (imagine the sentences of the language as molecules in the rose); the grammar serves to delineate its silhouette. A regular grammar only allows us straight horizontal and vertical line segments to describe the flower; ruler and T-square suffice, but the result is a coarse and mechanical-looking picture. A CF grammar would approximate the outline by straight lines at any angle and by circle segments; the drawing could still be made using the classical tools of compasses and ruler. The result is stilted but recognizable. A CS grammar would present us with a smooth curve tightly enveloping the flower, but the curve is too smooth: it cannot follow all the sharp turns and it deviates slightly at complicated points; still, a very realistic picture results. An unrestricted phrase structure grammar can represent the outline perfectly. The rose itself cannot be caught in a finite description; its essence remains forever out of our reach.

A more prosaic and practical example can be found in the successive sets of Pascal[†] programs that can be generated by the various grammar types.

☐ The set of all lexically correct Pascal programs can be generated by a regular grammar. A Pascal program is lexically correct if there are no newlines inside strings, comment is terminated before end-of-file, all numerical constants have the right form, etc.

☐ The set of all syntactically correct Pascal programs can be generated by a context-free grammar. These programs conform to the (CF) grammar in the manual.

☐ The set of all semantically correct Pascal programs can be generated by a CS grammar (although a VW grammar would be more practical). These are the

---

[†] We use the programming language Pascal here because we expect that most of our readers will be more or less familiar with it. Any programming language for which the manual gives a CF grammar will do.

Figure 2.29 The silhouette of a rose, approximated by Type 3 to Type 0 grammars

programs that pass through a Pascal compiler without drawing error messages.

☐ The set of all Pascal programs that would terminate in finite time when run with a given input can be generated by an unrestricted phrase structure grammar. Such a grammar would, however, be very complicated, even in van Wijngaarden form, since it would incorporate detailed descriptions of the Pascal library routines and the Pascal run-time system.

☐ The set of all Pascal programs that solve a given problem (for instance, play chess) cannot be generated by a grammar (although the description of the set is finite).

Note that each of the above sets is a subset of the previous set.

3

Introduction to parsing

To parse a string according to a grammar means to reconstruct the production tree (or trees) that indicate how the given string can be produced from the given grammar. There are two important points here; one is that we do require the entire production tree and the other is that there may be more than one such tree.

The requirement to recover the production tree is not natural. After all, a grammar is a condensed description of a set of strings, i.e., a language, and our input string either belongs or does not belong to that language; no internal structure or production path is involved. If we adhere to this formal view, the only meaningful question we can ask is if a given string can be recognized according to a grammar; any question as to how, would be a sign of senseless, even morbid curiosity. In practice, however, grammars have semantics attached to them; specific semantics is attached to specific rules, and in order to find out which rules were involved in the production of a string and how, we need the production tree. Recognition is (often) not enough, we need parsing to get the full benefit of the syntactic approach.

3.1 VARIOUS KINDS OF AMBIGUITY

A sentence from a grammar can easily have more than one production tree, i.e., there can easily be more than one way to produce the sentence. From a formal point of view this is again a non-issue (a set does not count how many times it contains an element), but as soon as we are interested in the semantics, the difference becomes significant. Not surprisingly, a sentence with more than one production tree is called *ambiguous*, but we must immediately distinguish between *essential ambiguity* and *spurious ambiguity*. The difference comes from the fact that we are not interested in the production trees per se, but rather in the semantics they describe. An ambiguous sentence is spuriously ambiguous if all its production trees describe the same semantics; if some of them differ in their semantics, the ambiguity is essential. The notion "ambiguity" can also be defined for grammars: a grammar is essentially ambiguous if it can produce an essentially ambiguous sentence, spuriously ambiguous if it can produce a spuriously ambiguous sentence (but not an essentially ambiguous one) and unambiguous if it cannot do either. Strangely enough, languages also can be ambiguous: there are (context-free) languages for which there is no unambiguous grammar; such languages belong in a research lab, in a cage. For testing the possible ambiguity of a grammar, see Section

9.10.

1.	Sum_S	->	Digit	$\{\ A_0:=A_1\ \}$
2.	Sum	->	Sum + Sum	$\{\ A_0:=A_1+A_3\ \}$
3a.	Digit	->	0	$\{\ A_0:=0\ \}$
	. . . .			
3j.	Digit	->	9	$\{\ A_0:=9\ \}$

Figure 3.1 A simple ambiguous grammar

A simple ambiguous grammar is given in Figure 3.1. Note that rule 2 differs from that in Figure 2.26. Now 3+5+1 has two production trees (Figure 3.2) but the semantics is the same in both cases: 9. The ambiguity is spurious. If we change the + into a −, however, the ambiguity becomes essential, Figure 3.3. The unambiguous grammar in Figure 2.26 remains unambiguous and retains the correct semantics if + is changed into −.

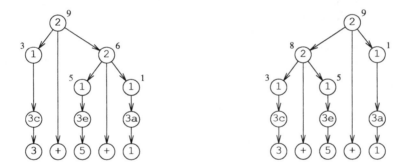

Figure 3.2 Spurious ambiguity: no change in semantics

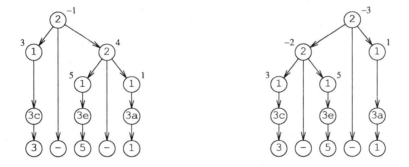

Figure 3.3 Essential ambiguity: the semantics differ

3.2 LINEARIZATION OF THE PARSE TREE

Often it is inconvenient and unnecessary to construct the actual production tree: many parsers produce a list of rule numbers instead, which means that they *linearize* the parse tree. There are three main ways to linearize a tree, *prefix*, *postfix* and *infix*. In prefix notation, each node is listed by listing its number followed by prefix listings of the subnodes in left-to-right order; this gives us the left-most derivation (for the right tree in Figure 3.2):

> left-most: 2 2 1 3c 1 3e 1 3a

In postfix notation, each node is listed by listing in postfix notation all the subnodes in left-to-right order, followed by the number of the rule in the node itself; this gives us the right-most derivation (for the same tree):

> right-most: 3c 1 3e 1 2 3a 1 2

In infix notation, each node is listed by first giving an infix listing between parentheses of the first n subnodes, followed by the rule number in the node, followed by an infix listing between parentheses of the remainder of the subnodes; n can be chosen freely and can even differ from rule to rule, but $n=1$ is normal. Infix notation is not common for derivations, but is occasionally useful. The case with $n=1$ is called the *left-corner derivation*; in our example we get:

> left-corner: (((3c)1) 2 ((3e)1))   2   ((3a)1)

The infix notation requires parentheses to enable us to reconstruct the production tree from it. The left-most and right-most derivations can do without, provided we have the grammar ready to find the number of subnodes for each node. Note that it is easy to tell if a derivation is left-most or right-most: a left-most derivation starts with a rule for the start symbol, a right-most derivation starts with a rule that produces terminal symbols only (if both conditions hold, there is only one rule, which is both left-most and right-most derivation).

The existence of several different derivations should not be confused with ambiguity. The different derivations are just notational variants for one and the same production tree. No semantic significance can be attached to their differences.

3.3 TWO WAYS TO PARSE A SENTENCE

The basic connection between a sentence and the grammar it derives from is the parse tree, which describes how the grammar was used to produce the sentence. For the reconstruction of this connection we need a parsing technique. When we consult the extensive literature on parsing techniques, we seem to find dozens of them, yet there are only two techniques to do parsing; all the rest is technical detail and embellishment.

The first method tries to imitate the original production process by rederiving the sentence from the start symbol. This method is called *top-down*, because the production tree is reconstructed from the top downwards.[†]

[†] Trees grow from their roots downwards in computer science; this is comparable to electrons

The second methods tries to roll back the production process and to reduce the sentence back to the start symbol. Quite naturally this technique is called *bottom-up*.

3.3.1 Top-down parsing
Suppose we have the monotonic grammar for the language $a^n b^n c^n$ from Figure 2.6, which we repeat here:

$$
\begin{array}{rcl}
S_S & -> & aSQ \\
S & -> & abc \\
bQc & -> & bbcc \\
cQ & -> & Qc
\end{array}
$$

and suppose the (input) sentence is aabbcc. First we try the top-down parsing method. We know that the production tree must start with the start symbol:

Now what could the second step be? We have two rules for S: S->aSQ and S->abc. The second rule would require the sentence to start with ab, which it does not; this leaves us S->aSQ:

This gives us a good explanation of the first a in our sentence. Again two rules apply: S->aSQ and S->abc. Some reflection will reveal that the first rule would be a bad choice here: all production rules of S start with an a, and if we would advance to the stage aaSQQ, the next step would inevitably lead to aaa...., which contradicts the input string. The second rule, however, is not without problems either:

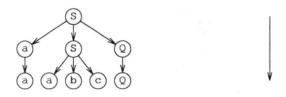

since now the sentence starts with aabc..., which also contradicts the input sentence. Here, however, there is a way out: cQ->Qc:

---

having a negative charge in physics.

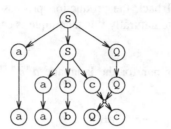

Now only one rule applies: bQc->bbcc, and we obtain our input sentence (together with the production tree):

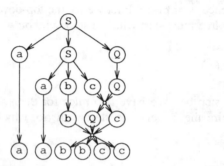

Top-down parsing tends to identify the production rules (and thus to characterize the parse tree) in prefix order.

3.3.2 Bottom-up parsing

Using the bottom-up technique, we proceed as follows. One production step must have been the last and its result must still be visible in the string. We recognize the right-hand side of bQc->bbcc in aabbcc. This gives us the final step in the production (and the first in the reduction):

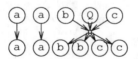

Now we recognize the Qc as derived by cQ->Qc:

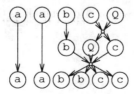

Again we find only one recognizable substring: abc:

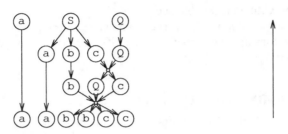

and also our last reduction step leaves us no choice:

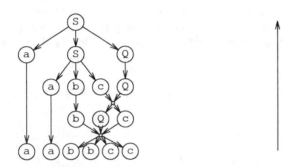

Bottom-up parsing tends to identify the production rules in postfix order. It is interesting to note that bottom-up parsing turns the parsing process into a production process. The above reduction can be viewed as a production with the reversed grammar:

$$
\begin{array}{rcl}
aSQ & -> & S \\
abc & -> & S \\
bbcc & -> & bQc \\
Qc & -> & cQ
\end{array}
$$

augmented with a rule that turns the start symbol into a new terminal symbol:

$$
S \quad -> \quad !
$$

and a rule which introduces a new start symbol, the original sentence:

$$
I_S \quad -> \quad aabbcc
$$

If, starting from I, we can produce ! we have recognized the input string, and if we have kept records of what we did, we also have obtained the parse tree.

3.3.3 Applicability

The above examples show that both the top-down and the bottom-up method will work under certain circumstances, but also that sometimes quite subtle considerations are involved, of which it is not at all clear how we can teach them to a computer. Almost the entire body of parser literature is concerned with formalizing these subtle considerations, and with considerable success.

   Note: It is also possible to reconstruct some parts of the production tree top-down and other parts bottom-up. Such methods identify the production rules in some infix order and are called *left-corner*.

3.4 NON-DETERMINISTIC AUTOMATA

Both examples above feature two components: a machine that can make substitutions and record a parse tree, and a control mechanism that decides which moves the machine should make. The machine is relatively simple since its substitutions are restricted to those allowed by the grammar, but the control mechanism can be made arbitrarily complex and may incorporate extensive knowledge of the grammar.

   This structure can be discerned in all parsing methods; there always is a substituting and record-keeping machine and a guiding control mechanism (Figure 3.4).

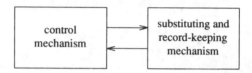

Figure 3.4 Global structure of a parser

The substituting machine is called a *non-deterministic automaton* or NDA; it is called "non-deterministic" since it often has several possible moves and the particular choice is not predetermined, and an "automaton" since it fits the Webster[†] definition "an apparatus that automatically performs certain actions by responding to preset controls or encoded instructions". It manages three items: the input string (actually a copy of it), the partial parse tree and some internal administration. Every move of the NDA transfers some information from the input string through the administration to the partial parse tree; each of the three items may be modified in the process:

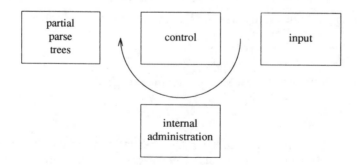

   The great strength of a NDA, and the main source of its usefulness, is that it can easily be constructed so that it can only make "correct" moves, that is, moves that keep

---

[†] *Webster's New Twentieth Century Dictionary*, The World Publ. Comp., Cleveland, 1970.

the system of partially processed input, internal administration and partial parse tree consistent. This has the consequence that we may move the NDA any way we choose: it may move in circles, it may even get stuck, but if it ever gives us an answer, i.e., a finished parse tree, that answer will be correct. It is also essential that the NDA *can* make all correct moves, so that it can produce all parsings if the control mechanism is clever enough to guide the NDA there. This property of the NDA is also easily arranged.

The inherent correctness of the NDA allows great freedom to the control mechanism, the "control" for short. It may be naive or sophisticated, it may be cumbersome or it may be efficient, it may even be wrong, but it can never cause the NDA to produce an incorrect parsing; and that is a comforting thought. (If it is wrong it may, however, cause the NDA to miss a correct parsing, to loop infinitely or to get stuck in a place where it should not).

3.4.1 Constructing the NDA
The NDA derives directly from the grammar. For a top-down parser its moves consist essentially of the production rules of the grammar and the internal administration is initially the start symbol. The control moves the machine until the internal administration is equal to the input string; then a parsing has been found. For a bottom-up parser the moves consist essentially of the reverse of the production rules of the grammar (see 3.3.2) and the internal administration is initially the input string. The control moves the machine until the internal administration is equal to the start symbol; then a parsing has been found. A left-corner parser works like a top-down parser in which a carefully chosen set of production rules has been reversed and which has special moves to undo this reversion when needed.

3.4.2 Constructing the control mechanism
Constructing the control of a parser is quite a different affair. Some controls are independent of the grammar, some consult the grammar regularly, some use large tables precalculated from the grammar and some even use tables calculated from the input string. We shall see examples of each of these: the "hand control" that was demonstrated at the beginning of this section comes in the category "consults the grammar regularly", backtracking parsers often use a grammar-independent control, LL and LR parsers use precalculated grammar-derived tables, the CYK parser uses a table derived from the input string and Earley's and Tomita's parsers use several tables derived from the grammar and the input string.

Constructing the control mechanism, including the tables, from the grammar is almost always done by a program. Such a program is called a *parser generator*; it is fed the grammar and perhaps a description of the terminal symbols and produces a program which is a parser. The parser often consists of a driver and one or more tables, in which case it is called *table-driven*. The tables can be of considerable size and of extreme complexity.

The tables that derive from the input string must of course be calculated by a routine that is part of the parser. It should be noted that this reflects the traditional setting in which a large number of different input strings is parsed according to a relatively static and unchanging grammar. The inverse situation is not at all unthinkable: many grammars are tried to explain a given input string (for instance, an observed sequence of events).

3.5 RECOGNITION AND PARSING FOR TYPE 0 TO TYPE 4 GRAMMARS

Parsing a sentence according to a grammar if we know in advance that the string indeed derives from the grammar, is in principle always possible. If we cannot think of anything better, we can just run the general production process of 2.5.1 on the grammar and sit back and wait until the sentence turns up (and we know it will); this by itself is not exactly enough, we must extend the production process a little, so that each sentential form carries its own partial production tree, which must be updated at the appropriate moments, but it is clear that this can be done with some programming effort. We may have to wait a little while (say a couple of million years) for the sentence to show up, but in the end we will surely obtain the parse tree. All this is of course totally impractical, but it still shows us that at least theoretically any string can be parsed *if* we know it is parsable, regardless of the grammar type.

3.5.1 Time requirements

When parsing strings consisting of more than a few symbols, it is important to have some idea of the *time requirements* of the parser, i.e., the dependency of the time required to finish the parsing on the number of symbols in the input string. Expected lengths of input range from some tens (sentences in natural languages) to some tens of thousands (large computer programs); the length of some input strings may even be virtually infinite (the sequence of buttons pushed on a coffee vending machine over its life-time). The dependency of the time requirements on the input length is also called *time complexity*.

Several characteristic time dependencies can be recognized. A time dependency is *exponential* if each following input symbol multiplies the required time by a constant factor, say 2: each additional input symbol doubles the parsing time. Exponential time dependency is written $O(C^n)$ where C is the constant multiplication factor. Exponential dependency occurs in the number of grains doubled on each field of the famous chess board; this way lies bankrupcy.

A time dependency is *linear* if each following input symbol takes a constant amount of time to process; doubling the input length doubles the processing time. This is the kind of behaviour we like to see in a parser; the time needed for parsing is proportional to the time spent on reading the input. So-called *real-time parsers* behave even better: they can produce the parse tree within a constant time after the last input symbol was read; given a fast enough computer they can keep up indefinitely with an input stream of constant speed. (Note that the latter is not necessarily true of linear-time parsers: they can in principle read the entire input of n symbols and then take a time proportional to n to produce the parse tree.)

Linear time dependency is written $O(n)$. A time dependency is called *quadratic* if the processing time is proportional to the square of the input length (written $O(n^2)$) and *cubic* if it is proportional to the to the third power (written $O(n^3)$). In general, a dependency that is proportional to any power of n is called *polynomial* (written $O(n^p)$).

3.5.2 Type 0 and Type 1 grammars

It is a remarkable result in formal linguistics that the *recognition* problem for a arbitrary Type 0 grammar cannot be solved. This means that there cannot be an algorithm that accepts an arbitrary Type 0 grammar and an arbitrary string and tells us in finite time if the grammar can produce the string or not. This statement can be proven, but the proof is very intimidating and, what is worse, does not provide any insight into the cause of the phenomenon. It is a proof by contradiction: we can prove that, if such an algorithm existed, we could construct a second algorithm of which we can prove that it only terminates if it never terminates. Since the latter is a logical impossibility and since all other premisses that went into the intermediate proof are logically sound we are forced to conclude that our initial premiss, the existence of a recognizer for Type 0 grammars, is a logical impossibility. Convincing, but not food for the soul. For the full proof see Hopcroft and Ullman [Books 1979, pp. 182-183] or Révész [Books 1985, p. 98].

It is quite possible to construct a recognizer that works for a certain number of Type 0 grammars, using a certain technique. This technique, however, will not work for all Type 0 grammars. In fact, however many techniques we collect, there will always be grammars for which they do not work. In a sense we just cannot make our recognizer complicated enough.

For Type 1 grammars, the situation is completely different. The seemingly inconsequential property that Type 1 production rules cannot make a sentential form shrink allows us to construct a control mechanism for a bottom-up NDA that will at least work in principle, regardless of the grammar. The internal administration of this control consists of a set of sentential forms that could have played a role in the production of the input sentence; it starts off containing only the input sentence. Each move of the NDA is a reduction according to the grammar. Now the control applies all possible moves of the NDA to all sentential forms in the internal administration in an arbitrary order, and adds each result to the internal administration if it is not already there. It continues doing so until each move on each sentential form results in a sentential form that has already been found. Since no move of the NDA can make a sentential form longer (because all right-hand sides are at least as long as their left-hand sides) and since there are only a finite number of sentential forms as long as or shorter than the input string, this must eventually happen. Now we search the sentential forms in the internal administration for one that consists solely of the start symbol; if it is there, we have recognized the input string, if it is not, the input string does not belong to the language of the grammar. And if we still remember, in some additional administration, how we got this start symbol sentential form, we have obtained the parsing. All this requires a lot of book-keeping, which we are not going to discuss, since nobody does it this way anyway.

To summarize the above, we cannot always construct a parser for a Type 0 grammar, but for a Type 1 grammar we always can. The construction of a practical and reasonably efficient parser for such grammars is a very difficult subject on which slow but steady progress has been made during the last 20 years (see the bibliography on "Unrestricted PS and CS Grammars"). It is not a hot research topic, mainly because Type 0 and Type 1 grammars are well-known to be human-unfriendly and will never see wide application. Yet it is not completely devoid of usefulness, since a good parser for Type 0 grammars would probably make a good starting point for a theorem prover.[†]

The human-unfriendliness consideration does not apply to two-level grammars. Having a practical parser for two-level grammars would be marvellous, since it would allow parsing techniques (with all their built-in automation) to be applied in many more

---

[†] A theorem prover is a program that, given a set of axioms and a theorem, proves or disproves the theorem without or with minimal human intervention.

areas than today, especially there where context conditions are important. The problems in constructing such a parser are at least as great as those seen above, but Fisher [VW 1985] has obtained some encouraging results.

All known parsing algorithms for Type 0, Type 1 and unrestricted VW grammars have exponential time dependency.

3.5.3 Type 2 grammars

Fortunately, much better parsing algorithms are known for CF (Type 2) grammars than for Type 0 and Type 1. Almost all practical parsing is done using CF and FS grammars, and almost all problems in context-free parsing have been solved. The cause of this large difference can be found in the *locality* of the CF production process: the evolution of one non-terminal in the sentential form is totally independent of the evolution of any other non-terminal, and, conversely, during parsing we can combine partial parse trees regardless of their histories. Neither is true in a context-sensitive grammar.

Both the top-down and the bottom-up parsing processes are readily applicable to CF grammars. In the examples below we shall use the simple grammar

```
Sentence_S   ->   Subject Verb Object
Subject      ->   the Noun | a Noun | ProperName
Object       ->   the Noun | a Noun | ProperName
Verb         ->   bit | chased
Noun         ->   cat | dog
ProperName   ->   ...
```

3.5.3.1 Top-down parsing

In top-down parsing we start with the start symbol and try to produce the input. The keywords here are *predict* and *match*. At any time there is a left-most non-terminal A in the sentential form and the parser tries systematically to predict a fitting alternative for A, as far as compatible with the symbols found in the input at the position where the result of A could start. Consider the example of Figure 3.5, where Object is the left-most non-terminal.

```
Input:                          the    cat    bit    a dog
Sentential form:                the    cat    bit    Object
(the internal administration)
```

Figure 3.5 Top-down parsing as the imitation of the production process

In this situation, the parser will first predict the Noun for Object, but will immediately reject this alternative since it requires the where the input has a. Next, it will try a Noun, which is temporarily accepted. The a is matched and the new left-most non-terminal is Noun. This parse will succeed when Noun eventually produces dog. The parser will then attempt a third prediction for Object, ProperName; this alternative is not immediately rejected as the parser cannot see that ProperName cannot start with a. It will fail at a later stage.

There are two serious problems with this approach. Although it can, in principle, handle arbitrary CF grammars, it will loop on some grammars if implemented naively. This can be avoided by using some special techniques, which result in general top-down parsers; these are treated in detail in Chapter 6. The second problem is that the algorithm requires exponential time since any of the predictions may turn out wrong and may have to be corrected by trial and error. The above example shows that some efficiency can be gained by preprocessing the grammar: it is advantageous to know in advance what tokens can start `ProperName`, to avoid predicting an alternative that is doomed in advance. This is true for most non-terminals in the grammar and this kind of information can be easily calculated from the grammar and stored in a table for use during parsing. For a reasonable set of grammars, linear time dependency can be achieved, as explained in Chapter 8.

3.5.3.2 *Bottom-up parsing*
In bottom-up parsing we start with the input and try to reduce it to the start symbol. Here the keywords are *shift* and *reduce*. When we are in the middle of the process, we have in our hands a sentential form reduced from the input. Somewhere in this sentential form there must be a segment (a substring) that was the result of the last production step that produced this sentential form; this segment is the right-hand side of a non-terminal to which it must now be reduced. This segment is called the *handle* of the sentential form, a quite adequate expression. See Figure 3.6. The trick is to find the handle. It must be the right-hand side of a rule, so we start looking for such a right-hand side by shifting symbols from the sentential form into the internal administration. When we find a right-hand side we reduce it to its left-hand side and repeat the process, until only the start symbol is left. We will not always find the correct handle this way; if we err, we will get stuck further on, will have to undo some steps, shift in more symbols and try again. In the above example we could have reduced the a Noun to Object, thereby boldly heading for a dead end.

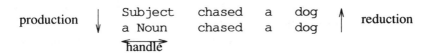

Figure 3.6 Bottom-up parsing as the inversion of the production process

There are essentially the same two problems with this approach as with the top-down technique. It may loop, and will do so on grammars with ε-rules: it will continue to find empty productions all over the place. This can be remedied by touching up the grammar. And it can take exponential time, since the correct identification of the handle may have to be done by trial and error. Again, doing preprocessing on the grammar often helps: it is easy to see from the grammar that `Subject` can be followed by `chased`, but `Object` cannot; so it is unprofitable to reduce a handle to `Object` if the next symbol is `chased`.

3.5.4 Type 3 grammars
A right-hand side in a regular grammar contains at most one non-terminal, so there is no difference between left-most and right-most production. Top-down methods are much more efficient for regular grammars than bottom-up methods.[†] When we take the

---

[†] Some regular grammars have, however, rules of the form $A \rightarrow a$ and $A \rightarrow Ba$ (and no others); in that case bottom-up methods work better.

production tree of Figure 2.14 and if we turn it 45° counterclockwise, we get the production line of Figure 3.7. The sequence of non-terminals roll on to the right, producing
terminals symbols as they go. In parsing, we are given the terminals symbols and are
supposed to construct the sequence of non-terminals. The first one is given, the start
symbol (hence the preference for top-down). If only one rule for the start symbol starts
with the first symbol of the input we are lucky and know which way to go. Very often,
however, there are many rules starting with the same symbol and then we are in need of
more wisdom. As with Type 2 grammars, we can of course find the correct continuation by trial and error, but far more efficient methods exist that can handle any regular
grammar. Since they form the basis of some advanced parsing techniques, they are
treated separately, in Chapter 5.

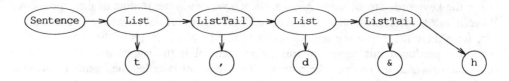

Figure 3.7 The production tree of Figure 2.14 as a production line

3.5.5 Type 4 grammars
Finite-choice (FC) grammars do not involve production trees, and membership of a
given input string to the language of the FC grammar can be determined by simple
look-up. This look-up is generally not considered to be "parsing", but is still mentioned
here for two reasons. First it can benefit from parsing techniques and second it is often
required in a parsing environment. Natural languages have some categories of words
that have only a very limited number of members; examples are the pronouns, the
prepositions and the conjunctions. It is often important to decide quickly if a given
word belongs to one of these finite-choice categories or will have to be analysed
further. The same applies to reserved words in a programming language.
    One approach is to consider the FC grammar as a regular grammar and apply the
techniques of Chapter 5. This is often amazingly efficient.
    A second often-used approach is that using a hash table. See any book on algo-
rithms, for instance, Smith [CSBooks 1989].

3.6 AN OVERVIEW OF PARSING METHODS
The reader of literature about parsing is confronted with a large number of techniques
with often unclear interrelationships. Yet (almost) all techniques can be placed in a single framework, according to some simple criteria; see Figure 3.10. We have already
seen that a parsing technique is either *top-down* or *bottom-up*. The next division is that
between *non-directional* and *directional*.

3.6.1 Directionality
A non-directional method constructs the parse tree while accessing the input in any
order it sees fit; this of course requires the entire input to be in memory before parsing
can start. There is a top-down and a bottom-up version.

3.6.1.1 Non-directional methods

The non-directional top-down method is simple and straightforward and has probably been invented independently by many people. It was first described by Unger [CF 1968] but in his article he gives the impression that the method already existed. The method has not received much attention in the literature but is more important than one might think, since it is used anonymously in a number of other parsers. We shall call it Unger's method; it is treated in Section 4.1.

The non-directional bottom-up method has also been discovered independently by a number of people, among whom Cocke, Younger [CF 1967] and Kasami [CF 1969]; an earlier description is by Sakai [CF 1962]. It is named CYK (or sometimes CKY) after the three best-known inventors. It has received considerable attention since its naive implementation is much more efficient than that of Unger's method. The efficiency of both methods can be improved, however, arriving at roughly the same performance (see Sheil [CF 1976]). The CYK method is treated in Section 4.2.

3.6.1.2 Directional methods

The directional methods process the input symbol by symbol, from left to right. (It is also possible to parse from right to left, using a mirror image of the grammar; this is occasionally useful.) This has the advantage that parsing can start, and indeed progress, considerably before the last symbol of the input is seen. The directional methods are all based explicitly or implicitly on the parsing automaton described in Section 3.5.3, where the top-down method performs predictions and matches and the bottom-up method performs shifts and reduces.

3.6.2 Search techniques

The next subdivision concerns the search technique used to guide the (non-deterministic!) parsing automaton through all its possibilities to find one or all parsings.

There are in general two methods for solving problems in which there are several alternatives in well-determined points: *depth-first search*, and *breadth-first search*. In depth-first search we concentrate on one half-solved problem; if the problem bifurcates at a given point P, we store one alternative for later processing and keep concentrating on the other alternative. If this alternative turns out to be a failure (or even a success, but we want all solutions), we roll back our actions until point P and continue with the stored alternative. This is called *backtracking*. In breadth-first search we keep a set of half-solved problems. From this set we calculate a new set of (better) half-solved problems by examining each old half-solved problem; for each alternative, we create a copy in the new set. Eventually, the set will come to contain all solutions.

Depth-first search has the advantage that it requires an amount of memory that is proportional to the size of the problem, unlike breadth-first search, which may require exponential memory. Breadth-first search has the advantage that it will find the simplest solution first. Both methods require in principle exponential time; if we want more efficiency (and exponential requirements are virtually unacceptable), we need some means to restrict the search. See any book on algorithms, for instance, Sedgewick [CSBooks 1988], for more information on search techniques.

These search techniques are not at all restricted to parsing and can be used in a wide array of contexts. A traditional one is that of finding an exit from a maze. Figure 3.8(*a*) shows a simple maze with one entrance and two exits. Figure 3.8(*b*) depicts the path a depth-first search will take; this is the only option for the human maze-walker:

he cannot duplicate himself and the maze. Dead ends make the depth-first search back-track to the most recent untried alternative. If the searcher will also backtrack at each exit, he will find all exits. Figure 3.8(c) shows which rooms are examined in each stage of the breadth-first search. Dead ends (in stage 3) cause the search branches in question to be discarded. Breadth-first search will find the shortest way to an exit (the shortest solution) first; if it continues until all there are no branches left, it will find all exits (all solutions).

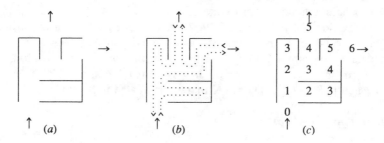

Figure 3.8 A simple maze with depth-first and breadth-first visits

3.6.3 General directional methods
Combining depth-first or breadth-first with top-down or bottom-up gives four classes of parsing techniques. The top-down techniques are treated in Chapter 6. The depth-first top-down technique allows a very simple implementation called recursive descent; this technique, which is explained in Section 6.6, is very suitable for writing parsers by hand. The bottom-up techniques are treated in Chapter 7. The combination of breadth-first and bottom-up leads to the class of Earley parsers, which have among them some very effective and popular parsers for general CF grammars. See Section 7.2.

3.6.4 Linear methods
Most of the general search methods indicated in the previous paragraph have exponential time dependency in the worst case: each symbol more in the input multiplies the parsing time by a constant factor. Such methods are unusable except for very small input length, where 20 symbols is about the maximum. Even the best of the above methods require cubic time in the worst case: for 10 tokens they do 1000 actions, for 100 tokens 1 000 000 actions and for 1000 tokens 1 000 000 000 actions, which, at 10 microseconds per action will already take almost 3 hours. It is clear that for real speed we should like to have a linear-time general parsing method. Unfortunately no such method has been discovered to date. On the other hand, there is no proof and not even an indication that such a method could not exist. (Compare this to the situation around unrestricted phrase structure parsing, where it has been proved that no algorithm for it can exist; see Section 3.5.2.) Worse even, nobody has ever come up with a specific CF grammar for which no ad hoc linear-time parser could be designed. The only thing is that we have at present no way to construct such a parser in the general case. This is a theoretically and practically unsatisfactory state of affairs that awaits further clarification.[†]

[†] There is a theoretically interesting but impractical method by Valiant [CF 1975] which does general CF parsing in $O(n^{2.81})$. Since this is only very slightly better than $O(n^{3.00})$ and since

In the meantime (and perhaps forever), we shall have to drop one of the two adjectives from our goal, a linear-time general parser. We can have a general parser, which will need cubic time at best, or we can have a linear-time parser, which will not be able to handle all CF grammars, but not both. Fortunately there are parsing methods (in particular LR parsing) that can handle very large classes of grammars but still, a grammar that is designed without regard for a parsing method and just describes the intended language in the most natural way has a small chance of allowing linear parsing automatically. In practice, grammars are often first designed for naturalness and then adjusted by hand to conform to the requirements of an existing parsing method. Such an adjustment is usually relatively simple, depending on the parsing method chosen. In short, making a linear-time parser for an arbitrary given grammar is 10% hard work; the other 90% can be done by computer.

We can achieve linear parsing time by restricting the number of possible moves of our non-deterministic parsing automaton to one in each situation. Since the moves of such an automaton involve no choice, it is called a *deterministic automaton*.

The moves of a deterministic automaton are determined unambiguously by the input stream (we can speak of a stream now, since the automaton operates from left to right); as a result it can give only one parsing for a sentence. This is all right if the grammar is unambiguous, but if it is not, the act of making the automaton deterministic has pinned us down to one specific parsing; we shall say more about this in Section 9.6.5.

All that remains is to explain how a deterministic control mechanism for a parsing automaton can be derived from a grammar. Since there is no single good solution to the problem, it is not surprising that quite a number of sub-optimal solutions have been found. From a very global point of view they all use the same technique: they analyse the grammar in depth to bring to the surface information that can be used to identify dead ends. These are then closed. If the method, applied to a grammar, closes enough dead ends so that no choices remain, the method succeeds for that grammar and gives us a linear-time parser. Otherwise it fails and we either have to look for a different method or adapt our grammar to the method.

A (limited) analogy with the maze problem can perhaps make this clearer. If we are allowed to do preprocessing on the maze (unlikely but instructive) the following method will often make our search through it deterministic. We assume that the maze consists of a grid of square rooms; see Figure 3.9(a). Now, if there is a room with three walls, add the fourth wall. Continue with this process until no rooms with three walls are left. If all rooms now have either two or four walls, there are no choices left and our method has succeeded; see Figure 3.9(b, c). We see how this method brings information about dead ends to the surface, to help restricting the choice.

It should be pointed out that the above analogy is a limited one. It is concerned with only one object, the maze, which is preprocessed. In parsing we are concerned with two objects, the grammar, which is static and can be preprocessed, and the input, which varies.

Returning to the parsing automaton, we can state the fact that it is deterministic

---

the actions required are very complicated and time-consuming, Valiant's algorithm is better
only for inputs of millions of symbols. Also, as it is a non-directional method, it would require
all these symbols to be in memory.

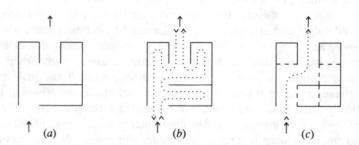

Figure 3.9 A single-exit maze made deterministic by preprocessing

more precisely: a parsing automaton is deterministic with look-ahead k if its control can, given the internal administration and the next k symbols of the input, decide unambiguously what to do next (to either match or predict and what to predict in the top-down case, and to either shift or reduce and how to reduce in the bottom-up case). Like grammar types, linear parsing methods are indicated by initials, like LL, LALR etc. If a method X uses a look-ahead of k symbols it is called $X(k)$.

3.6.5 Linear top-down and bottom-up methods
There is only one linear top-down method, called *LL*; the first L stands for Left-to-right, the second for "identifying the Left-most production", as directional top-down parsers do. LL parsing is treated in Chapter 8. LL parsing, especially LL(1) is very popular. LL(1) parsers are often generated by a parser generator but a simple variant can, with some effort, be written by hand, using recursive-descent techniques; see Section 8.2.6. Occasionally, the LL(1) method is used starting from the last token of the input backwards; it is then called *RR(1)*.

There are quite a variety of linear bottom-up methods, the most powerful being called *LR*, where again the L stand for Left-to-right and the R stand for "identifying the Right-most production". Linear bottom-up methods are treated in Chapter 9. Their parsers are invariably generated by a parser generator: the control mechanism of such a parser is so complicated that it is not humanly possible to construct it by hand. Some of the linear bottom-up methods are very popular and are perhaps used even more widely than the LL(1) method. LR(1) parsing is more powerful than LL(1) parsing, but also more difficult to understand and less convenient. The other methods cannot be compared easily to the LL(1) method. See Chapter 12 for a comparison of practical parsing methods. The LR(1) method can also be applied backwards and is then called *RL(1)*.

The great difference in variety between top-down and bottom-up methods is easily understood when we look more closely at the choices the corresponding parsers face. A top-down parser has by nature little choice: if a terminal symbol is predicted, it has no choice and can only ascertain that a match is present; only if a non-terminal is predicted it has a choice in the production of that non-terminal. A bottom-up parser can always shift the next input symbol, even if a reduction is also possible (and it often has to do so). If, in addition, a reduction is possible, it may have a choice between a number of right-hand sides. In general it has more choice than a top-down parser and more powerful methods are needed to make it deterministic.

3.6.6 Almost deterministic methods

When our attempt to construct a deterministic control for a parser fails and leaves us with an almost deterministic one, we need not despair yet. We can fall back on breadth-first search to solve the remnants of non-determinism at run-time. The better our original method was, the less non-determinism will be left, the less often breadth-first search will be needed and the more efficient our parser will be. This avenue of thought has been explored for bottom-up parsers by Tomita [CF 1986], who achieves with it what is probably the best general CF parser available today.

Of course, by reintroducing breadth-first search we are taking chances. The grammar and the input could conspire so that the non-determinism gets hit by each input symbol and our parser will again have exponential time dependency. In practice, however, they never do so and such parsers are very useful.

Tomita's parser is treated in Section 9.8. No corresponding research on top-down parsers has been reported in the literature. This is perhaps due to the fact that no amount of breadth-first searching can handle left-recursion in a grammar (left-recursion is explained in Section 6.3.2).

3.6.7 Left-corner parsing

In Section 3.6 we wrote that "almost" all parsing methods could be assigned a place in Figure 3.10. The principal class of methods that has been left out concerns "left-corner parsing". It is a third division alongside top-down and bottom-up, and since it is a hybrid between the two it should be assigned a separate column between these.

In left-corner parsing, the right-hand side of each production rule is divided into two parts: the left part is called the *left corner* and is identified by bottom-up methods. The division of the right-hand side is done so that once its left corner has been identified, parsing of the right part can proceed by a top-down method.

Although left-corner parsing has advantages of its own, it tends to combine the disadvantages or at least the problems of top-down and bottom-up parsing, and is hardly used in practice. For this reason it has not been included in Figure 3.10. From a certain point of view, top-down and bottom-up can each be considered special cases of left-corner, which gives it some theoretical significance. See Section 13.7 for literature references.

3.6.8 Conclusion

Figure 3.10 summarizes parsing techniques as they are treated in this book. Nijholt [Misc 1981] paints a more abstract view of the parsing landscape, based on left-corner parsing. See Deussen [Misc 1979] for an even more abstracted overview. An early systematic survey was given by Griffiths and Petrick [CF 1965].

	Top-down	Bottom-up
Non-directional methods	Unger parser	CYK parser

Directional methods	The predict/match automaton
	Depth-first search (backtrack)
	Breadth-first search
	    (Greibach)
	Recursive descent
	Definite Clause grammars
		The shift/reduce automaton
		Depth-first search (backtrack)
		Breadth-first search
		Breadth-first search, restricted
		    (Earley)

Linear directional methods:
breadth-first, with breadth restricted to 1
	There is only one top-down method:
	    LL(k)
		There is a whole gamut of methods:
		    precedence
		    bounded-context
		    LR(k)
		    LALR(1)
		    SLR(1)

Efficient general directional methods: maximally restricted breadth-first search	(no research reported)	Tomita

Figure 3.10 An overview of parsing techniques

4

General non-directional methods

In this chapter we will present two general parsing methods, both non-directional: Unger's method and the CYK method. These methods are called non-directional because they access the input in an seemingly arbitrary order. They require the entire input to be in memory before parsing can start.

Unger's method is top-down; if the input belongs to the language at hand, it must be derivable from the start symbol of the grammar. Therefore, it must be derivable from a right-hand side of the start symbol, say $A_1 A_2 \cdots A_m$. This, in turn, means that A_1 must derive a first part of the input, A_2 a second part, etc. If the input sentence is $z_1 z_2 \cdots z_n$, this demand can be depicted as follows:

Unger's method tries to find a partition of the input that fits this demand. This is a recursive problem: if a non-terminal A_i is to derive a certain part of the input, there must be a partition of this part that fits a right-hand side of A_i. Ultimately, such a right-hand side must consist of terminal symbols only, and these can easily be matched with the current part of the input.

The CYK method approaches the problem the other way around: it tries to find occurrences of right-hand sides in the input; whenever it finds one, it makes a note that the corresponding left-hand side derives this part of the input. Replacing the occurrence of the right-hand side with the corresponding left-hand side results in some sentential forms that derive the input. These sentential forms are again the subject of a search for right-hand sides, etc. Ultimately, we may find a sentential form that both derives the input sentence and is a right-hand side of the start symbol.

In the next two sections, these methods are investigated in detail.

4.1 UNGER'S PARSING METHOD

The input to Unger's parsing method [CF 1968] consists of a CF grammar and an input
sentence. We will first discuss Unger's parsing method for grammars without ε-rules
and without loops (see Section 2.8.4). Then, the problems introduced by ε-rules will be
discussed, and the parsing method will be modified to allow for all CF grammars.

4.1.1 Unger's method without ε-rules or loops

To see how Unger's method solves the parsing problem, let us consider a small example. Suppose we have a grammar rule

$$S \rightarrow ABC \mid DE \mid F$$

and we want to find out whether S derives the input sentence $pqrs$. The initial parsing
problem can then be schematically represented as:

S
pqrs

For each right-hand side we must first generate all possible partitions of the input sentence. Generating partitions is not difficult: if we have m cups, numbered from 1 to m,
and n marbles, numbered from 1 to n, we have to find all possible partitions such that
each cup contains at least one marble, the numbers of the marbles in any cup are consecutive, and any cup does not contain lower-numbered marbles than any marble in a
lower-numbered cup. We proceed as follows: first, we put marble 1 in cup 1, and then
generate all partitions of the other $n-1$ marbles over the other $m-1$ cups. This gives us
all partitions that have marble 1 in the first cup. Next, we put marbles 1 and 2 in the
first cup, and then generate all partitions of the other $n-2$ marbles over the other $m-1$
cups, etc. If n is less than m, no partition is possible.

Partitioning the input corresponds to partitioning the marbles (the input symbols)
over the cups (the right-hand side symbols). If a right-hand side has more symbols than
the sentence, no partition can be found (there being no ε-rules). For the first right-hand
side the following partitions must be tried:

S		
A	B	C
p	q	rs
p	qr	s
pq	r	s

The first partition results in the following sub-problems: does A derive p, does B derive
q, and does C derive rs? These sub-problems must all be answered in the affirmative,
or the partition is not the right one.

For the second right-hand side, we obtain the following partitions:

S	
D	E
p	qrs
pq	rs
pqr	s

The last right-hand side results in the following partition:

S
F
pqrs

All these sub-problems deal with shorter sentences, except the last one. They will all lead to similar split-ups, and in the end many will fail because a terminal symbol in a right-hand side does not match the corresponding part of the partition. The only partition that causes some concern is the last one. It is as complicated as the one we started with. This is the reason that we have disallowed loops in the grammar. If the grammar has loops, we may get the original problem back again and again. For instance, if there is a rule $F \rightarrow S$ in the example above, this will certainly happen.

The above demonstrates that we have a search problem here, and we can attack it with either the depth-first or the breadth-first search technique (see Section 3.6.2). Unger uses depth-first search.

In the following discussion, the grammar of Figure 4.1 will serve as an example.

$$
\begin{array}{rcl}
\text{Expr}_S & \rightarrow & \text{Expr + Term | Term} \\
\text{Term} & \rightarrow & \text{Term} \times \text{Factor | Factor} \\
\text{Factor} & \rightarrow & \text{(Expr) | i}
\end{array}
$$

Figure 4.1 A grammar describing simple arithmetic expressions

This grammar represents the language of simple arithmetic expressions, with operators + and ×, and operand i. We will use the sentence (i+i)×i as input example. So, the initial problem can be represented as:

Expr
(i+i)×i

Fitting the first right-hand side of Expr with the input results in the following partitions:

Expr		
Expr	+	Term
(	i	+i)×i
(	i+	i)×i
(	i+i	)×i
(	i+i)	×i
(	i+i)×	i
(i	+	i)×i
(i	+i	)×i
(i	+i)	×i
(i	+i)×	i
(i+	i	)×i
(i+	i)	×i
(i+	i)×	i
(i+i	)	×i
(i+i	)×	i
(i+i)	×	i

Even a small example like this already results in 15 partitions, and we will not examine them all here, although the unoptimized version of the algorithm requires this. We will only examine the partitions that have at least some chance of succeeding: we can eliminate all partitions that do not match the terminal symbol of the right-hand side. So, the only partition worth investigating further is:

Expr		
Expr	+	Term
(i	+	i)×i

The first sub-problem here is to find out whether and, if so, how Expr derives (i. We cannot partition (i into three non-empty parts because it only consists of 2 symbols. Therefore, the only rule that we can apply is the rule Expr -> Term. Similarly, the only rule that we can apply next is the rule Term -> Factor. So, we now have

Expr
Term
Factor
(i

However, this is impossible, because the first right-hand side of Factor has too many symbols, and the second one consists of one terminal symbol only. Therefore, the partition we started with does not fit, and it must be rejected. The other partitions were already rejected, so we can conclude that the rule Expr -> Expr + Term does not derive the input.

The second right-hand side of Expr consists of only one symbol, so we only have one partition here, consisting of one part. Partitioning this part for the first right-hand side of Term again results in 15 possibilities, of which again only one has a chance of succeeding:

	Expr		
	Term		
Term	×	Factor	
(i+i)	×	i	

Continuing our search, we will find the following derivation:

```
Expr ->
Term ->
Term × Factor ->
Factor × Factor ->
( Expr ) × Factor ->
( Expr + Term ) × Factor ->
( Term + Term ) × Factor ->
( Factor + Term ) × Factor ->
( i + Term ) × Factor ->
( i + Factor ) × Factor ->
( i + i ) × Factor ->
( i + i ) × i
```

and this is the only derivation to be found.

This example demonstrates several aspects of the method: even small examples require a considerable amount of work, but even some simple checks can result in huge savings. For instance, matching the terminal symbols in a right-hand side with the partition at hand often leads to the rejection of the partition without investigating it any further. Unger [CF 1968] presents several more of these checks. For instance, one can compute the minimum length of strings of terminal symbols derivable from each non-terminal. Once it is known that a certain non-terminal only derives terminal strings of length at least n, all partitions that fit this non-terminal with a substring of length less than n can be immediately rejected.

4.1.2 Unger's method with ε-rules

So far, we only have dealt with grammars without ε-rules, and not without reason. Complications arise when the grammar contains ε-rules, as is demonstrated by the following example: consider the grammar rule $S \rightarrow ABC$ and input sentence *pqr*. If we want to examine whether this rule derives the input sentence, and we allow for ε-rules, many more partitions will have to be investigated, because each of the non-terminals A, B, and C may derive the empty string. In this case, generating all partitions proceeds just as above, except that we first generate the partitions that have no marble at all in the first cup, then the partitions that have marble 1 in the first cup, etc.:

	S	
A	B	C
		pqr
	p	qr
	pq	r
	pqr	
p		qr
p	q	r
p	qr	
pq		r
pq	r	
pqr		

Now suppose that we are investigating whether B derives pqr, and suppose there is a rule $B \rightarrow SD$. Then, we will have to investigate the following partitions:

	B
S	D
	pqr
p	qr
pq	r
pqr	

It is the last of these partitions that will cause trouble: in the process of finding out whether S derives pqr, we end up asking the same question again, in a different context. If we are not careful and do not detect this, our parser will loop forever, or run out of memory.

When searching along this path, we are looking for a derivation that is using a loop in the grammar. This may even happen if the grammar does not contain loops. If this loop actually exists in the grammar, there are infinitely many derivations to be found along this path, provided that there is one, so we will never be able to present them all. The only interesting derivations are the ones without the loop. Therefore, we will cut off the search process in these cases. On the other hand, if the grammar does not contain such a loop, a cut-off will not do any harm either, because the search is doomed to fail anyway. So, we can avoid the problem altogether by cutting off the search process in these cases. Fortunately, this is not a difficult task. All we have to do is to maintain a list of questions that we are currently investigating. Before starting to investigate a new question (for instance "does S derive pqr?") we first check that the question does not already appear in the list. If it does, we do not investigate this question. Instead, we proceed as if the question were answered negatively.

Consider for instance the following grammar:

```
S   ->   LSD | D
L   ->   ε
D   ->   d
```

This grammar generates non-empty sequences of d's in a awkward way. The complete search for the questions S $\overset{*}{\to}$ d? and S $\overset{*}{\to}$ dd? is depicted in Figure 4.2.

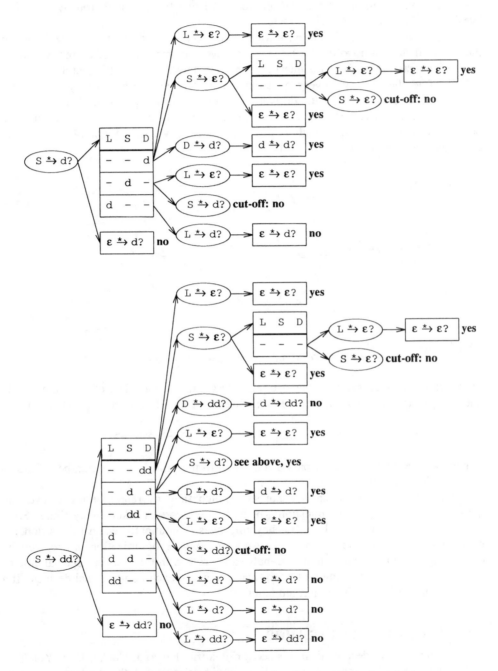

Figure 4.2 Unger's parser at work for the sentences d *and* dd

Figure 4.2 must be read from left to right, and from top to bottom. The questions are drawn in an ellipse, with the split-ups over the right-hand sides in boxes. A question is answered affirmatively if at least one of the boxes results in a "yes". In contrast, a partition only results in an affirmative answer if all questions arising from it result in a "yes".

Checking for cut-offs is easy: if a new question is asked, we follow the arrows in the reversed direction (to the left). This way, we traverse the list of currently investigated questions. If we meet the question again, we have to cut off the search.

To find the parsings, every question that is answered affirmatively has to pass back a list of rules that start the derivation asked for in the question. This list can be placed into the ellipse, together with the question. We have not done so in Figure 4.2, because it is complicated enough as it is. However, if we strip Figure 4.2 of its dead ends, and leave out the boxes, we get Figure 4.3.

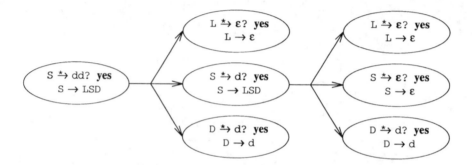

Figure 4.3 The result of Unger's parser for the sentence dd

In this case, every ellipse only has one possible grammar rule. Therefore, there is only one parsing, and we obtain it by reading Figure 4.3 from left to right, top to bottom:

$$S \ -> \ LSD \ -> \ SD \ -> \ LSDD \ -> \ SDD \ -> \ DD \ -> \ dD \ -> \ dd.$$

In general, the total number of parsings is equal to the product of the number of grammar rules in each ellipse.

This example shows that we can save much time by remembering answers to questions. For instance, the question whether L derives ε is asked many times. Sheil [CF 1976] has shown that the efficiency improves dramatically when this is done: it goes from exponential to polynomial. Another possible optimization is achieved by computing in advance which non-terminals can derive ε. In fact, this is a special case of computing the minimum length of a terminal string that each non-terminal derives. If a non-terminal derives ε, this minimum length is 0.

4.2 THE CYK PARSING METHOD

The parsing method described in this section is attributed to J. Cocke, D.H. Younger, and T. Kasami, who, independently, discovered variations of the method; it is now known as the Cocke-Younger-Kasami method, or the *CYK* method. The most accessible original description is that of Younger [CF 1967]. A much earlier description is by Sakai [CF 1962].

As with Unger's parsing method, the input to the CYK algorithm consists of a CF

grammar and an input sentence. The first phase of the algorithm constructs a table telling us which non-terminal(s) derive which substrings of the sentence. This is the
recognition phase. It ultimately also tells us whether the input sentence can be derived
from the grammar. The second phase uses this table and the grammar to construct all
possible derivations of the sentence.

We will first concentrate on the recognition phase, which really is the distinctive
feature of the algorithm.

4.2.1 CYK recognition with general CF grammars

To see how the CYK algorithm solves the recognition and parsing problem, let us consider the grammar of Figure 4.4. This grammar describes the syntax of numbers in
scientific notation. An example sentence produced by this grammar is 32.5e+1. We
will now use this grammar and sentence as an example.

$$
\begin{aligned}
\text{Number}_S &\rightarrow \text{Integer} \mid \text{Real} \\
\text{Integer} &\rightarrow \text{Digit} \mid \text{Integer Digit} \\
\text{Real} &\rightarrow \text{Integer Fraction Scale} \\
\text{Fraction} &\rightarrow . \text{ Integer} \\
\text{Scale} &\rightarrow \text{e Sign Integer} \mid \text{Empty} \\
\text{Digit} &\rightarrow 0 \mid 1 \mid 2 \mid 3 \mid 4 \mid 5 \mid 6 \mid 7 \mid 8 \mid 9 \\
\text{Empty} &\rightarrow \varepsilon \\
\text{Sign} &\rightarrow + \mid -
\end{aligned}
$$

Figure 4.4 A grammar describing numbers in scientific notation

The CYK algorithm first concentrates on substrings of the input sentence, shortest
substrings first, and then works its way up. The following derivations of substrings of
length 1 can be read directly from the grammar:

Digit	Digit		Digit		Sign	Digit
3	2	.	5	e	+	1

This means that Digit derives 3, Digit derives 2, etc. Note however, that this picture is not yet complete. For one thing, there are several other non-terminals deriving
3. This complication arises because the grammar contains so-called *unit rules*, rules of
the form $A \rightarrow B$, where A and B are non-terminals. Such rules are also often called *single rules* or *chain rules*. We can have chains of them in a derivation. So, the next step
consists of applying the unit rules, repetitively, for instance to find out which other
non-terminals derive 3. This gives us the following result:

Number, Integer, Digit	Number, Integer, Digit		Number, Integer, Digit		Sign	Number, Integer, Digit
3	2	.	5	e	+	1

Now, we already see some combinations that we recognize from the grammar: For instance, an `Integer` followed by a `Digit` is again an `Integer`, and a `.` (dot) followed by an `Integer` is a `Fraction`. We get (again also using unit rules):

Number, Integer		Fraction		Scale	
Number, Integer, Digit	Number, Integer, Digit	Number, Integer, Digit		Sign	Number, Integer, Digit
3	2	.	5	e	+	1

At this point, we see that the `Real`-rule is applicable in several ways, and then the `Number`-rule, so we get:

Number, Real						
Number, Real						
Number, Integer		Fraction		Scale		
Number, Integer, Digit	Number, Integer, Digit	Number, Integer, Digit		Sign	Number, Integer, Digit
3	2	.	5	e	+	1

We find that `Number` does indeed derive `32.5e+1`.

In the example above, we have seen that unit rules complicate things a bit. Another complication, one that we have avoided until now, is formed by ε-rules. For instance, if we want to recognize the input `43.1` according to the example grammar, we have to realize that `Scale` derives ε here, so we get the following picture:

Number, Real				
Number, Real				
Number, Integer		Fraction	Scale	
Number, Integer, Digit	Number, Integer, Digit	Number Integer Digit		
4	3	.	1	

In general this is even more complicated. We must take into account the fact that several non-terminals can derive ε between any two adjacent terminal symbols in the input sentence, and also in front of the input sentence or at the back. However, as we shall see, the problems caused by these kinds of rules can be solved, albeit at a certain cost.

In the meantime, we will not let these problems discourage us. In the example, we have seen that the CYK algorithm works by determining which non-terminals derive which substrings, shortest substrings first. Although we skipped them in the example, the shortest substrings of any input sentence are, of course, the ε-substrings. We shall have to be able to recognize them in arbitrary position, so let us first see if we can compute R_ε, the set of non-terminals that derive ε.

Initially, this set R_ε consists of the set of non-terminals A for which $A \rightarrow \varepsilon$ is a grammar rule. For the example grammar, R_ε is initially the set { Empty }. Next, we check each grammar rule: If a right-hand side consists only of symbols that are a member of R_ε, we add the left-hand side to R_ε (it derives ε, because all symbols in the right-hand side do). In the example, Scale would be added. This process is repeated until no new non-terminals can be added to the set. For the example, this results in

$$R_\varepsilon = \{ \text{Empty, Scale} \}.$$

Now, we direct our attention to the non-empty substrings of the input sentence. Suppose we have an input sentence $z = z_1 z_2 \cdots z_n$ and we want to compute the set of non-terminals that derive the substring of z starting at position i, of length l. We will use the notation $s_{i,l}$ for this substring, so,

$$s_{i,l} = z_i z_{i+1} \cdots z_{i+l-1}.$$

Figure 4.5 presents this notation graphically, using a sentence of 4 symbols.

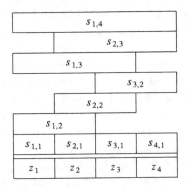

Figure 4.5 A graphical presentation of substrings

We will use the notation $R_{s_{i,l}}$ for the set of non-terminals deriving the substring $s_{i,l}$. This notation can be extended to deal with substrings of length 0: $s_{i,0} = \varepsilon$, and $R_{s_{i,0}} = R_\varepsilon$.

Because shorter substrings are dealt with first, we can assume that we are at a stage in the algorithm where all information on substrings with length smaller than a certain l is available. Using this information, we check each right-hand side in the grammar, to see if it derives $s_{i,l}$, as follows: suppose we have a right-hand side $A_1 \cdots A_m$. Then we divide $s_{i,l}$ into m (possibly empty) segments, such that A_1 derives the first segment, A_2 the second, etc. We start with A_1. If $A_1 \cdots A_m$ is to derive $s_{i,l}$, A_1 has to derive a first part of it, say of length k. That is, A_1 must derive $s_{i,k}$ (be a member of $R_{s_{i,k}}$), and $A_2 \cdots A_m$ must derive the rest:

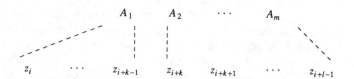

This is attempted for every k for which A_1 is a member of $R_{s_{i,k}}$, including 0. Naturally, if A_1 is a terminal, then A_1 must be equal to z_i, and k is 1. Checking if $A_2 \cdots A_m$ derives $z_{i+k} \cdots z_{i+l-1}$ is done in the same way. Unlike Unger's method, we do not have to try all partitions, because we already know which non-terminals derive which substrings.

Nevertheless, there are several problems with all this: in the first place, m could be 1 and A_1 a non-terminal, so we are dealing with a unit rule. In this case, A_1 must derive the whole substring $s_{i,l}$, and thus be a member of $R_{s_{i,l}}$, which is the set that we are computing now, so we do not know yet if this is the case. This problem can be solved by observing that if A_1 is to derive $s_{i,l}$, somewhere along the derivation there must be a first step not using a unit rule. So we have:

$$A_1 \to B \to \cdots \to C \stackrel{*}{\to} s_{i,l}$$

where C is the first non-terminal using a non-unit rule in the derivation. Disregarding ε-rules (the second problem) for a moment, this means that at a certain stage, C will be added to the set $R_{s_{i,l}}$. Now, if we repeat the process again and again, at some point, B will be added, and during the next repetition, A_1 will be added. So, we have to repeat the process until no new non-terminals are added to $R_{s_{i,l}}$. The second problem is caused by the ε-rules. If all but one of the A_t derive ε, we have a problem that is basically equivalent to the problem of unit rules. It can be solved in the same way.

In the end, when we have computed all the $R_{s_{i,l}}$, the recognition problem is solved: the start symbol S derives z ($= s_{1,n}$) if and only if S is a member of $R_{s_{1,n}}$.

This is a complicated process, but part of this complexity stems from the ε-rules and the unit rules. Their presence forces us to do the $R_{s_{i,l}}$ computation repetitively. Another, less serious source of the complexity is that a right-hand side may consist of arbitrary many non-terminals, so trying all possibilities can be a lot of work. So, imposing certain restrictions on the rules may simplify this process a great deal. However, these restrictions should not limit the generative power of the grammar significantly.

4.2.2 CYK recognition with a grammar in Chomsky Normal Form

Two of the restrictions that we want to impose on the grammar are obvious by now: no unit rules and no ε-rules. We would also like to limit the maximum length of a right-hand side to 2; this would simplify checking that a right-hand side derives a certain substring. It turns out that there is a form for CF grammars that exactly fits these restrictions: the Chomsky Normal Form. It is as if this normal form was invented for this algorithm. A grammar is in *Chomsky Normal Form* (CNF), when all rules either have the form $A \to a$, or $A \to BC$, where a is a terminal and A, B, and C are non-terminals. Fortunately, as we shall see later, almost all CF grammars can be mechanically transformed into a CNF grammar.

We will first discuss how the CYK-algorithm works for a grammar in CNF.

There are no ε-rules in a CNF grammar, so R_ε is empty. The sets $R_{s_{i,1}}$ can be read directly from the rules: they are determined by the rules of the form $A \to a$. A rule $A \to BC$ can never derive a single terminal, because there are no ε-rules.

Next, we proceed iteratively as before, first processing all substrings of length 2, then all substrings of length 3, etc. When a right-hand side BC is to derive a substring of length l, B has to derive the first part (which is non-empty), and C the rest (also non-empty).

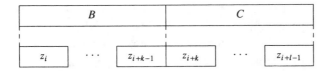

So, B must derive $s_{i,k}$, that is, B must be a member of $R_{s_{i,k}}$, and, likewise, C must derive $s_{i+k,l-k}$, that is, C must be a member of $R_{s_{i+k,l-k}}$. Determining if such a k exists is easy: just try all possibilities; they range from 1 to $l-1$. All sets $R_{s_{i,k}}$ and $R_{s_{i+k,l-k}}$ have already been computed at this point.

This process is much less complicated than the one we saw before, with a general CF grammar, for two reasons: the most important one is that we do not have to repeat the process again and again until no new non-terminals are added to $R_{s_{i,l}}$. Here, the substrings we are dealing with are really substrings. They cannot be equal to the string we started out with. The second reason is that we only have to find one place where the substring must be split in two, because the right-hand side only consists of two non-terminals. In ambiguous grammars, there can be several different splittings, but at this point, that does not worry us. Ambiguity is a parsing issue, not a recognition issue.

The algorithm results in a complete collection of sets $R_{s_{i,l}}$. The sentence z consists of only n symbols, so a substring starting at position i can never have more than $n+1-i$ symbols. This means that there are no substrings $s_{i,l}$ with $i+l>n+1$. Therefore, the $R_{s_{i,l}}$ sets can be organized in a triangular table, as depicted in Figure 4.6.

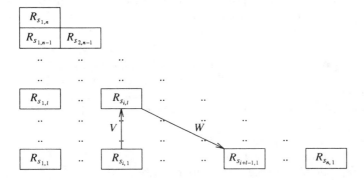

Figure 4.6 Form of the recognition table

This table is called the *recognition table*, or the *well-formed substring table*. $R_{s_{i,l}}$ is computed following the arrows V and W simultaneously, looking for rules $A \to BC$ with

B a member of a set on the V arrow, and C a member of the corresponding set on the W arrow. For B, substrings are taken starting at position i, with increasing length k. So the V arrow is vertical and rising, visiting $R_{s_{i,1}}, R_{s_{i,2}}, \cdots, R_{s_{i,k}}, \cdots, R_{s_{i,l-1}}$; for C, substrings are taken starting at position $i+k$, with length $l-k$, with end-position $i+l-1$, so the W arrow is diagonally descending, visiting $R_{s_{i+1,l-1}}, R_{s_{i+2,l-2}}, \cdots, R_{s_{i+k,l-k}}, \cdots,$ $R_{s_{i+l-1,1}}$.

As described above, the recognition table is computed in the order depicted in Figure 4.7(a). We could also compute the recognition table in the order depicted in Figure 4.7(b). In this last order, $R_{s_{i,l}}$ is computed as soon as all sets and input symbols needed for its computation are available. For instance, when computing $R_{s_{3,3}}$, $R_{s_{5,1}}$ is relevant, but $R_{s_{6,1}}$ is not, because the substring at position 3 with length 3 does not contain the substring at position 6 with length 1. This order makes the algorithm particularly suitable for on-line parsing, where the number of symbols in the input is not known in advance, and additional information is computed each time a symbol is entered.

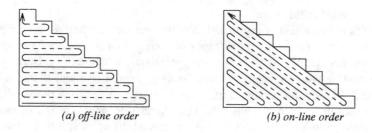

                (a) off-line order   *(b) on-line order*

Figure 4.7 Different orders in which the recognition table can be computed

Now, let us examine the cost of this algorithm. Figure 4.6 shows that there are $(n*(n+1))/2$ substrings to be examined. For each substring, at most $n-1$ different k-positions have to be examined. All other operations are independent of n, so the algorithm operates in a time at most proportional to the cube of the length of the input sentence. As such, it is far more efficient than exhaustive search, which needs a time that is exponential in the length of the input sentence.

4.2.3 Transforming a CF grammar into Chomsky Normal Form

The previous section has demonstrated that it is certainly worth while to try to transform a general CF grammar into CNF. In this section, we will discuss this transformation, using our number grammar as an example. The transformation is split up into several stages:
- first, ε-rules are eliminated.
- then, unit rules are eliminated.
- then, non-productive non-terminals are removed.
- then, non-reachable non-terminals are removed.
- then, finally, the remaining grammar rules are modified, and rules are added, until they all have the desired form, that is, either $A \rightarrow a$ or $A \rightarrow BC$.

All these transformations will not change the language defined by the grammar. This is not proven here. Most books on formal language theory discuss these transformations more formally and provide proofs, see for example Hopcroft and Ullman [Books 1979].

4.2.3.1 *Eliminating ε-rules*

Suppose we have a grammar G, with an ε-rule $A{\rightarrow}\varepsilon$, and we want to eliminate this rule. We cannot just remove the rule, as this would change the language defined by the non-terminal A, and also probably the language defined by the grammar G. So, something has to be done about the occurrences of A in the right-hand sides of the grammar rules. Whenever A occurs in a grammar rule $B{\rightarrow}\alpha A \beta$, we replace this rule with two others: $B{\rightarrow}\alpha A' \beta$, where A' is a new non-terminal, for which we shall add rules later (these rules will be the non-empty grammar rules of A), and $B{\rightarrow}\alpha\beta$, which handles the case where A derives ε in a derivation using the $B{\rightarrow}\alpha A \beta$ rule. Notice that the α and β in the rules above could also contain A; in this case, each of the new rules must be replaced in the same way, and this process must be repeated until all occurrences of A are removed. When we are through, there will be no occurrence of A left in the grammar.

Every ε-rule must be handled in this way. Of course, during this process new ε-rules may originate. This is only to be expected: the process makes all ε-derivations explicit. The newly created ε-rules must be dealt with in exactly the same way. Ultimately, this process will stop, because the number of of non-terminals deriving ε is limited and, in the end, none of these non-terminals occur in any right-hand side.

The next step in eliminating the ε-rules is the addition of grammar rules for the new non-terminals. If A is a non-terminal for which an A' was introduced, we add a rule $A'{\rightarrow}\alpha$ for all non-ε-rules $A{\rightarrow}\alpha$. Since all ε-rules have been made explicit, we can be sure that if a rule does not derive ε directly, it cannot do so indirectly. A problem that may arise here is that there may not be a non-ε-rule for A. In this case, A only derives ε, so we remove all rules using A'.

All this leaves us with a grammar that still contains ε-rules. However, none of the non-terminals having an ε-rule occurs in any right-hand side. These occurrences have just been carefully removed. So, these non-terminals can never play a role in any derivation from the start symbol S, with one important exception: S itself. In particular, we now have a rule $S{\rightarrow}\varepsilon$ if and only if ε is a member of the language defined by the grammar G. All other non-terminals with ε-rules can be removed safely. Cleaning up the grammar is left to later transformations.

```
S    ->    L a M
L    ->    L M
L    ->    ε
M    ->    M M
M    ->    ε
```

Figure 4.8 An example grammar to test ε-rule elimination schemes

The grammar of Figure 4.8 is a nasty grammar to test your ε-rule elimination scheme. Our scheme transforms this grammar into the grammar of Figure 4.9. This grammar still has ε-rules, but these will be eliminated by the removal of non-productive and/or non-reachable non-terminals. Cleaning up this mess will leave only one rule: $S{\rightarrow}a$. Removing the ε-rules in our number grammar results in the grammar of Figure 4.10. Note that the two rules to produce ε, Empty and Scale, are still

$$
\begin{array}{rcl}
\text{S} & \text{->} & \text{L}'\ \text{a}\ \text{M}'\ \mid\ \text{a}\ \text{M}'\ \mid\ \text{L}'\ \text{a}\ \mid\ \text{a} \\
\text{L} & \text{->} & \text{L}'\ \text{M}'\ \mid\ \text{L}'\ \mid\ \text{M}'\ \mid\ \varepsilon \\
\text{M} & \text{->} & \text{M}'\ \text{M}'\ \mid\ \text{M}'\ \mid\ \varepsilon \\
\text{L}' & \text{->} & \text{L}'\ \text{M}'\ \mid\ \text{L}'\ \mid\ \text{M}' \\
\text{M}' & \text{->} & \text{M}'\ \text{M}'\ \mid\ \text{M}'
\end{array}
$$

Figure 4.9 Result after our ε-rule elimination scheme

$$
\begin{array}{rcl}
\text{Number}_{\text{S}} & \text{->} & \text{Integer}\ \mid\ \text{Real} \\
\text{Integer} & \text{->} & \text{Digit}\ \mid\ \text{Integer Digit} \\
\text{Real} & \text{->} & \text{Integer Fraction Scale}'\ \mid\ \text{Integer Fraction} \\
\text{Fraction} & \text{->} & \text{. Integer} \\
\text{Scale}' & \text{->} & \text{e Sign Integer} \\
\text{Scale} & \text{->} & \text{e Sign Integer}\ \mid\ \varepsilon \\
\text{Empty} & \text{->} & \varepsilon \\
\text{Digit} & \text{->} & 0\ \mid\ 1\ \mid\ 2\ \mid\ 3\ \mid\ 4\ \mid\ 5\ \mid\ 6\ \mid\ 7\ \mid\ 8\ \mid\ 9 \\
\text{Sign} & \text{->} & +\ \mid\ -
\end{array}
$$

Figure 4.10 Our number grammar after elimination of ε-rules

present but are not used any more.

4.2.3.2 Eliminating unit rules
The next trouble-makers to be eliminated are the unit rules, that is, rules of the form
$A \rightarrow B$. It is important to realize that, if such a rule $A \rightarrow B$ is used in a derivation, it must
be followed at some point by the use of a rule $B \rightarrow \alpha$. Therefore, if we have a rule
$A \rightarrow B$, and the rules for B are

$$B \rightarrow \alpha_1 \mid \alpha_2 \mid \cdots \mid \alpha_n,$$

we can replace the rule $A \rightarrow B$ with

$$A \rightarrow \alpha_1 \mid \alpha_2 \mid \cdots \mid \alpha_n.$$

In doing this, we can of course introduce new unit rules. In particular, when repeating
this process, we could at some point again get the rule $A \rightarrow B$. In this case, we have an
infinitely ambiguous grammar, because B derives B. Now this may seem to pose a
problem, but we can just leave such a unit rule out; the effect is that we short-cut
derivations like

$$A \rightarrow B \rightarrow \cdots \rightarrow B \rightarrow \cdots$$

Also rules of the form $A \rightarrow A$ are left out. In fact, a pleasant side-effect of removing ε-
rules and unit rules is that the resulting grammar is not infinitely ambiguous any more.

　　　Removing the unit rules in our ε-free number grammar results in the grammar of
Figure 4.11.

4.2.3.3 Removing non-productive non-terminals
Non-productive non-terminals are non-terminals that have no terminal derivation.
Every sentential form that can be derived from it will contain non-terminals. These are

Number$_S$	->	0 | 1 | 2 | 3 | 4 | 5 | 6 | 7 | 8 | 9
Number$_S$	->	Integer Digit
Number$_S$	->	Integer Fraction Scale' | Integer Fraction
Integer	->	0 | 1 | 2 | 3 | 4 | 5 | 6 | 7 | 8 | 9
Integer	->	Integer Digit
Real	->	Integer Fraction Scale' | Integer Fraction
Fraction	->	. Integer
Scale'	->	e Sign Integer
Scale	->	e Sign Integer | ε
Empty	->	ε
Digit	->	0 | 1 | 2 | 3 | 4 | 5 | 6 | 7 | 8 | 9
Sign	->	+ | −

Figure 4.11 Our number grammar after eliminating unit rules

not pleasant things to have in a grammar. Naturally, "proper" grammars do not have them. Nevertheless, we must be able to determine which non-terminals do have a terminal derivation, if only to check that a grammar is "proper".

To find out which non-terminals have a terminal derivation we use a scheme that hinges on the fact that a non-terminal has a terminal derivation if and only if it has a right-hand side consisting of symbols that all have a terminal derivation. Of course, terminals have themselves a terminal derivation. The scheme works as follows: First, we mark the non-terminals that have a right-hand side containing only terminals: they obviously have a terminal derivation. Next, we mark all non-terminals that have a right-hand side consisting only of terminals and marked non-terminals: they too have a terminal derivation. We keep on doing this until there are no more non-terminals to be marked.

Now, the non-productive non-terminals are the ones that have not been marked in the process. We remove all rules that contain a non-marked non-terminal in either the left-hand side or the right-hand side. This process does not remove all rules of a marked non-terminal, as there must be at least one rule for it with a right-hand side consisting only of terminals and marked non-terminals, or it would not have been marked in the first place. (This may remove all rules, including those for the start-symbol, in which case the grammar describes the empty language).

Our number grammar does not contain non-productive non-terminals, so it will not be changed by this phase.

4.2.3.4 Removing non-reachable non-terminals

A non-terminal is called *reachable* or *accessible* if there exists at least one sentential form, derivable from the start symbol, in which it occurs. So, a non-terminal A is reachable if $S \xrightarrow{*} \alpha A \beta$ for some α and β. A non-terminal is *non-reachable* if it is not reachable. For non-reachable non-terminals the same holds as for non-productive non-terminals: they do not occur in "proper" grammars. However, they can be introduced by some of the transformations that we have seen before, so we must be able to find them to "clean up" a grammar again.

We found the non-productive non-terminals by finding the "useful" ones. Likewise, we find the non-reachable non-terminals by finding the reachable ones. For this, we can use the following scheme: First, the start symbol is marked: it is reachable. Then, any time an as yet unmarked non-terminal is marked, all non-terminals occurring in any of its right-hand sides are marked. In the end, the unmarked non-terminals are not reachable and their rules can be removed. They do not occur in any right-hand side of a reachable non-terminal, for otherwise it would have been marked in the process.

It is interesting to note that removing non-reachable non-terminals does not introduce non-productive non-terminals. However, first removing non-reachable non-terminals and then removing non-productive non-terminals may produce a grammar which contains again non-reachable non-terminals. Finding an example demonstrating this is left to the reader.

In our number grammar, the non-terminals Real, Scale, and Empty are non-reachable, which leaves us with the grammar of Figure 4.12.

```
Number_S  ->  0 | 1 | 2 | 3 | 4 | 5 | 6 | 7 | 8 | 9
Number_S  ->  Integer Digit
Number_S  ->  Integer Fraction Scale' | Integer Fraction
Integer   ->  0 | 1 | 2 | 3 | 4 | 5 | 6 | 7 | 8 | 9
Integer   ->  Integer Digit
Fraction  ->  . Integer
Scale'    ->  e Sign Integer
Digit     ->  0 | 1 | 2 | 3 | 4 | 5 | 6 | 7 | 8 | 9
Sign      ->  + | -
```

Figure 4.12 Our number grammar after removal of non-reachable rules

4.2.3.5 Finally, to Chomsky Normal Form

After all these grammar transformations, we have a grammar without ε-rules or unit rules, all non-terminal are reachable, and there are no non-productive non-terminals. So, we are left with two types of rules: rules of the form $A \rightarrow a$, which are already in the proper form, and rules of the form $A \rightarrow X_1 X_2 \cdots X_m$, with $m \geq 2$. For every terminal b occurring in such a rule we create a new non-terminal T_b with as only rule $T_b \rightarrow b$, and we replace each occurrence of b in a rule $A \rightarrow X_1 X_2 \cdots X_m$ with T_b. Now, the only rules not yet in CNF are of the form $A \rightarrow X_1 X_2 \cdots X_m$, with $m \geq 3$, and all X_i a non-terminal. These rules can now just be split up:

$$A \quad \rightarrow \quad X_1 X_2 \cdots X_m$$

is replaced by the following two rules:

$$A \quad \rightarrow \quad A_1 X_3 \cdots X_m$$
$$A_1 \quad \rightarrow \quad X_1 X_2$$

where A_1 is a new non-terminal. Now, we have replaced the original rule with one that is one shorter, and one that is in CNF. This splitting can be repeated until all parts are in CNF. Figure 4.13 represents our number grammar in CNF.

Number$_S$	->	0 | 1 | 2 | 3 | 4 | 5 | 6 | 7 | 8 | 9
Number$_S$	->	Integer Digit
Number$_S$	->	N1 Scale' | Integer Fraction
N1	->	Integer Fraction
Integer	->	0 | 1 | 2 | 3 | 4 | 5 | 6 | 7 | 8 | 9
Integer	->	Integer Digit
Fraction	->	T1 Integer
T1	->	.
Scale'	->	N2 Integer
N2	->	T2 Sign
T2	->	e
Digit	->	0 | 1 | 2 | 3 | 4 | 5 | 6 | 7 | 8 | 9
Sign	->	+ | -

Figure 4.13 Our number grammar in CNF

4.2.4 The example revisited

Now, let us see how the CYK algorithm works with our example grammar, which we have just transformed into CNF. Again, our input sentence is 32.5e+1. The recognition table is given in Figure 4.14. The bottom row is read directly from the grammar; for instance, the only non-terminals having a production rule with right-hand side 3 are Number, Integer, and Digit. Notice that for each symbol a in the sentence there must be at least one non-terminal A with a production rule $A{\rightarrow}a$, or else the sentence cannot be derived from the grammar.

The other rows are computed as described before. Actually, there are two ways to compute a certain $R_{s_{i,l}}$. The first method is to check each right-hand side in the grammar; for instance, to check whether the right-hand side N1 Scale' derives the substring 2.5e ($= s_{2,4}$). The recognition table derived so far tells us that

☐   N1 is not a member of $R_{s_{2,1}}$ or $R_{s_{2,2}}$,

☐   N1 is a member of $R_{s_{2,3}}$, but Scale' is not a member of $R_{s_{5,1}}$,

so the answer is no. Using this method, we have to check each right-hand side in this way, adding the left-hand side to $R_{s_{2,4}}$ if we find that the right-hand side derives $s_{2,4}$.

The second method is to compute possible right-hand sides from the recognition table computed so far; for instance, $R_{s_{2,4}}$ is the set of non-terminals that have a right-hand side AB where either

☐ A is a member of $R_{s_{2,1}}$ and B is a member of $R_{s_{3,3}}$, or

☐ A is a member of $R_{s_{2,2}}$ and B is a member of $R_{s_{4,2}}$, or

☐ A is a member of $R_{s_{2,3}}$ and B is a member of $R_{s_{5,1}}$.

This gives as possible combinations for AB: N1 T2 and Number T2. Now we check all rules in the grammar to see if they have a right-hand side that is a member of this set. If so, the left-hand side is added to $R_{s_{2,4}}$.

4.2.5 CYK parsing with Chomsky Normal Form

We now have an algorithm that determines whether a sentence belongs to a language or not, and it is much faster than exhaustive search. Most of us, however, not only want to know whether a sentence belongs to a language, but also, if so, how it can be derived

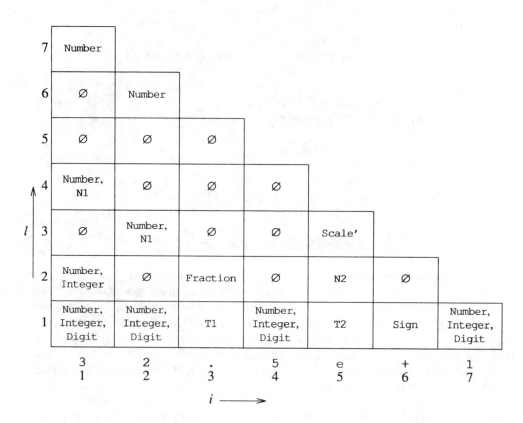

Figure 4.14 The recognition table for the input sentence 32.5e+1

from the grammar. If it can be derived in more than one way, we probably want to know all possible derivations. As the recognition table contains the information on all derivations of substrings of the input sentence that we could possible make, it also contains the information we want. Unfortunately, this table contains too much information, so much that it hides what we want to know. The table may contain information about non-terminals deriving substrings, where these derivations cannot be used in the derivation of the input sentence from the start symbol S. For instance, in the example above, $R_{s_{2,3}}$ contains N1, but the fact that N1 derives 2.5 cannot be used in the derivation of 32.5e+1 from Number.

The key to the solution of this problem lies in the simple observation that the derivation must start with the start-symbol S. The first step of the derivation of the input sentence z, with length n, can be read from the grammar, together with the recognition table. If $n=1$, there must be a rule $S \rightarrow z$; if $n \geq 2$, we have to examine all rules $S \rightarrow AB$, where A derives the first k symbols of z, and B the rest, that is, A is a member of $R_{s_{1,k}}$ and B is a member of $R_{s_{k+1,n-k}}$, for some k. There must be at least one such a rule, or else S would not derive z.

Now, for each of these combinations AB we have the same problem: how does A derive $s_{1,k}$ and B derive $s_{k+1,n-k}$? These problems are solved in exactly the same way. It does not matter which non-terminal is examined first. Consistently taking the left-

most one results in a left-most derivation, consistently taking the right-most one results
in a right-most derivation.

Notice that we can use an Unger-style parser for this. However, it would not have
to generate all partitions any more, because we already know which partitions will
work.

Let us try to find a left-most derivation for the example sentence and grammar,
using the recognition table of Figure 4.14. We begin with the start symbol, Number.
Our sentence contains seven symbols, which is certainly more than one, so we have to
use one of the rules with a right-hand side of the form AB. The Integer Digit rule is
not applicable here, because the only instance of Digit that could lead to a derivation
of the sentence is the one in $R_{s_{7,1}}$, but Integer is not a member of $R_{s_{1,6}}$. The
Integer Fraction rule is not applicable either, because there is no Fraction
deriving the last part of the sentence. This leaves us with the production rule Number
-> N1 Scale', which is indeed applicable, because N1 is a member of $R_{s_{1,4}}$, and
Scale' is a member of $R_{s_{5,3}}$, so N1 derives 32.5 and Scale' derives e+1.

Next, we have to find out how N1 derives 32.5. There is only one applicable
rule: N1 -> Integer Fraction, and it is indeed applicable, because Integer is a
member of $R_{s_{1,2}}$, and Fraction is a member of $R_{s_{3,2}}$, so Integer derives 32, and
Fraction derives .5. In the end, we find the following derivation:

```
Number ->
N1 Scale' ->
Integer Fraction Scale' ->
Integer Digit Fraction Scale' ->
3 Digit Fraction Scale' ->
3 2 Fraction Scale' ->
3 2 T1 Integer Scale' ->
3 2 . Integer Scale' ->
3 2 . 5 Scale' ->
3 2 . 5 N2 Integer ->
3 2 . 5 T2 Sign Integer ->
3 2 . 5 e Sign Integer ->
3 2 . 5 e + Integer ->
3 2 . 5 e + 1
```

Unfortunately, this is not exactly what we want, because this is a derivation that uses
the rules of the grammar of Figure 4.13, not the rules of the grammar of Figure 4.4, the
one that we started with.

4.2.6 Undoing the effect of the CNF transformation

When we examine the grammar of Figure 4.4 and the recognition table of Figure 4.14,
we see that the recognition table contains the information we need on most of the non-
terminals of the original grammar. However, there are a few non-terminals missing in
the recognition table: Scale, Real, and Empty. Scale and Empty were removed
because they became non-reachable, after the elimination of ε-rules. Empty was
removed altogether, because it only derived the empty string, and Scale was replaced
by Scale', where Scale' derives exactly the same as Scale, except for the empty

string. We can use this to add some more information to the recognition table: at every occurrence of Scale', we add Scale.

The non-terminal Real was removed because it became non-reachable after eliminating the unit rules. Now, the CYK algorithm does not *require* that all non-terminals in the grammar be reachable. We could just as well have left the non-terminal Real in the grammar, and have transformed its rules to CNF. The CYK algorithm would then have added Real to the recognition table, wherever that would be appropriate. The rules for Real that would be added to the grammar of Figure 4.13 are:

Real   ->   N1 Scale' | Integer Fraction

The resulting recognition table is presented in Figure 4.15. In this figure, we have also added an extra row at the bottom of the triangle. This extra row represents the non-terminals that derive the empty string. These non-terminals can be considered as possibly occurring between any two adjacent symbols in the sentence, and also in front of or at the end of the sentence. The set $R_{s_{i,0}}$ represents the non-terminals that can be considered as possibly occurring just in front of symbol z_i and the set $R_{s_{n+1,0}}$ represents the ones that can occur at the end of the sentence.

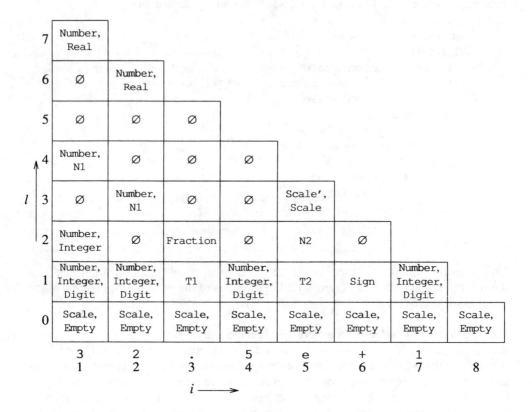

Figure 4.15 The recognition table with Scale, Real, *and* Empty *added*

Now, we have a recognition table which contains all the information we need to parse a sentence with the original grammar. Again, a derivation starts with the start-symbol S. If $A_1 A_2 \cdots A_m$ is a right-hand side of S, we want to know if this rule can be applied, that is, if $A_1 A_2 \cdots A_m$ derives $s_{1,n}$. This is checked, starting with A_1. There are two cases:

☐ A_1 is a terminal symbol. In this case, it must be the first symbol of $s_{1,n}$, or this rule is not applicable. Then, we must check if $A_2 \cdots A_m$ derives $s_{2,n-1}$, in the same way that we are now checking if $A_1 A_2 \cdots A_m$ derives $s_{1,n}$.

☐ A_1 is a non-terminal. In this case, it must be a member of a $R_{s_{1,k}}$, for some k, or this rule is not applicable. Then, we must check if $A_2 \cdots A_m$ derives $s_{k+1,n}$, in the same way that we are now checking if $A_1 A_2 \cdots A_m$ derives $s_{1,n}$. If we want all parsings, we must do this for every k for which A_1 is a member of $R_{s_{1,k}}$. Notice that non-terminals deriving the empty string pose no problem at all, because they appear as a member of $R_{s_{i,0}}$ for all i.

We have now determined whether the rule is applicable, and if it is, which parts of the rule derive which substrings. The next step now is to determine how the substrings can be derived. These tasks are similar to the task we started with, and are solved in the same way. This process terminates at some time, as long as the grammar does not contain loops. This is simply an Unger parser that knows in advance which partitions will lead to a successful parse.

Let us go back to the grammar of Figure 4.4 and the recognition table of Figure 4.15, and see how this works for our example input sentence. We now know that Number does derive 32.5e+1, and want to know how. We first ask ourselves: can we use the Number -> Integer rule? Integer is a member of $R_{s_{1,1}}$ and $R_{s_{1,2}}$, but there is nothing behind the Integer in the rule to derive the rest of the sentence, so we cannot use this rule. Can we use the Number -> Real rule? Yes we can, because Real is a member of $R_{s_{1,7}}$, and the length of the sentence is 7. So, we start our derivation with

       Number -> Real -> ...

Now, we get similar questions for the Real non-terminal: can we use the Real -> Integer Fraction Scale rule? Well, Integer is a member of $R_{s_{1,1}}$, but we cannot find a Fraction in any of the $R_{s_{2,k}}$ sets. However, Integer is also a member of $R_{s_{1,2}}$, and Fraction is a member of $R_{s_{3,2}}$. Now, Scale is a member of $R_{s_{5,0}}$; this does not help because it would leave nothing in the rule to derive the rest. Fortunately, Scale is also a member of $R_{s_{5,3}}$, and that matches exactly to the end of the string. So, this rule is indeed applicable, and we continue our derivation:

       Number -> Real -> Integer Fraction Scale -> ...

The sentence is now split up into three parts:

Number		
Real		
Integer	Fraction	Scale
3 2	. 5	e + 1

It is left to the reader to verify that we will find only one derivation, and that this is it:

```
Number ->
Real ->
Integer Fraction Scale ->
Integer Digit Fraction Scale ->
Digit Digit Fraction Scale ->
3 Digit Fraction Scale ->
3 2 Fraction Scale ->
3 2 . Integer Scale ->
3 2 . Digit Scale ->
3 2 . 5 Scale ->
3 2 . 5 e Sign Integer ->
3 2 . 5 e + Integer ->
3 2 . 5 e + Digit ->
3 2 . 5 e + 1
```

4.2.7 A short retrospective of CYK

We have come a long way. We started with building a recognition table using the original grammar. Then we found that using the original grammar with its unit rules and ε-rules is somewhat complicated, although it can certainly be done. We proceeded by transforming the grammar to CNF. CNF does not contain unit rules or ε-rules; our gain in this respect was that the algorithm for constructing the recognition table became much simpler. The limitation of the maximum length of a right-hand side to 2 was a gain in efficiency, and also a little in simplicity. However, Sheil [CF 1976] has demonstrated that the efficiency only depends on the maximum number of non-terminals occurring in a right-hand side of the grammar, not on the length of the right-hand sides. This can easily be understood, once you realize that the efficiency depends (among others) on the number of cuts in a substring that are "difficult" to find, when checking whether a right-hand side derives this substring. This number of "difficult" cuts only depends on the number of non-terminals in the right-hand side. So, for efficiency, CNF is a bit too restrictive.

A disadvantage of this transformation to CNF is that the resulting recognition table lacks some information that we need to construct a derivation using the original grammar. In the transformation process, some non-terminals were thrown away, because they became non-productive. Fortunately, the missing information could easily be added. Ultimately, this process resulted in almost the same recognition table that we would get with our first attempt using the original grammar. It only contains some extra information on non-terminals that were added during the transformation of the grammar to CNF. More importantly, however, it was obtained in a simpler and much more efficient way.

4.2.8 Chart parsing

The CYK algorithm is also known under the name of *chart parsing*. More precisely, both techniques have a number of variants and some variants of the CYK algorithm are identical to some variants of chart parsing. The most striking difference between them lies in the implementation; conceptually both algorithms do the same thing: they collect possible parsings for larger and larger chunks of the input.

Although often presented in a different format, a *chart* is just a recognition table. Figure 4.16 shows the recognition table of Figure 4.14 in a chart format: each arc represents a non-terminal deriving the part of the sentence spanned by the arc.

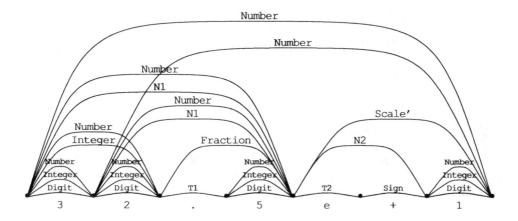

Figure 4.16 The recognition table of Figure 4.14 in chart format

Several variants of chart parsing are discussed and compared in Bolc [NatLang 1987].

5

Regular grammars and finite-state automata

Regular grammars are the simplest form of grammars that still have generative power. They can describe concatenation (joining two texts together) and repetition and can specify alternatives, but they cannot express nesting. Regular grammars are probably the best-understood part of formal linguistics and almost all questions about them can be answered.

5.1 APPLICATIONS OF REGULAR GRAMMARS

In spite of their simplicity there are many applications of regular grammars, of which we will briefly mention the most important ones.

5.1.1 CF parsing

In some parsers for CF grammars, a subparser can be discerned that handles a regular grammar; such a subparser is based implicitly or explicitly on the following surprising phenomenon. Consider the sentential forms in left-most or right-most derivations. Such a sentential form consists of a closed (finished) part, which contains terminal symbols only and an open (unfinished) part which contains non-terminals as well. In left-most derivations, the open part starts at the left-most non-terminal and extends to the right, in right-most derivations, the open part starts at the right-most non-terminal and extends to the left; see Figure 5.1 which uses sentential forms from Section 2.5.2.

$$d \ , \ N \ \& \ N \qquad\qquad N \ , \ N \ \& \ h$$
$$\longmapsto \qquad\qquad\qquad \longleftarrow$$

Figure 5.1 Open parts in left-most and right-most productions

Now it can be proved (and it is not difficult to show) that these open parts can be described by a regular grammar (which follows from the CF grammar). Furthermore, these open parts of the sentential form play an important role in some CF parsing methods which explains the significance of regular grammars for CF parsing.

5.1.2 Systems with finite memory

Since CF (or stronger) grammars allow nesting and since nesting can, in principle, be arbitrarily deep, the generation of correct CF (or stronger) sentences may, in principle, require an arbitrary amount of memory to temporarily hold the unprocessed nesting information. Mechanical systems do not possess an arbitrary amount of memory and consequently cannot exhibit CF behaviour and are restricted to regular behaviour. This is immediately clear for simple mechanical systems like vending machines, traffic lights and video-recorders: they all behave according to a regular grammar. It is also in principle true for more complicated mechanical systems, like a country's train system or a computer. Here, the argument gets, however, rather vacuous since nesting information can be represented very efficiently and a little memory can take care of a lot of nesting. Consequently, although these systems in principle exhibit regular behaviour, it is often easier to describe them with CF or stronger means, even though that would incorrectly ascribe infinite memory to them.

Conversely, the global behaviour of many systems that do have much memory can still be described by a regular grammar, and many CF grammars are already for a large part regular. This is because regular grammars already take adequate care of concatenation, repetition and choice; context-freeness is only required for nesting. If we call a rule that produces a regular (sub)language (and which consequently could be replaced by a regular rule) "quasi-regular", we can observe the following. If all alternatives of a rule contain terminals only, that rule is quasi-regular (choice). If all alternatives of a rule contain only terminals and non-terminals the rules of which are quasi-regular and non-recursive, then that rule is quasi-regular (concatenation). And if a rule is recursive but recursion occurs only at the end of an alternative and involves only quasi-regular rules, then that rule is again quasi-regular (repetition). This often covers large parts of a CF grammar. See Krzemień and Łukasiewicz [FS 1976] for an algorithm to identify all quasi-regular rules in a grammar.

Natural languages are a case in point. Although CF or stronger grammars seem necessary to delineate the set of correct sentences (and they may very well be, to catch many subtleties), quite a good rough description can be obtained through regular languages. Consider the stylized grammar for the main clause in an Subject-Verb-Object (SVO) language in Figure 5.2.

```
MainClause   ->   Subject Verb Object
   Subject   ->   [ a | the ] Adjective* Noun
    Object   ->   [ a | the ] Adjective* Noun
      Verb   ->   verb1 | verb2 | ...
 Adjective   ->   adj1 | adj2 | ...
      Noun   ->   noun1 | noun2 | ...
```

Figure 5.2 A not obviously quasi-regular grammar

This grammar is quasi-regular: Verb, Adjective and Noun are regular by themselves, Subject and Object are concatenations of repetitions of regular forms (regular nonterminals and choices) and are therefore quasi-regular, and so is MainClause. It takes some work to bring this grammar into standard regular form, but it can be done, as shown in Figure 5.3, in which the lists for verbs, adjectives and nouns have been abbreviated to verb, adjective and noun, to save space. Even (finite) context-

```
            MainClause      ->    a SubjAdjNoun_verb_Object
            MainClause      ->    the SubjAdjNoun_verb_Object

SubjAdjNoun_verb_Object     ->    noun verb_Object
SubjAdjNoun_verb_Object     ->    adjective SubjAdjNoun_verb_Object

         verb_Object        ->    verb Object

              Object        ->    a ObjAdjNoun
              Object        ->    the ObjAdjNoun

         ObjAdjNoun         ->    noun
         ObjAdjNoun         ->    adjective ObjAdjNoun

                verb        ->    verb1 | verb2 | ...
           adjective        ->    adj1 | adj2 | ...
                noun        ->    noun1 | noun2 | ...
```

Figure 5.3 A regular grammar in standard form for that of Figure 5.2

dependency can be incorporated: for languages that require the verb to agree in number with the subject, we duplicate the first rule:

```
    MainClause    ->    SubjectSingular VerbSingular Object
                  |     SubjectPlural VerbPlural Object
```

and duplicate the rest of the grammar accordingly. The result is still regular. Nested subordinate clauses may seem a problem, but in practical usage the depth of nesting is severely limited. In English, a sentence containing a subclause containing a subclause containing a subclause will baffle the reader, and even in German and Dutch nestings over say five deep are frowned upon. We replicate the grammar the desired number of times and remove the possibility of further levels from the deepest level. Then the deepest level is regular, which makes the other levels regular in turn. The resulting grammar will be huge but regular and will be able to profit from all simple and efficient techniques known for regular grammars. The required duplications and modifications are mechanical and can be done by a program. Dewar, Bratley and Thorne [NatLang 1969] describe an early example of this approach, Blank [NatLang 1989] a recent one.

5.1.3 Pattern searching

Many linear patterns, especially text patterns, have a structure that is easily expressed by a (quasi-)regular grammar. Notations that indicate amounts of money in various currencies, for instance, have the structure given by the grammar of Figure 5.4, where _ has been used to indicate a space symbol. Examples are $_19.95 and ¥_1600. Such notations, however, do not occur in isolation but are usually embedded in long stretches of text that itself does not conform to the grammar of Figure 5.4. To isolate the notations, a recognizer (rather than a parser) is derived from the grammar that will accept arbitrary text and will indicate where sequences of symbols are found that conform to

$$\begin{array}{rcl}
\text{Amount}_S & -> & \text{CurrencySymbol Space}^* \text{ Digit}^+ \text{ Cents}^? \\
\text{CurrencySymbol} & -> & f \mid \$ \mid ¥ \mid £ \mid \dots \\
\text{Space} & -> & \_ \\
\text{Digit} & -> & [0123456789] \\
\text{Cents} & -> & . \text{ Digit Digit} \mid .\text{--}
\end{array}$$

Figure 5.4 A quasi-regular grammar for currency notations

the grammar. Parsing (or an other form of analysis) is deferred to a later stage. A technique for constructing such a recognizer is given in Section 5.3.4.

5.2 PRODUCING FROM A REGULAR GRAMMAR

When producing from a regular grammar, the producer needs to remember only one thing: which non-terminal is next. We shall illustrate this and further concepts using the simple regular grammar of Figure 5.5.

$$\begin{array}{rcl}
S_S & -> & a\ A \\
S & -> & a\ B \\
A & -> & b\ B \\
A & -> & b\ C \\
B & -> & c\ A \\
B & -> & c\ C \\
C & -> & a
\end{array}$$

Figure 5.5 Sample regular grammar

This grammar produces sentences consisting of an a followed by an alternating sequence of b's and c's followed by a terminating a. For the moment we shall restrict ourselves to regular grammars in standard notation; further on we shall extend our methods to more convenient forms.

The one non-terminal the producer remembers is called its *state* and the producer is said to be *in* that state. When a producer is in a given state, for instance, A, it chooses one of the rules belonging to that state, for instance, A->bC, produces the b and moves to state C. Such a move is called a *state transition*. It is customary to represent the states and the possible transitions of a producer in a *transition diagram*, Figure 5.6, where the above state transition is represented by the arc marked b from A to C.

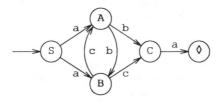

Figure 5.6 Transition diagram for the regular grammar of Figure 5.5

S is the initial state and the accepting state is marked ◊; another convention (not used here) is to draw an accepting state as a double circle. The symbols on the arcs are those produced by the corresponding move. The producer stops when it is in an accepting state. Like the non-deterministic automaton we saw in Section 3.4, the producer is an automaton, a finite non-deterministic automaton, or *finite-state automaton*, to be exact. "Finite" because it can only be in a finite number of states (5 in this case; 3 bits of internal memory would suffice) and "non-deterministic" because, for instance, in state S it has more than one way to produce an a.

5.3 PARSING WITH A REGULAR GRAMMAR

The above automaton for producing a sentence can in principle also be used for parsing. If we have a sentence, for instance, abcba, and want to check and parse it, we can view the above transition diagram as a maze and the (tokens in the) sentence as a guide. If we manage to follow a path through the maze, matching symbols from our sentence to those on the walls of the corridors as we go and end up in ◊ exactly at the end of the sentence, we have checked the sentence and the names of the rooms we have visited form the backbone of the parse tree. See Figure 5.7, where the path is shown as a dotted line.

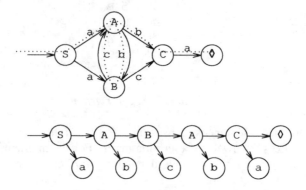

Figure 5.7 Actual and linearized passage through the maze

Now this is easier said than done. How did we know, for instance, to turn left in room S rather than right? Of course we could employ general maze-solving techniques (and they would give us our answer in exponential time) but a much simpler and much more efficient answer is available here: we split ourselves in two and head both ways. After the first a of abcba we are in the set of rooms {A, B}. Now we have a b to follow; from B there are no exits marked b but from A there are two, which lead to B and C. So we are now in rooms {B, C}. Our path is now more difficult to depict but still easy to linearize, as shown in Figure 5.8. We can find the parsing by starting at the end and following the pointers backwards: ◊ <- C <- A <- B <- A <- S. If the grammar is ambiguous the backward pointers may bring us to a fork in the road: an ambiguity has been found and both paths have to be followed separately to find both parsings. With regular grammars, however, one is often not interested in the parse, but only in the recognition: the fact that the input is correct and it ends here suffices.

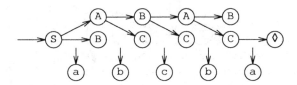

Figure 5.8 Linearized set-based passage through the maze

5.3.1 Replacing sets by states

Although the process described above is linear in the length of the input (each next token takes an amount of work that is not dependent on the length of the input), still a lot of work has to be done for each token. What is worse, the grammar has to be consulted repeatedly and so we expect the speed of the process to depend adversely on the size of the grammar. Fortunately there is a surprising and fundamental improvement possible: from the NFA in Figure 5.6 we construct a new automaton with a new set of states, where each new state is equivalent to a set of old states. Where the original (non-deterministic) automaton was in doubt after the first a, a situation we represented as {A, B}, the new automaton firmly knows that after the first a it is in state AB.

The states of the new automaton can be constructed systematically as follows. We start with the initial state of the old automaton, which is also the initial state of the new one. For each new state we create, we examine its contents in terms of the old states, and for each token in the language we determine to which set of old states the given set leads. These sets of old states are then considered states of the new automaton. If we create the same state a second time, we do not analyse it again. This process is called the *subset construction* and results initially in a (deterministic) state tree. The state tree for the grammar of Figure 5.5 is depicted in Figure 5.9. To stress that it systematically checks all new states for all symbols, outgoing arcs leading nowhere are also shown. Newly generated states that have already been generated before are marked with a ✔.

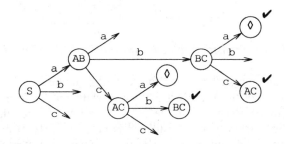

Figure 5.9 Deterministic state tree for the grammar of Figure 5.5

The state tree of Figure 5.9 is turned into a transition diagram by leading the arrows to states marked ✔ to their first-time representatives and removing the dead ends. The new automaton is shown in Figure 5.10. When we now use the sentence abcba as a guide for traversing this transition diagram, we find that we are never in doubt and that we safely arrive at the accepting state. All outgoing arcs from a state

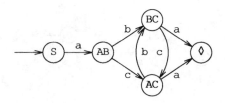

Figure 5.10 Deterministic automaton for the grammar of Figure 5.5

bear different symbols, so when following a list of symbols, we are always pointed to at most one direction. If in a given state there is no outgoing arc for a given symbol, then that symbol may not occur in that position. If it is, the input is in error.

There are two things to be noted here. The first is that we see that most of the possible states of the new automaton do not actually materialize: the old automaton had 5 states, so there were $2^5=32$ possible states for the new automaton while in fact it has only 5; states like SB or ABC do not occur. This is usual; although there are nondeterministic finite-state automata with n states that turn into a DFA with 2^n states, these are rare and have to be constructed on purpose. The average garden variety NFA with n states typically results in a DFA with less than or around $10*n$ states.

The second is that consulting the grammar is no longer required; the state of the automaton together with the input token fully determine the next state. To allow efficient look-up the next state can be stored in a table indexed by the old state and the input token. The table for our DFA is given in Figure 5.11.

		input symbol		
		a	b	c
	S	AB		
	AB		BC	AC
old state				
	AC	◊	BC	
	BC	◊		AC

Figure 5.11 Transition table for the automaton of Figure 5.10

Using such a table, an input string can be checked at the expense of only a few machine instructions per token. For the average DFA, most of the entries in the table are empty (cannot be reached by correct input and refer to error states). Since the table can be of considerable size (300 states times 100 tokens is normal), several techniques exist to exploit the empty space by compressing the table. Dencker, Dürre and Heuft [Misc 1984] give a survey of some techniques.

The parse tree obtained looks as follows:

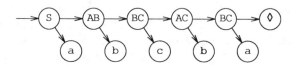

which is not the original parse tree. If the automaton is used only to recognize the input string this is no drawback; if the parse tree is required, it can be reconstructed in the following fairly obvious bottom-up way. Starting from the last state ◊ and the last token a, we conclude that the last right-hand side (the "handle" in bottom-up parsing) was a. Since the state was BC, a combination of B and C, we look through the rules for B and C. We find that a derived from C–>a, which narrows down BC to C. The right-most b and the C combine into the handle bC which in the set {A, C} must derive from A. Working our way backwards we find the parsing:

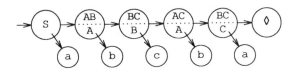

This method again requires the grammar to be consulted repeatedly; moreover, the way back will not always be so straight as in the above example and we will have problems with ambiguous grammars. Efficient full parsing of regular grammars has received relatively little attention; substantial information can be found in Ostrand, Paull and Weyuker [FS 1981].

5.3.2 Non-standard notation

A regular grammar in standard form can only have rules of the form $A \rightarrow a$ and $A \rightarrow aB$. We shall now first extend our notation with two other types of rules, $A \rightarrow B$ and $A \rightarrow \varepsilon$, and show how to construct NFA's and DFA's for them. We shall then turn to regular expressions and rules that have regular expressions as right-hand sides (for instance, $P \rightarrow a^* bQ$) and show how to convert them into rules in the extended notation.

The grammar in Figure 5.12 contains examples of both new types of rules; Figure 5.13 presents the usual trio of NFA, state tree and DFA for this grammar. First consider the NFA. When we are in state S we see the expected transition to state B on the token a, resulting in the standard rule S–>aB. The non-standard rule S–>A indicates that we can get from state S to state A without reading (or producing) a symbol; we then say that we read the zero-length string ε and that we make an ε-transition (or ε-move). The rule A–>aA creates a transition from A to A marked a and B–>bB does something similar. The standard rule B–>b creates a transition marked b to the accepting state, and the non-standard rule A–>ε creates an ε-transition to the accepting state. ε-transitions should not be confused with ε-rules: unit rules create ε-transitions to non-accepting states and ε-rules create ε-transitions to accepting states.

$$
\begin{array}{rcl}
S_S & \rightarrow & A \\
S & \rightarrow & a\ B \\
A & \rightarrow & a\ A \\
A & \rightarrow & \varepsilon \\
B & \rightarrow & b\ B \\
B & \rightarrow & b
\end{array}
$$

Figure 5.12 Sample regular grammar with ε-rules

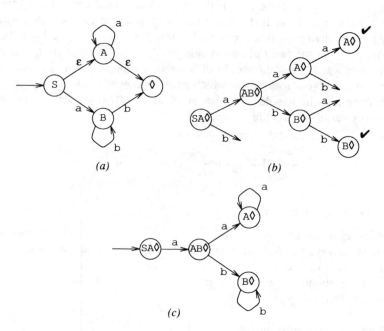

Figure 5.13 NFA (a), state tree (b) and DFA (c) for the grammar of Figure 5.12

Now that we have constructed an NFA with ε-moves, the question arises how we can process the ε-moves to obtain a DFA. To answer this question we use the same reasoning as before; in Figure 5.6, after having seen an a we did not know if we were in state A or state B and we represented that as {A, B}. Here, when we enter state S, even before having processed a single symbol, we already do not know if we are in states S, A or ◊, since the latter two are reachable from S through ε-moves. So the initial state of the DFA is already compound: SA◊. We now have to consider where this state leads to for the symbols a and b. If we are in S then a will bring us to B and if we are in A, a will bring us to A. So the new state includes A and B, and since ◊ is reachable from A through ε-moves, it also includes ◊ and its name is AB◊. Continuing in this vein we can construct the complete state tree (Figure 5.13(b)) and collapse it into a DFA (c). Note that all states of the DFA contain the NFA state ◊, so the input may end in all of them.

The set of NFA states reachable from a given state through ε-moves is called the ε-*closure* of that state. The ε-closure of, for instance, S is {S, A, ◊}.

5.3.3 DFA's from regular expressions
As mentioned in Section 2.3.3, regular languages are often specified by regular expressions rather than by regular grammars. Examples of regular expressions are $[0-9]^+ (. [0-9]^+)^?$ which should be read as "one or more symbols from the set 0 through 9, possibly followed by a dot which must then be followed by one or more symbols from 0 through 9" (and which represents numbers with possibly a dot in them) and $(ab)^* (p|q)^+$, which should be read as "zero or more strings ab followed by one or more p's or q's" (and which is not directly meaningful). The usual forms occurring in regular expressions are recalled in the table in Figure 5.14; some systems provide more possibilities, some provide fewer. In computer input, no difference is generally made

Form	Meaning	Name
R_1R_2	R_1 followed by R_2	concatenation
$R_1 \mid R_2$	R_1 or R_2	alternative
R^*	zero or more R's	optional sequence (Kleene star)
R^+	one or more R's	(proper) sequence
$R^?$	zero or one R	optional
(R)	R	nesting
$[abc \cdots]$	any symbol from the set $abc \cdots$	
a	the symbol a itself	

Figure 5.14 Some usual elements of regular expressions

between the metasymbol * and the symbol $\ast$, etc. Special notations will be necessary if the language to be described contains any of the symbols $\mid$ $\ast$ $+$? ( ) [or] .

Rule pattern	replaced by:
$P \rightarrow a$	(standard)
$P \rightarrow aQ$	(standard)
$P \rightarrow Q$	(extended standard)
$P \rightarrow \varepsilon$	(extended standard)
$P \rightarrow a \cdots$	$P \rightarrow aT$
	$T \rightarrow \cdots$
$P \rightarrow (R_1 \mid R_2 \mid \cdots) \cdots$	$P \rightarrow R_1 \cdots$
	$P \rightarrow R_2 \cdots$
	$\cdots$
$P \rightarrow (R) \cdots$	$P \rightarrow R \cdots$
$P \rightarrow R^* \cdots$	$P \rightarrow T$
	$T \rightarrow RT$
	$T \rightarrow \cdots$
$P \rightarrow R^+ \cdots$	$P \rightarrow RT$
	$T \rightarrow RT$
	$T \rightarrow \cdots$
$P \rightarrow R^? \cdots$	$P \rightarrow R \cdots$
	$P \rightarrow \cdots$
$P \rightarrow [abc \cdots] \cdots$	$P \rightarrow (a \mid b \mid c \mid \cdots) \cdots$

Figure 5.15 Transformations on regular grammars

A regular expression can be converted into a regular grammar by using the transformations given in Figure 5.15; this regular grammar can then be used to produce a DFA as described above. There is also a method to create an NFA directly form the regular expression, which requires, however, some preprocessing on the regular expression; see Thompson [FS 1968].

We shall illustrate the method using the expression $(ab)^*(p \mid q)^+$. Our method will also work for regular grammars that contain regular expressions (like $A{\rightarrow}ab^{*}cB$) and we shall in fact immediately turn our regular expression into such a grammar:

$$S_S \quad \rightarrow \quad (\text{ab})^{*}\,(\text{p}|\text{q})^{+}$$

The T in the transformations stands for an intermediate non-terminal, to be chosen fresh for each application of a transformation; we use A, B, C $\cdots$ in the example since that is less confusing than $T_1, T_2, T_3, \cdots$. The transformations are to be applied until all rules are in (extended) standard form.

The first transformation that applies is $P{\rightarrow}R^{*}\cdots$, which replaces $S_S{\rightarrow}(\text{ab})^{*}\,(\text{p}|\text{q})^{+}$ by

$$
\begin{array}{lll}
S_S & \rightarrow & A \qquad\qquad\qquad\qquad ✔\\
A & \rightarrow & (\text{ab})\ A\\
A & \rightarrow & (\text{p}|\text{q})^{+}
\end{array}
$$

The first rule is already in the desired form and has been marked ✔. The transformations $P{\rightarrow}(R)\cdots$ and $P{\rightarrow}a\cdots$ work on A${\rightarrow}$(ab) A and result in

$$
\begin{array}{lll}
A & \rightarrow & a\ B \qquad\qquad\qquad ✔\\
B & \rightarrow & b\ A \qquad\qquad\qquad ✔
\end{array}
$$

Now the transformation $P{\rightarrow}R^{+}\cdots$ must be applied to A${\rightarrow}$(p|q)$^{+}$, yielding

$$
\begin{array}{lll}
A & \rightarrow & (\text{p}|\text{q})\ C\\
C & \rightarrow & (\text{p}|\text{q})\ C\\
C & \rightarrow & \varepsilon \qquad\qquad\qquad\quad ✔
\end{array}
$$

The ε originated from the fact that $(\text{p}|\text{q})^{+}$ in A${\rightarrow}$(p|q)$^{+}$ is not followed by anything (of which ε is a faithful representation). Now A${\rightarrow}$(p|q) C and C${\rightarrow}$(p|q) C are easily decomposed into

$$
\begin{array}{lll}
A & \rightarrow & \text{p}\ C \qquad\qquad\qquad ✔\\
A & \rightarrow & \text{q}\ C \qquad\qquad\qquad ✔\\
C & \rightarrow & \text{p}\ C \qquad\qquad\qquad ✔\\
C & \rightarrow & \text{q}\ C \qquad\qquad\qquad ✔
\end{array}
$$

The complete extended-standard version can be found in Figure 5.16; an NFA and DFA can now be derived using the methods of Section 5.3.1 (not shown).

5.3.4 Fast text search using finite-state automata

Suppose we are looking for the occurrence of a short piece of text, for instance, a word or a name (the "search string") in a large piece of text, for instance, a dictionary or an encyclopedia. One naive way of finding a search string of length n in a text would be to try to match it to the characters 1 to n; if that fails, shift the pattern one position and try to match against characters 2 to $n+1$, etc., until we find the search string or reach the end of the text. (Dictionaries and encyclopedias may be organized better, but a file containing a million business letters almost certainly would not.)

$$
\begin{array}{lll}
S_S & \text{->} & A \\
A & \text{->} & a\ B \\
B & \text{->} & b\ A \\
A & \text{->} & p\ C \\
A & \text{->} & q\ C \\
C & \text{->} & p\ C \\
C & \text{->} & q\ C \\
C & \text{->} & \varepsilon \\
\end{array}
$$

Figure 5.16 Extended-standard regular grammar for $(ab)^* (p\,|\,q)^+$

Finite automata offer a much more efficient way to do text search. We derive a DFA from the string, let it run down the text and when it reaches an accepting state, it has found the string. Assume for example that the search string is ababc and that the text will contain only a's, b's and c's. The NFA that searches for this string is shown in Figure 5.17(*a*); it was derived as follows. At each character in the text there are two possibilities: either the search string starts there, which is represented by the chain of states going to the right, or it does not start there, in which case we have to skip the present character and return to the initial state. The automaton is non-deterministic, since when we see an a in state A, we have two options: to believe that it is the start of an occurrence of ababc or not to believe it.

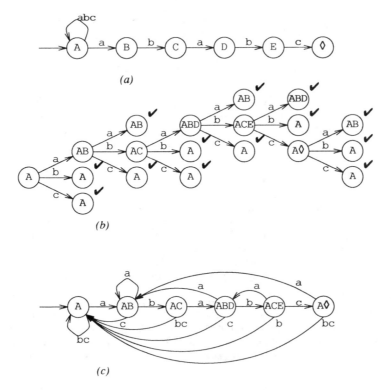

(a)

(b)

(c)

Figure 5.17 NFA (a), state tree (b) and DFA (c) to search for ababc

Using the traditional techniques, this NFA can be used to produce a state tree (*b*) and then a DFA (*c*). Figure 5.18 shows the states the DFA goes through when fed the text aabababca.

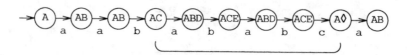

Figure 5.18 State transitions of the DFA of Figure 5.17(c) on aabababca

This application of finite-state automata is known as the *Aho and Corasick bibliographic search algorithm* [FS 1975]. Like any DFA, it requires only a few machine instructions per character. As an additional bonus it will search for several strings for the price of one. The DFA corresponding to the NFA of Figure 5.19 will search simultaneously for Kawabata, Mishima and Tanizaki; note that three different accepting states result, $\lozenge_K$, $\lozenge_M$ and $\lozenge_T$.

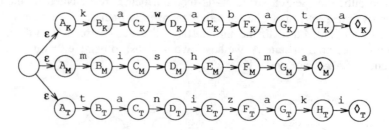

Figure 5.19 Example of an NDA for searching multiple strings

The Aho and Corasick algorithm is not the last word in string search; it faces stiff competition from the Rabin-Karp algorithm[†] and the Boyer-Moore algorithm[‡] neither of which will be treated here, since they are based on different principles.

[†] R.M. Karp, M.O. Rabin, "Efficient randomized pattern matching algorithms", Technical Report TR-31-81, Harvard Univ., Cambridge, Mass., 1981. We want to find a string S of length l in a text T. First we choose a hash function H that assigns a large integer to any string of length l and calculate $H(S)$ and $H(T[1..l])$. If they are equal, we compare S and $T[1..l]$. If either fails we calculate $H(T[2..l+1])$ and repeat the process. The trick is to choose H so that $H(T[p+1..p+l])$ can be calculated cheaply from $H(T[p..p+l-1])$. See also Sedgewick [CSBooks 1988], page 289.

[‡] Robert S. Boyer, J. Strother Moore, "A fast string searching algorithm", *Commun. ACM*, vol. 20, no. 10, p. 762-772, Oct 1977. We want to find a string S of length l in a text T and start by positioning $S[1]$ at $T[1]$. Now suppose that $T[l]$ does not occur in S; then we can shift S to $T[l+1]$ without missing a match, and thus increase the speed of the search process. This principle can be extended to blocks of more characters. See also Sedgewick [CSBooks 1988], page 286.

6
General directional top-down methods

In this chapter, we will discuss top-down parsing methods that try to rederive the input sentence by prediction. As explained in Section 3.3.1, we start with the start symbol and try to produce the input from it. At any point in time, we have a sentential form that represents our prediction of the rest of the input sentence:

rest of input
prediction

This sentential form consists of both terminals and non-terminals. If a terminal symbol is in front, we match it with the current input symbol. If a non-terminal is in front, we pick one of its right-hand sides and replace the non-terminal with this right-hand side. This way, we all the time replace the left-most non-terminal, and in the end, when we succeed, we have imitated a left-most production.

6.1 IMITATING LEFT-MOST PRODUCTIONS

Let us see how such a rederiving process could proceed with an example. Consider the example grammar of Figure 6.1. This grammar produces all sentences with equal numbers of a's and b's.

$$
\begin{array}{lll}
S & -> & aB \mid bA \\
A & -> & a \mid aS \mid bAA \\
B & -> & b \mid bS \mid aBB
\end{array}
$$

Figure 6.1 A grammar producing all sentences with equal numbers of a's *and* b's

Let us try to parse the sentence aabb, by trying to rederive it from the start-symbol, S. S is our first prediction. The first symbol of our prediction is a non-terminal, so we have to replace it by one of its right-hand sides. In this grammar, there are two choices for S: either we use the rule S->aB, or we use the rule S->bA. The sentence starts with an a and not with a b, so we cannot use the second rule here. Applying the first rule leaves us with the prediction aB. Now, the first symbol of the prediction is a terminal symbol. Here, we have no choice:

a	abb
a	B

We have to match this symbol with the current symbol of the sentence, which is also an a. So, we have a match, and accept the a. This leaves us with the prediction B for the rest of the sentence: abb. The first symbol of the prediction is again a non-terminal, so it has to be replaced by one of its right-hand sides. Now, we have three choices. However, the first and the second are not applicable here, because they start with a b, and we need another a. Therefore, we take the third choice, so now we have prediction aBB:

a	a	bb
a	a	BB

Again, we have a match with the current input symbol, so we accept it and continue with the prediction BB for bb. Again, we have to replace the left-most B by one of its choices. The next terminal in the sentence is a b, so the third choice is not applicable here. This still leaves us with two choices, b and bS. So, we can either try them both, or be a bit more intelligent about it. If we would take bS, then we would get at least another a (because of the S), so this cannot be the right choice. So, we take the b choice, and get the prediction bB for bb. Again, we have a match, and this leaves us with prediction B for b. For the same reason, we take the b choice again. After matching, this leaves us with an empty prediction. Luckily, we are also at the end of the input sentence, so we accept it. If we had made notes of the production rules used, we would have found the following derivation:

    S -> aB -> aaBB -> aabB -> aabb.

Figure 6.2 presents the steps of the parse in a tree-form. The dashed line separates the already processed part from the prediction. All the time, the left-most symbol of the prediction is processed.

This example demonstrates several aspects that the parsers discussed in this chapter have in common:

☐   we always process the left-most symbol of the prediction;
☐   if this symbol is a terminal, we have no choice: we have to match it with the current input symbol or reject the parse;
☐   if this symbol is a non-terminal, we have to make a prediction: it has to be replaced by one of its right-hand sides. Thus, we always process the left-most non-terminal first, so we get a left-most derivation.

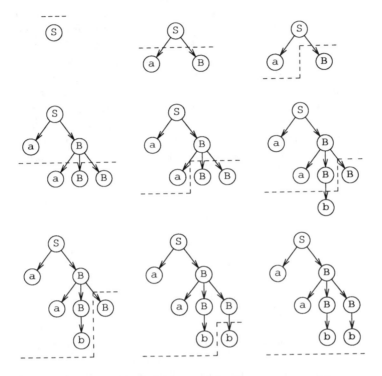

Figure 6.2 Production trees for the sentence aabb

6.2 THE PUSHDOWN AUTOMATON

The steps we have taken in the example above resemble very much the steps of a so-called *pushdown automaton*. A pushdown automaton (PDA) is a device that reads input and has control over a stack. The stack can contain symbols that belong to a so-called *stack alphabet*. A *stack* is a list that can only be accessed at one end: the last symbol entered on the list ("pushed") is the first symbol to be taken from it ("popped"). This is also sometimes called a "first-in, last-out" list, or a FILO list: the first symbol that goes in is the last symbol to come out. In the example above, the prediction works like a stack, and this is what the pushdown automaton uses the stack for too. We therefore often call this stack the *prediction stack*. The stack also explains the name "pushdown" automaton: the automaton "pushes" symbols on the stack for later processing.

The pushdown automaton operates by popping a stack symbol and reading an input symbol. These two symbols then in general give us a choice of several lists of stack symbols to be pushed on the stack. So, there is a mapping of (input symbol, stack symbol) pairs to lists of stack symbols. The automaton accepts the input sentence when the stack is empty at the end of the input. If there are choices (so an (input symbol, stack symbol) pair maps to more than one list), the automaton accepts a sentence when there are choices that lead to an empty stack at the end of the sentence.

This automaton is modeled after context-free grammars with rules in the so-called *Greibach Normal Form* (GNF). In this normal form, all grammar rules have either the form $A\rightarrow a$ or $A\rightarrow aB_1B_2\cdots B_n$, with a a terminal and $A, B_1, \ldots , B_n$ non-terminals. The stack symbols are, of course, the non-terminals. A rule of the form $A\rightarrow aB_1B_2\cdots B_n$ leads to a mapping of the (a, A) pair to the list $B_1B_2\cdots B_n$. This means that if the input symbol is an a, and the prediction stack starts with an A, we could accept the a, and replace the A part of the prediction stack with $B_1B_2\cdots B_n$. A rule of the form $A\rightarrow a$ leads to a mapping of the (a, A) pair to an empty list. The automaton starts with the start symbol of the grammar on the stack. Any ε-free context-free grammar can be put into Greibach Normal Form. Most books on formal language theory discuss how to do this (see for instance Hopcroft and Ullman [Books 1979]).

The example grammar of Figure 6.1 already is in Greibach Normal Form, so we can easily build a pushdown automaton for it. The automaton is characterized by the mapping shown in Figure 6.3.

```
(a, S)    ->    B
(b, S)    ->    A
(a, A)    ->
(a, A)    ->    S
(b, A)    ->    AA
(b, B)    ->
(b, B)    ->    S
(a, B)    ->    BB
```

Figure 6.3 Mapping of the PDA for the grammar of Figure 6.1

An important remark to be made here is that many pushdown automata are non-deterministic. For instance, the pushdown automaton of Figure 6.3 can choose between an empty list and an S for the pair (a, A). In fact, there are context-free languages for which we cannot build a deterministic pushdown automaton, although we can build a non-deterministic one. We should also mention that the pushdown automata as discussed here are a simplification of the ones we find in automata theory. In automata theory, pushdown automata have so-called states, and the mapping is from (state, input symbol, stack symbol) triplets to (state, list of stack symbols) pairs. Seen in this way, they are like finite-state automata (discussed in Chapter 5), extended with a stack. Pushdown automata also come in two different kinds: some accept a sentence by empty stack, others accept by ending up in a state that is marked as an accepting state. Perhaps surprisingly, having states does not make the pushdown automaton concept more powerful. Pushdown automata with states still only accept languages that can be described with a context-free grammar. In our discussion, the pushdown automaton only has one state, so we have taken the liberty of leaving it out.

Pushdown automata as described above have several shortcomings that must be resolved if we want to convert them into parsing automata. Firstly, pushdown automata require us to put our grammar into Greibach Normal Form. While grammar transformations are no problem for the formal linguist, we would like to avoid them as much as possible, and use the original grammar if we can. Now we could relax the Greibach Normal Form requirement a little by also allowing terminals as stack symbols, and adding

$(a, a) \rightarrow$

to the mapping for all terminals *a*. We could then use grammars having only right-hand sides starting with a terminal. We could also split the steps of the pushdown automaton into separate "match" and "predict" steps, as we did in the example of Section 6.1. The "match" steps then correspond to usage of the

$$(a, a) \rightarrow$$

mappings, and the "predict" step then corresponds to a

$$(, A) \rightarrow \cdots$$

mapping, that is, a non-terminal on the top of the stack is replaced by one of its right-hand sides, without consuming a symbol from the input. For the grammar of Figure 6.1, this would result in the mapping shown in Figure 6.4, which is in fact just a rewrite of the grammar of Figure 6.1.

(, S)	->	aB
(, S)	->	bA
(, A)	->	a
(, A)	->	aS
(, A)	->	bAA
(, B)	->	b
(, B)	->	bS
(, B)	->	aBB
(a, a)	->	
(b, b)	->	

Figure 6.4 Match and predict mappings of the PDA for the grammar of Figure 6.1

We will see later that, even using this approach, we may have to modify the grammar anyway, but in the meantime, this looks very promising so we adopt this strategy. This strategy also solves another problem: ε-rules do not need special treatment any more. To get Greibach Normal Form, we would have to eliminate them. This is not necessary any more, because they now just correspond to a

$$(, A) \rightarrow$$

mapping.

The second shortcoming is that the pushdown automaton does not keep a record of the rules (mappings) it uses. Therefore, we introduce an *analysis stack* into the automaton. For every prediction step, we push the non-terminal being replaced onto the analysis stack, suffixed with the number of the right-hand side taken (numbering the right-hand sides of a non-terminal from 1 to *n*). For every match, we push the matched terminal onto the analysis stack. Thus, the analysis stack corresponds exactly to the parts to the left of the dashed line in Figure 6.2, and the dashed line represents the separation between the analysis stack and the prediction stack. This results in an automaton that at any point in time has a configuration as depicted in Figure 6.5. In the literature, such a configuration, together with its current state, stacks, etc. is sometimes called an *instantaneous description*. In Figure 6.5, matching can be seen as pushing the vertical line to the right.

matched input	rest of input
analysis	prediction

Figure 6.5 An instantaneous description

The third and most important shortcoming, however, is the non-determinism. Formally, it may be satisfactory that the automaton accepts a sentence if and only if there is a sequence of choices that leads to an empty stack at the end of the sentence, but for our purpose it is not, because it does not tell us how to obtain this sequence. We have to guide the automaton to the correct choices. Looking back to the example of Section 6.1, we had to make a choice at several points in the derivation, and we did so based on some ad hoc considerations that were specific for the grammar at hand: sometimes we looked at the next symbol in the sentence, and there were also some points where we had to look further ahead, to make sure that there were no more a's coming. In the example, the choices were easy, because all the right-hand sides start with a terminal symbol. In general, however, finding the correct choice is much more difficult. The right-hand sides could for instance equally well have started with a non-terminal symbol that again has right-hand sides starting with a non-terminal, etc.

In Chapter 8 we will see that many grammars still allow us to decide which right-hand side to choose, given the next symbol in the sentence. In this chapter, however, we will focus on top-down parsing methods that work for a larger class of grammars. Rather than trying to pick a choice based on ad hoc considerations, we would like to guide the automaton through all the possibilities. In Chapter 3 we saw that there are in general two methods for solving problems in which there are several alternatives in well-determined points: depth-first search and breadth-first search. We shall now see how we can make the machinery operate for both search methods. Since the effects can be exponential in size, even a small example can get quite big. We will use the grammar of Figure 6.6, with test input aabc. This grammar generates a rather complex language: sentences consist either of a number of a's followed by a number of b's followed by an equal number of c's, or of a number of a's followed by an equal number of b's followed by a number of c's. Example sentences are for instance: abc, aabbc.

```
S   ->   DC | AB
A   ->   a | aA
B   ->   bc | bBc
D   ->   ab | aDb
C   ->   c | cC
```

Figure 6.6 A more complicated example grammar

6.3 BREADTH-FIRST TOP-DOWN PARSING

The breadth-first solution to the top-down parsing problem is to maintain a list of all possible predictions. Each of these predictions is then processed as described in Section 6.2 above, that is, if there is a non-terminal in front, the prediction stack is replaced by several new prediction stacks, as many as there are choices for this non-terminal. In each of these new prediction stacks, the non-terminal is replaced by the corresponding choice. This prediction step is repeated for all prediction stacks it applies to (including the new ones), until all prediction stacks have a terminal in front. Then, for each of the prediction stacks we match the terminal in front with the current input symbol, and strike out all prediction stacks that do not match. If there are no prediction stacks left, the sentence does not belong to the language. So, instead of one prediction stack/analysis stack pair, our automaton now maintains a list of prediction stack/analysis stack pairs, one for each possible choice, as depicted in Figure 6.7.

matched input	rest of input
analysis1	prediction1
analysis2	prediction2
...	...

Figure 6.7 An instantaneous description of our extended automaton

The method is suitable for on-line parsing, because it processes the input from left to right. Any parsing method that processes its input from left to right and results in a left-most derivation is called an LL parsing method. The first L stands for Left to right, and the second L for Left-most derivation.

Now, we almost know how to write a parser along these lines, but there is one detail that we have not properly dealt with yet: termination. Does the input sentence belong to the language defined by the grammar when, ultimately, we have an empty prediction stack? Only when the input is exhausted! To avoid this extra check, and to avoid problems about what to do when we arrive at the end of sentence but haven't finished parsing yet, we introduce a special so-called *end-marker* #, that is appended at the end of the sentence. Also, a new grammar rule S' –>S# is added to the grammar, where S' is a new non-terminal that serves as a new start symbol. The end-marker behaves like an ordinary terminal symbol; when we have an empty prediction, we know that the last step taken was a match with the end-marker, and that this match succeeded. This also means that the input is exhausted, so it must be accepted.

6.3.1 An example

Figure 6.8 presents a complete breadth-first parsing of the sentence aabc#. At first there is only one prediction stack: it contains the start-symbol; no symbols have been accepted yet *(a)*. The step leading to *(b)* is a simple predict step; there is no other right-hand side for S'. Another predict step leads us to *(c)*, but this time there are two possible right-hand sides, so we obtain two prediction stacks; note that the difference of the prediction stacks is also reflected in the analysis stacks, where the different suffixes of S represent the different right-hand sides predicted. Another predict step with several right-hand sides leads to *(d)*. Now, all prediction stacks have a terminal on top;

(a)

	aabc#
S'	

(b)

	aabc#
S'_1	S#

(c)

	aabc#
$S'_1 S_1$	DC#
$S'_1 S_2$	AB#

(d)

	aabc#
$S'_1 S_1 D_1$	abC#
$S'_1 S_1 D_2$	aDbC#
$S'_1 S_2 A_1$	aB#
$S'_1 S_2 A_2$	aAB#

(e)

a	abc#
$S'_1 S_1 D_1 a$	bC#
$S'_1 S_1 D_2 a$	DbC#
$S'_1 S_2 A_1 a$	B#
$S'_1 S_2 A_2 a$	AB#

(f)

a	abc#
$S'_1 S_1 D_1 a$	bC#
$S'_1 S_1 D_2 a D_1$	abbC#
$S'_1 S_1 D_2 a D_2$	aDbbC#
$S'_1 S_2 A_1 a B_1$	bc#
$S'_1 S_2 A_1 a B_2$	bBc#
$S'_1 S_2 A_2 a A_1$	aB#
$S'_1 S_2 A_2 a A_2$	aAB#

(g)

aa	bc#
$S'_1 S_1 D_2 a D_1 a$	bbC#
$S'_1 S_1 D_2 a D_2 a$	DbbC#
$S'_1 S_2 A_2 a A_1 a$	B#
$S'_1 S_2 A_2 a A_2 a$	AB#

(h)

aa	bc#
$S'_1 S_1 D_2 a D_1 a$	bbC#
$S'_1 S_1 D_2 a D_2 a D_1$	abbbC#
$S'_1 S_1 D_2 a D_2 a D_2$	aDbbbC#
$S'_1 S_2 A_2 a A_1 a B_1$	bc#
$S'_1 S_2 A_2 a A_1 a B_2$	bBc#
$S'_1 S_2 A_2 a A_2 a A_1$	aB#
$S'_1 S_2 A_2 a A_2 a A_2$	aAB#

(i)

aab	c#
$S'_1 S_1 D_2 a D_1 ab$	bC#
$S'_1 S_2 A_2 a A_1 a B_1 b$	c#
$S'_1 S_2 A_2 a A_1 a B_2 b$	Bc#

(j)

aab	c#
$S'_1 S_1 D_2 a D_1 ab$	bC#
$S'_1 S_2 A_2 a A_1 a B_1 b$	c#
$S'_1 S_2 A_2 a A_1 a B_2 b B_1$	bcc#
$S'_1 S_2 A_2 a A_1 a B_2 b B_2$	bBcc#

(k)

aabc	#
$S'_1 S_2 A_2 a A_1 a B_1 bc$	#

(l)

aabc#	
$S'_1 S_2 A_2 a A_1 a B_1 bc\#$	

Figure 6.8 The breadth-first parsing of the sentence aabc#

all happen to match, resulting in *(e)*. Next, we again have some predictions with a non-terminal in front, so another predict step leads us to *(f)*. The next step is a match step, and fortunately, some matches fail; these are just dropped as they can never lead to a successful parse. From *(g)* to *(h)* is again a predict step. Another match where, again, some matches fail, leads us to *(i)*. A further prediction results in *(j)* and then two matches result in *(k)* and *(l)*, leading to a successful parse (the predict stack is empty). The analysis is

$S'_1S_2A_2aA_1aB_1bc\#.$

For now, we do not need the terminals in the analysis; discarding them gives

$S'_1S_2A_2A_1B_1.$

This means that we get a left-most derivation by first applying rule S'_1, then rule S_2, then rule A_2, etc., all the time replacing the left-most non-terminal. Check:

$$S' \rightarrow S\# \rightarrow AB\# \rightarrow aAB\# \rightarrow aaB\# \rightarrow aabc\#.$$

The breadth-first method described here was first presented by Greibach [CF 1964]. However, in that presentation, grammars are first transformed into Greibach Normal Form, and the steps taken are like the ones our initial pushdown automaton makes. The predict and match steps are combined.

6.3.2 A counterexample: left-recursion

The method discussed above clearly works for this grammar, and the question arises whether it works for all context-free grammars. One would think it does, because all possibilities are systematically tried, for all non-terminals, in any occurring prediction. Unfortunately, this reasoning has a serious flaw that is demonstrated by the following example: let us see if the sentence ab belongs to the language defined by the simple grammar

$$S \quad \rightarrow \quad Sb \mid a$$

Our automaton starts off in the following state:

	ab#
	S'

As we have a non-terminal at the beginning of the prediction, we use a predict step, resulting in:

	ab#
S'_1	S#

Now, another predict step results in:

	ab#
S'_1S_1	Sb#
S'_1S_2	a#

As one prediction again starts with a non-terminal, we predict again:

	ab#
$S'_1 S_1 S_1$	Sbb#
$S'_1 S_1 S_2$	ab#
$S'_1 S_2$	a#

By now, it is clear what is happening: we seem to have ended up in an infinite process leading us nowhere. The reason for this is that we keep trying the S->Sb rule without ever coming to a state where a match can be attempted. This problem can occur whenever there is a non-terminal that derives an infinite sequence of sentential forms, all starting with a non-terminal, so no matches can take place. As all these sentential forms in this infinite sequence start with a non-terminal, and the number of non-terminals is finite, there is at least one non-terminal A occurring more than once at the start of those sentential forms. So, we have: $A \rightarrow \cdots \rightarrow A\alpha$. A non-terminal that derives a sentential form starting with itself is called *left-recursive*. Left recursion comes in two kinds: we speak of *immediate left-recursion* when there is a grammar rule $A \rightarrow A\alpha$, like in the rule S->Sb; we speak of *indirect left-recursion* when the recursion goes through other rules, for instance $A \rightarrow B\alpha$, $B \rightarrow A\beta$. Both forms of left-recursion can be concealed by ε-producing non-terminals. For instance in the grammar

$$
\begin{array}{lcl}
S & -> & ABc \\
B & -> & Cd \\
B & -> & ABf \\
C & -> & Se \\
A & -> & \varepsilon
\end{array}
$$

the non-terminals S, B, and C are all left-recursive. Grammars with left-recursive non-terminals are called left-recursive as well.

If a grammar has no ε-rules and no loops, we could still use our parsing scheme if we use one extra step: if a prediction stack has more symbols than the unmatched part of the input sentence, it can never derive the sentence (no ε-rules), so it can be dropped. However, this little trick has one big disadvantage: it requires us to know the length of the input sentence in advance, so the method no longer is suitable for on-line parsing. Fortunately, left-recursion can be eliminated: given a left-recursive grammar, we can transform it into a grammar without left-recursive non-terminals that defines the same language. As left-recursion poses a major problem for any top-down parsing method, we will now discuss this grammar transformation.

6.4 ELIMINATING LEFT-RECURSION

We will first discuss the elimination of immediate left-recursion. We will assume that ε-rules and unit rules already have been eliminated (see Section 4.2.3.1 and 4.2.3.2). Now, let A be a left-recursive rule, and

$$ A \quad \rightarrow \quad A\alpha_1 \mid \cdots \mid A\alpha_n \mid \beta_1 \mid \cdots \mid \beta_m $$

be all the rules for A. None of the α_i are equal to ε, or we would have a rule $A \rightarrow A$, a unit rule. None of the β_j are equal to ε either, or we would have an ε-rule. The sentential forms generated by A using only the $A \rightarrow A\alpha_k$ rules all have the form

$$A\alpha_{k_1}\alpha_{k_2}\cdots\alpha_{k_j}$$

and as soon as one of the $A\rightarrow\beta_i$ rules is used, the sentential form has no longer an A in front; it has the following form:

$$\beta_i\alpha_{k_1}\alpha_{k_2}\cdots\alpha_{k_j}$$

for some i, and some $k_1, \cdots, k_j$, where j could be 0. These same sentential forms are generated by the following set of rules:

$$
\begin{array}{rcl}
A\_head & \rightarrow & \beta_1 \mid \cdots \mid \beta_m \\
A\_tail & \rightarrow & \alpha_1 \mid \cdots \mid \alpha_n \\
A\_tails & \rightarrow & A\_tail\ A\_tails \mid \varepsilon \\
A & \rightarrow & A\_head\ A\_tails
\end{array}
$$

or, without re-introducing ε-rules,

$$
\begin{array}{rcl}
A\_head & \rightarrow & \beta_1 \mid \cdots \mid \beta_m \\
A\_tail & \rightarrow & \alpha_1 \mid \cdots \mid \alpha_n \\
A\_tails & \rightarrow & A\_tail\ A\_tails \mid A\_tail \\
A & \rightarrow & A\_head\ A\_tails \mid A\_head
\end{array}
$$

where A_head, A_tail, and A_tails are newly introduced non-terminals. None of the α_i is ε, so A_tail does not derive ε, so A_tails is not left-recursive. A could still be left-recursive, but it is not immediately left-recursive, because none of the β_j start with an A. They could, however, derive a sentential form starting with an A.

In general, eliminating the indirect left-recursion is more complicated. The idea is that first the non-terminals are numbered, say $A_1, A_2, \cdots, A_n$. Now, for a left-recursive non-terminal A there is a derivation

$$A \rightarrow B\alpha \rightarrow \cdots \rightarrow C\gamma \rightarrow A\delta$$

with all the time a non-terminal at the left of the sentential form, and repeatedly replacing this non-terminal using one of its right-hand sides. All these non-terminals have a number associated with them, say $i_1, i_2, \cdots, i_m$, and in the derivation we get the following sequence of numbers: $i_1, i_2, \cdots, i_m, i_1$. Now, if we did not have any rules $A_i\rightarrow A_j\alpha$ with $j\leq i$, this would be impossible, because $i_1 < i_2 < \cdots < i_m < i_1$ is impossible.

The idea now is to eliminate all rules of this form. We start with A_1. For A_1, the only rules to eliminate are the immediately left-recursive ones, and we already have seen how to do just that. Next, it is A_2's turn. Each production rule of the form $A_2\rightarrow A_1\alpha$ is replaced by the production rules

$$A_2 \rightarrow \alpha_1\alpha \mid \cdots \mid \alpha_m\alpha$$

where

$$A_1 \rightarrow \alpha_1 \mid \cdots \mid \alpha_m$$

are the A_1-rules. This cannot introduce new rules of the form $A_2 \to A_1 \gamma$ because we have just eliminated A_1's left-recursive rules, and the α_i's are not equal to ε. Next, we eliminate the immediate left-recursive rules of A_2. This finishes the work we have to do for A_2. Likewise, we deal with A_3 through A_n, in this order, always first replacing rules $A_i \to A_1 \gamma$, then rules $A_i \to A_2 \delta$, etc. We have to obey this ordering, however, because for instance replacing a $A_i \to A_2 \delta$ rule could introduce a $A_i \to A_3 \gamma$ rule, but not a $A_i \to A_1 \alpha$ rule.

6.5 DEPTH-FIRST (BACKTRACKING) PARSERS

The breadth-first method presented in the previous section has the disadvantage that it uses a lot of memory. The depth-first method also has a disadvantage: in its general form it is not suitable for on-line parsing. However, there are many applications where parsing does not have to be done on-line, and then the depth-first method is advantageous since it does not need much memory.

In the depth-first method, when we are faced with a number of possibilities, we choose one and leave the other possibilities for later. First, we fully examine the consequences of the choice we just made. If this choice turns out to be a failure (or even a success, but we want all solutions), we roll back our actions until the present point and continue with the other possibilities.

Let us see how this search technique applies to top-down parsing. Our depth-first parser follows the same steps as our breadth-first parser, until it encounters a choice: a non-terminal that has more than one right-hand side lies on top of the prediction stack. Now, instead of creating a new analysis stack/prediction stack pair, it chooses the first right-hand side. This is reflected on the analysis stack by the appearance of the non-terminal involved, with suffix 1, exactly as it was in our breadth-first parser. This time however, the analysis stack is not only used for remembering the parse, but also for backtracking.

The parser continues in this way, until a match fails, or the prediction stack is empty. If the prediction stack is empty, we have found a parse, which is represented by the analysis stack (we know that the input is also exhausted, because of the end-marker #). If a match fails, the parser will backtrack. This backtracking consists of the following steps: first, any terminal symbols at the end of the analysis stack are popped from this stack, and pushed back on top of the prediction stack. Also, these symbols are removed from the matched input and added to the beginning of the rest of the input (this is the reversal of the "match" steps), that is, backtracking over a terminal is done by moving the vertical line backwards, as is demonstrated in Figure 6.9.

Figure 6.9 Backtracking over a terminal

Then, there are two possibilities: if the analysis stack is empty, there are no other possibilities to try, and the parsing stops; otherwise, there is a non-terminal on top of the analysis stack, and the top of the prediction stack corresponds to a right-hand side of this non-terminal. The choice of this right-hand side just resulted in a failed match. In the latter case, we pop the non-terminal from the analysis stack and replace the right-hand side part in the prediction stack with this non-terminal (this is the reversal of a prediction step). This is demonstrated in Figure 6.10.

Figure 6.10 Backtracking over a A→γ choice

Next, there are again two possibilities: if this was the last right-hand side of this non-terminal, we have already tried its right-hand sides and have to backtrack further; if not, we start parsing again, first using a predict step that replaces the non-terminal with its next right-hand side.

Now, let us try to parse the sentence aabc, this time using the backtracking parser. Figure 6.11 presents the parsing process step by step; the backtracking steps are marked with a *B*. The example demonstrates another disadvantage of the backtracking method: it can make wrong choices and find out about this only much later. Of course, it could also start with the right choices and be finished rapidly.

As presented here, the parsing stops when a parsing is found. If we want to find all parsings, we should not stop when the prediction stack is empty. We can continue by backtracking just as if we had not found a successful parse, and write down the analysis stack (that represents the parse) every time that the prediction stack is empty. Ultimately, we will end with an empty analysis part, indicating that we have exhausted all analysis possibilities, and the parsing stops.

6.6 RECURSIVE DESCENT

In the previous sections, we have seen several automata at work, using a grammar to decide the parsing steps while processing the input sentence. Now this is just another way of stating that these automata use a grammar as a program. Looking at a grammar as a program for a parsing machine is not as far-fetched as it may seem at first. After all, a grammar is a prescription for deriving sentences of the language that the grammar describes, and what we are doing in top-down parsing is rederiving a sentence from the grammar. This only differs from the classic view of a grammar as a generating device in that we are now trying to rederive a particular sentence, not just any sentence. Seen in this way, grammars are programs, written in a programming language with a declarative style (that is, it specifies what to do, but not the steps that need to be done to achieve the result).

If we want to write a top-down parser for a certain context-free grammar in one of the more common programming languages, like Pascal, C, or Modula-2, there are several options. The first option is to write a program that emulates one of the automata described in the previous sections. This program can then be fed a grammar and an input sentence. This is a perfectly sound approach and is easy to program. The difficulty comes when the parser must perform some other actions as parts of the input are recognized. For instance, a compiler must build a symbol table when it processes a

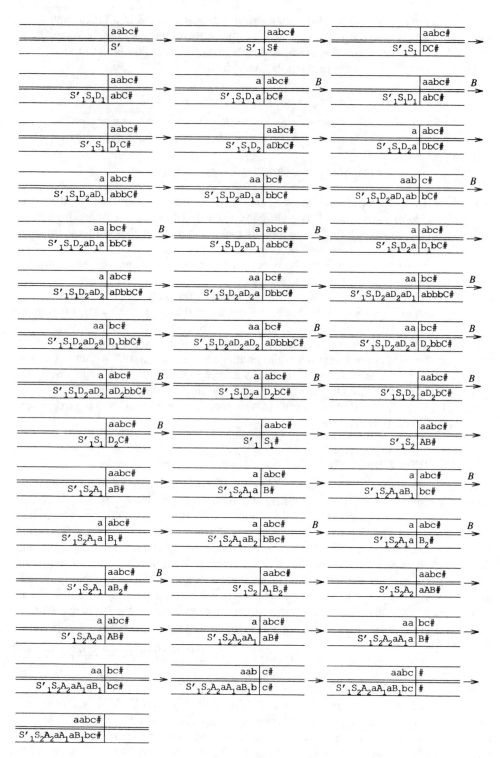

Figure 6.11 Parsing the sentence aabc

declaration sequence. This, and efficiency considerations lead to a second option: to write a special purpose parser for the grammar at hand. Many of these special purpose parsers have been written, and most of them use an implementation technique called *recursive descent*. We will assume that the reader has some programming experience, and knows about procedures and recursion. If not, this section can be skipped. It does not describe a different parsing method, but merely an implementation technique that is often used in hand-written parsers and also in some machine-generated parsers.

6.6.1 A naive approach
As a first approach, we regard a grammar rule as a procedure for recognizing its left-hand side. The rule

```
S    ->    aB | bA
```

is regarded as a procedure to recognize an S. This procedure then states something like the following:

> S succeeds if
>   a succeeds and then B succeeds
> or else
>   b succeeds and then A succeeds

This does not differ much from the grammar rule, but it does not look like a piece of Pascal or C either. Like a cookbook recipe that usually does not tell us that we must peel the potatoes, let alone how to do that, the procedure is incomplete.

There are several bits of information that we must maintain when carrying out such a procedure. First, there is the notion of a "current position" in the rule. This current position indicates what must be tried next. When we implement rules as procedures, this current position is maintained automatically, by the program counter, which tells us where we are within a procedure. Next, there is the input sentence itself. When implementing a backtracking parser, we usually keep the input sentence in a global array, with one element for each symbol in the sentence. The array must be global, because it contains information that must be accessible equally easily from all procedures. Then, there is the notion of a current position in the input sentence. When the current position in the rule indicates a terminal symbol, and this symbol corresponds to the symbol at the current position in the input sentence, both current positions will be advanced one position. The current position in the input sentence is also global information. We will therefore maintain this position in a global variable, of a type that is suitable for indexing the array containing the input sentence. Also, when starting a rule we must remember the current position in the input sentence, because we need it for the "or else" clauses. These must all be started at the same position in the input sentence. For instance, starting with the rule for S of grammar 6.1, suppose that the a matches the symbol at the current position of the input sentence. The current position is advanced and then B is tried. For B, we have a rule similar to that of S. Now suppose that B fails. We then have to try the next choice for S, and backup the position in the input sentence to what it was when we started the rule for S. This is backtracking, just as we have seen it earlier.

All this tells us how to deal with one rule. However, usually we are dealing with a grammar that has more than one non-terminal, so there will be more than one rule. When we arrive at a non-terminal in a rule, we have to execute the rule for that non-terminal, and, if it succeeds, return to the current invocation and continue there. We achieve this automatically by using the procedure-call mechanism of the implementation language.

Another detail that we have not covered yet is that we have to remember the grammar rules that we use. If we do not remember them, we will not know afterwards how the sentence was derived. Therefore we note them in a separate list, striking them out when they fail. Each procedure must keep its own copy of the index in this list, again because we need it for the "or else " clauses: if a choice fails, all choices that have been made after the choice now failing must be discarded. In the end, when the rule for S' succeeds, the grammar rules left in this list represent a left-most derivation of the sentence.

Now, let us see how a parser, as described above, works for an example. Let us consider again grammar of Figure 6.6, and input sentence abbcc. As before, we add a rule S'->S# to the grammar and a # to the end of the sentence, so our parser starts in the following state:

Active rules	Sentence	Parse
1: S' -> •S#	•abc#	1: S' -> S#

Our administration is divided into three parts; the "Active rules" part indicates the active rules, with a dot (•) indicating the current position within that rule. The bottom rule in this part is the rule that we are currently working on. The "Sentence" part indicates the sentence, including a position marker indicating the current position in the sentence. The "Parse" part will be used to remember the rules that we use (not only the currently active ones). The entries in this part are numbered, and each entry in the "Active rules" part also contains its index in the "Parse" part. As we shall see later, this is needed to backup after having taken a wrong choice.

There is only one possibility here: the current position in the procedure indicates that we must invoke the procedure for S, so let us do so:

Active rules	Sentence	Parse
1: S' -> S•#	•abc#	1: S' -> S#
2: S -> •DC | AB	•abc#	2: S -> DC

Notice that we have advanced the position in the S' rule. It now indicates where we have to continue when we are finished with S (the return address). Now we try the first alternative for S. There is a choice here, so the current position in the input sentence is saved. We have not made this explicit in the pictures, because this position is already present in the "Sentence"-part of the entry that invoked S.

Active rules	Sentence	Parse
1: S' -> S•#	•abc#	1: S' -> S#
2: S -> D•C | AB	•abc#	2: S -> DC
3: D -> •ab | aDb	•abc#	3: D -> ab

Now, the first choice for D is tried. The a succeeds, and next the b also succeeds, so we get:

	Active rules	Sentence	Parse
1:	S′ -> S•#	•abc#	1: S′ -> S#
2:	S -> D•C ǀ AB	•abc#	2: S -> DC
3:	D -> ab• ǀ aDb	ab•c#	3: D -> ab

Now, we are at the end of a choice for D. This means that it succeeds, and we remove this entry from the list of active rules, after updating the current positions in the entry above. Next, it is C's turn:

	Active rules	Sentence	Parse
1:	S′ -> S•#	•abc#	1: S′ -> S#
2:	S -> DC• ǀ AB	ab•c#	2: S -> DC
4:	C -> •c ǀ cC	ab•c#	3: D -> ab
			4: C -> c

Now, the c succeeds, so the C succeeds, and then the S also succeeds.

	Active rules	Sentence	Parse
1:	S′ -> S•#	abc•#	1: S′ -> S#
			2: S -> DC
			3: D -> ab
			4: C -> c

Now, the # also succeeds, and thus S′ succeeds, resulting in:

	Active rules	Sentence	Parse
1:	S′ -> S#•	abc#•	1: S′ -> S#
			2: S -> DC
			3: D -> ab
			4: C -> c

The "Parse" part now represents a left-most derivation of the sentence:

S′ -> S# -> DC# -> abC# -> abc#.

This method is called *recursive descent*. Descent, because it operates top-down, and recursive, because each non-terminal is implemented as a procedure that can directly or indirectly (through other procedures) invoke itself. It should be stressed that "recursive descent" is merely an implementation issue, albeit an important one. It should also be stressed that the parser described above is a backtracking parser, independent of the implementation method used. Backtracking is a property of the parser, not of the implementation.

The backtracking method developed above is aesthetically pleasing, because we in fact use the grammar itself as a program (or we transform the grammar rules into procedures, which can be done mechanically). There is only one problem: the recursive descent method, as described above, does not always work! We already know that it does not work for left-recursive grammars, but the problem is worse than that. For instance, aabc and abcc are sentences that are not recognized, but should be. Parsing of the aabc sentence gets stuck after the first a, and parsing of the abcc sentence gets stuck after the first c. Yet, aabc can be derived as follows:

$$S \rightarrow AB \rightarrow aAB \rightarrow aaB \rightarrow aabc,$$

and abcc can be derived with

$$S \rightarrow DC \rightarrow abC \rightarrow abcC \rightarrow abcc.$$

So, let us examine why our method fails. A little investigation shows that we never try the A->aA choice when parsing aabc, because the A->a choice succeeds. Such a problem arises whenever more than one right-hand side can succeed, and this is the case whenever a right-hand side can derive a prefix of a string derivable from another right-hand side of the same non-terminal. The method developed so far is too optimistic, in that it assumes that if a choice succeeds, it must be the right choice. It does not allow us to backtrack over such a choice, when it was the wrong one. This is a particularly serious problem if the grammar has ε-rules, because ε-rules always succeed. Another consequence of being unable to backup over a succeeding choice is that it does not allow us to get all parses when there is more than one (this is possible for ambiguous grammars). Improvement is certainly needed here. Our criterion for determining whether a choice is the right one clearly is wrong. Looking back at the backtracking parser of the beginning of this section, we see that that parser does not have this problem, because it does not consider choices independently of their context. One can only decide that a choice is the right one if taking it results in a successful parse; even if the choice ultimately succeeds, we have to try the other choices as well if we want all parses. In the next section, we will develop a recursive-descent parser that solves all the problems mentioned above. Meanwhile, the method above only works for grammars that are *prefix-free*. A non-terminal A is prefix-free if $A \xrightarrow{*} x$ and $A \xrightarrow{*} xy$, where x and y are strings of terminal symbols, implies that $y = \varepsilon$. A grammar is called prefix-free if all its non-terminals are prefix-free,

6.6.2 Exhaustive backtracking recursive descent

In the previous section we saw that we have to be careful not to accept a choice too early; it can only be accepted when it leads to a successful parse. Now this demand is difficult to express in a recursive-descent parser; how do we obtain a procedure that tells us whether a choice leads to a successful parse? In principle, there are infinitely many of these procedures, depending on the sentential form (the prediction) that must derive the rest of the input. We cannot just write them all. However, at any point during the parsing process we are dealing with only one such sentential form: the current prediction, so we could try to build a parsing procedure for this sentential form dynamically, during parsing. Many programming languages offer a useful facility for this purpose: procedure parameters. One procedure can accept a procedure as parameter, and call it, or pass it on to another procedure, or whatever other things one does with procedures. Some languages (for instance Pascal) require these procedures to be named, that is, the actual parameter must be declared as a procedure; other languages, like Algol 68, allow a procedure body for an actual parameter.

Let us see how we can write a parsing procedure for a symbol X, given that it is passed a procedure, which we will call *tail*, that parses the rest of the sentence (the part that follows the *X*). This is the approach taken for all non-terminals, and, for the time being, for terminals as well.

The parsing procedure for a terminal symbol *a* is easy: it matches the current input symbol with *a*; if it succeeds, it advances the input position, and calls the *tail* parameter; then, when *tail* returns, it restores the input position and returns.

Obviously, the parsing procedure for a non-terminal *A* is more complicated. It depends on the type of grammar rule we have for *A*. The simplest case is $A \rightarrow \varepsilon$. This is implemented as a call to *tail*. The next simple case is $A \rightarrow X$, where *X* is either a terminal or a non-terminal symbol. To deal with this case, we must remember that we assume that we have a parsing procedure for *X*, so the implementation of this case consists of a call to *X*, with the *tail* parameter. The next case is $A \rightarrow XY$, with *X* and *Y* symbols. The procedure for *X* expects a procedure for "what comes after the *X*" as parameter. Here, this parameter procedure is built using the *Y* and the *tail* procedures: we create a new procedure out of these two. This, by itself, is a simple procedure: it calls *Y*, with *tail* as parameter. If we call this procedure *Y_tail*, we can implement *A* by calling *X* with *Y_tail* as parameter.[†] And finally, if the right-hand side contains more than two symbols, this technique has to be repeated: for a rule $A \rightarrow X_1 X_2 \cdots X_n$ we create a procedure for $X_2 \cdots X_n$ and *tail* using a procedure for $X_3 \cdots X_n$ and *tail*, and so on. Finally, if we have a choice, that is, we have $A \rightarrow \alpha \mid \beta$, the parsing procedure for *A* has two parts: one part for α, followed by a call to *tail*, and another part for β, followed by a call to *tail*. We have already seen how to implement these parts. If we only want one parsing, all parsing procedures may be implemented as functions that return either **false** or **true**, reflecting whether they result in a successful parse; the part for β is then only started if the part for α, followed by *tail*, fails. If we want all parses, we have to try both choices.

Applying this technique to all grammar rules almost results in a parser. Only, we don't have a starting point yet; this is easily obtained: we just call the procedure for the start-symbol, with the procedure for recognizing the end-marker as parameter. This end-marker procedure is probably a bit different from the others, because this is the procedure where we finally find out whether a parsing attempt succeeds.

Figure 6.12 presents a fully backtracking recursive-descent parser for the grammar of Figure 6.6, written in Pascal. The program has a mechanism to remember the rules used, so these can be printed for each successful parse. Figure 6.13 presents a sample session with this program.

```
{$C+: distinguish between upper and lower case }
program parse(input, output);
{   This is an exhaustive backtracking recursive-descent parser that will
    correctly parse according to the grammar
        S -> D C | A B
        A -> a | a A
        B -> b c | b B c
```

[†] For some programming languages this is difficult. The problem is that *tail* must be accessible from *Y_tail*. Therefore, *Y_tail* should be a local procedure within the procedure for *A*. But, some languages do not allow for local procedures (for instance C), and others do not allow local procedures to be passed as parameters (like Modula-2). Some extensive trickery is required for these languages, but this is beyond the scope of this book.

```
      D -> a b | a D b
      C -> c | c C
```
It implements proper backtracking by only checking one symbol at a
time and passing the rest of the alternative as a parameter for
evaluation on a lower level. A more naive backtracking parser will not
accept e.g. aabc.
}

```
const    infinity = 100;                          { large enough }

type     str = packed array[1..10] of char;

var      tp: integer;                             { index in text }
         length: integer;                         { number of symbols in text }
         rp: integer;                             { index in rules }
         text: array [1..infinity] of char;       { input text }
         rules: array [1..infinity] of str;       { store rules used }

{ administration of rules used }
procedure pushrule (s: str); begin rp := rp + 1; rules[rp] := s end;
procedure poprule; begin rp := rp - 1 end;

procedure endmark;                { recognize end and report success }
         var      i: integer;
begin    if text[tp] = '#' then begin
              writeln('Derivation:');
              for i := 1 to rp do writeln('    ', rules[i]);
         end
end;

procedure a(procedure tail);     { recognize an 'a' and call tail }
begin if text[tp] = 'a' then begin tp := tp + 1; tail; tp := tp - 1 end end;

procedure b(procedure tail);     { recognize a 'b' and call tail }
begin if text[tp] = 'b' then begin tp := tp + 1; tail; tp := tp - 1 end end;

procedure c(procedure tail);     { recognize a 'c' and call tail }
begin if text[tp] = 'c' then begin tp := tp + 1; tail; tp := tp - 1 end end;

procedure A(procedure tail);     { recognize an 'A' and call tail }
         { procedures for the alternative tails }
         procedure t; begin tail end;
         procedure At; begin A(tail) end;
begin
         pushrule('A -> a    '); a(t); poprule;
         pushrule('A -> aA   '); a(At); poprule
end;

procedure B(procedure tail);     { recognize a 'B' and call tail }
         procedure ct; begin c(tail) end;
         procedure Bct;
              procedure ct; begin c(tail) end;
         begin B(ct) end;
begin
         pushrule('B -> bc   '); b(ct); poprule;
         pushrule('B -> bBc  '); b(Bct); poprule
```

```
end;

procedure D(procedure tail);      { recognize a 'D' and call tail }
        procedure bt; begin b(tail) end;
        procedure Dbt;
                procedure bt; begin b(tail) end;
        begin D(bt) end;
begin
        pushrule('D -> ab    ');   a(bt); poprule;
        pushrule('D -> aDb   ');   a(Dbt); poprule
end;

procedure C(procedure tail);      { recognize a 'C' and call tail }
        procedure t; begin tail end;
        procedure Ct; begin C(tail) end;
begin
        pushrule('C -> c     ');   c(t); poprule;
        pushrule('C -> cC    ');   c(Ct); poprule
end;

procedure S(procedure tail);      { recognize a 'S' and call tail }
        procedure Ct; begin C(tail) end;
        procedure Bt; begin B(tail) end;
begin
        pushrule('S -> DC    ');   D(Ct); poprule;
        pushrule('S -> AB    ');   A(Bt); poprule
end;

function readline: boolean;
begin
        write('> '); length := 1;
        if not eof then
        begin   while not eoln do begin
                        read(text[length]); length := length + 1;
                end;
                readln; readline := true
        end
        else readline := false;
end;

procedure parser;
begin   text[length] := '#'; tp := 1; rp := 0; S(endmark) end;

begin while readline do parser end.
```

Figure 6.12 A parser for the grammar of Figure 6.6

6.7 DEFINITE CLAUSE GRAMMARS

In the previous sections, we have seen how to create parsers that retain much of the original structure of the grammar. The programming language Prolog allows us to take this even one step further. Prolog has its foundations in logic. The programmer declares some facts about objects and their relationships, and asks questions about these. The Prolog system uses a built-in search and backtrack mechanism to answer

```
> aabc
Derivation:
       S -> AB
       A -> aA
       A -> a
       B -> bc
> abcc
Derivation:
       S -> DC
       D -> ab
       C -> cC
       C -> c
> abc
Derivation:
       S -> DC
       D -> ab
       C -> c
Derivation:
       S -> AB
       A -> a
       B -> bc
```

Figure 6.13 A session with the program of Figure 6.12

the questions with "yes" or "no". For instance, if we have told the Prolog system about the fact that a table and a chair are pieces of furniture, as follows:

```
furniture(table).
furniture(chair).
```

and we then ask if a bread is a piece of furniture:

```
| ?- furniture(bread).
```

the answer will be "no", but the answer to the question

```
| ?- furniture(table).
```

will, of course, be "yes". We can also use variables, which can be either instantiated (have a value), or not. Variables start with a capital letter or an underscore (_). We can use them for instance as follows:

```
| ?- furniture(X).
```

This is asking for an instantiation of the variable X. The Prolog system will search for a possible instantiation and respond:

```
X = table
```

We can then either stop by typing a RETURN, or continue searching by typing a semicolon (and then a RETURN). In the last case, the Prolog system will search for another instantiation of X.

Not every fact is as simple as the one in the example above. For instance, a Prolog clause that could tell us something about antique furniture is the following:

```
antique_furniture(Obj, Age)  :- furniture(Obj), Age>100.
```

Here we see a conjunction of two goals: an object Obj with age Age is an antique piece of furniture if it is a piece of furniture AND its age is more than a 100 years.

An important data structure in Prolog is the *list*. The empty list is denoted by [], [a] is a list with head a and tail [], [a,b,c] is a list with head a and tail [b,c].

Many Prolog systems allow us to specify grammars. For instance, the grammar of Figure 6.6, looks like the one in Figure 6.14, when written in Prolog. The terminal symbols appear as lists of one element.

```
% Our example grammar in Definite Clause Grammar format.

sn --> dn, cn.
sn --> an, bn.
an --> [a].
an --> [a], an.
bn --> [b], [c].
bn --> [b], bn, [c].
cn --> [c].
cn --> [c], cn.
dn --> [a], [b].
dn --> [a], dn, [b].
```

Figure 6.14 An example grammar in Prolog

The Prolog system translates these rules into Prolog clauses, also sometimes called *definite clauses*, which we can investigate with the listing question:

```
| ?- listing(dn).

dn(_3,_4)  :-
    c(_3,a,_13),
    c(_13,b,_4).
dn(_3,_4)  :-
    c(_3,a,_13),
    dn(_13,_14),
    c(_14,b,_4).

yes

| ?- listing(sn).

sn(_3,_4)  :-
```

```
        dn(_3,_13),
        cn(_13,_4).
    sn(_3,_4) :-
        an(_3,_13),
        bn(_13,_4).
```

yes

We see that the clauses for the non-terminals have two parameter variables. The first one represents the part of the sentence that has yet to be parsed, and the second one represents the tail end of the first one, being the part that is not covered by the current invocation of this non-terminal.

The built-in c-clause matches the head of its first parameter with the second parameter, and the tail of this parameter with the third parameter. A sample Prolog session with this grammar is presented below:

```
& prolog
C-Prolog version 1.5
| ?- [gram1].
gram1 consulted 968 bytes .133333 sec.
```

yes

We have now started the Prolog system, and requested it to consult the file containing the grammar. Here, the grammar resides in a file called gram1.

```
| ?- sn(A,[]).

A = [a,b,c] ;

A = [a,b,c,c] ;

A = [a,b,c,c,c] .
```

yes

We have now asked the system to generate some sentences, by passing an uninstantiated variable to sn, and requesting the system to find other instantiations twice. The Prolog system uses a depth-first searching mechanism, which is not suitable for sentence generation. It will only generate sentences starting with an a, followed by a b, and then followed by an ever increasing number of c's.

```
| ?- sn([a,b,c],[]).

yes
| ?- sn([a,a,b,c],[]).

yes
```

```
| ?- sn([a,b,c,c],[]).
```

yes
```
| ?- sn([a,a,a,b,b,c,c,c],[]).
```

no
```
| ?- halt.
```

```
[ Prolog execution halted ]
&
```

Here, we have asked the system to recognize some sentences, including one on which the naive backtracking parser failed. This session demonstrates that we can use Definite Clause Grammars for recognizing sentences, and to a lesser extent also for generating sentences.

Cohen and Hickey [CF 1987] discuss this and other applications of Prolog in parsers in more detail. For more information on Prolog, see *Programming in Prolog* by William F. Clocksin and Christopher S. Mellish (Springer-Verlag, Berlin, 1981).

7

General bottom-up parsing

As explained in Section 3.3.2, bottom-up parsing is conceptually very simple. At all times we are in the possession of a sentential form that derives from the input text through a series of left-most reductions (which mirrored right-most productions). There is a cut somewhere in this sentential form which separates the already reduced part (on the left) from the yet unexamined part (on the right). See Figure 7.1. The part on the left is called the "stack" and the part on the right "rest of input". The latter contains terminal symbols only, since it is an unprocessed part of the original sentence, while the stack contains a mixture of terminals and non-terminals, resulting from recognized right-hand sides. We can complete the picture by keeping the partial parse trees created by the reductions attached to their non-terminals. Now all the terminal symbols of the original input are still there; the terminals in the stack are one part of them, another part is semi-hidden in the partial parse trees and the rest is untouched in the rest of the input. No information is lost, but some structure has been added. When the bottom-up parser has reached the situation where the rest of the input is empty and the stack contains only the start symbol, we have achieved a parsing and the parse tree will be dangling from the start symbol. This view clearly exposes the idea that parsing is nothing but structuring the input.

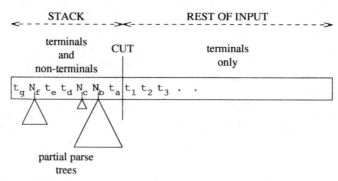

Figure 7.1 The structure of a bottom-up parse

The cut between stack and rest of input is often drawn as a gap, for clarity and since in actual implementations the two are often represented quite differently in the parser.

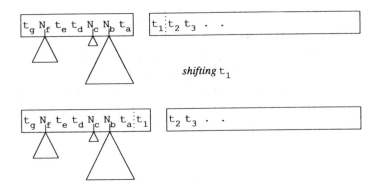

shifting t_1

Figure 7.2 A shift move in a bottom-up automaton

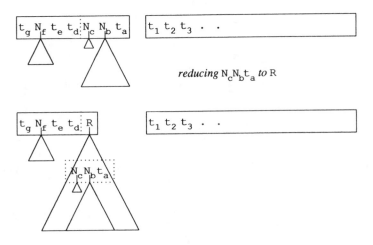

reducing $N_c N_b t_a$ *to* R

Figure 7.3 A reduce move in a bottom-up automaton

Our non-deterministic bottom-up automaton can make only two moves: shift and reduce; see Figures 7.2 and 7.3. During a shift, a (terminal) symbol is shifted from the rest of input to the stack; t_1 is shifted in Figure 7.2. During a reduce move, a number of symbols from the right end of the stack, which form the right-hand side of a rule for a non-terminal, are replaced by that non-terminal and are attached to that non-terminal as the partial parse tree. $N_c N_b t_a$ is reduced to R in Figure 7.3; note that the original $N_c N_b t_a$ are still present inside the partial parse tree. There would, in principle, be no harm in performing the instructions backwards, an *unshift* and *unreduce*, although they would seem to move us away from our goal, which is to obtain a parse tree. We shall see that we need them to do backtracking.

At any point in time the machine can either shift (if there is an input symbol left) or not, or it can do one or more reductions, depending on how many right-hand sides can be recognized. If it cannot do either, it will have to resort to the backtrack moves, to find other possibilities. And if it cannot even do that, it is finished, and has found all (zero or more) parsings.

7.1 PARSING BY SEARCHING

The only problem left is how to guide the automaton through all of the possibilities. This is easily recognized as a search problem, which can be handled by a depth-first or a breadth-first method. We shall now see how the machinery operates for both search methods. Since the effects are exponential in size, even the smallest example gets quite big and we shall use the unrealistic grammar of Figure 7.4. The test input is aaaab.

$$
\begin{array}{llll}
1. & S_S & \text{->} & a\ S\ b \\
2. & S & \text{->} & S\ a\ b \\
3. & S & \text{->} & a\ a\ a \\
\end{array}
$$

Figure 7.4 A simple grammar for demonstration purposes

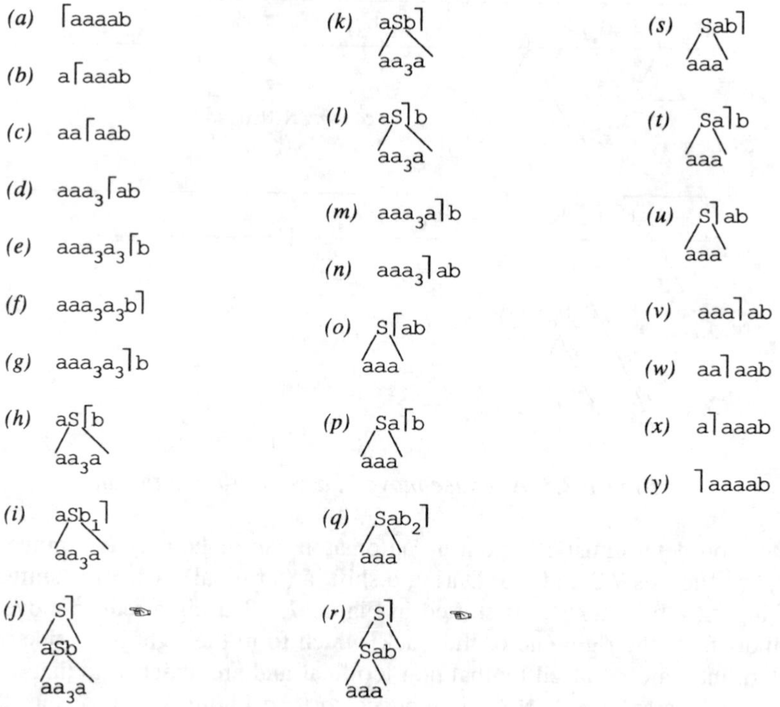

(a) $\lceil$aaaab

(b) a$\lceil$aaab

(c) aa$\lceil$aab

(d) aaa$_3\lceil$ab

(e) aaa$_3$a$_3\lceil$b

(f) aaa$_3$a$_3$b$\rceil$

(g) aaa$_3$a$_3\rceil$b

(h) aS$\lceil$b   (tree: aa$_3$a)

(i) aSb$_1\rceil$ (tree: aa$_3$a)

(j) S$\rceil$ (tree: aSb / aa$_3$a)

(k) aSb$\rceil$ (tree: aa$_3$a)

(l) aS$\rceil$b   (tree: aa$_3$a)

(m) aaa$_3$a$\rceil$b

(n) aaa$_3\rceil$ab

(o) S$\lceil$ab   (tree: aaa)

(p) Sa$\lceil$b   (tree: aaa)

(q) Sab$_2\rceil$ (tree: aaa)

(r) S$\rceil$ (tree: Sab / aaa)

(s) Sab$\rceil$ (tree: aaa)

(t) Sa$\rceil$b   (tree: aaa)

(u) S$\rceil$ab   (tree: aaa)

(v) aaa$\rceil$ab

(w) aa$\rceil$aab

(x) a$\rceil$aaab

(y) $\rceil$aaaab

Figure 7.5 Stages for the depth-first parsing of aaaab

7.1.1 Depth-first (backtracking) parsing

Refer to Figure 7.5, where the gap for a shift is shown as $\lceil$ and that for an unshift as $\rceil$. At first the gap is to the left of the entire input (a) and shifting is the only alternative; likewise with (b) and (c). In (d) we have a choice, either to shift, or to reduce using rule 3; we shift, but remember the possible reduction(s); the rule numbers of these are shown as subscripts to the symbols in the stack. Idem in (*e*). In (*f*) we have reached a position in which shift fails, reduce fails (there are no right-hand sides aaaab, aaab, aab, ab or b) and there are no stored alternatives. So we start backtracking by unshifting (*g*). Here we find a stored alternative, "reduce by 3", which we apply (*h*), deleting the index for the stored alternative in the process; now we can shift again (*i*). No more shifts are possible, but a reduce by 1 gives us a parsing (*j*). After having enjoyed our success we unreduce (*k*); note that (*k*) only differs from (*i*) in that the stored alternative 1 has been consumed. Unshifting, unreducing and again unshifting brings us to (*n*) where we find a stored alternative, "reduce by 3". After reducing (*o*) we can shift again, twice (*p*, *q*). A "reduce by 2" produces the second parsing (*r*). The rest of the road is barren: unreduce, unshift, unshift, unreduce (*v*) and three unshifts bring the automaton to a halt, with the input reconstructed (*y*).

(*a1*)		initial	(*f1*)	aaaab	shifted from *e1*
(*b1*)	a	shifted from *a1*	(*f2*)	Sab / aaa	shifted from *e2*
(*c1*)	aa	shifted from *b1*			
(*d1*)	aaa	shifted from *c1*	(*f3*)	aSb / aaa	shifted from *e3*
(*d2*)	S / aaa	reduced from *d1*	(*f4*)	S / Sab / aaa	reduced from *f2* ☜
(*e1*)	aaaa	shifted from *d1*			
(*e2*)	Sa / aaa	shifted from *d2*	(*f5*)	S / aSb / aaa	reduced from *f3* ☜
(*e3*)	aS / aaa	reduced from *e2*			

Figure 7.6 Stages for the breadth-first parsing of aaaab

7.1.2 Breadth-first (on-line) parsing

Breadth-first bottom-up parsing is simpler than depth-first, at the expense of a far larger memory requirement. Since the input symbols will be brought in one by one (each causing a shift, possibly followed by some reduces), our representation of a partial parse will consist of the stack only, together with its attached partial parse trees. We shall never need to do an unshift or unreduce. Refer to Figure 7.6. We start our solution set with only one empty stack (*a1*). Each parse step consist of two phases; in phase one the next input symbol is appended to the right of all stacks in the solution set; in phase two all stacks are examined and if they allow one or more reductions, one or more copies are made of it, to which the reductions are applied. This way we will never miss a solution. The first and second a are just appended (*b1*, *c1*), but the third allows a reduction (*d2*). The fourth causes one more reduction (*e2*) and the fifth gives rise to two reductions, each of which produces a parsing (*f4* and *f5*).

7.1.3 A combined representation

The configurations of the depth-first parser can be combined into a single graph; see Figure 7.7(*a*) where numbers indicate the order in which the various shifts and reduces are performed. Shifts are represented by lines to the right and reduces by upward arrows. Since a reduce often combines a number of symbols, the additional symbols are brought in by arrows that start upwards from the symbols and then turn right to reach the resulting non-terminal. These arrows constitute at the same time the partial parse tree for that non-terminal. Start symbols in the right-most column with partial parse trees that span the whole input head complete parse trees.

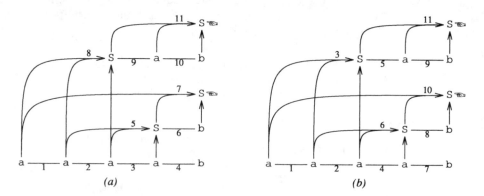

(*a*)   (*b*)

Figure 7.7 The configurations of the parsers combined

If we complete the stacks in the solution sets in our breadth-first parser by appending the rest of the input to them, we can also combine them into a graph, and, what is more, into the same graph; only the action order as indicated by the numbers is different, as shown in Figure 7.7(*b*). This is not surprising, since both represent the total set of possible shifts and reduces; depth-first and breadth-first are just two different ways to visit all nodes of this graph. Figure 7.7(*b*) was drawn in the same form as Figure 7.7(*a*); if we had drawn the parts of the picture in the order in which they are executed by the breadth-first search, many more lines would have crossed. The picture would have been equivalent to (*b*) but much more complicated to look at.

7.1.4 A slightly more realistic example

The above algorithms are relatively easy to understand and implement[†] and although they require exponential time in general, they behave reasonably well on a number of grammars. Sometimes, however, they will burst out in a frenzy of senseless activity, even with an innocuous-looking grammar (especially with an innocuous-looking grammar!). The grammar of Figure 7.8 produces algebraic expressions in one variable, a, and two operators, + and −. Q is used for the operators, since O (oh) looks too much like 0 (zero). This grammar is unambiguous and for a−a+a it has the correct production tree

---

[†] See, for instance, Hext and Roberts [CF 1970] for Dömölki's method to find all possible reductions simultaneously.

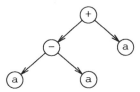

which restricts the minus to the following a rather than to a+a. Figure 7.9 shows the graph searched while parsing a−a+a. It contains 108 shift lines and 265 reduce arrows and would fit on the page only thanks to the exceedingly fine print the phototypesetter is capable of. This is exponential explosion.

$$
\begin{array}{rcl}
S_S & -> & E \\
E & -> & E\ Q\ F \\
E & -> & F \\
F & -> & a \\
Q & -> & + \\
Q & -> & -
\end{array}
$$

Figure 7.8 A grammar for expressions in one variable

7.2 TOP-DOWN RESTRICTED BREADTH-FIRST BOTTOM-UP PARSING

In spite of their occasionally vicious behaviour, breadth-first bottom-up parsers are attractive since they work on-line, can handle left-recursion without any problem and can generally be doctored to handle ε-rules. So the question remains how to curb their needless activity. Many methods have been invented to restrict the search breadth to at most 1, at the expense of the generality of the grammars these methods can handle; see Chapter 9. A method that will restrict the fan-out to reasonable proportions while still retaining full generality was developed by Earley [CF 1970].

7.2.1 The Earley parser without look-ahead

When we take a closer look at Figure 7.9, we see after some thought that many reductions are totally pointless. It is meaningful to reduce the third a to E or S since these can only occur at the end if they represent the entire input; likewise the reduction of a−a to S is absurd, since S can only occur at the end. Earley noticed that what was wrong with these spurious reductions was that they were incompatible with a top-down parsing, that is: they could never derive from the start symbol. He then gave a method to restrict our reductions only to those that derive from the start symbol. We shall see that the resulting parser takes at most n^3 units of time for input of length n rather than C^n.

Earley's parser can also be described as a breadth-first top-down parser with bottom-up recognition, which is how it is explained by the author [CF 1970]. Since it can, however, handle left-recursion directly but needs special measures to handle ε-rules, we prefer to treat it as a bottom-up method.

We shall again use the grammar from Figure 7.8 and parse the input a−a+a. Just as in the non-restricted algorithm, we have at all times a set of partial solutions which is modified by each symbol we read. We shall write the sets between the input symbols

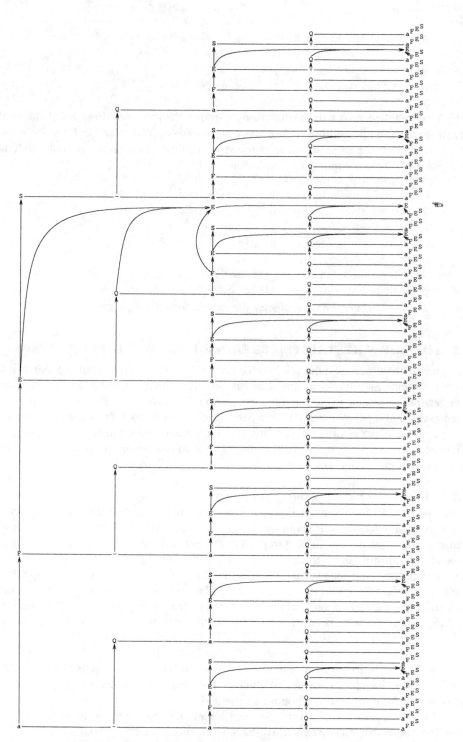

Figure 7.9 The graph searched while parsing a–a+a

as we go; we have to keep earlier sets, since they will still be used by the algorithm. Unlike the non-restricted algorithm, in which the sets contained stacks, the sets consist of what is technically known as *items*, or *Earley items* to be more precise. An *item* is a grammar rule with a gap in its right-hand side; the part of the right-hand side to the left of the gap (which may be empty) has already been recognized, the part to the right of the gap is predicted. The gap is traditionally shown as a fat dot: •. Items are for instance: E–>•EQF, E–>E•QF, E–>EQ•F, E–>EQF•, F–>a•, etc. It is unfortunate when a vague every-day term gets endowed with a very specific technical meaning, but the expression has taken hold, so it will have to do. An *Earley item* is an item with an indication of the position of the symbol at which the recognition of the recognized part started. Notations vary, but we shall write @n after the item (read: "at n"). If the set at the end of position 7 contains the item E–>E•QF@3, we have recognized an E in positions 3, 4, 5, 6, 7 and are looking forward to recognizing QF.

The sets of items contain exactly those items a) of which the part before the dot has been recognized so far and b) of which we are certain that we shall be able to use the result when they will happen to be recognized in full (but we cannot, of course, be certain that that will happen). If a set contains the item E–>E•QF@3, we can be sure that when we will have recognized the whole right-hand side EQF, we can go back to the set at the beginning of symbol number 3 and find there an item that was looking forward to recognizing an E, i.e., that had an E with a dot in front of it. Since that is true recursively, no recognition will be in vain.

7.2.1.1 *The Scanner, Completer and Predictor*
The construction of an item set from the previous item set proceeds in three phases. The first two correspond to those of the non-restricted algorithm, where they were called "shift" and "reduce"; here they are called "Scanner" and "Completer". The third is new and is related to the top-down component; it is called "Predictor".

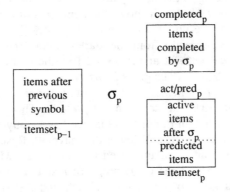

Figure 7.10 The Earley items sets for one input symbol

The Scanner, Completer and Predictor deal with four sets of items for each token in the input. Refer to Figure 7.10, where the input symbol σ_p at position p is surrounded by the four sets: *itemset*$_{p-1}$, which contains the items available just before σ_p; *completed*$_p$, the set of items that have become completed due to σ_p; *active*$_p$, which contains the non-completed items that passed σ_p; and *predicted*$_p$, the set of newly predicted items. The sets *active*$_p$ and *predicted*$_p$ together form *itemset*$_p$; the internal division will be indicated in the drawings by a dotted line. Initially, $itemset_{p-1}$ is filled (as a result of processing σ_{p-1}) and the other sets are empty; the construction of $itemset_0$ is special.

The Scanner looks at σ_p, goes through $itemset_{p-1}$ and makes copies of all items that contain $\bullet\sigma$ (all other items are ignored); in those, the part before the dot was already recognized and now σ is recognized. Consequently, the Scanner changes $\bullet\sigma$ into $\sigma\bullet$. If the dot is now at the end, it stores the item in the set $completed_p$; otherwise it stores it in the set $active_p$.

Next the Completer inspects $completed_p$, which contains the items that have just been recognized completely and can now be reduced. This reduction goes as follows. For each item of the form $R\rightarrow\cdots\bullet @m$ the Completer goes to $itemset_{m-1}$, and calls the Scanner; the Scanner, which was used to work on the σ_p found in the input and $itemset_{p-1}$, is now directed to work on the R recognized by the Completer and $itemset_{m-1}$. It will make copies of all items in $itemset_{m-1}$ featuring a $\bullet R$, replace the $\bullet R$ by $R\bullet$ and store them in either $completed_p$ or $active_p$, as appropriate. This can add indirectly recognized items to the set $completed_p$, which means more work for the Completer. After a while, all completed items have been reduced, and the Predictor's turn has come.

The Predictor goes through the sets $active_p$ (which was filled by the Scanner) and $predicted_p$ (which is empty initially), and considers all non-terminals which have a dot in front of them; these we expect to see in the input. For each expected (predicted) non-terminal N and for each rule for that non-terminal $N\rightarrow P\cdots$, the Predictor adds an item $N\rightarrow\bullet P\cdots @p$ to the set $predicted_p$. This may introduce new predicted non-terminals (for instance, P) in $predicted_p$ which cause more predicted items. After a while, this too will stop.

The sets $active_p$ and $predicted_p$ together form the new $itemset_p$. If the $completed$ set for the last symbol in the input contains an item $S\rightarrow\cdots\bullet @1$, i.e., an item spanning the entire input and reducing to the start symbol, we have found at least one parsing.

Now refer to Figure 7.11, which shows the items sets of the Earley parser working on a–a+a. The initial active item set $active_0$ is {S->•E@1}, indicating that this is the only item that can derive directly from the start symbol. The Predictor first predicts E->•EQF@1, from this E->•EQF@1 and E->•F@1 (but the first one is in the set already) and from the last one F->•a@1. This gives $itemset_0$.

The Scanner working on $itemset_0$ and scanning for an a, only catches F->•a@1, which it turns into F->a•@1 and stores in $completed_1$. This not only means that we have recognized and reduced an F, but also that we have a buyer for it. The Completer goes to the set $itemset_0$ and copies all items that have •F. Result: one item, E->•F@1, which turns into E->F•@1 and is again stored in $completed_1$. More work for the Completer, which will now copy items containing •E; result: two items, S->•E@1 which becomes S->E•@1 and goes to the completed set, and E->•EQF@1 which becomes E->E•QF@1 and which becomes the first and only member of $active_1$. The completion of S yields no new information.

The Predictor working on $active_1$ has an easy job: •Q causes two items for Q, both with @2, since that is where recognition will have started, if it occurs at all. Nothing spectacular happens until the Scanner processes the second a; from $itemset_2$ it extracts F->•a@3 which gives F->a•@3 which is passed to the Completer (through $completed_3$). The latter sees the reduction of a to F starting at position 3, goes to $itemset_2$ to see who ordered an F, and finds E->EQ•F@1; given the F, this turns into E->EQF•@1,

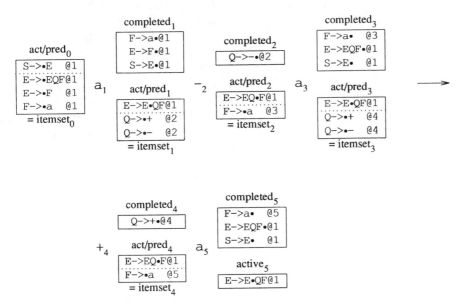

Figure 7.11 Items sets of the Earley parser working on a−a+a

which in its turn signals the reduction to E of the substring from 1 to 3 (again through *completed 3*). The Completer checks *itemset 0* and finds two clients there for the E: S->•E@1 and E->•EQF@1; the first ends up as S->E•@1 in *completed 3*, the second as E->E•QF@1 in *active 3*.

After the last symbol has been processed by the Scanner, we still run the Completer to do the final reductions, but running the Predictor is useless, since there is nothing to predict any more. Note that the parsing started by calling the Predictor on the initial active set and that there is one Predictor/Scanner/Completer action for each symbol. Since the last completed set indeed contains an item S->E•@1, there is at least one parsing.

7.2.1.2 Constructing a parse tree
All this does not directly give us a parse tree. As is more often the case in parser construction (see, for instance, Section 4.1) we have set out to build a parser and have ended up building a recognizer. The intermediate sets, however, contain enough information about fragments and their relations to construct a parse tree easily. As with the CYK parser, a simple top-down Unger-type parser can serve for this purpose, since the Unger parser is very interested in the lengths of the various components of the parse tree and that is exactly what the sets in the Earley parser provide. In his 1970 article, Earley gives a method of constructing the parse tree(s) while parsing, by keeping with each item a pointer back to the item that caused it to be present. Tomita [CF 1986, p. 74-77] has, however, shown that this method will produce incorrect parse trees on certain ambiguous grammars.

From the set *completed 5* in Figure 7.11, which is the first we inspect after having finished the set construction, we see that there is a parse possible with S for a root and extending over symbols 1 to 5; we designate the parse root as S_{1-5} in Figure 7.12.

Given the completed item S->E•@1 in *completed* $_5$ there must be a parse node E $_{1-5}$, which is completed at 5. Since all items completed after 5 are contained in *completed* $_5$, we scan the latter to find a completed E starting at 1; we find E->EQF•@1. This gives us parse tree (*a*), where the values at the question marks are still to be seen. Since items are recognized at their right ends, we start by finding a parse for the F $_{?-5}$, to be found in *completed* $_5$. We find F->a•@5, giving us parse tree (*b*). It suggests that we find a parse for Q $_{?-4}$ completed after 4; in *completed* $_4$ we find Q->+•@4. Consequently Q $_{?-4}$ is Q $_{4-4}$ and the E $_{1-?}$ in (*b*) must be E $_{1-3}$. This makes us look in *completed* $_3$ for an E->...@1, where we find E->EQF•@1. We now have parse tree (*c*), and, using the same techniques, we easily complete it (*d*).

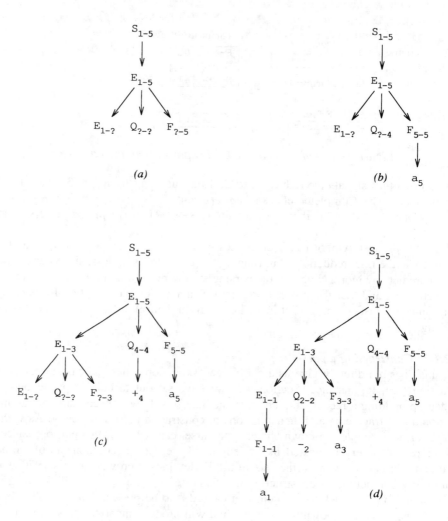

Figure 7.12 Construction of the parse trees

7.2.1.3 Space and time requirements

It is interesting to have a look at the space and time needed for the construction of the sets. First we calculate the maximum size of the sets just after symbol number p. There is only a fixed number of different items, I, limited by the size of the grammar; for our grammar it is $I=14$. However, each item can occur with any of the additions @1 to @$p+1$, of which there are $p+1$. So the number of items in the set $itemset_p$ is limited to $I\times(p+1)$. The exact calculation of the maximum number of items in each of the sets is complicated by the fact that different rules apply to the first, last and middle items. Disregarding these complications, we find that the maximum number of items in all $itemsets$ up to p is roughly $I\times p^2/2$. The same applies to the *completed* sets. So, for an input of length n, the memory requirement is $O(n^2)$, as with the CYK algorithm. In actual practice, the amount of memory used is often far less than this theoretical maximum. In our case all sets together could conceivably contain about $14\times5^2=350$ items, with which the actual number of $4+3+3+1+2+3+3+1+2+3+1=26$ items compares very favourably.

Although a set at position p can contain a maximum of $O(p)$ items, it may require an amount of work proportional to p^2 to construct that set, since each item could, in principle, be inserted by the Completer once from each preceding position. Under the same simplifying assumptions as above, we find that the maximum number of actions needed to construct all sets up to p is roughly $I\times p^3/6$. So the total amount of work involved in parsing a sentence of length n with the Earley algorithm is $O(n^3)$, as it is with the CYK algorithm. Again, in practice it is much better: on many grammars, including the one from Figure 7.8, it will work in linear time ($O(n)$) and on any unambiguous grammar it will work in $O(n^2)$. In our example, a maximum of about $14\times5^3/6\approx300$ actions might be required, compared to the actual number of 28 (both items for E in $predicted_0$ were inserted twice).

It should be noted that once the calculation of the sets is finished, only the *completed* sets are consulted. The *active* and *predicted* sets can be thrown away to make room for the parse tree(s).

The practical efficiency of this and the CYK algorithms is not really surprising, since in normal usage most arbitrary fragments of the input will not derive from any non-terminal. The sentence fragment "*letter into the upper left-most*" does not represent any part of speech, nor does any fragment of it of a size larger than one. The $O(n^2)$ and $O(n^3)$ bounds only materialize for grammars in which almost all non-terminals produce almost all substrings in almost all combinatorially possible ways, as for instance in the grammar S->SS, S->x.

7.2.2 The relation between the Earley and CYK algorithms

The similarity in the time and space requirement between the Earley and the CYK algorithm suggest a deeper relation between the two and indeed there is one. The Earley sets can be accommodated in a CYK-like grid; see Figure 7.13 To stress the similarity, the sets are distributed over diagonals of boxes slanting from north-west to south-east. Since the columns indicate the beginnings of possibly recognized fragments, all items with the same @p come in the same column. This arrangement assigns a natural position to each item. Completed items are drawn in the top left corner of a box, active items in the bottom right corner. Predicted items have not yet recognized anything and live in the bottom layer.

When we compare this picture to that produced by the CYK parser (Figure 7.14)

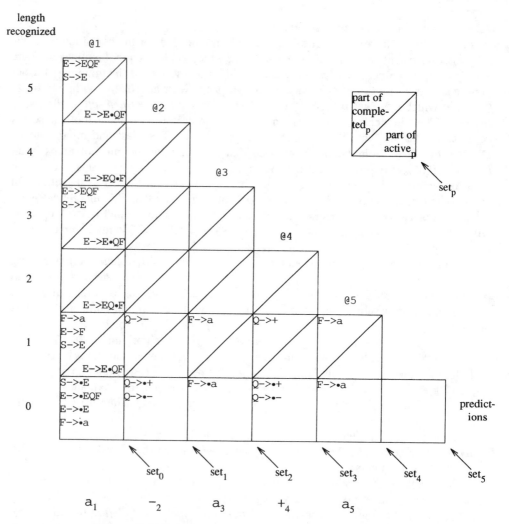

Figure 7.13 The Earley sets represented in CYK fashion

we see correspondences and differences. Rather than having items, the boxes contain non-terminals only. All active and predicted items are absent. The left-hand sides of the completed items also occur in the CYK picture, but the latter features more recognized non-terminals; from the Earley picture we know that these will never play a role in any parse tree. The costs and the effects of the top-down restriction are clearly shown.

The correspondence between the Earley and the CYK algorithms has been analysed by Graham and Harrison [CF 1976]. This has resulted in a combined algorithm described by Graham, Harrison and Ruzzo [CF 1980].

7.2.3 Ambiguous sentences
Calculating the sets for a parsing of an ambiguous sentence does not differ from that for an unambiguous one. Some items will be inserted more than once into the same set, but that can happen even with unambiguous sentences. The parse trees will be faithfully produced by the Unger parser; when searching a completed set for items of the

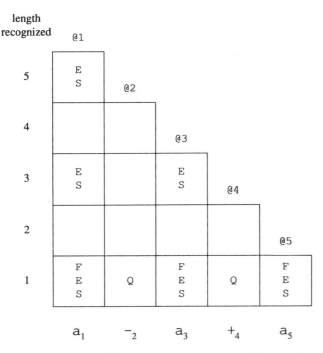

Figure 7.14 CYK sets for the parsing of Figure 7.11

form $A \rightarrow \cdots \bullet @p$, it may find several. Each will produce a different parse tree (or set of parse trees if further ambiguities are found). There may be exponentially many parse trees (even though the work to produce the sets is limited to $O(n^3)$) or even infinitely many of them. Infinite ambiguity is cut out automatically by the Unger parser, but exponential numbers of parse trees will just have to be suffered. If they are essential to the application, Tomita [CF 1986, p. 17-20] has given an efficient packing method for them.

The enumeration of all possible parse trees is often important, since many methods augment the CF grammar with more long-range restrictions formulated outside the CF framework, to thus approximate a context-sensitive analysis. To this end, all parse trees are produced and checked; only those that meet the restrictions are accepted.

Figure 7.15 shows the sets for the parsing of an ambiguous sentence xxx according to the grammar S->SS, S->x; again an artificial example is the only one which can be shown, for reasons of size. Figure 7.16 gives the parse trees. There is only one root in $completed_3$: S->SS•@1, leading to parse tree (*a*). Looking up a parsing for S_{2-3} in $completed_3$, we come up with three possibilities: S->•x@3, S->SS•@2 and S->SS•@1. The first and second lead to parse trees (*b*) and (*c*) but the third is suppressed by the Unger parser (it would lead to infinite recursion). No further ambiguities occur and the final parse trees are found in (*d*) and (*e*). All this is the same as in the CYK parser.

7.2.4 Handling ε-rules

Like most parsers, the above parser cannot handle ε-rules without special measures. ε-rules show up first as an anomaly in the work of the Predictor. While predicting items of the form $A \rightarrow \bullet \cdots @p+1$ as a consequence of having a •A in an item in $active_p$ or

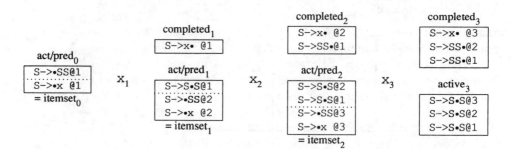

Figure 7.15 Parsing of xxx according to S->SS, S->x

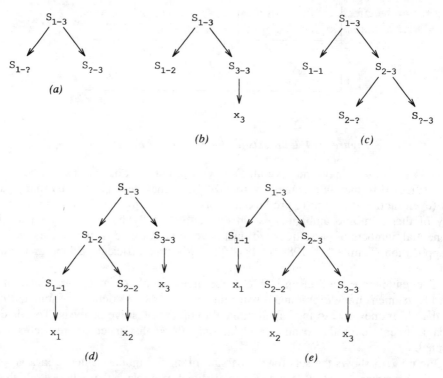

Figure 7.16 Parse tree construction for the parsing of Figure 7.15

$predicted_p$, it may stumble upon an empty prediction $A \rightarrow \bullet$ @$p+1$; this means that the non-terminal A has been completed just before symbol number $p+1$ and this completed item should be added to the set $completed_p$, which up to now only contained items with @p at most. So we find that there was more work for the Completer after all. But that is not the end of the story. If we now run the Completer again, it will draw the consequences of the newly completed item(s) which have @$p+1$. So it will consult $itemset_p$, which is, however, incomplete since items are still being added to its constituents, $active_p$ and $predicted_p$. If it finds occurrences of $\bullet A$ there, it will add copies with $A \bullet$ instead; part of these may require new predictions to be done (if the dot lands in front of another non-terminal), part may be completed items, which will have to go into *completed$_p$* and which mean more work for the Completer. The latter items can have a starting point lower than p, which brings in items from further back, which may or may not now be completed through this action or through empty completed items at p.

The easiest way to handle this mare's nest is to stay calm and keep running the Predictor and Completer in turn until neither has anything more to add. Since the number of items is finite this will happen eventually, and in practice it happens rather sooner than later.

The Completer and Predictor loop has to be viewed as a single operation called "X" by Graham, Harrison and Ruzzo [CF 1980]. Just like the Predictor it has to be applied to the initial state, to honour empty productions before the first symbol; just like the Completer it has to be applied to the final state, to honour empty productions after the last symbol.

Part of the effects are demonstrated by the grammar of Figure 7.17 which is based on a grammar similar to that of Figure 7.8. Rather than addition and subtraction, this one handles multiplication and division, with the possibility to omit the multiplication sign: aa means a×a.

$$
\begin{array}{rcl}
S_S & -> & E \\
E & -> & E \; Q \; F \\
E & -> & F \\
F & -> & a \\
Q & -> & \times \\
Q & -> & / \\
Q & -> & \varepsilon
\end{array}
$$

Figure 7.17 A grammar with an ε-rule

The parsing is given in Figure 7.18. The items pointed at by a ☞ have been added by a second pass of the Completer/Predictor. The Q->•@2, inserted by the Predictor into *completed$_1$* as a consequence of E->E•QF@1 in *active$_1$*, is picked up by the second pass of the Completer, and is used to clone E->E•QF@1 in *active$_1$* into E->EQ•F@1. This in turn is found by the Predictor which predicts the item F->•a@2 from it. Note that we now do have to consider the full *active/predicted* set after the last symbol; its processing by the Completer/Predictor may insert an item of the form S->...@1 in the last *completed* set, indicating a parsing.

7.2.5 Prediction look-ahead

In the following we shall describe a series of increasingly complicated (and more effi-cient) parsers of the Earley type; somewhere along the line we will also meet a parser that is (almost) identical to the one described by Earley in his paper.

When we go back to Figure 7.11 and examine the actions of the Predictor, we see that it sometimes predicts items that it could know were useless if it could look ahead at the next symbol. When the next symbol is a −, it is kind of foolish to proudly predict Q->•+@2. The Predictor can of course easily be modified to check such simple cases, but it is possible to have a Predictor that will *never* predict anything obviously errone-ous; all its predicted items will be either completed or active in the next set. (The pred-ictions may, however, fail on the symbol after that; after all, it is a Predictor, not an

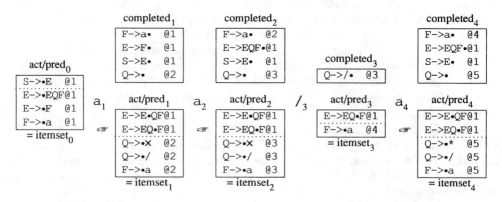

Figure 7.18 Recognition of empty productions in an Earley parser

Oracle.)

To see how we can obtain such a perfect Predictor we need a different example (after removing Q->•+@2 and Q->•-@4 from Figure 7.11 all predictions there come true, so nothing can be gained any more).

$$
\begin{array}{llll}
S'_S & -> & S \\
S & -> & A \mid AB \mid B & \text{FIRST}(S) = \{p, q\} \\
A & -> & C & \text{FIRST}(A) = \{p\} \\
B & -> & D & \text{FIRST}(B) = \{q\} \\
C & -> & p & \text{FIRST}(C) = \{p\} \\
D & -> & q & \text{FIRST}(D) = \{q\}
\end{array}
$$

Figure 7.19 A grammar for demonstrating prediction look-ahead and its FIRST sets

The artificial grammar of Figure 7.19 produces nothing but the three sentences p, q and pq, and does so in a straightforward way. The root is S' rather than S, which is a convenient way to have a grammar with only one rule for the root. This is not necessary but it simplifies the following somewhat, and it is usual in practice.

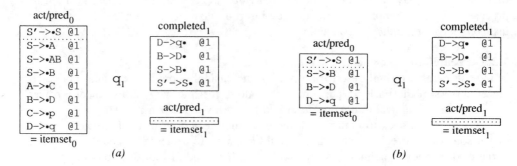

Figure 7.20 Parsing the sentence q without look-ahead (a) and with look-ahead (b)

The parsing of the sentence q is given in Figure 7.20(a) and (b). Starting from the initial item, the Predictor predicts a list of 7 items (*a*). Looking at the next symbol, q, the Predictor could easily avoid the prediction C–>•p@1, but several of the other predictions are also false, for instance, A–>•C@1. The Predictor could avoid the first since it sees that it cannot begin with q; if it knew that C cannot begin with a q, it could also avoid A–>•C@1. (Note that *itemset*₁ is empty, indicating that there is no way for the input to continue.)

The required knowledge can be obtained by calculating the FIRST sets of all non-terminals in the grammar (FIRST sets and a method of calculating them are explained in Sections 8.2.1.1 and 8.2.2.1). The use of the FIRST sets is very effective: the Predictor again starts from the initial item, but since it knows that q is not in FIRST(A), it will not predict S–>•A@1. Items like a–>•C@1 do not even have to be avoided, since their generation will never be contemplated in the first place. Only the B-line will be predicted (*b*) and it will consist of three predictions, all of them to the point.

$$
\begin{array}{lll}
S' & \to & S \\
S & \to & A \mid AB \mid B \qquad \text{FIRST}(S) = \{\varepsilon, p, q\} \\
A & \to & C \qquad\qquad\qquad \text{FIRST}(A) = \{\varepsilon, p\} \\
B & \to & D \qquad\qquad\qquad \text{FIRST}(B) = \{q\} \\
C & \to & p \mid \varepsilon \qquad\qquad\; \text{FIRST}(C) = \{\varepsilon, p\} \\
D & \to & q \qquad\qquad\qquad \text{FIRST}(D) = \{q\}
\end{array}
$$

Figure 7.21 A grammar with an ε-rule and its FIRST sets

Handling ε-rules is easier now: we know for every non-terminal whether it can produce ε (in which case ε is in the FIRST set of that non-terminal). If we add a rule C–>ε to our grammar (Figure 7.21), the entire picture changes. Starting from the initial item S'–>•S@1 (Figure 7.22), the Predictor will still not predict S–>•A@1 since FIRST(A) does not contain q, but it *will* predict S–>•AB@1 since FIRST(AB) does contain a q (B combined with the transparency of A). The line continues by predicting A–>•C@1, but C–>•@1 is a completed item and goes into *completed*₀. When the Completer starts, it finds C–>•@1, applies it to A–>•C@1 and produces A–>C•@1, likewise completed. The latter is then applied to S–>•AB@1 to produce the active item S–>A•B@1. This causes another run of the Predictor, to follow the new •B, but all those items have already been added.

Bouckaert, Pirotte and Snelling, who have analysed variants of the Earley parsers for two different look-ahead regimes [CF 1975], show that predictive look-ahead reduces the number of items by 20 to 50% or even more on "practical" grammars.

7.2.6 Reduction look-ahead
Once we have gone through the trouble of calculating the FIRST sets, we can use them for a second type of look-ahead: *reduction look-ahead*. Prediction look-ahead reduces the number of predicted items, reduction look-ahead reduces the number of completed items. Referring back to Figure 7.11, which depicted the actions of an Earley parser without look-ahead, we see that it does two silly completions: S–>E•@1 in *completed*₁, and S–>E•@1 in *completed*₃. The redundancy of these completed items stems from the fact that they are only meaningful at the end of the input. Now this may seem a very special case, not worth testing for, but the phenomenon can be put in a more general

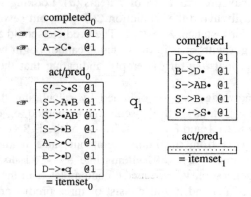

Figure 7.22 Parsing the sentence q with the grammar of Figure 7.21

setting: if we introduce an explicit symbol for end-of-file (for instance, #), we can say that the above items are redundant because they are followed by a symbol (− and +, respectively) which is not in the set of symbols the item should be followed by on completion.

The trick is now to keep, together with any item, a set of symbols which may come after that item, the *reduction look-ahead set*; if the item seems completed but the next symbol is not in this set, the item is discarded. The rules for constructing the look-ahead set for an item are straightforward, but unlike the prediction look-ahead it cannot be calculated in advance; it must be constructed as we go. (A limited and less effective set could be calculated statically, using the FOLLOW sets explained in 8.2.2.2.)

The initial item starts with a look-ahead set of [#] (the look-ahead set will be shown between square brackets at the end of the item). When the dot advances in an item, its look-ahead set remains the same, since what happens inside an item does not affect what may come after it. When a new item is created by the Predictor, a new look-ahead set must be composed. Suppose the item is

$P \rightarrow A \cdot BCD$ [abc] @n

and predicted items for B must be created. We now ask ourselves what symbols may follow the occurrence of B in this item. It is easy to see that they are:
- □ any symbol C can start with,
- □ if C can produce the empty string, any symbol D can start with,
- □ if D can also produce the empty string, any of the symbols a, b and c.

Given the FIRST sets for all non-terminals, which can also tell us if a non-terminal can produce empty, the resulting new reduction look-ahead set is easily calculated. It is also written as FIRST(CD [abc]), which is of course the set of first symbols of anything produced by $CDa \mid CDb \mid CDc$.

The Earley sets with reduction look-ahead for our example a−a+a are given in Figure 7.23, where we have added a # symbol in position 6. The calculation of the sets follow the above rules. The look-ahead of the item E−>•EQF@1 [#+−] in *predicted*$_0$ results from its being inserted twice: once predicted from S−>•E@1 [#], which contributes the #, and once from E−>•EQF@1 [?], which contributes the +− from FIRST(Q).

Note that the item S->E•@1[#] is not placed in *completed*$_1$, since the actual symbol ahead ($-_2$) is not in the item's look-ahead set; something similar occurs in *completed*$_3$, but not in *completed*$_5$.

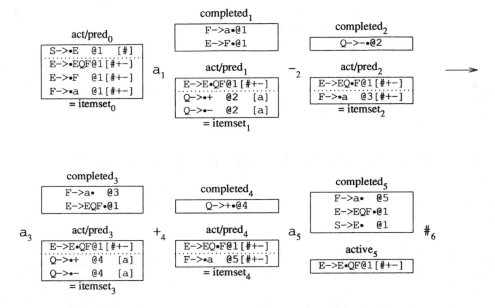

Figure 7.23 Item sets with reduction look-ahead

As with prediction look-ahead, the gain in our example is meagre. The effectiveness in the general case is not easily determined. Earley recommends the reduction look-ahead, but does not take into account the effort required to calculate and maintain the look-ahead sets. Bouckaert, Pirotte and Snelling definitely condemn the reduction look-ahead, on the grounds that it may easily double the number of items to be carried around, but they count, for instance, E->•F@1[+-] as two items. All in all, since the gain from reduction look-ahead cannot be large and its implementation cost and overhead are probably considerable, it is likely that its use should not be recommended. The well-tuned Earley/CYK parser by Graham, Harrison and Ruzzo [CF 1980] does not feature reduction look-ahead.

8

Deterministic top-down methods

In Chapter 6 we discussed two general top-down methods: one using breadth-first search and one using depth-first search. These methods have in common the need to search to find derivations, and thus are not efficient. In this chapter and the next we will concentrate on parsers that do not have to search: there will always be only one possibility to choose from. Parsers with this property are called *deterministic*. Deterministic parsers are much faster than non-deterministic ones, but there is a penalty: the class of grammars that the parsing method is suitable for, while depending on the method chosen, is more restricted than that of the grammars suitable for non-deterministic parsing methods.

In this chapter, we will focus our attention on deterministic top-down methods. As has been explained in Section 3.6.5, there is only one such method, this in contrast with the deterministic bottom-up methods, which will be discussed in the next chapter. From Chapters 3 and 6 we know that in a top-down parser we have a prediction for the rest of the input, and that this prediction has either a terminal symbol in front, in which case we "match", or a non-terminal, in which case we "predict".

It is the predict step that, until now, has caused us so much trouble. The predict step consists of replacing a non-terminal by one of its right-hand sides, and if we have no means to decide which right-hand side to select, we have to try them all. One restriction we could impose on the grammar, one that immediately comes to mind, is limiting the number of right-hand sides of each non-terminal to one. Then we would need no search, because no selection would be needed. However, such a restriction is far too severe, as it would leave us with only finite languages. So, limiting the number of right-hand sides per non-terminal to one is not a solution.

There are two sources of information that could help us in selecting the right right-hand side. First of all, there is the partial derivation as it is constructed so far. However, apart from the prediction this does not give us any information about the rest of the input. The other source of information is the rest of the input. We will see that looking at the next symbol or the next few symbols will, for certain grammars, tell us which choice to take.

8.1 REPLACING SEARCH BY TABLE LOOK-UP

Grammars that make it particularly easy to at least limit the search are ones in which each right-hand side starts with a terminal symbol. In this case, a predict step is always immediately followed by a match step, matching the next input symbol with the symbol starting the right-hand side selected in the prediction. This match step can only succeed for right-hand sides that start with this input symbol. The other right-hand sides will immediately lead to a match step that will fail. We can use this fact to limit the number of predictions as follows: only the right-hand sides that start with a terminal symbol that is equal to the next input symbol will be considered. For instance, consider the grammar of Figure 6.1, repeated in Figure 8.1, and the input sentence aabb.

$$
\begin{array}{lll}
S & \rightarrow & aB \mid bA \\
A & \rightarrow & a \mid aS \mid bAA \\
B & \rightarrow & b \mid bS \mid aBB
\end{array}
$$

Figure 8.1 A grammar producing sentences with an equal number of a's *and* b's

Using the breadth-first top-down method of Chapter 6, extended with the observation described above, results in the steps of Figure 8.2: *(a)* presents the start of the automaton; we have added the # end-marker; only one right-hand side of S starts with an a, so this is the only applicable right-hand side; this leads to *(b)*; next, a match step leads to (c) ; the next input symbol is again an a, so only one right-hand side of B is applicable, resulting in *(d)*; *(e)* is the result of a match step; this time, the next input symbol is a b, so two right-hand sides of B are applicable; this leads to *(f)*; *(g)* is the result of a match step; again, the next input symbol is a b, so two right-hand sides of B are applicable; only one right-hand side of S is applicable; this leads to *(h)*, and this again calls for a match step, leading to *(i)*; now, there are no applicable right-hand sides for S and A, because there are no right-hand sides starting with a #; thus, these predictions are dead ends; this leaves a match step for the only remaining prediction, leading to *(j)*.

   We could enhance the efficiency of this method even further by precomputing the applicable right-hand sides for each non-terminal/terminal combination, and enter these in a table. For the grammar of Figure 8.1, this would result in the table of Figure 8.3. Such a table is called a *parse table*.

   Despite its title, most of this chapter concerns the construction of these parse tables. Once such a parse table is obtained, the actions of the parser are obvious. The parser does not need the grammar any more. Instead, every time a predict step is called for, the parser uses the next input symbol and the non-terminal at hand as indices in the parse table. The corresponding table entry contains the right-hand sides that have to be considered. For instance, in Figure 8.2(*e*), the parser would use input symbol b and non-terminal B to determine that it has to consider the right-hand sides B_1 and B_2. If the corresponding table entry is empty, we have found an error in the input and the input sentence cannot be derived from the grammar. Using the parse table of Figure 8.3 instead of the grammar of Figure 8.1 for parsing the sentence aabb will again lead to Figure 8.2. The advantage of using a parse table is that we do not have to check all right-hand sides of a non-terminal any more, to see if they start with the right terminal symbol.

   Still, we have a search process, albeit a more limited one than we had before. The search is now confined to the elements of the parse table entries. In fact, we now only

(a)		aabb#
		S#

(b)		aabb#
	S_1	aB#

(c)	a	abb#
	S_1a	B#

(d)	a	abb#
	S_1aB_3	aBB#

(e)	aa	bb#
	S_1aB_3a	BB#

(f)	aa	bb#
	$S_1aB_3aB_1$	bB#
	$S_1aB_3aB_2$	bSB#

(g)	aab	b#
	$S_1aB_3aB_1$b	B#
	$S_1aB_3aB_2$b	SB#

(h)	aab	b#
	$S_1aB_3aB_1bB_1$	b#
	$S_1aB_3aB_1bB_2$	bS#
	$S_1aB_3aB_2bS_2$	bAB#

(i)	aabb	#
	$S_1aB_3aB_1bB_1$b	#
	$S_1aB_3aB_1bB_2$b	S#
	$S_1aB_3aB_2bS_2$b	AB#

(j)	aabb#	
	$S_1aB_3aB_1bB_1$b#	

Figure 8.2 The limited breadth-first parsing of the sentence aabb#

	a	b	#
S	S_1: aB	S_2: bA	
A	A_1: a A_2: aS	A_3: bAA	
B	B_3: aBB	B_1: b B_2: bS	

Figure 8.3 The parse table for the grammar of Figure 8.1

need a search because of the (A,a) and the (B,b) entry of the table. These entries have more than one element, so we need the search to determine which one results in a derivation of the input sentence.

This last observation is an important one: it immediately leads to a restriction that we could impose on the grammar, to make the parsing deterministic: we could require that each parse table entry contain at most one element. In terms of the grammar, this means that all right-hand sides of a non-terminal start with a different terminal symbol. A grammar that fulfills this requirement is called a *simple LL(1) grammar (SLL(1))*, or an *s-grammar*. Here, LL(1) means that the grammar allows a deterministic parser that operates from Left to right, produces a Left-most derivation, using a look-ahead of one (1) symbol.

Consider for instance the grammar of Figure 8.4.

$$
\begin{array}{lcl}
S & -> & aB \\
B & -> & b \mid aBb
\end{array}
$$

Figure 8.4 An example SLL(1) grammar

This grammar generates all sentences starting with a number of a's, followed by an equal number of b's. The grammar is clearly SLL(1). It leads to the parse table of Figure 8.5.

	a	b	#
S	S_1: aB		
B	B_2: aBb	B_1: b	

Figure 8.5 The parse table for the grammar of Figure 8.4

The parsing of the sentence aabb is presented in Figure 8.6. Again we have added the # end-marker.

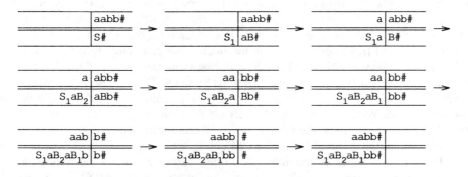

Figure 8.6 The SLL(1) parsing of the sentence aabb#

As expected, there is always only one prediction, so no search is needed. Thus, the process is deterministic, and therefore very efficient. The efficiency could be enhanced even further by combining the predict step with the match step that always follows the predict step.

So, SLL(1) grammars lead to simple and very efficient parsers. However, the restrictions that we have placed on the grammar are severe. Not many practical grammars are SLL(1), although many can be transformed into SLL(1) form. In the next section, we will consider a more general class of grammars that still allows for the same kind of parser.

8.2 LL(1) GRAMMARS

For the deterministic top-down parser described in the previous section, the crucial restriction placed on the grammar is that all right-hand sides of a non-terminal start with a different terminal symbol. This ensures that each parse table entry contains at most one element. In this section, we will drop the requirement that right-hand sides start with a terminal symbol. We will see that we can still construct a parse table in that case. Later on, we will see that we can even construct a parse table for grammars with ε-rules.

8.2.1 LL(1) grammars without ε-rules

If a grammar has no ε-rules, there are no non-terminals that derive the empty string. In other words, each non-terminal ultimately derives strings of terminal symbols of length at least one, and this also holds for each right-hand side. The terminal symbols that start these strings are the ones that we are interested in. Once we know for each right-hand side which terminal symbols can start a string derived from this right-hand side, we can construct a parse table, just as we did in the previous section. So, we have to compute this set of terminal symbols for each right-hand side.

8.2.1.1 *FIRST$_1$ sets*

These sets of terminal symbols are called the *FIRST*$_1$ sets: if we have a non-empty sentential form x, then $FIRST_1(x)$ is the set of terminal symbols that can start a sentential form derived from x in zero or more production steps. The subscript $_1$ indicates that the set contains single terminal symbols only. Later, we will see $FIRST_k$ sets, consisting of strings of terminal symbols of length at most k. For now, we will drop the subscript $_1$: we will use *FIRST* instead of $FIRST_1$. If x starts with a terminal symbol, then $FIRST(x)$ is a set that has this symbol as its only member. If x starts with a non-terminal A, then $FIRST(x)$ is equal to $FIRST(A)$, because A cannot produce ε. So, if we can compute the FIRST set for any non-terminal A, we can compute it for any sentential form x. However, $FIRST(A)$ depends on the right-hand sides of the A-rules: it is the union of the FIRST sets of these right-hand sides. These FIRST sets may again depend on the FIRST set of some non-terminal. This could even be A itself, if the rule is directly or indirectly left-recursive. This observation suggests the iterative process described below to compute the FIRST sets of all non-terminals:

☐   We first initialize the FIRST sets to the empty set.
☐   Then we process each grammar rule in the following way: if the right-hand side starts with a terminal symbol, we add this symbol to the FIRST set of the left-hand side, since it can be the first symbol of a sentential form derived from the left-hand side. If the right-hand side starts with a non-terminal symbol, we add all symbols of the present FIRST set of this non-terminal to the FIRST set of the left-hand side. These are all symbols that can be the first terminal symbol of a sentential form derived from the left-hand side.
☐   The previous step is repeated until no more new symbols are added to any of the FIRST sets.

Eventually, no more new symbols can be added, because the maximum number of elements in a FIRST set is the number of symbols, and the number of FIRST sets is equal to the number of non-terminals. Therefore, the total number of times that a new symbol can be added to any FIRST set is limited by the product of the number of symbols and the number of non-terminals.

8.2.1.2 Producing the parse table

With the help of these FIRST sets, we can now construct a parse table for the grammar. We process each grammar rule $A \rightarrow \alpha$ in the following way: if α starts with a terminal symbol a, we add α to the (A,a) entry of the parse table; if α starts with a non-terminal, we add α to the (A,a) entry of the parse table for all symbols a in FIRST(A).

Now let us compute the parse table for the example grammar of Figure 8.7. This grammar describes a simple language that could be used as the input language for a rudimentary consulting system: the user enters some facts, and then asks a question. There is also a facility for sub-sessions. The contents of the facts and questions are of no concern here. They are represented by the word STRING, which is regarded as a terminal symbol.

```
Session   ->   Fact Session
Session   ->   Question
Session   ->   ( Session ) Session
   Fact   ->   ! STRING
Question   ->   ? STRING
```

Figure 8.7 An example grammar

We first compute the FIRST sets. Initially, the FIRST sets are all empty Then, we process all grammar rules in the order of Figure 8.7. The rule Session -> Fact Session results in adding the symbols from FIRST(Fact) to FIRST(Session), but FIRST(Fact) is still empty. The rule Session -> Question results in adding the symbols from FIRST(Question) to FIRST(Session), but FIRST(Question) is still empty too. The rule Session -> (Session) Session results in adding (to FIRST(Session). The rule Fact -> ! STRING results in adding ! to FIRST(Fact), and the rule Question -> ? STRING results in adding ? to FIRST(Question). So, after processing all right-hand sides once, we have the following:

FIRST(Session)	FIRST(Fact)	FIRST(Question)
(	!	?

Next, we process all grammar rules again. This time, the rule Session -> Fact Session will result in adding ! (from FIRST(Fact)) to FIRST(Session), the rule Session -> Question will result in adding ? to FIRST(Session), and no other changes will take place. So now we get:

FIRST(Session)	FIRST(Fact)	FIRST(Question)
(! ?	!	?

There were some changes, so we have to repeat this process again. This time, there are no changes, so the table above presents the FIRST sets of the non-terminals. Now we have all the information we need to create the parse table. We have to add Fact

Session to the (Session,*a*) entry for all terminal symbols *a* in FIRST(Fact Session). The only terminal symbol in FIRST(Fact Session) is !, so we add Fact Session to the (Session,!) entry. Likewise, we add Question to the (Session,?) entry. Next we add (Session) Session to the (Session, () entry, ! STRING to the (Fact,!) entry, and ? STRING to the (Question,?) entry. This results in the parse table of Figure 8.8.

	!	?	(	)	STRING	#
Session	Fact Session	Question	(Session) Session			
Question		? STRING				
Fact	! STRING					

Figure 8.8 The parse table for the grammar of Figure 8.7

All parse table entries have at most one element, so the parser will be deterministic. A grammar without ε-rules is called *LL(1)* if all entries of the parse table, as constructed above, have at most one element, or, in other words, if for every non-terminal *A* the FIRST sets of *A* are pairwise disjoint (no symbol occurs in more than one). We have lost the S (simplicity) of SLL(1), but the parser is still as simple as before. Producing the parse table has become more difficult, but we have gained a lot: many practical grammars are LL(1), or are easily transformed into an LL(1) grammar.

8.2.2 LL(1) grammars with ε-rules
Not allowing for ε-rules is, however, still a major drawback. Certain language constructs are difficult, if not impossible, to describe with an LL(1) grammar without ε-rules. For instance, non-terminals that describe lists of terminals or non-terminals are difficult to express without ε-rules. Of course, we could write

$$A \rightarrow aA \mid a$$

for a list of *a*'s, but this is not LL(1). Compare also the grammar of Figure 8.7 with the one of Figure 8.9. They describe the same language, but the one of Figure 8.9 is much clearer.

```
Session    ->    Facts Question | ( Session ) Session
  Facts    ->    Fact Facts | ε
   Fact    ->    ! STRING
Question    ->    ? STRING
```

Figure 8.9 The grammar of Figure 8.7 rewritten

8.2.2.1 Extending the FIRST sets
The main problem with allowing ε-rules is that the FIRST sets, as we have discussed them in the previous section, are not sufficient any more. For instance, the Facts non-terminal in the grammar of Figure 8.9 has an ε-rule. The FIRST set for this right-hand side is empty, so it does not tell us on which look-ahead symbols we should choose this right-hand side. Also, in the presence of ε-rules, the computation of the FIRST sets itself needs some revision. For instance, if we compute the FIRST set of

the first right-hand side of Session using the method of the previous section, ? will not be a member, but it should, because Facts can derive ε (it is transparent), and then ? starts a sentential form that can be derived from Session.

Let us first extend the FIRST definition to also deal with ε-rules. This time, in addition to terminal symbols, ε will also be allowed as a member of a FIRST set. We will now also have to deal with empty sentential forms, so we will sometimes need the FIRST(ε) set. We will define it as the set containing only the empty string ε. We will also add ε to the FIRST set of a sentential form if this sentential form derives ε.

These may seem minor changes, but the presence of ε-rules affects the computation of the FIRST sets. FIRST($u_1 u_2 \cdots u_n$) is now equal to FIRST(u_1), ε excluded, but extended with FIRST($u_2 \cdots u_n$) if u_1 derives ε. In particular, FIRST(uε) (= FIRST(u)) is equal to FIRST(u), ε excluded, but extended with FIRST(ε) (= {ε}) if u derives ε.

Apart from this, the computation of the revised FIRST sets proceeds in exactly the same way as before. When we need to know whether a non-terminal A derives ε, we have two options: we could compute this information separately, using the method described in Section 4.2.1, or we could check if ε is a member of the FIRST(A) set as it is computed so far. This last option uses the fact that if a non-terminal derives ε, ε will ultimately be a member of its FIRST set.

Now let us compute the FIRST sets for the grammar of Figure 8.9. They are first initialized to the empty set. Then, we process each grammar rule: the rule Session -> Facts Question results in adding the terminal symbols from FIRST(Facts) to FIRST(Session). However, FIRST(Facts) is still empty. The rule Session -> (Session) Session results in adding (to FIRST(Session). Then, the rule Facts -> Fact Facts results in adding the symbols from FIRST(Fact) to FIRST(Facts), and the rule Facts -> ε results in adding ε to FIRST(Facts). Then, the rule Fact -> ! STRING results in adding ! to FIRST(Fact), and the rule Question -> ? STRING results in adding ? to FIRST(Question). This completes the first pass over the grammar rules, resulting in:

FIRST(Session)	FIRST(Facts)	FIRST(Fact)	FIRST(Question)
(	ε	!	?

The second pass is more interesting: this time, we know that Facts derives ε, and therefore, the rule Session -> Facts Question results in adding the symbols from FIRST(Question) to FIRST(Session). The rule Facts -> Fact Facts results in adding ! to FIRST(Facts). So we get:

FIRST(Session)	FIRST(Facts)	FIRST(Fact)	FIRST(Question)
(?	ε !	!	?

In the third pass, the only change is the addition of ! to FIRST(Session), because it is now a member of FIRST(Facts). So we have:

FIRST(Session)	FIRST(Facts)	FIRST(Fact)	FIRST(Question)
(? !	ε !	!	?

The fourth pass does not result in any new additions.

The question remains how to decide when an ε right-hand side or, for that matter, a right-hand side that derives ε is to be predicted. Suppose that we have a grammar rule

$$A \to \alpha_1 \mid \alpha_2 \mid \cdots \mid \alpha_n$$

and also suppose that α_m is or derives ε. Now suppose we find A at the front of a prediction, as in

$$
\begin{array}{c|l}
\cdots & a \cdots \# \\
\hline
\cdots & Ax\#
\end{array}
$$

where we again have added the # end-marker. A breadth-first parser would have to investigate the following predictions:

$$
\begin{array}{c|l}
\cdots & a \cdots \# \\
\hline
\cdots & \alpha_1 x\# \\
\cdots & \quad . \\
\cdots & \quad . \\
\cdots & \alpha_n x\#
\end{array}
$$

None of these predictions derive ε, because of the end-marker (#). We know how to compute the FIRST sets of these predictions. If the next input symbol is not a member of any of these FIRST sets, either the prediction we started with ($Ax\#$) is wrong, or there is an error in the input sentence. Otherwise, the next input symbol is a member of one or more of these FIRST sets, and we can strike out the predictions that do not have the symbol in their FIRST set. If none of these FIRST sets have a symbol in common with any of the other FIRST sets, the next input symbol can only be a member of at most one of these FIRST sets, so at most one prediction remains, and the parser is deterministic at this point.

A context-free grammar is called LL(1) if this is always the case. In other words, a grammar is LL(1) if for any prediction $Ax\#$, with A a non-terminal with right-hand sides α_1, ..., and α_n, the sets $\text{FIRST}(\alpha_1 x\#)$, ..., and $\text{FIRST}(\alpha_n x\#)$ are pairwise disjoint (no symbol is a member of more than one set). This definition does not conflict with the one that we gave in the previous section for grammars without ε-rules, because in this case $\text{FIRST}(\alpha_i x\#)$ is equal to $\text{FIRST}(\alpha_i)$, so in this case the sets $\text{FIRST}(\alpha_1)$, ..., and $\text{FIRST}(\alpha_n)$ are pairwise disjoint.

8.2.2.2 The need for FOLLOW sets

So, what do we have now? We can construct a deterministic parser for any LL(1) grammar. This parser operates by starting with the prediction $S\#$, and its prediction steps consist of replacing the non-terminal at hand with each of its right-hand sides, computing the FIRST sets of the resulting predictions, and checking whether the next input symbol is a member of any of these sets. We then continue with the predictions for which this is the case. If there is more than one, the parser announces that the grammar is not LL(1) and stops. Although this is a deterministic parser, it is not very efficient, because it has to compute several FIRST sets at each prediction step. We cannot compute all these FIRST sets before starting the parser, because such a FIRST set depends on the whole prediction (of which there are infinitely many), not just on the non-terminal. So, we still do not know if, and if so, how we can construct a parse table for an LL(1) grammar with ε-rules, nor do we have a method to determine if a grammar is LL(1).

Now suppose we have a prediction $Ax\#$ and a rule $A \rightarrow \alpha$, and α is or derives ε. The input symbols that lead to the selection of $A \rightarrow \alpha$ are the symbols in the set $FIRST(\alpha x\#)$, and this set of symbols is formed by the symbols in $FIRST(\alpha)$, extended with the symbols in $FIRST(x\#)$ (because of the transparency of α). The selection of $A \rightarrow \alpha$ on an input symbol that is not a member of $FIRST(\alpha)$ is called an ε-*move*. The set $FIRST(x\#)$ is the problem: we cannot compute it at parser generation time. What we *can* calculate, though, is the union of all $FIRST(x\#)$ sets such that $x\#$ can follow A in any prediction. This is just the set of all terminal symbols that can follow A in any sentential form derivable from $S\#$ (not just the present prediction) and is called, quite reasonably, the *FOLLOW* set of A, $FOLLOW(A)$.

Now it would seem that such a gross approximation would seriously weaken the parser or even make it incorrect. This is not so. Suppose that this set contains a symbol a that is not a member of $FIRST(x\#)$, and a is the next input symbol. If a is not a member of $FIRST(A)$, we will predict $A \rightarrow \alpha$, and we will ultimately end up with a failing match, because $\alpha x\#$ does not derive a string starting with an a. So, the input string will (correctly) be rejected, although the error will be detected a bit later than before, because the parser will make some ε-moves before finding out that something is wrong. If a is a member of $FIRST(A)$ then we may have a problem if a is a member of one of the FIRST sets of the other right-hand sides of A. We will worry about this a bit later.

The good thing about the FOLLOW set is that we can compute it at parser generation time. Each non-terminal has a FOLLOW set, and they can be computed as follows:
□   as with the computation of the FIRST sets, we start with the FOLLOW sets all empty.
□   Next we process all right-hand sides, including the $S\#$ one. Whenever a right-hand side contains a non-terminal, as in $A \rightarrow \cdots By$, we add all symbols from $FIRST(y)$ to $FOLLOW(B)$; these symbols can follow a B. In addition, if y derives ε, we add all symbols from $FOLLOW(A)$ to $FOLLOW(B)$.
□   The previous step is repeated until no more new symbols can be added to any of the FOLLOW sets.

Now let us go back to our example and compute the FOLLOW sets. Starting with Session #, # is added to FOLLOW(Session). Next, the symbols of FIRST(Question) are added to FOLLOW(Facts), because of the rule Session -> Facts Question. This rule also results in adding all symbols of FOLLOW(Session) to FOLLOW(Question). The rule Session -> (Session) Session results in adding the) symbol to FOLLOW(Session) and the addition of all symbols of FOLLOW(Session) to FOLLOW(Session), which does not add much. The next rule is the rule Facts -> Fact Facts. All symbols from FIRST(Facts) are added to FOLLOW(Fact), and all symbols from FOLLOW(Facts) are added to FOLLOW(Facts). The other rules do not result in any additions. So, after the first pass we have:

FOLLOW(Session)	FOLLOW(Facts)	FOLLOW(Fact)	FOLLOW(Question)
) #	?	!	#

In the second pass,) is added to FOLLOW(Question), because it is now a member of FOLLOW(Session), and all members of FOLLOW(Session) become a member of FOLLOW(Question) because of the rule Session -> Facts Question. No other changes take place. The resulting FOLLOW sets are presented below:

FOLLOW(Session)	FOLLOW(Facts)	FOLLOW(Fact)	FOLLOW(Question)
) #	?	!	#)

8.2.2.3 Using the FOLLOW sets to produce a parse table

Once we know the FOLLOW set for each non-terminal that derives ε, we can once again construct a parse table: first, we compute the FIRST set of each non-terminal. This also tells us which non-terminals derive ε. Next, we compute the FOLLOW set of each non-terminal. Then, starting with an empty parse table, we process each grammar rule $A \rightarrow \alpha$ as follows: we add α to the (A,a) entry of the parse table for all terminal symbols a in FIRST(α), as we did before. This time however, we also add α to the (A,a) entry of the parse table for all terminal symbols a in FOLLOW(A) when α is or derives ε (when FIRST(α) contains ε). A shorter way of saying this is that we add α to the (A,a) entry of the parse table for all terminal symbols a in FIRST(α FOLLOW(A)). This last set consists of the union of the FIRST sets of the sentential forms αb for all symbols b in FOLLOW(A).

Now let us produce a parse table for our example. The Session -> Facts Question rule does not derive ε, because Question does not. Therefore, only the terminal symbols in FIRST(Facts Question) lead to addition of this rule to the table. These symbols are ! and ? (because Facts also derives ε). Similarly, all other rules are added, resulting in the parse table presented in Figure 8.10.

	(	)	#	!	?	STRING
Session	(Session) Session			Facts Question	Facts Question	
Facts				Fact Facts	ε	
Fact				! STRING		
Question					? STRING	

Figure 8.10 The parse table for the grammar of Figure 8.9

8.2.3 LL(1) versus strong-LL(1)

If all entries of the resulting parse table have at most one element, the parser is again deterministic. In this case, the grammar is called *strong-LL(1)* and the parser is called a strong-LL(1) parser. In the literature, strong-LL(1) is referred to as "strong LL(1)" (note that there is a space between the words "strong" and "LL"). However, we find this term a bit misleading because it suggests that the class of strong-LL(1) grammars is more powerful than the class of LL(1) grammars, but this is not the case. Every strong-LL(1) grammar is LL(1).

It is perhaps more surprising that every LL(1) grammar is strong-LL(1). In other words, every grammar that is not strong-LL(1) is not LL(1), and this is demonstrated with the following argument: if a grammar is not strong-LL(1), there is a parse table entry, say (A,a), with at least two elements, say α and β. This means that a is a member of both FIRST(α FOLLOW(A)) and FIRST(β FOLLOW(A)). Now, there are three possibilities:

☐ a is a member of both FIRST(α) and FIRST(β). In this case, the grammar cannot be LL(1), because for any prediction $Ax\#$, a is a member of both FIRST($\alpha x\#$) and FIRST($\beta x\#$).

☐ a is a member of either FIRST(α) or FIRST(β), but not both. Let us say that a is a member of FIRST(α). In this case, a still is a member of FIRST(β FOLLOW(A)) so there is a prediction $Ax\#$, such that a is a member of FIRST($\beta x\#$). However, a is also a member of FIRST($\alpha x\#$), so the grammar is not LL(1). In other words, in this case there is a prediction in which an LL(1) parser cannot decide which right-hand side to choose either.

☐ a is neither a member of FIRST(α), nor a member of FIRST(β). In this case α and β must derive ε and a must be a member of FOLLOW(A). This means that there is a prediction $Ax\#$ such that a is a member of FIRST($x\#$) and thus a is a member of both FIRST($\alpha x\#$) and FIRST($\beta x\#$), so the grammar is not LL(1). This means that in an LL(1) grammar at most one right-hand side of any non-terminal derives ε.

8.2.4 Full LL(1) parsing

We already mentioned briefly that the difference between LL(1) parsing and strong-LL(1) parsing is that the strong-LL(1) parser sometimes makes ε-moves before detecting an error. Consider for instance the following grammar:

$$S \quad \to \quad a\ A\ b\ |\ b\ A\ a$$
$$A \quad \to \quad c\ S\ |\ \varepsilon$$

The parse table of this grammar is:

	a	b	c	#
S	a A b	b A a		
A	ε	ε	c S	

Now, on input sentence aacabb, the strong-LL(1) parser makes the following moves:

	aacabb#
	S#

$\to$

	aacabb#
S_1	aAb#

$\to$

a	acabb#
S_1a	Ab#

$\to$

a	acabb#
S_1aA$_2$	b#

The problem here is that the prediction is destroyed by the time the error is detected. In contrast, an LL(1) parser would not do the last step, because neither FIRST(b#), nor FIRST(cSb#) contain a, so the LL(1) parser would detect the error before choosing a right-hand side for A. A full LL(1) parser has the *immediate error detection property*, which means that an error is detected as soon as the erroneous symbol is first examined, whereas a strong-LL(1) parser only has the *correct-prefix property*, which means that the parser detects an error as soon as an attempt is made to match (or shift) the erroneous symbol. In Chapter 10, we will see that the immediate error detection property will help improve error recovery.

Given a prediction $A \cdots \#$, a full LL(1) parser bases its parsing decisions on FIRST($A \cdots \#$) rather than on the approximation FIRST(A FOLLOW(A)); this avoids any parsing decisions on erroneous input symbols (which can never occur in FIRST($A \cdots \#$) but may occur in FIRST(A FOLLOW(A))). So, if we have prediction $A \cdots \#$ and input symbol a, we first have to determine if a is a member of FIRST($A \cdots \#$), before consulting the parse table to choose a right-hand side for A. The penalty for this is in efficiency: every time that parse table has to be consulted, a FIRST set has to be computed and a check made that the input symbol is a member.

Fortunately, we can do better than this. A first step to improvement is the following: suppose that we maintain between all symbols in the prediction a set of terminal symbols that are correct at this point, like this:

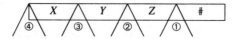

Here, ① is the set of symbols that are legal at this point; this is just the FIRST set of the remaining part of the prediction: FIRST($\#$); likewise, ② is FIRST($Z\#$), ③ is FIRST($YZ\#$), and ④ is FIRST($XYZ\#$) (none of these sets contain ε). These sets can easily be computed, from right to left. For instance, ③ consists of the symbols in FIRST(Y), with the symbols from ② added if Y derives ε (if ε is a member of FIRST(Y)). When a non-terminal is replaced by one of its right-hand sides, the set behind this right-hand side is available, and we can use this to compute the sets within this right-hand side and in front of it.

Now let us see how this works for our example. As the reader can easily verify,

FIRST(S) = { a, b}, and
FIRST(A) = { c, ε}.

The parser starts with the prediction S$\#$. We have to find a starting point for the sets: it makes sense to start with an empty one to the right of the $\#$, because no symbols are correct after the $\#$. So, the parser starts in the following state:

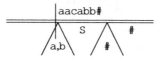

The first input symbol is a member of the current FIRST set, so it is correct. The (S, a) entry of the parse table contains aAb so we get parser state

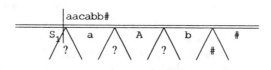

Computing the sets marked with a question mark from right to left results in the

following parser state:

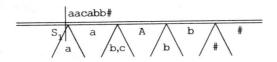

Note that b now is a member of the set in front of A, but a is not, although it is a member of FOLLOW(A). After the match step, the parser is in the following state:

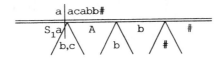

The next input symbol is not a member of the current FIRST set, so an error is detected, and no right-hand side of A is chosen. Instead, the prediction is left intact, so error recovery can profit from it.

It is not clear that all this is more efficient than computing the FIRST set of a prediction to determine the correctness of an input symbol before choosing a right-hand side. However, it does suggest that we can do this at parser generation time, by combining non-terminals with the FIRST sets that can follow it in a prediction. For our example, we always start with non-terminal S and the set {#}. We will indicate this with the pair [S,{#}]. Starting with this pair, we will try to make rules for the behaviour of each pair that turns up, for each valid look-ahead. We know from the FIRST sets of the alternatives for S that on look-ahead symbol a, [S,{#}] results in right-hand side aAb. Now the only symbol that can follow A here is a b. So in fact, we have:

      on look-ahead symbol a, [S,{#}] results in right-hand side a [A,{b}] b.

Similarly we find:

      on look-ahead symbol b, [S,{#}] results in right-hand side b [A,{a}] a.

We have now obtained pairs for A followed by a b, and A followed by an a. So we have to make rules for them: We know that on look-ahead symbol c, [A,{b}] results in right-hand side cS. Because A can only be followed by a b in this context, the same holds for this S. This gives:

      on look-ahead symbol c, [A,{b}] results in right-hand side c [S,{b}].

Likewise, we get the following rules:

      on look-ahead symbol b, [A,{b}] results in right-hand side ε;
      on look-ahead symbol c, [A,{a}] results in right-hand side c [S,{a}];
      on look-ahead symbol a, [A,{a}] results in right-hand side ε.

Now we have to make rules for the pairs S followed by an a, and S followed by a b:

on look-ahead symbol a, [S,{a}] results in right-hand side a [A,{b}] b;
on look-ahead symbol b, [S,{a}] results in right-hand side b [A,{a}] a;
on look-ahead symbol a, [S,{b}] results in right-hand side a [A,{b}] b;
on look-ahead symbol b, [S,{b}] results in right-hand side b [A,{a}] a.

In fact, we find that we have rewritten the grammar, using the [non-terminal, followed-by set] pairs as non-terminals, into the following form:

$$
\begin{aligned}
[S,\{\#\}] &\rightarrow & a\ [A,\{b\}]\ b\ |\ b\ [A,\{a\}]\ a \\
[S,\{a\}] &\rightarrow & a\ [A,\{b\}]\ b\ |\ b\ [A,\{a\}]\ a \\
[S,\{b\}] &\rightarrow & a\ [A,\{b\}]\ b\ |\ b\ [A,\{a\}]\ a \\
[A,\{a\}] &\rightarrow & c\ [S,\{a\}]\ |\ \varepsilon \\
[A,\{b\}] &\rightarrow & c\ [S,\{b\}]\ |\ \varepsilon
\end{aligned}
$$

For this grammar, the following parse table can be produced:

	a	b	c	#
[S,{#}]	a [A,{b}] b	b [A,{a}] a		
[S,{a}]	a [A,{b}] b	b [A,{a}] a		
[S,{b}]	a [A,{b}] b	b [A,{a}] a		
[A,{a}]	ε		c [S,{a}]	
[A,{b}]		ε	c [S,{b}]	

The entries for the different [S,...] rules are identical so we can merge them. After that, the only change with respect to the original parse table is the duplication of the A-rule: now there is one copy for each context in which A has a different set behind it in a prediction.

Now, after accepting the first a of aacabb, the prediction is now [A,{b}]b#; since the parse table entry ([A,{b}], a) is empty, parsing will stop here and now.

The resulting parser is exactly the same as the strong-LL(1) one. Only the parse table is different. Often, the LL(1) table is much larger than the strong-LL(1) one. As the benefit of having an LL(1) parser only lies in that it detects some errors a bit earlier, this usually is not considered worth the extra cost, and thus most parsers that are advertised as LL(1) parsers are actually strong-LL(1) parsers.

8.2.5 Solving LL(1) conflicts
If a parse table entry has more than one element, we have what we call an *LL(1) conflict*. In this section, we will discuss how to deal with them. One way to deal with conflicts is one that we have seen before: use a depth-first or a breadth-first parser with a one symbol look-ahead. This, however, has several disadvantages: the resulting parser is not deterministic any more, it is less efficient (often to such an extent that it becomes unacceptable), and it still does not work for left-recursive grammars. Therefore, we have to try and eliminate these conflicts, so we can use an ordinary LL(1) parser.

8.2.5.1 *Eliminating left-recursion*
The first step to take is the elimination of left-recursion. Left-recursive grammars always lead to LL(1) conflicts, because the right-hand side causing the left-recursion has a FIRST set that contains all symbols from the FIRST set of the non-terminal.

Therefore, it also contains all terminal symbols of the FIRST sets of the other right-hand sides of the non-terminal. Eliminating left-recursion has already been discussed in Section 6.4.

8.2.5.2 *Left-factoring*
Another technique for removing LL(1) conflicts is *left-factoring*. Left-factoring of grammar rules is like factoring arithmetic expressions:

$$a * b + a * c = a * (b + c).$$

The grammatical equivalent to this is a rule

$$A \rightarrow xy \mid xz,$$

which clearly has an LL(1) conflict on the terminal symbols in FIRST(x). We replace this grammar rule with the two rules

$$A \rightarrow xN$$
$$N \rightarrow y \mid z$$

where N is a new non-terminal. There have been some attempts to automate this process; see Foster [Transform 1968] and Rosenkrantz and Hunt [Transform 1987].

8.2.5.3 *Conflict resolvers*
Sometimes, these techniques do not help much. We could for instance deal with a language for which no LL(1) grammar exists. In fact, many languages can be described by a context-free grammar, but not by an LL(1) grammar. Another method of handling conflicts is to resolve them by so-called *disambiguating* rules. An example of such a disambiguating rule is: "on a conflict, the textually first one of the conflicting right-hand sides is chosen". With this disambiguating rule, the order of the right-hand sides within a grammar rule becomes crucial, and unexpected results may occur if the grammar-processing program does not clearly indicate where conflicts occur and how they are resolved.

A better method is to have the grammar writer specify explicitly how each conflict must be resolved, using so-called *conflict resolvers*. One option is to resolve conflicts at parser generation time. Parser generators that allow for this kind of conflict resolver usually have a mechanism that enables the user to indicate (at parser generation time) which right-hand side must be chosen on a conflict. Another, much more flexible method is to have conflicts resolved at parse time. When the parser meets a conflict, it calls a user-specified conflict resolver. Such a user-specified conflict resolver has the complete left-context at its disposal, so it could base its choice on this left-context. It is also possible to have the parser look further ahead in the input, and then resolve the conflict based on the symbols found. See Milton, Kirchhoff and Rowland [LL 1979] and Grune and Jacobs [LL 1988], for similar approaches using attribute grammars.

8.2.6 LL(1) and recursive descent

Most hand-written parsers are LL(1) parsers. They usually are written in the form of a non-backtracking recursive-descent parser (see Section 6.6). In fact, this is a very simple way to implement an LL(1) parser. For a non-terminal A with grammar rule

$$A \rightarrow \alpha_1 \mid \cdots \mid \alpha_n$$

the parsing routine has the following structure:

```
procedure A;
    if lookahead ∈ FIRST(α₁ FOLLOW(A)) then
        code for α₁ ...
    else if lookahead ∈ FIRST(α₂ FOLLOW(A)) then
        code for α₂ ...
        .
        .
        .
    else if lookahead ∈ FIRST(αₙ FOLLOW(A)) then
        code for αₙ ...
    else ERROR;
end A;
```

The look-ahead symbol always resides in a variable called "lookahead". The procedure ERROR announces an error and stops the parser.

The code for a right-hand side consists of the code for the symbols of the right-hand side. A non-terminal symbol results in a call to the parsing routine for this non-terminal, and a terminal symbol results in a call to a MATCH routine with this symbol as parameter. This MATCH routine has the following structure:

```
procedure MATCH(sym);
    if lookahead = sym then
        lookahead := NEXTSYM
    else ERROR;
end MATCH;
```

The NEXTSYM procedure reads the next symbol from the input.

Several LL(1) parser generators produce a recursive descent parser instead of a parse table that is to be interpreted by a grammar-independent parser. The advantages of generating a recursive descent parser are numerous:

☐   Semantic actions are easily embedded in the parsing routines.
☐   A parameter mechanism or attribute mechanism comes virtually for free: the parser generator can use the parameter mechanism of the implementation language.
☐   non-backtracking recursive descent parsers are quite efficient, often more efficient than the table-driven ones.
☐   Dynamic conflict resolvers are implemented easily.

The most important disadvantage of generating a recursive descent parser is the size of the parser. A recursive descent parser is usually larger than a table-driven one (including the table). However, this becomes less of a problem as computer memories get bigger and bigger. See Waite and Carter [Misc 1985] for measurements of table-driven parsers versus recursive descent parsers.

8.3 LL(k) GRAMMARS

Up until now, we have limited the look-ahead to just one symbol, and one might wonder if having a look-ahead of k symbols instead of one makes the method more powerful. It does, so let us define LL(k) grammars. For this, we need a definition of $FIRST_k$ sets: if x is a sentential form, then $FIRST_k(x)$ is the set of terminal strings w such that $|w|$ (the length of w) is less than k and $x \overset{*}{\rightarrow} w$, or $|w|$ is equal to k, and $x \overset{*}{\rightarrow} wy$, for some sentential form y. For $k = 1$ this definition coincides with the definition of the FIRST sets as we have seen it before.

We now have the instruments needed to define LL(k): a grammar is *LL(k)* if for any prediction $Ax\#$, with A a non-terminal with right-hand sides α_1, ..., and α_n, the sets $FIRST_k(\alpha_1 x\#)$, are pairwise disjoint. Obviously, for any k, the set of LL(k) grammars is a subset of the set of LL($k+1$) grammars, and in fact, for any k there are LL($k+1$) grammars that are not LL(k). A trivial example of this is given in Figure 8.11.

$$S_s \;\; \rightarrow \;\; a^k b \;\; | \;\; a^k a$$

Figure 8.11 An LL(k+1) grammar that is not LL(k)

Less obvious is that for any k there are languages that are LL($k+1$), but not LL(k). An example of such a language is given in Figure 8.12.

$$
\begin{aligned}
S_S &\rightarrow aSA \;\; | \;\; \varepsilon \\
A &\rightarrow a^k bS \;\; | \;\; c
\end{aligned}
$$

Figure 8.12 A grammar defining an LL(k+1) language that is not LL(k)

See Kurki-Suonio [LL 1969] for more details.

With LL(k) grammars we have the same problem as with the LL(1) grammars: producing a parse table is difficult. In the LL(1) case, we solved this problem with the aid of the FOLLOW sets, obtaining strong-LL(1) parsers. We can try the same with LL(k) grammars using $FOLLOW_k$ sets. For any non-terminal A, $FOLLOW_k(A)$ is now defined as the union of the sets $FIRST_k(x\#\# \cdots \#\#)$, for any prediction $Ax\#\# \cdots \#\#$ (in LL(k) parsing, we add k end-markers instead of just one).

Once we have the $FIRST_k$ sets and the $FOLLOW_k$ sets, we can produce a parse table for the grammar. Like the LL(1) parse table, this parse table will be indexed with pairs consisting of a non-terminal and a terminal string of length equal to k. Every grammar rule $A \rightarrow \alpha$ is processed as follows: α is added to the (A, w) entry of the table for every w in $FIRST_k(\alpha \; FOLLOW_k(A))$ (as we have seen before, this last set denotes the union of several $FIRST_k$ sets: it is the union of all $FIRST_k(\alpha v)$ sets with v an element of $FOLLOW_k(A)$). All this is just an extension to k look-ahead symbols of what we did earlier with one look-ahead symbol.

If this results in a parse table where all entries have at most one element, the grammar is *strong-LL(k)*. Unlike the LL(1) case however, for $k > 1$ there are grammars that are LL(k), but not strong-LL(k). An example of such a grammar is given in Figure

8.13.

$$S \quad \rightarrow \quad aAaa \mid bAba$$
$$A \quad \rightarrow \quad b \mid \epsilon$$

Figure 8.13 An LL(2) grammar that is not strong-LL(2)

This raises an interesting question, one that has kept the authors busy for quite a while: how come? Why is it different for $k = 1$? If we try to repeat our proof from Section 8.2.3 for a look-ahead $k > 1$, we see that we fail at the very last step: let us examine a strong-LL(k) conflict: suppose that the right-hand sides α and β both end up in the (A, w) entry of the parse table. This means that a is a member of both $\text{FIRST}_k(\alpha$ $\text{FOLLOW}_k(A))$ and $\text{FIRST}_k(\beta$ $\text{FOLLOW}_k(A))$. Now, there are three cases:

☐ w is a member both $\text{FIRST}_k(\alpha)$ and $\text{FIRST}_k(\beta)$. In this case, the grammar cannot be LL(k), because for any prediction $Ax\#\#\cdots\#\#$, w is a member of both $\text{FIRST}_k(\alpha x\#\#\cdots\#\#)$ and $\text{FIRST}_k(\beta x\#\#\cdots\#\#)$.

☐ w is a member of either $\text{FIRST}_k(\alpha)$ or $\text{FIRST}_k(\beta)$, but not both. Let us say that w is a member of $\text{FIRST}_k(\alpha)$. In this case, w still is a member of $\text{FIRST}_k(\beta$ $\text{FOLLOW}_k(A))$ so there is a prediction $Ax\#\#\cdots\#\#$, such that w is a member of $\text{FIRST}_k(\beta x\#\#\cdots\#\#)$. However, w is also a member of $\text{FIRST}_k(\alpha x\#\#\cdots\#\#)$, so the grammar is not LL(k). In other words, in this case there is a prediction in which an LL(k) parser cannot decide which right-hand side to choose either.

☐ w is neither a member of $\text{FIRST}_k(\alpha)$ nor a member of $\text{FIRST}_k(\beta)$. Here, we have to deviate from the reasoning we used in the LL(1) case. As w is an element of $\text{FIRST}_k(\alpha$ $\text{FOLLOW}_k(A))$, w can now be split into two parts $w_{1.1}$ and $w_{1.2}$, such that $w_{1.1}$ is an element of $\text{FIRST}_k(\alpha)$ and $w_{1.2}$ is a non-empty start of an element of $\text{FOLLOW}_k(A)$. Likewise, w can be split into two parts $w_{2.1}$ and $w_{2.2}$ such that $w_{2.1}$ is an element of $\text{FIRST}_k(\beta)$ and $w_{2.2}$ is a non-empty start of an element of $\text{FOLLOW}_k(A)$. So, we have the following situation:

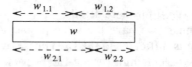

Now, if $w_{1.1}=w_{2.1}$, $w_{1.1}$ is a member of $\text{FIRST}_k(\alpha)$, as well as $\text{FIRST}_k(\beta)$, and there is a prediction $Ax\#\#\cdots\#\#$ such that $x\#\#\cdots\#\# \overset{*}{\rightarrow} w_{1.2}\cdots$. So, $\text{FIRST}_k(\alpha x\#\#\cdots\#\#)$ contains w and so does $\text{FIRST}_k(\beta x\#\#\cdots\#\#)$, and therefore, the grammar is not LL(k). So the only case left is that $w_{1.1}\neq w_{2.1}$. Neither $w_{1.2}$ nor $w_{2.2}$ are ϵ, and this is just impossible if $|w|=1$.

Strong-LL(k) parsers with $k > 1$ are seldom used in practice, because the parse tables are huge, and there are not many languages that are LL(k) for some $k > 1$, but not LL(1). Even the languages that are LL(k) for some $k > 1$, but not LL(1), are usually for the most part LL(1), and can be parsed using an LL(1) parser with conflict resolvers at the places where the grammar is not LL(1).

To obtain a full LL(k) parser, the method that we used to obtain a full LL(1) parser can be extended to deal with pairs $[A, L]$, where L is a FIRST_k set of $\cdots\#\#\cdots\#\#$ in some prediction $A\cdots\#\#\cdots\#\#$. This extension is straightforward and will not be discussed further.

8.4 EXTENDED LL(1) GRAMMARS

Several parser generators accept an extended context-free grammar instead of an ordinary one. See for instance Lewi et al.[LL 1978], Heckmann [LL 1986], Grune and Jacobs[LL 1988]. Extended context-free grammars have been discussed in Chapter 2. To check that an extended context-free grammar is LL(1), we have to transform the extended context-free grammar into an ordinary one, in a way that will avoid introducing LL(1) conflicts. For instance, the transformation for Something^+ given in Chapter 2:

$$\text{Something}^+ \rightarrow \text{Something} \mid \text{Something Something}^+$$

will not do, because it will result in an LL(1) conflict on the symbols in FIRST(Something). Instead, we will use the following transformations:

$$
\begin{aligned}
\text{Something}^* &\rightarrow \varepsilon \mid \text{Something Something}^* \\
\text{Something}^+ &\rightarrow \text{Something Something}^* \\
\text{Something}^? &\rightarrow \varepsilon \mid \text{Something}
\end{aligned}
$$

If the resulting grammar is LL(1), the original extended context-free grammar was ELL(1) (Extended LL(1)). This is the recursive interpretation of Chapter 2. Parser generation usually proceeds as follows: first transform the grammar to an ordinary context-free grammar, and then produce a parse table for it.

Extended LL(1) grammars allow for a more efficient implementation in recursive descent parsers. In this case, $\text{Something}^?$ can be implemented as an **if** statement:

```
if lookahead ∈ FIRST(Something) then
    code for Something ...
else if lookahead ∉ FOLLOW(Something?) then
    ERROR;
```

Something^* can be implemented as a **while** loop:

```
while lookahead ∈ FIRST(Something) do
    code for Something ...
if lookahead ∉ FOLLOW(Something*) then
    ERROR;
```

and Something^+ can be implemented as a **repeat** loop:

```
repeat
    if lookahead ∉ FIRST(Something) then
        ERROR;
    code for Something ...
until lookahead ∈ FOLLOW(Something+);
```

Here, procedure calls are replaced by much more efficient repetitive constructs.

9

Deterministic bottom-up parsing

There is a great variety of deterministic bottom-up parsing methods. The first deterministic parsers (Wolpe [Precedence 1958], Wegstein [Precedence 1959]) were bottom-up parsers and interest has only increased since. The annotated bibliography in this book contains about 140 entries on deterministic bottom-up parsing against some 30 on deterministic top-down parsing. These figures may not reflect the relative importance of the methods, they are certainly indicative of the fascination and complexity of the subject of this chapter.

There are two families of deterministic bottom-up parsers, those that are purely bottom-up and those that have an additional top-down component. The first family comprises the precedence and bounded-context techniques, which are treated in Sections 9.1 to 9.3; the second family, which is both more powerful and more complicated, contains the LR techniques and is treated in Sections 9.4 to 9.7. Tomita's parser in Section 9.8 is not purely deterministic but leans so heavily on the LR techniques that its treatment in this chapter is warranted. The chapter closes with a short section on non-canonical bottom-up parsing and one on the use of $LR(k)$ as an ambiguity test.

The proper setting for the subject at hand can best be obtained by summarizing a number of relevant facts from previous chapters.

☐   A right-most production expands the right-most non-terminal in a sentential form, by replacing it by one of its right-hand sides. A sentence is produced by repeated right-most production until no non-terminal remains. See Figure 9.1 (a), where the sentential forms are right-aligned to show how the production process creeps to the left, where it terminates. The grammar used is that of Figure 7.8.

☐   Each step of a bottom-up parser, working on a sentential form, identifies the latest right-most production in it and undoes it by reducing a segment of the input to the non-terminal it derived from. The identified segment is called the *handle*. Since the parser starts with the final sentential form of the production process (that is, the input) it finds its first reduction rather to the left end, which is convenient. A bottom-up parser identifies right-most productions in reverse order. See Figure 9.1(b) where the handles are aligned.

☐   To obtain an efficient parser we have to have an efficient method to identify handles, without elaborate searching. The identified handle has to be correct (or the input is in error); we do not want to consider alternative choices for handles.

Although this chapter is called "Deterministic Bottom-Up *Parsing*", it is almost

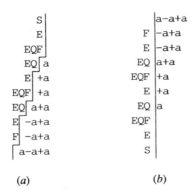

(a)   (b)

Figure 9.1 Right-most production (a) and right-most reduction (b)

exclusively concerned with methods for finding handles. Once the handle is found, parsing is (almost always) trivial. The exceptions will be treated separately.

Unlike top-down parsing, which identifies production right at their beginning, that is, before any of its constituents have been identified, bottom-up parsing identifies a production only at its very end, when all its constituents have already been identified. A top-down parser allows semantic actions to be performed at the beginning of a production and these actions can help in determining the semantics of the constituents. In a bottom-up parser, semantic actions are only performed during a reduction, which occurs at the end of a production, and the semantics of the constituents have to be determined without the benefit of knowing in which production they occur. We see that the increased power of bottom-up parsing comes at a price: since the decision what production applies is postponed to the latest possible moment, that decision can be based upon the fullest possible information, but it also means that the actions that depend on this decision come very late.

9.1 SIMPLE HANDLE-ISOLATING TECHNIQUES

There is a situation in (more or less) daily life in which the (more or less) average citizen is called upon to identify a handle. If one sees a formula like

$$4 + 5 \times 6 + 8$$

one immediately identifies the handle and evaluates it:

$$4 + \underline{5 \times 6} + 8$$

$$4 + \quad 30 \quad + 8$$

The next handle is

$$4 + \underline{\quad 30 \quad + 8}$$

$$34 \quad\quad + 8$$

and then

$$
\begin{array}{r}
34 \qquad + 8 \\
\hline
42
\end{array}
$$

If we look closely, we can discern in this process shifts and reduces. The person doing the arithmetic shifts symbols until he reaches the situation

4 + 5 × 6   + 8

in which the control mechanism in his head tells him that this is the right moment to do a reduce. If asked why, he might answer something like: "Ah, well, I was taught in school that multiplication comes before addition". Before we can formalize this notion and turn it into a parsing method, we consider an even simpler case below (Section 9.1.1).

$$
\begin{array}{rcl}
S_S & -> & \# \ E \ \# \\
E & -> & E + T \\
E & -> & T \\
T & -> & T \times F \\
T & -> & F \\
F & -> & n \\
F & -> & (\ E \ )
\end{array}
$$

Figure 9.2 A grammar for simple arithmetic expressions

Meanwhile we note that formulas like the one above are called "arithmetic expressions" and are produced by the grammar of Figure 9.2. S is the start symbol, E stands for "expression", T for "term", F for "factor" and n for any number. The last causes no problems, since the exact value of the number is immaterial to the parsing process. We have demarcated the beginning and the end of the expression with # marks; the blank space that normally surrounds a formula is not good enough for automatic processing. This also simplifies the stop criterion: the parser accepts the input as correct and stops when the terminating # is shifted, or upon the subsequent reduce.

9.1.1 Fully parenthesized expressions

$$
\begin{array}{rcl}
S_S & -> & \# \ E \ \# \\
E & -> & (\ E + T \ ) \\
E & -> & T \\
T & -> & (\ T \times F \ ) \\
T & -> & F \\
F & -> & n \\
F & -> & (\ E \ )
\end{array}
$$

Figure 9.3 A grammar for fully parenthesized arithmetic expressions

An arithmetic expression is *fully parenthesized* if each operator together with its operands has parentheses around it. Such expressions are generated by the grammar of Figure 9.3. Our example expression would have the form

$$\# \ (\ (\ 4 \ + \ (\ 5 \ \times \ 6 \ ) \ ) \ + \ 8 \ ) \ \#$$

Now finding the handle is trivial: go to the first closing parenthesis and then back to the nearest opening parenthesis. The segment between and including the parentheses is the handle. Reduce it and repeat the process as often as required. Note that after the reduction there is no need to start all over again, looking for the first closing parenthesis: there cannot be any closing parenthesis on the left of the reduction spot, so we can start searching right where we are. In the above example we find the next right parenthesis immediately and do the next reduction:

$$\# \ (\ (\ 4 \ + \ 30 \ ) \ + \ 8 \ ) \ \#$$

9.2 PRECEDENCE PARSING

Of course, grammars are not normally kind enough to have begin- and end-markers to each compound right-hand side, and the above parsing method has little practical value (as far as we know it does not even have name). Yet, suppose we had a method for inserting the proper parentheses into an expression that was lacking them. At a first glance this seems trivial to do: when we see +n× we know we can replace this by + (n× and we can replace ×n+ by ×n) +. There is a slight problem with +n+, but since the first + has to be performed first, we replace this by +n) +. The #'s are easy; we can replace #n by # (n and n# by n) #. For our example we get:

$$\# \ (\ 4 \ + \ (\ 5 \ \times \ 6 \ ) \ + \ 8 \ ) \ \#$$

This is, however, not completely correct – it should have been # ((4+ (5×6)) +8) # – and for 4+5×6 we get the obviously incorrect form # (4+ (5×6) #.

The problem is that we do not know how many parentheses to insert in, for instance, +n×; in 4+5×6×7 we should replace it by + ((n×: # (4+ ((5×6) ×7)) #. We solve this problem by inserting *parentheses generators* rather than parentheses. A generator for open parentheses is traditionally written as <, one for closing parentheses as >; we shall also use a "non-parenthesis", ≐. These symbols look confusingly like <, > and =, to which they are only remotely related. Now, our tentatively inserted parentheses become firmly inserted parentheses generators; see Figure 9.4 in which we have left out the n since its position can be inferred from the pattern. Still, the table in Figure 9.4 is incomplete: the pattern × × is missing and so are all patterns involving parentheses. In principle there should be a pattern for each combination of two operators (where we count the genuine parentheses as operators too), and only the generator to be inserted is relevant for each combination. This generator is called the *precedence relation* between the two operators. It is convenient to collect all combinations of operators in a table, the *precedence table*. The precedence table for the grammar of

$$
\begin{array}{rcl}
+ \times & \rightarrow & + \lessdot \times \\
\times + & \rightarrow & \times \gtrdot + \\
+ + & \rightarrow & + \gtrdot + \\
\# \ldots & \rightarrow & \# \lessdot \ldots \\
\ldots \# & \rightarrow & \ldots \gtrdot \#
\end{array}
$$

Figure 9.4 Preliminary table of precedence relations

Figure 9.2 is given in Figure 9.5; the left-most column contains the left-hand symbols and the top-most row the right-hand symbols.

	#	+	×	(	)
#	≐	⋖	⋖	⋖	
+	⋗	⋗	⋖	⋖	⋗
×	⋗	⋗	⋗	⋖	⋗
(		⋖	⋖	⋖	≐
)	⋗	⋗	⋗		⋗

Figure 9.5 Operator-precedence table to the grammar of Figure 9.2

There are three remarks to be made about this precedence table. First, we have added a number of ⋖ and ⋗ tokens not covered above (for instance, ×⋗×). Second, there is #≐# and (≐) (but not)≐(!); we shall shortly see what they mean. And third, there are three empty entries, meaning that when we find these combinations in the input, it contains an error (and is not produced by the grammar for which we made our precedence table).

Such a table is called a precedence table because for symbols that are normally regarded as operators it gives their relative precedence. An entry like +⋖× indicates that in the combination +×, the × has a higher precedence than the +. We shall first show how the precedence table is used in parsing and then how such a precedence table can be constructed systematically for a given grammar, if the grammar allows it.

The stack in an operator-precedence parser differs from the normal bottom-up parser stack in that it contains "important" symbols, the operators, between which relations are defined, and "unimportant" symbols, the numbers, which are only consulted to determine the value of a handle and which do not influence the parsing. Moreover, we need places on the stack to insert the parentheses generators (one can, in principle, do without these, by reevaluating them whenever necessary). Since there is a parentheses generator between each pair of operators and there is also (almost) always a value between such a pair, we shall indicate both in the same position on the stack, with the parentheses generator in line and the value below it; see Figure 9.6.

To show that, contrary to what is sometimes thought, operator-precedence can do more than just calculate a value (and since we have seen too often now that $4+5\times6+8=42$), we shall have the parser construct the parse tree rather than the value. The stack starts with a #. Values and operators are shifted onto it, interspersed with parentheses generators, until a ⋗ generator is met; the following operator is not shifted and is left in the input (Figure 9.6(b)). It is now easy to identify the handle, which is

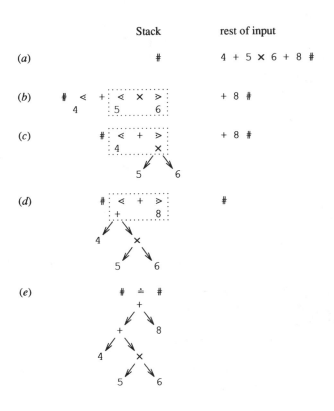

	Stack	rest of input

Figure 9.6 Operator-precedence parsing of 4+5×6+8

demarcated by a dotted rectangle in the figure and which is reduced to a tree; see (*c*), in which also the next > has already appeared between the + on the stack and the + in the input. Note that the tree and the new generator have come in the position of the < of the handle. A further reduction brings us to (*d*) in which the + and the 8 have already been shifted, and then to the final state of the operator-precedence parser, in which the stack holds #≐# and the parse tree dangles from the value position.

We see that the stack only holds < markers and values, plus a > on the top each time a handle is found. The meaning of the ≐ becomes clear when we parse an input text which includes parentheses, like 4×(5+6); see Figure 9.7, in which we have the parser calculate the value rather than the parse tree. We see that the ≐ is used to allow handles consisting of more than one operator and two operands; the handle in (*c*) has two operators, the (and the) and one operand, the 11. Note that as already indicated in Section 5.1.1, the set of stack configurations can be described by a regular expression; for this type of parsers the expression is:

$$\texttt{\#} \quad | \quad \texttt{\#<q ([<\dot{=}]q)}^{*} \texttt{>}^{?} \quad | \quad \texttt{\#\dot{=}\#}$$

where q is any operator; the first alternative is the start situation and the third alternative is the end situation.

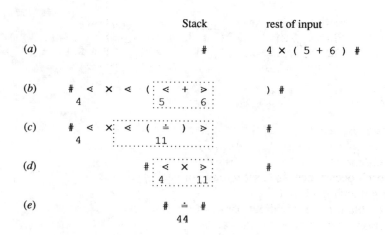

Figure 9.7 An operator-precedence parsing involving $\doteq$

9.2.1 Constructing the operator-precedence table

The above hinges on the difference between operators, which are terminal symbols and between which precedence relations are defined, and operands, which are non-terminals. This distinction is captured in the following definition of an operator grammar:

☐   A CF grammar is an *operator grammar* if (and only if) each right-hand side contains at least one terminal and no right-hand side contains two consecutive non-terminals.

So each pair of non-terminals is separated by at least one terminal; all the terminals except those carrying values (n in our case) are called operators.

For such grammars, setting up the precedence table is relatively easy. First we calculate for each non-terminal A the set $FIRST_{OP}(A)$, which is the set of all operators that can occur as the first operator in any sentential form deriving from A, and $LAST_{OP}(A)$, which is defined similarly. Note that this first operator in a sentential form can be preceded by at most one non-terminal in an operator grammar. The $FIRST_{OP}$'s of all non-terminals are constructed simultaneously as follows:

1.   For each non-terminal A, find all right-hand sides of all rules for A; now for each right-hand side R we insert the first terminal in R (if any) into $FIRST_{OP}(A)$. This gives us the initial values of all $FIRST_{OP}$'s.
2.   For each non-terminal A, find all right-hand sides of all rules for A; now for each right-hand side R that starts with a non-terminal, say B, we add the elements of $FIRST_{OP}(B)$ to $FIRST_{OP}(A)$. This is reasonable, since a sentential form of A may start with B, so all terminals in $FIRST_{OP}(B)$ should also be in $FIRST_{OP}(A)$.
3.   Repeat step 2 above until no $FIRST_{OP}$ changes any more.

We have now found the $FIRST_{OP}$ of all non-terminals. A similar algorithm, using the *last* terminal in R in step 1 and a B which *ends* A in step 2 provides the $LAST_{OP}$'s. The sets for the grammar of Figure 9.2 are shown in Figure 9.8.

Now we can fill the precedence table using the following rules, in which q, q_1 and q_2 are operators and A is a non-terminal.

☐   For each occurrence in a right-hand side of the form q_1q_2 or q_1Aq_2, set $q_1\doteq q_2$.

$$FIRST_{OP}(S) = \{ \# \} \qquad LAST_{OP}(S) = \{ \# \}$$
$$FIRST_{OP}(E) = \{ +, \times, (\} \qquad LAST_{OP}(E) = \{ +, \times,) \}$$
$$FIRST_{OP}(T) = \{ \times, (\} \qquad LAST_{OP}(T) = \{ \times,) \}$$
$$FIRST_{OP}(F) = \{ (\} \qquad LAST_{OP}(F) = \{) \}$$

Figure 9.8 FIRST$_{OP}$ and LAST$_{OP}$ sets for the grammar of Figure 9.2

This keeps operators from the same handle together.

□   For each occurrence $q_1 A$, set $q_1 \lessdot q_2$ for each q_2 in $FIRST_{OP}(A)$. This demarcates the left end of a handle.

□   For each occurrence $A q_1$, set $q_2 \gtrdot q_1$ for each q_2 in $LAST_{OP}(A)$. This demarcates the right end of a handle.

If we obtain a table without conflicts this way, that is, if we never find two different relations between two operators, then we call the grammar *operator-precedence*. It will now be clear why ($\doteq$) and not) $\doteq$ (, and why $+ \gtrdot +$ (because E+ occurs in E−>E+T and + is in $LAST_{OP}(E)$).

In this way, the table can be derived from the grammar by a program and be passed on to the operator-precedence parser. A very efficient linear-time parser results. There is, however, one small problem we have glossed over: Although the method properly identifies the handle, it often does not identify the non-terminal to which to reduce it. Also, it does not show any unit rule reductions; nowhere in the examples did we see reductions of the form E−>F or T−>F. In short, operator-precedence parsing generates only skeleton parse trees.

Operator-precedence parsers are very easy to construct (often even by hand) and very efficient to use; operator-precedence is the method of choice for all parsing problems that are simple enough to allow it. That only a skeleton parse tree is obtained, is often not an obstacle, since operator grammars often have the property that the semantics is attached to the operators rather than to the right-hand sides; the operators are identified correctly.

It is surprising how many grammars are (almost) operator-precedence. Almost all formula-like computer input is operator-precedence. Also, large parts of the grammars of many computer languages are operator-precedence. An example is a construction like CONST total = head + tail; from a Pascal-like language, which is easily rendered as:

						Stack			rest of input
#	$\lessdot$	CONST	$\lessdot$	$\doteq$	$\lessdot$	+	$\gtrdot$		; #
			total		head		tail		

Ignoring the non-terminals has other bad consequences besides producing a skeleton parse tree. Since non-terminals are ignored, a missing non-terminal is not noticed. As a result, the parser will accept incorrect input without warning and will produce an incomplete parse tree for it. A parser using the table of Figure 9.5 will blithely accept the empty string, since it immediately leads to the stack configuration #$\doteq$#. It produces a parse tree consisting of one empty node.

The theoretical analysis of this phenomenon turns out to be inordinately difficult; see Levy [Precedence 1975], Williams [Precedence 1977, 1979, 1981] and many others in Section 13.8. In practice it is less of a problem than one would expect; it is easy to check for the presence of required non-terminals, either while the parse tree is being constructed or afterwards.

9.2.2 Precedence functions

Several objections can be raised against operator-precedence. First, it cannot handle all grammars that can be handled by other more sophisticated methods. Second, its error detection capabilities are weak. Third, it constructs skeleton parse trees only. And fourth, the two-dimensional precedence table, which for say a 100 tokens has 10000 entries, may take too much room. The latter objection can be overcome for those precedence tables that can be represented by so-called *precedence functions*. The idea is the following. Rather than having a *table T* such that for any two operators q_1 and q_2, $T[q_1,q_2]$ yields the relation between q_1 and q_2, we have two integer *functions f* and *g* such that $f_{q_1} < g_{q_2}$ means that $q_1 \lessdot q_2$, $f_{q_1} = g_{q_2}$ means $q_1 \doteq q_2$ and $f_{q_1} > g_{q_2}$ means $q_1 \gtrdot q_2$. f_q is called the *left priority* of q, g_q the *right priority*; they would probably be better indicated by l and r, but the use of f and g is traditional. Note that we write f_{q_1} rather than $f(q_1)$; this allows us to write, for instance, $f_{(}$ for the left priority of (rather than the confusing $f(()$. It will be clear that *two* functions are required: with just one function one cannot express, for instance, +>+. Precedence functions take much less room than precedence tables. For our 100 tokens we need 200 function values rather than 10000 tables entries. Not all tables allow a representation with precedence functions, but many do.

Finding the proper f and g for a given table seems simple enough and can indeed often be done by hand. The fact, however, that there are two functions rather than one, the size of the tables and the occurrence of the $\doteq$ complicate things. A well-known algorithm to construct the functions was given by Bell [Precedence 1969] of which several variants exist. The following technique is a straightforward and easily implemented variant of Bell's algorithm.

First we turn the precedence table into a list of numerical relations, as follows:

☐   for each $q_1 \lessdot q_2$ we have $f_{q_1} < g_{q_2}$,

☐   for each $q_1 \doteq q_2$ we have $f_{q_1} = g_{q_2}$,

☐   for each $q_1 \gtrdot q_2$ we have $f_{q_1} > g_{q_2}$,

Here we no longer view forms like f_q as function values but rather as variables; reinterpretation as function values will occur later. Making such a list is easier done by computer than by hand; see Figure 9.9(a). Next we remove all equals-relations, as follows:

☐   for each relation $f_{q_1} = g_{q_2}$ we create a new variable $f_{q_1} g_{q_2}$ and replace all occurrences of f_{q_1} and g_{q_2} by $f_{q_1} g_{q_2}$.

Note that $f_{q_1} g_{q_2}$ is not the product of f_{q_1} and g_{q_2} but rather a new variable, i.e., the name of a new priority value. Now a relation like $f_{q_1} = g_{q_2}$ has turned into $f_{q_1} g_{q_2} = f_{q_1} g_{q_2}$ and can be deleted trivially. See (b).

Third we flip all > relations:

☐   we replace each relation $p_1 > p_2$ by $p_2 < p_1$, where p_1 and p_2 are priority variables. See (c).

The list has now assumed a very uniform appearance and we can start to assign numerical values to the variables. We shall do this by handing out the numbers $0, 1, \cdots$ as follows:

<table>
<tr><td>

(a)
$f_\# = g_\#$
$f_\# < g_+$
$f_\# < g_\times$
$f_\# < g_($
$f_+ > g_\#$
$f_+ > g_+$
$f_+ < g_\times$
$f_+ < g_($
$f_+ > g_)$
$f_\times > g_\#$
$f_\times > g_+$
$f_\times > g_\times$
$f_\times < g_($
$f_\times > g_)$
$f_(< g_+$
$f_(< g_\times$
$f_(< g_($
$f_(= g_)$
$f_) > g_\#$
$f_) > g_+$
$f_) > g_\times$
$f_) > g_)$

</td><td>

(b)
$f_{\#g\#} < g_+$
$f_{\#g\#} < g_\times$
$f_{\#g\#} < g_($
$f_+ > f_{\#g\#}$
$f_+ > g_+$
$f_+ < g_\times$
$f_+ < g_($
$f_+ > f_{(g)}$
$f_\times > f_{\#g\#}$
$f_\times > g_+$
$f_\times > g_\times$
$f_\times < g_($
$f_\times > f_{(g)}$
$f_{(g)} < g_+$
$f_{(g)} < g_\times$
$f_{(g)} < g_($
$f_) > f_{\#g\#}$
$f_) > g_+$
$f_) > g_\times$
$f_) > f_{(g)}$

</td><td>

(c)
$f_{\#g\#} < g_+$
$f_{\#g\#} < g_\times$
$f_{\#g\#} < g_($
$f_{\#g\#} < f_+$
$g_+ < f_+$
$f_+ < g_\times$
$f_+ < g_($
$f_{(g)} < f_+$
$f_{\#g\#} < f_\times$
$g_+ < f_\times$
$g_\times < f_\times$
$f_\times < g_($
$f_{(g)} < f_\times$
$f_{(g)} < g_+$
$f_{(g)} < g_\times$
$f_{(g)} < g_($
$f_{\#g\#} < f_)$
$g_+ < f_)$
$g_\times < f_)$
$f_{(g)} < f_)$

</td></tr>
</table>

(d)
$f_{\#g\#} = 0$
$f_{(g)} = 0$
$g_+ < f_+$
$f_+ < g_\times$
$f_+ < g_($
$g_+ < f_\times$
$g_\times < f_\times$
$f_\times < g_($
$g_+ < f_)$
$g_\times < f_)$

(e)
$f_{\#g\#} = 0$
$f_{(g)} = 0$
$g_+ = 1$
$f_+ < g_\times$
$f_+ < g_($
$g_\times < f_\times$
$f_\times < g_($
$g_\times < f_)$

(f)
$f_{\#g\#} = 0$
$f_{(g)} = 0$
$g_+ = 1$
$f_+ = 2$
$g_\times < f_\times$
$f_\times < g_($
$g_\times < f_)$

(g)
$f_{\#g\#} = 0$
$f_{(g)} = 0$
$g_+ = 1$
$f_+ = 2$
$g_\times = 3$
$f_\times < g_($

(h)
$f_{\#g\#} = 0$
$f_{(g)} = 0$
$g_+ = 1$
$f_+ = 2$
$g_\times = 3$
$f_\times = 4$

(i)
$f_\# = 0$
$g_\# = 0$
$f_(= 0$
$g_) = 0$
$g_+ = 1$
$f_+ = 2$
$g_\times = 3$
$f_\times = 4$

(j)
$f_\# = 0$
$f_(= 0$
$f_+ = 2$
$f_\times = 4$
$f_) = 5$

$g_\# = 0$
$g_) = 0$
$g_+ = 1$
$g_\times = 3$
$g_(= 5$

Figure 9.9 Calculating precedence functions

☐   Find all variables that occur only on the left of a relation; since they are clearly smaller than all the others, they can all be given the value 0.

In our example we find $f_{\#g\#}$ and $f_{(g)}$, which both get the value 0. Since the relations that have these two variables on their left will be satisfied provided we hand out no more 0's, we can remove them (see (d)):

☐   Remove all relations that have the identified variables on their left sides.

This removal causes another set of variables to occur on the left of a relation only, to which we now hand out the value 1. We repeat this process with increasing values until the list of relations has become empty; see (e) through (h).

□   Decompose the compound variables and give each component the numerical value of the compound variable. This decomposes, for instance, $f_{(g)}=0$ into $f_{(}=0$ and $g_{)}=0$; see (i).

This leaves without a value those variables that occurred on the right-hand side only in the comparisons under (c):

□   To all still unassigned priority values, assign the lowest value that has not yet been handed out.

$f_{)}$ and $g_{(}$ both get the value 5 (see (j) where the values have also been reordered) and indeed these occur at the high side of a comparison only. It is easily verified that the priority values found satisfy the initial comparisons as derived from the precedence table.

It is possible that we reach a stage in which there are still relations left but there are no variables that occur on the left only. It is easy to see that in that case there must be a circularity of the form $p_1 < p_2 < p_3 \cdots < p_1$ and that no integer functions representing these relations can exist: the table does not allow precedence functions.

	#	)	+	×	(
#	≐		⋖	⋖	⋖
(		≐	⋖	⋖	⋖
+	⋗	⋗	⋗	⋖	⋖
×	⋗	⋗	⋗	⋗	⋖
)	⋗	⋗	⋗	⋗	

Figure 9.10 The precedence table of Figure 9.5 reordered

Note that finding precedence functions is equivalent to reordering the rows and columns of the precedence table so that the latter can be divided into three regions: a ⋗ region on the lower left, a ⋖ region on the upper right and a ≐ border between them. See Figure 9.10.

There is always a way to represent a precedence table with more than two functions; see Bertsch [Precedence 1977] on how to construct such functions.

9.2.3 Simple-precedence parsing

The fact that operator-precedence parsing produces skeleton parse trees only is a serious obstacle to its application outside formula handling. The defect seems easy to remedy. When a handle is identified in an operator-precedence parser, it is reduced to a node containing the value(s) and the operator(s), without reference to the grammar. For serious parsing the matching right-hand side of the pertinent rule has to be found. Now suppose we require all right-hand sides in the grammar to be different. Then, given a handle, we can easily find the rule to be used in the reduction (or to find that there is no matching right-hand side, in which case there was an error in the input).

This is, however, not quite good enough. To properly do the right reductions and to find reductions of the form $A \rightarrow B$ (unit reductions), the non-terminals themselves have to play a role in the identification of the right-hand side. They have to be on the stack like any other symbol and precedence relations have to be found for them. This has the additional advantage that the grammar need no longer be an operator grammar and that the stack entries have a normal appearance again.

A grammar is *simple precedence* if (and only if):
☐   it has a conflict-free precedence table over all its symbols, terminals and non-terminals alike,
☐   none of its right-hand sides is ε,
☐   all of its right-hand sides are different.

The construction of the simple-precedence table is again based upon two sets, $FIRST_{ALL}(A)$ and $LAST_{ALL}(A)$. $FIRST_{ALL}(A)$ is similar to the set FIRST(A) introduced in Section 8.2.2.1 and differs from it in that it also contains all non-terminals that can start a sentential form derived from A (whereas FIRST(A) contains terminals only). $LAST_{ALL}(A)$ contains all terminals and non-terminals that can end a sentential form of A. Their construction is similar to that given in Section 8.2.2.1 for the FIRST set. Figure 9.11 shows the pertinent sets for our grammar.

$$FIRST_{ALL}(S) = \{\#\} \qquad\qquad LAST_{ALL}(S) = \{\#\}$$
$$FIRST_{ALL}(E) = \{E, T, F, n, (\} \qquad LAST_{ALL}(E) = \{T, F, n,)\}$$
$$FIRST_{ALL}(T) = \{T, F, n, (\} \qquad\quad LAST_{ALL}(T) = \{F, n,)\}$$
$$FIRST_{ALL}(F) = \{n, (\} \qquad\qquad\; LAST_{ALL}(F) = \{n,)\}$$

Figure 9.11 FIRST$_{ALL}$ and LAST$_{ALL}$ for the grammar of Figure 9.2

A simple-precedence table is now constructed as follows: For each two juxtaposed symbols X and Y in a right-hand side we have:
☐ $X \doteq Y$; this keeps X and Y together in the handle;
☐   if X is a non-terminal: for each symbol s in $LAST_{ALL}(X)$ and each terminal t in FIRST(Y) (or Y itself if Y is a terminal) we have $s > t$; this allows X to be reduced completely when the first sign of Y appears in the input; note that we have FIRST(Y) here rather than $FIRST_{ALL}(Y)$;
☐   if Y is a non-terminal: for each symbol s in $FIRST_{ALL}(Y)$ we have $X < s$; this protects X while Y is being recognized.

	#	E	T	F	n	+	×	(	)
#		<⋅/≐	<⋅	<⋅	<⋅			<⋅	
E	≐					≐			≐
T	⋅>					⋅>	≐		⋅>
F	⋅>					⋅>	⋅>		⋅>
n	⋅>					⋅>	⋅>		⋅>
+			<⋅/≐	<⋅	<⋅			<⋅	
×				≐	<⋅			<⋅	
(		<⋅/≐	<⋅	<⋅	<⋅			<⋅	
)	⋅>					⋅>	⋅>		⋅>

Figure 9.12 Simple-precedence table to Figure 9.2, with conflicts

Simple precedence is not the answer to all our problems as is evident from Figure 9.12 which displays the results of an attempt to construct the precedence table for the operator-precedence grammar of Figure 9.2. Not even this simple grammar is simple-precedence, witness the conflicts for #⋖/≐E, (⋖/≐E and +⋖/≐T.

$$
\begin{array}{rcl}
S_S & \rightarrow & E' \\
E' & \rightarrow & E \\
E & \rightarrow & E + T' \\
E & \rightarrow & T' \\
T' & \rightarrow & T \\
T & \rightarrow & T \times F \\
T & \rightarrow & F \\
F & \rightarrow & n \\
F & \rightarrow & (\ E\ )
\end{array}
$$

$\text{FIRST}_{ALL}(E') = \{E, T', T, F, n, (\}$	$\text{LAST}_{ALL}(E') = \{T', T, F, n,)\}$
$\text{FIRST}_{ALL}(E) = \{E, T', T, F, n, (\}$	$\text{LAST}_{ALL}(E) = \{T, F, n,)\}$
$\text{FIRST}_{ALL}(T') = \{T, F, n, (\}$	$\text{LAST}_{ALL}(T') = \{F, n,)\}$
$\text{FIRST}_{ALL}(T) = \{T, F, n, (\}$	$\text{LAST}_{ALL}(T) = \{F, n,)\}$
$\text{FIRST}_{ALL}(F) = \{n, (\}$	$\text{LAST}_{ALL}(F) = \{n,)\}$

	#	E'	E	T'	T	F	n	+	×	(	)
#		≐	⋖	⋖	⋖	⋖	⋖			⋖	
E'	≐										
E	⋗							≐			≐
T'	⋗							⋗			⋗
T	⋗							⋗	≐		⋗
F	⋗							⋗	⋗		⋗
n	⋗							⋗	⋗		⋗
+				≐	⋖	⋖	⋖			⋖	
×						≐	⋖			⋖	
(				≐	⋖	⋖	⋖	⋖			⋖
)	⋗							⋗	⋗		⋗

Figure 9.13 A modified grammar with its simple-precedence table, without conflicts

There are two ways to remedy this. We can adapt the grammar by inserting extra levels around the troublesome non-terminals. This is done in Figure 9.13 and works in this case; it brings us, however, farther away from our goal, to produce a correct parse tree, since we now produce a parse tree for a different grammar. Or we can adapt the parsing method, as explained in the next section.

9.2.4 Weak-precedence parsing

It turns out that most of the simple-precedence conflicts are ⋖/≐ conflicts. Now the difference between ⋖ and ≐ is in a sense less important than that between either of them and ⋗. Both ⋖ and ≐ result in a shift and only ⋗ asks for a reduce. Only when a reduce is found will the difference between ⋖ and ≐ become significant for finding the head of the handle. Now suppose we drop the difference between ⋖ and ≐ and combine them into ≤; then we need a different means of identifying the handle and the proper right-hand side. This can be done by requiring not only that all right-hand sides be different, but also that no right-hand side be equal to the tail of another right-hand side. A grammar that conforms to this and has a conflict-free ≤/⋗ precedence table is called *weak precedence*. Figure 9.14 gives the (conflict-free) weak-precedence table for the grammar of Figure 9.2. It is of course possible to retain the difference between ⋖ and ≐ where it exists; this will improve the error detection capability of the parser.

	#	E	T	F	n	+	×	(	)
#		≤	⋖	⋖	⋖			⋖	
E	≐					≐			≐
T	⋗					⋗	≐		⋗
F	⋗					⋗	⋗		⋗
n	⋗					⋗	⋗		⋗
+			≤	⋖	⋖			⋖	
×				≐	⋖			⋖	
(		≤	⋖	⋖	⋖			⋖	
)	⋗					⋗	⋗		⋗

Figure 9.14 Weak-precedence table to the grammar of Figure 9.2

The rule that no right-hand side should be equal to the tail of another right-hand side is more restrictive than necessary. More lenient rules exist in several variants, which, however, all require more work in identifying the reduction rule. See, for instance, Ichbiah and Morse [Precedence 1970] or Sekimoto [Precedence 1972].

Weak precedence is a useful method that applies to a relatively large group of grammars. Especially if parsing is used to roughly structure an input stream, as in the first pass or scan of a complicated system, weak precedence can be of service.

9.2.5 Extended precedence and mixed-strategy precedence

The above methods determine the precedence relations by looking at 1 symbol on the stack and 1 token in the input. Once this has been said, the idea suggests itself to replace the 1's by m and n respectively, and to determine the precedence relations from the topmost m symbols on the stack and the first n tokens in the input. This is called *(m,n)-extended precedence*.

We can use the same technique to find the left end of the handle on the stack when using weak precedence: use k symbols on the left and l on the right to answer the question if this is the head of the handle. This is called *(k,l)(m,n)-extended [weak] precedence*.

By increasing its parameters, extended precedence can be made reasonably powerful. Yet the huge tables required ($2 \times 300 \times 300 \times 300 = 54$ million entries for (1,2)(2,1) extended precedence with 300 symbols) severely limit its applicability. Moreover, even with large values of k, l, m and n it is inferior still to LR(1), which we treat in Section 9.5.

If a grammar is $(k,l)(m,n)$-extended precedence, it is not always necessary to test the full k, l, m and n symbols. Indeed it is almost never necessary and large parts of the grammar can almost always be handled by (normal) weak-precedence methods; the full $(k,l)(m,n)$-extended precedence power is needed only in one or two spots in the grammar. This phenomenon has led to techniques in which the (normal) weak-precedence table has a (small) number of exception entries that refer to further, more powerful tables. This technique is called *mixed-strategy precedence*. Mixed-strategy precedence has been investigated by McKeeman [Books 1970].

9.2.6 Actually finding the correct right-hand side

All the above methods identify only the bounds of the handle; the actual right-hand side is still to be determined. It may seem that a search through all right-hand sides is necessary for each reduction, but this is not so. The right-hand sides can be arranged in a tree structure with their right-most symbols forming the root of the tree, as in Figure 9.15. When we have found a > relation, we start walking down the stack looking for a < and at the same time we follow the corresponding path through the tree; when we find the < we should be at the beginning of a rule in the tree, or we have found an error in the input; see Figure 9.15. The tree can be constructed by sorting the grammar rules on their symbols in backward order and taking equal tails together. As an example, the path followed for < T ≐ × ≐ F > has been indicated by a dotted line.

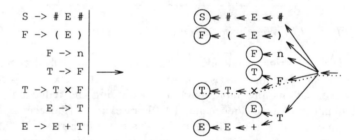

Figure 9.15 Tree structure for efficiently finding right-hand sides

For several methods to improve upon this, see the literature (Section 13.8).

9.3 BOUNDED-CONTEXT PARSING

There is a different way to solve the annoying problem of the identification of the right-hand side: let the identity of the rule be part of the precedence relation. A grammar is *(m,n) bounded-context* $(BC(m,n))$ if (and only if) for each combination of m symbols on the stack and n tokens in the input there is a unique parsing decision which is either "shift" ($\lessgtr$) or "reduce using rule X" ($>_X$), as obtained by a variant of the rules for extended precedence. Figure 9.16 gives the $BC(2,1)$ tables for the grammar of Figure 9.2. Note that the rows correspond to stack symbol pairs; the entry Accept means that the input has been parsed and Error means that a syntax error has been found. Blank entries will never be accessed; all-blank rows have been left out. See, for instance, Loeckx [Precedence 1970] for the construction of such tables.

Bounded-context (especially $BC(2,1)$) was once very popular but has been

	#	+	×	n	(	)
#S	Accept					
#E	$>_{S\to E}$	$<$				Error
#T	$>_{E\to T}$	$>_{E\to T}$	$<$			Error
#F	$>_{T\to F}$	$>_{T\to F}$	$>_{T\to F}$			Error
#n	$>_{F\to n}$	$>_{F\to n}$	$>_{F\to n}$	Error	Error	Error
#(	Error	Error	Error	$<$	$<$	Error
E+	Error	Error	Error	$<$	$<$	Error
E)	$>_{F\to (E)}$	$>_{F\to (E)}$	$>_{F\to (E)}$	Error	Error	$>_{F\to (E)}$
T×	Error	Error	Error	$<$	$<$	Error
+T	$>_{E\to E+T}$	$>_{E\to E+T}$	$<$			$>_{E\to E+T}$
+F	$>_{T\to F}$	$>_{T\to F}$	$>_{T\to F}$			$>_{T\to F}$
+n	$>_{F\to n}$	$>_{F\to n}$	$>_{F\to n}$	Error	Error	$>_{F\to n}$
+(	Error	Error	Error	$<$	$<$	Error
×F	$>_{T\to T\times F}$	$>_{T\to T\times F}$	$>_{T\to T\times F}$			$>_{T\to T\times F}$
×n	$>_{F\to n}$	$>_{F\to n}$	$>_{F\to n}$	Error	Error	$>_{F\to n}$
×(	Error	Error	Error	$<$	$<$	Error
(E	Error	$<$				$<$
(T	Error	$>_{E\to T}$	$<$			$>_{E\to T}$
(F	Error	$>_{T\to F}$	$>_{T\to F}$			$>_{T\to F}$
(n	Error	$>_{F\to n}$	$>_{F\to n}$	Error	Error	$>_{F\to n}$
((	Error	Error	Error	$<$	$<$	Error

Figure 9.16 BC(2,1) tables for the grammar of Figure 9.2

superseded almost completely by LALR(1) (Section 9.6). Recently, interest in bounded-context grammars has been revived, since it has turned out that such grammars have some excellent error recovery properties; see Section 10.8. This is not completely surprising if we consider that bounded-context grammars have the property that a small number of symbols in the sentential form suffice to determine completely what is going on.

9.3.1 Floyd productions

Bounded-context parsing steps can be summarized conveniently by using Floyd productions. *Floyd productions* are rules for rewriting a string that contains a marker, Δ, on which the rules focus. A Floyd production has the form $\alpha\Delta\beta \Rightarrow \gamma\Delta\delta$ and means that if the marker in the string is preceded by α and is followed by β, the construction must be replaced by $\gamma\Delta\delta$. The rules are tried in order starting from the top and the first one to match is applied; processing then resumes on the resulting string, starting from the top of the list, and the process is repeated until no rule matches.

Although Floyd productions were not primarily designed as a parsing tool but rather as a general string manipulation language, the identification of the Δ in the string with the gap in a bottom-up parser suggests itself and was already made in Floyd's original article [Misc 1961]. Floyd productions for the grammar of Figure 9.2 are given in Figure 9.17. The parser is started with the Δ at the left of the input.

The apparent convenience and conciseness of Floyd productions makes it very tempting to write parsers in them by hand, but Floyd productions are very sensitive to the order in which the rules are listed and a small inaccuracy in the order can have a

$$
\begin{array}{lll}
\Delta\ n & => & n\ \Delta \\
\Delta\ (& => & (\ \Delta \\
n\ \Delta & => & F\ \Delta \\
T\ \Delta\ * & => & T*\ \Delta \\
T*F\ \Delta & => & T\ \Delta \\
F\ \Delta & => & T\ \Delta \\
E+T\ \Delta & => & E\ \Delta \\
T\ \Delta & => & E\ \Delta \\
(E)\ \Delta & => & F\ \Delta \\
\Delta\ + & => & +\ \Delta \\
\Delta\ ) & => &)\ \Delta \\
\Delta\ \# & => & \#\ \Delta \\
\#E\#\ \Delta & => & S\ \Delta
\end{array}
$$

Figure 9.17 Floyd productions for the grammar of Figure 9.2

devastating effect.

9.4 LR METHODS

The LR methods are based on the combination of two ideas that have already been touched upon in previous sections. To reiterate, the problem is to find the handle in a sentential form as efficiently as possible, for as large a class of grammars as possible. Such a handle is searched for from left to right. Now, from Section 5.3.4 we recall that a very efficient way to find a string in a left-to-right search is by constructing a finite-state automaton. Just doing this is, however, not good enough. It is quite easy to construct an FS automaton that would recognize any of the right-hand sides in the grammar efficiently, but it would just find the left-most reducible substring in the sentential form. This substring is, however, often not the handle.

The idea can be made practical by applying the same trick that was used in Earley's parser to drastically reduce the fan-out of the breadth-first search (see Section 7.2): start the automaton with the start rule of the grammar and only consider, in any position, right-hand sides that could be derived from the start symbol. This top-down restriction device served in the Earley parser to reduce the cost to $O(n^3)$, here we require the grammar to be such that it reduces the cost to $O(n)$. The resulting automaton is started in its initial state at the left end of the sentential form and allowed to run to the right; it has the property that it stops at the right end of the handle and that its accepting state tells us how to reduce the handle. How this is done will be explained in the next section.

Since practical FS automata easily get so big that their states cannot be displayed on a single page of a book, we shall use the grammar of Figure 9.18 for our examples. It is a simplified version of that of Figure 9.2, in which only one binary operator is left, for which we have chosen the − rather than the +. Although this is not essential, it serves to remind us that the proper parse tree must be derived, since (a−b) −c is not the same as a− (b−c) (whereas (a+b) +c and a+ (b+c) are). The # indicates the end of the input.

$$
\begin{array}{rcl}
S_S & \to & E\ \# \\
E & \to & E\ -\ T \\
E & \to & T \\
T & \to & n \\
T & \to & (\ E\ )
\end{array}
$$

Figure 9.18 A very simple grammar for differences of numbers

9.4.1 LR(0)

We shall now set out to construct a top-down-restricted handle-recognizing FS automaton for the grammar of Figure 9.18, and start by constructing a non-deterministic version. We recall that a non-deterministic automaton can be drawn as a set of states connected by arrows (transitions), each marked with one symbol or with ε. Each state will contain one *item*. Like in the Earley parser, an item consists of a grammar rule with a dot • embedded in its right-hand side. An item $X \to \cdots Y \bullet Z \cdots$ in a state means that the (non-deterministic!) automaton bets on $X \to \cdots YZ \cdots$ being the handle and that it has already recognized $\cdots Y$. Unlike the Earley parser there are no back-pointers. To simplify the explanation of the transitions involved, we introduce a second kind of state, which we call a *station*. It has only ε arrows incoming and outgoing, contains something of the form $\bullet X$ and is drawn in a rectangle rather than in an ellipse. When the automaton is in such a station at some point in the sentential form, it thinks that at this point a handle starts that reduces to X. Consequently each $\bullet X$ station has ε-transitions to items for all rules for X, each with the dot at the left end, since no part of the rule has yet been recognized; see Figure 9.19. Equally reasonably, each state holding an item $X \to \cdots \bullet Z \cdots$ has an ε-transition to the station $\bullet Z$, since the bet on an X may be over-optimistic and the automaton may have to settle for a Z. The third and last source of arrows in the non-deterministic automaton is straightforward. From each state containing $X \to \cdots \bullet P \cdots$ there is a P-transition to the state containing $X \to \cdots P \bullet \cdots$, for P a terminal or a non-terminal. This corresponds to the move the automaton makes when it really meets a P. Note that the sentential form may contain non-terminals, so transitions on *non*-terminals should also be defined.

With this knowledge we refer to Figure 9.19. The stations for S, E and T are drawn at the top of the picture, to show how they lead to all possible items for S, E and T, respectively. From each station, ε-arrows fan out to all states containing items with the dot at the left, one for each rule for the non-terminal in that station; from each such state, non-ε-arrows lead down to further states. Now the picture is almost complete. All that needs to be done is to scan the items for a dot followed by a non-terminal (readily discernable from the outgoing arrow marked with it) and to connect each such item to the corresponding station through an ε-arrow. This completes the picture.

There are two things to be noted on this picture. First, for each grammar rule with a right-hand side of length l there are $l+1$ items and they are easily found in the picture. Moreover, for a grammar with r different non-terminals, there are r stations. So the number of states is roughly proportional to the size of the grammar, which assures us that the automaton will have a modest number of states. For the average grammar of a hundred rules something like 300 states is usual. The second is that all states have outgoing arrows except the ones which contain an item with the dot at the right end. These are accepting states of the automaton and indicate that a handle has been found; the item in the state tells us how to reduce the handle.

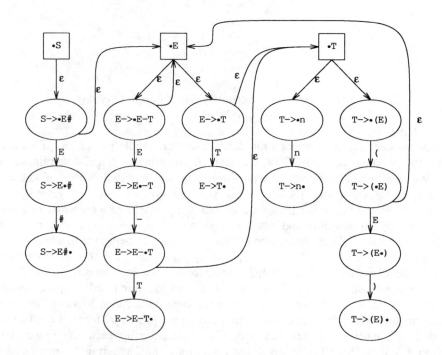

Figure 9.19 A non-deterministic handle recognizer for the grammar of Figure 9.18

We shall now run this NDA on the sentential form E–n–n, to see how it works. As in the FS case we can do so if we are willing to go through the trouble of resolving the non-determinism on the fly. The automaton starts at the station •S and can immediately make ε-moves to S–>•E#, •E, E–>•E–T, E–>•T, •T, T–>•n and T–>• (E) . Moving over the E reduces the set of states to S–>E•# and E–>E•–T; moving over the next – brings us at E–>E–•T from which ε-moves lead to •T, T–>•n and T–>• (E) . Now the move over n leaves only one item: T–>n•, which tells us through the dot at the end of the item, that we have found a handle, n, and that we should reduce it to T using T–>n. See Figure 9.20. This reduction gives us a new sentential form, E–T–n, on which we can repeat the process.

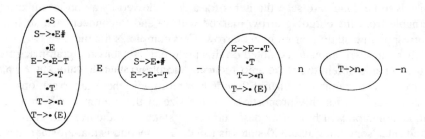

Figure 9.20 The sets of NDA states while analysing E–n–n

Just as in the FS case, we will soon tire of doing it this way, and the first thing we need to do is to make the NDA deterministic, if we are to use it in earnest. We use the subset construction of Section 5.3.1 to construct a deterministic automaton that has sets of the items of Figure 9.19 as its states. The result is shown in Figure 9.21, where we have left out the stations to avoid clutter and since they are evident from the other items. We see that the deterministic automaton looks a lot less understandable than Figure 9.19; this is the price to be paid for having determinism. Yet we see that the subset construction has correctly identified the subsets we had already constructed by hand in the previous paragraph. This type of automaton is called an *LR(0) automaton*.

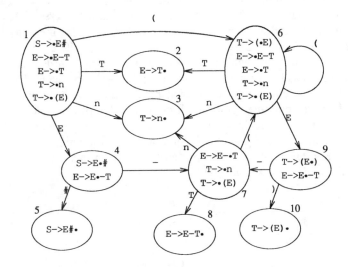

Figure 9.21 The corresponding deterministic handle recognizer

It is customary to number the states of the deterministic automaton, as has already been done in Figure 9.21 (the order of the numbers is arbitrary, they serve identification purposes only). Now it has become much easier to represent the sentential form with its state information, both implementationwise in a computer and in a drawing:

    ① E ④ – ⑦ n ③   – n

The sequence ① ④ ⑦ ③ can be read from Figure 9.21 using the path E–n. We start with state ① on the stack and shift in symbols from the sentential form, all the while assessing the new states. As soon as an accepting state shows up on the top of the stack (and it cannot show up elsewhere on the stack) the shifting stops and a reduce is called for; the accepting state indicates how to reduce. Accepting state ③ calls for a reduction T–>n, so our new sentential form will be E–T–n.

    Repeating the handle-finding process on this new form we obtain:

    ① E ④ – ⑦ T ⑧   – n

which shows us two things. First, the automaton has identified a new reduce, E–>E–T, from state ⑧, which is correct. The second thing is that by restarting the automaton at the beginning of the sentential form we have done superfluous work: up to state 7, that is, up to the left end of the handle, nothing has changed. We can save work as follows: after a reduction of a handle to X, we look at the new exposed state on the stack and follow the path marked X in the automaton, starting from that state. In our example we have reduced to T, found a ⑦ exposed on the stack and the automaton leads us from there to ⑧ along the path marked T. This type of shift on a non-terminal that has just resulted from a reduction is called a *GOTO-action*. Note that the state exposed after a reduction can never call for a reduction: if it did so, that reduction would already have been performed earlier.

It is convenient to represent the LR(0) automaton by means of table in which the rows correspond to states and the columns to symbols. In the intersection we find what to do with a given symbol in a given state. The LR(0) table for the automaton of Figure 9.21 is given in Figure 9.22. An entry like s3 means "shift the input symbol onto the stack and go to state ③", which is often abbreviated to "shift to 3". The entry e means that an error has been found: the corresponding symbol cannot legally appear in that position. A blank entry will never even be consulted: either the state calls for a reduction or the corresponding symbol will never at all appear in that position, regardless of the form of the input. In state 4, for instance, we will never meet an E: the E would have originated from a previous reduction, but no reduction would do that in that position. Since non-terminals are only put on the stack in legal places no empty entry on a non-terminal will ever be consulted.

	n	–	(	)	#	E	T	reduce by
1	s3	e	s6	e	e	s4	s2	
2								E -> T
3								T -> n
4	e	s7	e	e	s5			
5								S -> E #
6	s3	e	s6	e	e	s9	s2	
7	s3	e	s6	e	e		s8	
8								E -> E – T
9	e	s7	e	s10	e			
10								T -> (E)

Figure 9.22 LR(0) table for the grammar of Figure 9.18

In practice the "reduce by" entries for the reducing states do not directly refer to the rules to be used, but to routines that have built-in knowledge of these rules, that know how many entries to unstack and that perform the semantic actions associated with the recognition of the rule in question. Parts of these routines will be generated by a parser generator.

The table in Figure 9.22 contains much empty space and is also quite repetitious. As grammars get bigger, the parsing tables get larger and they contain progressively more empty space and redundancy. Both can be exploited by data compression techniques and it is not uncommon that a table can be reduced to 15% of its original size by the appropriate compression technique. See, for instance, Al-Hussainin and Stone [LR 1986] and Dencker, Dürre and Heuft [Misc 1984].

The advantages of LR(0) over precedence and bounded-context are clear. Unlike precedence, LR(0) immediately identifies the rule to be used for reduction, and unlike bounded-context, LR(0) bases its conclusions on the entire left context rather than on the last *m* symbols of it. Actually, LR(0) can be seen as a clever implementation of BC(∞,0), i.e., bounded-context with unrestricted left context and zero right context.

9.4.2 LR(0) grammars

By now the reader may have the vague impression that something is wrong. On the one hand we claim that there is no method to make a linear-time parser for an arbitrary grammar; on the other we have demonstrated above a method that seems to work for an arbitrary grammar. A non-deterministic automaton as in Figure 9.19 can certainly be constructed for any grammar, and the subset construction will certainly turn it into a deterministic one, which will definitely not require more than linear time. Voilà, a linear-time parser.

The problem lies in the accepting states of the deterministic automaton. An accepting state may still have an outgoing arrow, say on a symbol +, and if the next symbol is indeed a +, the state calls for both a reduction and for a shift: the automaton is not really deterministic after all. Or an accepting state may be an honest accepting state but call for two different reductions. The first problem is called a *shift/reduce conflict* and the second a *reduce/reduce conflict*. Figure 9.23 shows examples (that derive from a slightly different grammar than in Figure 9.18).

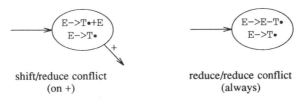

shift/reduce conflict   reduce/reduce conflict
(on +)   (always)

Figure 9.23 Two types of conflict

Note that there cannot be a shift/shift conflict. A shift/shift conflict would imply that two different arrows leaving the same state would carry the same symbol. This is, how-ever, prevented by the subset algorithm (which would have made into one the two states the arrows point to).

A state that contains a conflict is called an *inadequate state*. A grammar that leads to a deterministic LR(0) automaton with no inadequate states is called *LR(0)*. The grammar of Figure 9.18 is LR(0).

9.5 LR(1)

Our initial enthusiasm about the clever and efficient LR(0) parsing technique will soon be damped considerably when we find out that very few grammars are in fact LR(0). If we augment the grammar of Figure 9.18 by a single non-terminal S' and replace S->E# by S'->S# and S->E to better isolate the end-marker, the grammar ceases to be LR(0). The new grammar is given in Figure 9.24, the non-deterministic automaton in Figure 9.25 and the deterministic one in Figure 9.26.

Apart from the split of state 5 in the old automaton into states 5 and 11, we observe to our dismay that state 4 (marked ✗) is now inadequate, exhibiting a

$$
\begin{array}{llll}
1. & S'_S & -> & S \ \# \\
2. & S & -> & E \\
3. & E & -> & E \ - \ T \\
4. & E & -> & T \\
5. & T & -> & n \\
6. & T & -> & (\ E \ )
\end{array}
$$

Figure 9.24 A non-LR(0) grammar for differences of numbers

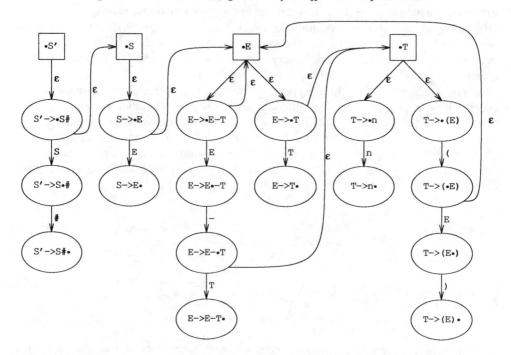

Figure 9.25 Non-deterministic automaton for the grammar in Figure 9.24

shift/reduce conflict on –, and the grammar is not LR(0). We are the more annoyed since this is a rather stupid inadequacy: S->E• can never occur in front of a – but only in front of a #, so there is no real problem at all. If we had developed the parser by hand, we could easily test in state 4 if the symbol ahead was a – or a # and accordingly (or else there was an error in the input). Since, however, practical parsers have hundreds of states, such manual intervention is not acceptable and we have to find algorithmic ways to look at the symbol ahead.

Taking our clue from the the explanation of the Earley parser,[†] we attach to each dotted item a look-ahead symbol, which we shall again write between [ ]'s, to avoid confusion with the rule itself. The construction of a non-deterministic handle-finding automaton using this kind of items, and the subsequent subset construction yield an LR(1) parser.

[†] This is historically incorrect: LR(1) parsing was invented (Knuth [LR 1965]) before Earley parsing (Earley [CF 1970]).

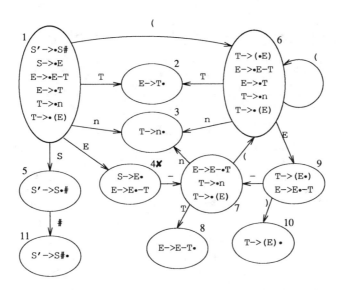

Figure 9.26 Inadequate LR(0) automaton for the grammar in Figure 9.24

We shall now examine Figure 9.27, the non-deterministic automaton. Like the items, the stations have to carry a look-ahead symbol too. Actually, a look-ahead symbol in a station is more natural than that in an item. A station like •E# just means: hoping to see an E followed by a #. The parser starts at station •S′, which has an invisible look-ahead. From it we have ε-moves to all production rules for S′, of which there is only one; this yields the item S′ –>•S#, again with empty look-ahead. This item necessitates the station •S#; we do not automatically construct all possible stations as we did for the LR(0) automaton, but only those to which there are actual moves from elsewhere in the automaton. The station •S# has # for a look-ahead and produces one item, S–>•E #. It is easy to see how the look-ahead propagates. The station •E#, arrived at from the previous item, causes the item E–>•E–T #, which in its turn necessitates the station •E–, since now the automaton can be in the state "hoping to find an E followed by a –". The rest of the automaton will hold no surprises.

The look-ahead derives either from the symbol following the non-terminal:

the item E–>•E–T leads to station •E–

or from the previous look-ahead if the non-terminal is the last symbol in the item:

the item S–>•E # leads to station •E#

There is a complication which does not occur in our example. When a non-terminal is followed by another non-terminal:

$P \rightarrow \bullet QR \ x$

there will be ε-moves from this item to all stations •Q y, where for y we have to fill in all terminals in FIRST(R). This is reasonable since all these and only these symbols

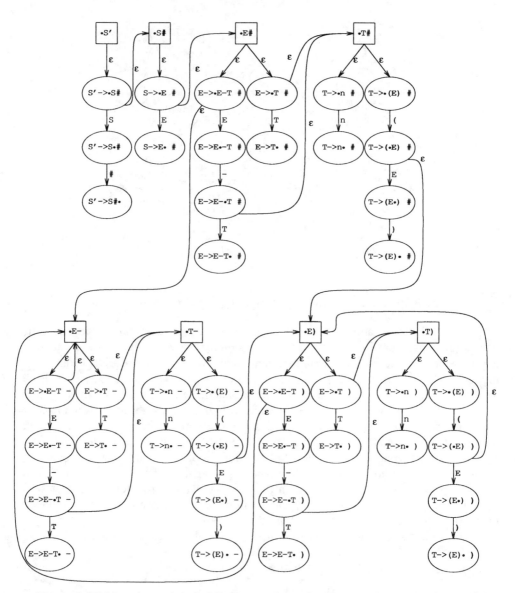

Figure 9.27 Non-deterministic LR(1) automaton for the grammar in Figure 9.24

can follow Q in this particular item. It will be clear that this is a rich source of stations.

The next step is to run the subset algorithm on this automaton to obtain the deterministic automaton; if the automaton has no inadequate states, the grammar was LR(1) and we have obtained an LR(1) parser. The result is given in Figure 9.28. As was to be expected, it contains many more states than the LR(0) automaton although the 60% increase is very modest, due to the simplicity of the grammar. An increase of a factor of 10 or more is more likely in practice. (Although Figure 9.28 was constructed by hand, LR automata are normally created by a parser generator exclusively.)

We are glad but not really surprised to see that the problem of state 4 in Figure

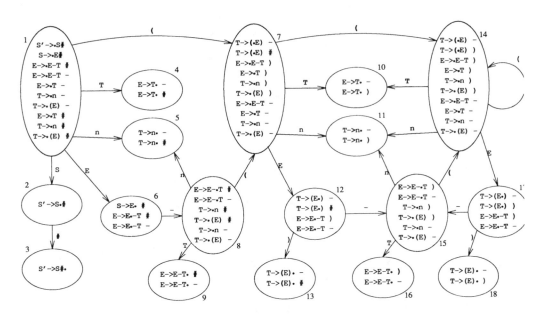

Figure 9.28 Deterministic LR(1) automaton for the grammar in Figure 9.24

9.26, which is now state ⑥ in Figure 9.28, has been resolved: on # reduce using S->E, on – shift to ⑧ and on any other symbol give an error message.

It is again useful to represent the LR(1) automaton in a table, the LR(1) parsing table. Since some reduction rules now occur several times in the table, it is convenient to number the rules, so they can be referred to by number in the table. The table gives for each (state, symbol) pair whether:

☐   to shift the symbol onto the stack and go to state N (written sN),
☐   to reduce using rule R, remove the entries corresponding to the right-hand side from the stack and enter the table again with the pair ($state_{new}$, lhs), where $state_{new}$ is the state just uncovered and now on top of the stack and lhs is the left-hand side of R (written rR), or
☐   to announce an error (written e).

Figure 9.29 shows the LR(1) table; the blank entries can never be accessed.

The sentential form E–n–n leads to the following stack:

① E ⑥ – ⑧ n ⑤   – n

and since the look-ahead is –, the correct reduction T->n is indicated.

Note that if the sentential form had been E–nn, the LR(1) parser would find an error:

① E ⑥ – ⑧ n ⑤   n

since the pair (5, n) yields e. It is instructive to see that the LR(0) parser of Figure 9.22 would do the reduction:

	n	−	(	)	#	S	E	T
1	s5	e	s7	e	e	s2	s6	s4
2	e	e	e	e	s3			
3/acc								
4	e	r4	e	e	r4			
5	e	r5	e	e	r5			
6	e	s8	e	e	r2			
7	s11	e	s14	e	e		s12	s10
8	s5	e	s7	e	e			s9
9	e	r3	e	e	r3			
10	e	r4	e	r4	e			
11	e	r5	e	r5	e			
12	e	s15	e	s13	e			
13	e	r6	e	e	r6			
14	s11	e	s14	e	e		s17	s10
15	s11	e	s14	e	e			s16
16	e	r3	e	r3	e			
17	e	s15	e	s18	e			
18	e	r6	e	r6	e			

Figure 9.29 LR(1) table for the grammar of Figure 9.24

① E ④ – ⑦ n ③   n

since state 3 is an accepting state. Even a second reduction would follow:

① E ④ – ⑦ T ⑧   n

which through E->E−T yields

① E ④   n

Only now is the error found, since the pair (4, n) in Figure 9.22 yields e. Not surprisingly, the LR(0) automaton is less alert than the LR(1) automaton.

All stages of the LR(1) parsing of the string n−n−n are given in Figure 9.30. Note that state ⑥ in h causes a shift (look-ahead −) while in l it causes a reduce 2 (look-ahead #).

9.5.1 LR(1) with ε-rules
In Section 3.3.2 we have seen that one has to be careful with ε-rules in bottom-up parsers: they are hard to recognize bottom-up. Fortunately LR(1) parsers are strong enough to handle them without problems. In the non-deterministic automaton, an ε-rule is nothing special; it is just an exceptionally short list of moves starting from a station (see station •Bc in Figure 9.32(*a*). In the deterministic automaton, the ε-reduction is possible in all states of which the ε-rule is a member, but hopefully its look-ahead sets it apart from all other rules in those states. Otherwise a shift/reduce or reduce/reduce conflict results, and indeed the presence of ε-rules in a grammar raises

a	①	n–n–n#	shift
b	① n ⑤	–n–n#	reduce 5
c	① T ④	–n–n#	reduce 4
d	① E ⑥	–n–n#	shift
e	① E ⑥ – ⑧	n–n#	shift
f	① E ⑥ – ⑧ n ⑤	–n#	reduce 5
g	① E ⑥ – ⑧ T ⑨	–n#	reduce 3
h	① E ⑥	–n#	shift
i	① E ⑥ – ⑧	n#	shift
j	① E ⑥ – ⑧ n ⑤	#	reduce 5
k	① E ⑥ – ⑧ T ⑨	#	reduce 3
l	① E ⑥	#	reduce 2
m	① S ②	#	shift
n	① S ② # ③		reduce 1
o	① S′ ③		accept

Figure 9.30 LR(1) parsing of the string n–n–n

the risks of such conflicts and reduces the likelihood of the grammar to be LR(1).

$$
\begin{array}{lll}
S' & -> & S \; \# \\
S & -> & A \; B \; c \\
A & -> & a \\
B & -> & b \\
B & -> & \varepsilon
\end{array}
$$

Figure 9.31 A simple grammar with an ε-rule

To avoid page-filling drawings, we demonstrate the effect using the trivial grammar of Figure 9.31. Figure 9.32(*a*) shows the non-deterministic automaton, Figure 9.32(*b*) the resulting deterministic one. Note that no special actions were necessary to handle the rule B–>ε.

The only complication occurs again in determining the look-ahead sets in rules in which a non-terminal is followed by another non-terminal; here we meet the same phenomenon as in an LL(1) parser (Section 8.2.2.1). Given an item, for instance, $P \rightarrow \bullet ABC$ [*d*], we are required to produce the look-ahead set for the station •*A* [· · ·]. If *B* had been a terminal, it would have been the look-ahead. Now we take the FIRST set of *B*, and if *B* produces ε (is nullable) we add the FIRST set of *C* since *B* can be transparent and allow us to see the first token of *C*. If *C* is also nullable, we may even see [*d*], so in that case we also add *d* to the look-ahead set. The result of these operations is written as FIRST(*BC* [*d*]) (which is, in fact, equal to FIRST(*BCd*)).

9.5.2 Some properties of LR(*k*) parsing

Instead of a look-ahead of one token, *k* tokens can be used. It is not difficult to do so but it is extremely tedious and the resulting tables assume gargantuan size (see, e.g., Ukkonen [LR 1985]). Moreover it does not really help much. Although an LR(2) parser is more powerful than an LR(1) parser, in that it can handle some grammars that

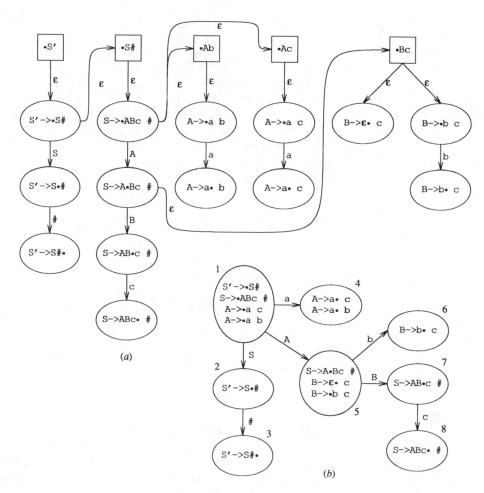

Figure 9.32 Non-deterministic and deterministic LR(1) automata for Figure 9.31

the other cannot, the emphasis is on "some". If a common-or-garden variety grammar is not LR(1), chances are minimal that it is LR(2) or higher.

Some theoretically interesting properties of varying practical significance are briefly mentioned here. It can be proved that any LR(k) grammar with $k>1$ can be transformed into an LR($k-1$) grammar (and so to LR(1), but not always to LR(0)), often at the expense of an enormous increase in size; see, e.g. Mickunas, Lancaster and Schneider [LR 1976]. It can be proved that if a language allows parsing with a push-down automaton as described in Section 3.4, it has an LR(1) grammar; such languages are called *deterministic languages*. It can be proved that if a grammar can be handled by any of the deterministic methods of Chapters 8 and 9 (except the non-canonical methods of 9.9), it can be handled by an LR(k) parser (that is, all deterministic methods are weaker than or equally strong as LR(k)).

An LR(1) parser has the *immediate error detection property*: the parser will stop at the first incorrect token in the input and not even perform another shift or reduce. This is important because this early error detection property allows a maximum amount of context to be preserved for error recovery; see Section 10.2.6.

In summary, LR(k) parsers are the strongest deterministic parsers possible and they are the strongest linear-time parsers known (with the possible exception of some non-canonical parsers; see Section 9.9). They react to errors immediately, are paragons of virtue and beyond compare. They are also not widely used.

9.6 LALR(1) PARSING

The reader will have sensed that our journey has not yet come to an end; the goal of a practical, powerful, linear-time parser has still not be attained. Even at their inception by Knuth in 1965 [LR 1965], it was realized that LR(1) parsers would be impractical in that the space required for their deterministic automata would be prohibitive. A modest grammar might already require hundreds of thousands or even millions of states, numbers that were totally incompatible with the computer memories of those days and that would even tax present-day memories.

In the face of this difficulty, development of this line of parsers came to a standstill, partially interrupted by Korenjak's invention of a method to partition the grammar, build LR(1) parsers for each of the parts and combine these into a single over-all parser (Korenjak [LR 1969]). This helped, but not much, in view of the added complexity.

The problem was finally solved by using an unlikely and discouraging-looking method. Consider the LR(1) automaton in Figure 9.28 and imagine boldly discarding all look-ahead information from it. Then we see that each state in the LR(1) automaton reverts to a specific state in the LR(0) automaton; for instance, LR(1) states 7 and 14 collapse into LR(0) state 6 and LR(1) states 4 and 10 collapse into LR(0) state 3. There is not a single state in the LR(1) automaton that was not already present in a rudimentary form in the LR(0) automaton. Also, the transitions remain intact during the collapse: both LR(1) states 7 and 14 have a transition to state 10 on T, but so has LR(0) state 6 to 3. By striking out the look-ahead information from an LR(1) automaton, it collapses into an LR(0) automaton for the same grammar, with a great gain as to memory requirements but also at the expense of the look-ahead power. This will probably not surprise the reader too much, although a formal proof of this phenomenon is not trivial.

The idea is now to collapse the automaton but to keep the look-ahead information (and collapse it too, but not discard it). The surprising fact is that this preserves almost all the original look-ahead power (and still saves an enormous amount of memory). The resulting automaton is called an *LALR(1) automaton*, for "Look Ahead LR[(0)] with a look-ahead of 1 token." *LALR(k)* also exists and is LR(0) with an add-on look-ahead of k tokens.

The LALR(1) automaton for our grammar of Figure 9.24 is given in Figure 9.33, where the look-aheads are sets now and are shown between [and]. We see that the original conflict in state 4 is indeed still resolved, as it was in the LR(1) automaton, but that its size is equal to that of the LR(0) automaton. That now is a very fortunate state of affairs!

We have finally reached our goal. LALR(1) parsers are powerful, almost as powerful as LR(1) parsers, they have fairly modest memory requirements, only slightly inferior to (= larger than) those of LR(0) parsers,[†] and they are time-efficient. LALR(1)

[†] Since the LALR(1) tables contain more information than the LR(0) tables (although they have the same size), they lend themselves less well to data compression. So practical LALR(1)

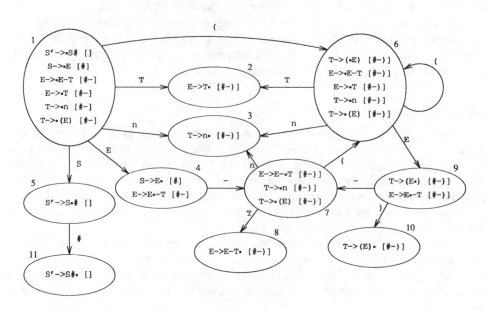

Figure 9.33 The LALR(1) automaton for the grammar of Figure 9.24

parsing may very well be the most-used parsing method in the world today.

9.6.1 Constructing the LALR(1) parsing tables

When we have sufficiently drunk in the beauty of the vista that spreads before us on these heights, and start thinking about returning home and actually building such a parser, it will come to us that there is a small but annoying problem left. We have understood how the desired parser should look and also seen how to construct it, but during that construction we used the unacceptably large LR(1) parser as an intermediate step.

So the problem is to find a shortcut by which we can produce the LALR(1) parse table without having to construct the one for LR(1). This particular problem has fascinated scores of computer scientists to this day (see the references in 13.6, for instance, Park and Choe [LR 1987]), and several good (and some very clever) algorithms are known.

We shall treat here only one algorithm, one that is both intuitively relatively clear and reasonably efficient. It was (probably) first described in rather vague terms by Anderson, Eve and Horning [LR 1973], it is used in the well-known parser generator *yacc* (Johnson [LR 1978]) and is described in more detail by Aho, Sethi and Ullman [Books 1986]. The algorithm does not seem to have a name; we shall call it the *channel algorithm* here.

We again use the grammar of Figure 9.24, which we now know is LALR(1) (but not LR(0)). Since we want to do look-ahead but do not yet know what to look for, we use LR(0) items extended with a yet unknown look-ahead field, indicated by an empty

---

parsers will be bigger than LR(0) parsers.

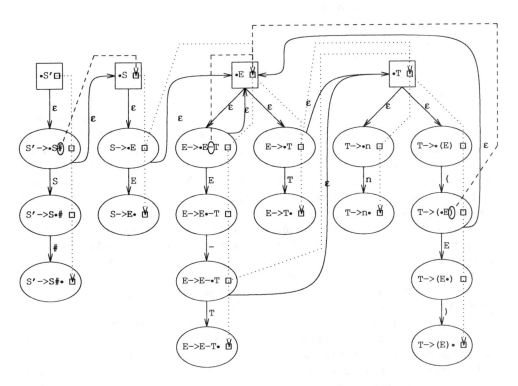

Figure 9.34 Non-deterministic automaton with channels

square; a possible item would be A–>bC•De □. Using such items, we construct the non-deterministic LR(0) automaton in the usual fashion; see Figure 9.34. Now suppose that we were told by some oracle what the look-ahead set of the item S–>•E □ is (second column, second row in Figure 9.34); call this look-ahead set *L*. Then we could draw a number of conclusions. The first is that the item S–>E• □ also has *L*. The next is that the look-ahead set of the station •E□ is also *L*, and from there *L* spreads to E–>•E–T, E–>E•–T, E–>E–•T, E–>E–T•, E–>•T and E–>T•. From E–>E–•T and E–>•T it flows to the station •T and from there it again spreads on.

The flow possibilities of look-ahead information from item to item once it is known constitute "channels" which connect items. Each channel connects two items and is one-directional. There are two kinds of channels. From each station channels run down to each item that derives from it; the input to these channels comes from elsewhere. From each item that has the dot in front of a non-terminal *A*, a channel runs parallel to the ε-arrow to the station •A□. If *A* is the last symbol in the right-hand side, the channel propagates the look-ahead of the item it starts from. If *A* is not the last symbol, but is followed by, for instance, *CDe* (so the entire item would be something like *P→B•ACDe* □), the input to the channel is FIRST(*CDe*); such input is said to be "generated spontaneously", as opposed to "propagated" input. The full set of channels has been drawn as dotted lines (carrying propagated input) and as dashed lines (carrying spontaneous input) in Figure 9.34. It can be represented in a computer as a list of input and output ends of channels:

Input end	leads to	output end
•S'□	==>	S'->•S# □
S'->•S# □	==>	S'->S•# □
[#]	==>	•S□
S'->S•# □	==>	S'->S#• □

· · ·

Next we run the subset algorithm on this (channelled) non-deterministic automaton in slow motion and watch carefully where the channels go. This procedure severely taxes the human brain; a more practical way is to just construct the deterministic automaton without concern for channels and then use the above list (in its complete form) to re-establish the channels. This is easily done by finding the input and output end items and stations in the states of the deterministic automaton and construct the corresponding channels. Note that a single channel in the non-deterministic automaton can occur many times in the deterministic automaton, since items can (and will) be duplicated by the subset algorithm. The result can best be likened to a bowl of mixed spaghetti and tagliatelli (the channels and the transitions) with occasional chunks of ham (the item sets) and will not be printed in this book.

Now we are close to home. For each channel we pump its input to the channel's end. First this will only have effect for channels that have spontaneous input: a # will flow in state 1 from item S'->•S# [□] to station •S [□], which will then read •S [#]; a − from E->•E−T [□] flows to the •E [□], which changes to •E [−]; etc. etc. We go on pumping until all look-ahead sets are stable and nothing changes any more. We have now obtained the LALR(1) automaton and can discard the channels (although we must, of course, keep the transitions).

It is interesting to look more closely at state 4 (see Figure 9.33) and to see how S->E• [#] gets its look-ahead which *excludes* the −, although the latter is present in the look-ahead set of E->E•−T [#−] in state 4. To this end, a magnified view of the top left corner of the full channelled LALR(1) automaton is presented in Figure 9.35; it comprises the states 1 to 4. Again channels with propagated input are dotted, those with spontaneous input are dashed and transitions are drawn. We can now see more clearly that S->E• [#] derives its look-ahead from S->•E [#] in 1, while E->E•−T [#−] derives its look-ahead (indirectly) from •E [−] in 1. The latter has a look-ahead − generated spontaneously in E->•E−T [□] in 1. The channel from S->•E [#] to •E [#−] only works "downstream", which prevents the − from flowing back. LALR(1) parsers often give one the feeling that they succeed by a narrow margin!

9.6.2 LALR(1) with ε-rules

The same complications arise as in Section 9.5.1 in the determination of the FIRST set of the rest of the right-hand side: when a non-terminal is nullable we have to also include the FIRST set of what comes after it, and so on. We meet a special complication if the entire rest of the right-hand side can be empty: then we may see the look-ahead □, which we do not know yet. In fact this creates a third kind of channel that has to be watched in the subset algorithm. We shall not be so hypocritical as to suggest the construction of the LALR(1) automaton for the grammar of Figure 9.31 as an exercise to the reader, but we hope the general principles are clear. Let a parser generator do the rest.

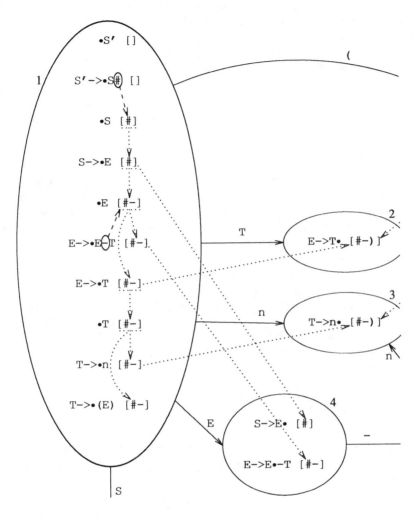

Figure 9.35 Part of the deterministic automaton with channels (magnified cut)

9.6.3 Identifying LALR(1) conflicts

When a grammar is not LR(1), the constructed LR(1) automaton will have conflicts, and the user of the parser generator will have to be notified. Such notification often takes such forms as:

    Reduce/reduce conflict
    in state 213 on look-ahead #
        S -> E versus A -> T + E

This may seem cryptic but the user soon learns to interpret such messages and to reach the conclusion that indeed "the computer can't see this". This is because LR(1) parsers can handle all deterministic grammars and our idea of "what a computer can see" coincides reasonably well with what is deterministic.

The situation is worse for those (relatively rare) grammars that are LR(1) but not LALR(1). The user never really understands what is wrong with the grammar: the computer should be able to make the right parsing decisions, but it complains that it cannot. Of course there is nothing wrong with the grammar; the LALR(1) method is just marginally too weak to handle it.

To alleviate the problem, some research has gone into methods to elicit from the faulty automaton a possible input string that would bring it into the conflict state. See DeRemer and Pennello [LR 1982]. The parser generator can then display such input with both its possible parse trees.

9.6.4 SLR(1)

There is a simpler way to proceed with the non-deterministic automaton of Figure 9.34. We can first pump around the look-ahead sets until they are all known and then apply the subset algorithm, rather than vice versa. This gives us the *SLR(1)* automaton (for Simple LR(1)); see DeRemer [LR 1971]. The same automaton can be obtained without using channels at all: construct the LR(0) automaton and then add to each item $A \rightarrow \cdots$ a look-ahead set that is equal to FOLLOW(A). Pumping around the look-ahead sets in the non-deterministic automaton effectively calculates the FOLLOW sets of each non-terminal and spreads these over each item derived from it.

The SLR(1) automaton is shown in Figure 9.36. FOLLOW(S)={#}, FOLLOW(E)={#, −,) } and FOLLOW(T)={#, −,) }; consequently, only states 1 and 4 differ from those in the LALR(1) automaton of Figure 9.33. The increased look-ahead sets do not spoil the adequateness of all states: the grammar is also SLR(1).

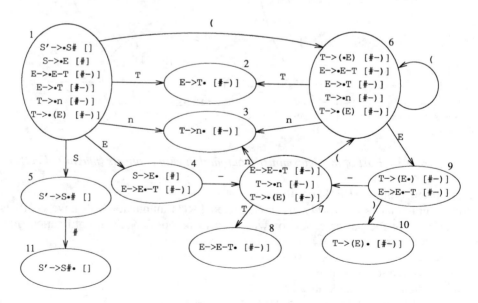

Figure 9.36 SLR(1) automaton for the grammar of Figure 9.24

SLR(1) parsers are intermediate in power between LR(0) and LALR(1). Since

SLR(1) parsers have the same size as LALR(1) parsers, are considerably less powerful and are only marginally easier to construct, LALR(1) parsers are generally preferred.

9.6.5 Conflict resolvers

When states in an automaton have conflicts and no stronger method is available, the automaton can still be useful, provided we can find other ways to resolve the conflicts. Most LR parser generators have built-in automatic conflict resolvers that will make sure that a deterministic automaton results, whatever properties the input grammar may have. Such a system will just enumerate the problems it has encountered and indicate how it has solved them.

Two useful and popular rules of thumb to solve LR conflicts are:

☐   on a shift/reduce conflict, shift (only on those look-aheads for which the conflict occurs);
☐   on a reduce/reduce conflict, reduce using the longest rule.

Both rules implement the same idea: take the largest bite possible. If you find that there is a production of A somewhere, make it as long as possible, including as much material on both sides as possible. This is very often what the grammar writer wants.

Systems with built-in conflict resolvers are a mixed blessing. On the one hand they allow very weak or even ambiguous grammars to be used (see for instance, Aho, Johnson and Ullman [Misc 1975]). This can be a great help in formulating grammars for difficult and complex analysis jobs; see, for instance, Kernighan and Cherry [Misc 1975], who make profitable use of automatic conflict resolution for the specification of typesetter input.

On the other hand a system with conflict resolvers may impose a structure on the input where there is none. Such a system does no longer correspond to any grammar-like sentence-generating mechanism, and it may be very difficult to specify exactly what strings will be accepted and with what structure. How severe a drawback this is depends on the application and of course on the capabilities of the parser generator user.

Note that it is not humanly possible to have dynamic (parse-time) conflict-resolvers as in the LL case (Section 8.2.5.3). The conflict-resolver would be called upon in a context that is still under construction, and its user would be required to fully understand the underlying LR automaton. Some experiments have been done with interactive conflict resolvers, which consult the user of the parser when a conflict actually arises: a large chunk of text around the conflict point is displayed and the user is asked to resolve the conflict. This is useful in, for instance, document conversion. See Share [Misc 1988].

9.7 FURTHER DEVELOPMENTS OF LR METHODS

Although the LALR(1) method as explained in Section 9.6 is quite satisfactory for most applications, a number of extensions to and improvements of the LR methods have been studied. The most important of these will be briefly explained in this section; for details see the literature, Section 13.6 and the original references. Most of the more advanced methods have not yet found their way into existing parser generators.

9.7.1 Elimination of unit rules

Many rules in practical grammars are of the form $A \rightarrow B$; examples can be found in Figures 2.9, 4.4, 5.2, 7.8, 8.7, 9.37 and many others. Such rules are called *unit rules*, *single rules* or *chain rules*. They generally serve naming purposes only and have no semantics attached to them. Consequently, their reduction is a matter of stack manipulation and state transition only, to no visible purpose for the user. Such "administrative reductions" can take a considerable part of the parsing time (50% is not unusual). Simple methods to short-cut such reductions are easily found (for instance, removal by systematic substitution) but may result in an exponential increase in table size. Better methods were found but turned out to be complicated and to impair the error detection properties of the parser. The latter can again be corrected, at the expense of more complication. See Heilbrunner [LR 1985] for a thorough treatment and Chapman [LR 1987] for much practical information.

Note that the term "elimination of unit rules" in this case is actually a misnomer: the unit rules themselves are not removed from the grammar, but rather their effect from the parser tables. Compare this to the actual elimination of unit rules in Section 4.2.3.2.

```
Metre    ->    Iambic | Trochaic | Dactylic | Anapestic
```

Figure 9.37 A (multiple) unit rule

9.7.2 Regular right part grammars

As shown in Section 2.3.2.3, there are two interpretations of a regular right-hand side of a rule: the recursive and the iterative interpretation. The recursive interpretation is no problem: for a form like A^+ anonymous non-terminals are introduced, the reduction of which entails no semantic actions. The burden of constructing a list of the recognized A's lies entirely on the semantic routines attached to the A's.

The iterative interpretation causes more problems. When an A^+ has been recognized and is about to be reduced, the stack holds an indeterminate number of A's:

```
... A···AAA|
```

The right end of the handle has been found, but the left end is doubtful. Scooping up all A's from the right may be incorrect since some may belong to another rule; after all, the top of the stack may derive from a rule $P \rightarrow QAAA^+$. A possible solution is to have for each reducing state and look-ahead a FS automaton that scans the stack backwards while examining states in the stack to determine the left end and the actual rule to reduce to. The part to be reduced (the handle) can then be shown to a semantic routine which can, for instance, construct a list of A's, thereby relieving the A's from a task that is not structurally theirs. The resulting tables can be enormous and clever algorithms have been designed for their construction and reduction. See for instance, LaLonde [LR 1981]. Sassa and Nakata [LR 1987] provide a different and simpler technique.

9.7.3 Improved LALR(1) table construction

The channel algorithm for the construction of LALR(1) parse tables explained in Section 9.6.1 is relatively fast as it is, but the underlying automata have a rich structure and many other algorithms are known for this problem. There exist simple and complicated variants and improvements, gaining factors of 5 or 10 over the simple channel algorithm. See for instance, DeRemer and Pennello [LR 1982] and the Park, Choe and Chang [LR 1985, 1987] versus Ives [LR 1986, 1987] discussion. Bermudez and Logothetis [LR 1989] present a remarkably elegant interpretation of LALR(1) parsing.

9.7.4 Incremental parsing
In incremental parsing, the structured input (a program text, a structured document, etc.) is kept in linear form together with a parse tree. When the input is (incrementally) modified by the user, for instance, by typing or deleting a character, it is the task of the incremental parser to update the corresponding parse tree, preferably at minimum cost. This requires serious measures inside the parser, to quickly determine the extent of the damage done to the parse tree, localize its effect and take remedial steps. Formal requirements for the grammar to make this easier have been found. See for instance, Degano, Mannucci and Mojana [LR 1988] and many others in Section 13.6.

9.7.5 Incremental parser generation
In incremental parser generation, the parser generator keeps the grammar together with its parsing table(s) and has to respond quickly to user-made changes in the grammar, by updating and checking the tables. Research on this is in its infancy. See Heering, Klint and Rekers [LR 1989] and Horspool [LR 1989].

9.7.6 LR-regular
Rather than trying to resolve inadequate states by looking ahead a fixed number of tokens, we can have an FS automaton for each inadequate state that is sent off up the input stream; the state in which this automaton stops is used as a look-ahead. This parsing technique is called *LR-regular*. See Čulik and Cohen [LR 1973].

A variant of this method reads in the entire input into an array and runs a single FS automaton (derived from the grammar) backwards over the array, recording the state of the automaton with each token. Next, during (forward) LR parsing, these recorded states rather than the tokens are used as look-aheads.

9.7.7 Recursive ascent
In Sections 8.2.6 and 8.4 we have seen that an LL parser can be implemented conveniently using recursive descent. Analogously, an LR parser can be implemented using *recursive ascent*, but the required technique is not nearly as obvious as in the LL case. The key idea is to have the recursion stack mimic the LR parsing stack. To this end there is a procedure for each state; when a token is to be shifted to the stack, the procedure corresponding to the resulting state is called instead. This indeed constructs the correct recursion stack, but causes problems when a reduction has to take place: a dynamically determined number of procedures has to return in order to unstack the right-hand side. A simple technique to achieve this is to have two global variables, one, Nt, holding the non-terminal recognized and the second, l, holding the length of the right-hand side. All procedures will check l and if it is non-zero, they will decrease l by one and return immediately. Once l is zero, the procedure that finds that situation will call the appropriate state procedure based on Nt. For details see Roberts [LR 1988, 1989, 1990] and Kruseman Aretz [LR 1988]. The advantage of recursive ascent over table-driven is its potential for high-speed parsing.

9.8 TOMITA'S PARSER

Now that we have seen the precise criteria for the existence of an LR-like parser for a grammar, i.e., that there is a handle-recognizing finite-state automaton with no inadequate states for that grammar, we become interested in the grammars for which the criteria are not completely fulfilled and for which the automaton has some inadequate states. Tomita [CF 1986] has given an efficient and very effective approach to such grammars.

Tomita's method can be summarized as doing breadth-first search as in Section 7.1.2 over those parsing decisions that are not solved by the LR automaton (which can be LR(1), LALR(1), SLR(1), LR(0), precedence or even simpler), while at the same time keeping the partial parse trees in a form akin to the common representation of Section 7.1.3. More precisely, whenever an inadequate state is encountered on the top of the stack, the following steps are taken:

1.   For each possible reduce in the state, a copy of the stack is made and the reduce is applied to it. This removes part of the right end of the stack and replaces it with a non-terminal; using this non-terminal as a move in the automaton, we find a new state to put on the top of the stack. If this state allows again reductions, this copy step is repeated until all reduces have been treated, resulting in equally many stack copies.

2.   Stacks that have a right-most state that does not allow a shift on the next input token are discarded (since they resulted from incorrect guesses). Copies of the next input token are shifted onto the remaining stacks.

There are a number of things to be noted here. First, if the automaton uses look-ahead, this is of course taken into account in deciding which reduces are possible in step 1 (ignoring this information would not be incorrect but would cause more stacks to be copied and subsequently discarded). Second, the process in step 1 may not terminate. If a grammar has loops (rules of the form $A \to B$, $B \to A$) reduction will alternate between A and B. There are two solutions: upon creating a stack, check if it is already there (and then ignore it) or check the grammar in advance for loops (and then reject it). Third, if all stacks are discarded in step 2 the input was in error, at that specific point.

$$
\begin{array}{lll}
S_S & \to & E\ \# \\
E & \to & E + E \\
E & \to & d
\end{array}
$$

Figure 9.38 A moderately ambiguous grammar

The above forms the basic mechanism of the Tomita parser. Since simple stack duplication may cause a proliferation of stacks and is apt to duplicate much information that is not in need of duplication, two optimizations are used in the practical form of the parser: combining equal states and combining equal stack prefixes. We shall demonstrate all three techniques using the grammar of Figure 9.38 as an example. The grammar is a variant of that of Figure 3.1 and is moderately ambiguous. Its LR(0) automaton is shown in Figure 9.39; it has one inadequate state, ⑤. Since the grammar is ambiguous, there is not much point in using a stronger LR method. For more (and larger!) examples see Tomita [CF 1986].

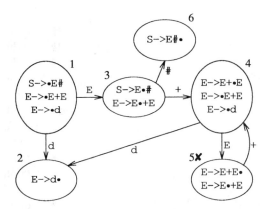

Figure 9.39 LR(0) automaton to the grammar of Figure 9.38

9.8.1 Stack duplication

Refer to Figure 9.40, in which we assume the input d+d+d#. The automaton starts in state ① (*a*). The steps shift (*b*), reduce, shift, shift (*c*) and reduce (*d*) are problem-free and bring us to state ⑤. The last state, however, is inadequate, allowing a reduce and a shift. True to the breadth-first search method and in accordance with step 1 above, the stack is now duplicated and the top of one of the copies is reduced (*e1*) while the other one is left available for a subsequent shift (*e2*). Note that no further reduction is possible and that both stacks now have a different top state. Both states allow a shift and then another (*f1, f2*) and then a reduce (*g1, g2*). Now both stacks carry an inadequate state on top and need to be duplicated, after which operation one of the copies undergoes a reduction (*h1.1, h1.2, h2.1, h2.2*). It now turns out that the stack in *h2.1* again features an inadequate state ⑤ after the reduction; it will again have to be duplicated and have one copy reduced. This gives the stack in *h2.1a*. Now all possible reductions have been done and it is time for a shift again. Only state ③ allows a shift on #, so the other stacks are discarded and we are left with *i1.1* and *i2.1a*. Both require a reduction, yielding *j1.1* and *j2.1a*, which are accepting states. The parser stops and has found two parsings.

In order to save space and to avoid cluttering up the pictures, we have not shown the partial parse trees that resulted from the various reductions that have taken place. If we had done so, we would have found the two S's in *j.1.1* and *j.2.1a* holding the parse trees of Figure 9.41.

9.8.2 Combining equal states

Examining Figure 9.40 *f* and *g*, we see that once both stacks have the same state on top, further actions on both stacks will be identical, and the idea suggests itself to combine the two stacks to avoid duplicate work. This approach is depicted in Figure 9.42(*f*) and (*g*) (Figure 9.42(*a*) to (*e*) are identical to those of Figure 9.40 and are not shown). That this is, however, not entirely without problems becomes evident as soon as we need to do a reduce that spans the merge point. This happens in (*g*), which also features an inadequate state. Now a number of things happen. First, since the state is inadequate, the whole set of combined stacks connected to it are duplicated. One copy (*h3*) is left for the shift, the other is subjected to the reduce. This reduce, however, spans the merge

	stack configuration	input	action
a	①	d+d+d#	shift
b	① d ②	+d+d#	reduce, shift, shift
c	① E ③ + ④ d ②	+d#	reduce
d	① E ③ + ④ E ⑤	+d#	duplicate to *e1* and *e2*; reduce *e1*
e1	① E ③	+d#	shift, shift, to *f1*
e2	① E ③ + ④ E ⑤	+d#	shift, shift, to *f2*
f1	① E ③ + ④ d ②	#	reduce to *g1*
f2	① E ③ + ④ E ⑤ + ④ d ②	#	reduce to *g2*
g1	① E ③ + ④ E ⑤	#	duplicate to *h1.1* and *h1.2*; reduce *h1.1*
g2	① E ③ + ④ E ⑤ + ④ E ⑤	#	duplicate to *h2.1* and *h2.2*; reduce *h2.1*
h1.1	① E ③	#	shift to *i1.1*
h1.2	① E ③ + ④ E ⑤	#	discard
h2.1	① E ③ + ④ E ⑤	#	reduce again, to *h2.1a*
h2.2	① E ③ + ④ E ⑤ + ④ E ⑤	#	discard
h2.1a	① E ③	#	shift to *i2.1a*
i1.1	① E ③ # ⑥		reduce to *j1.1*
i2.1a	① E ③ # ⑥		reduce to *j2.1a*
j1.1	① S		accept
j2.1a	① S		accept

Figure 9.40 Sequence of stack configurations while parsing d+d+d#

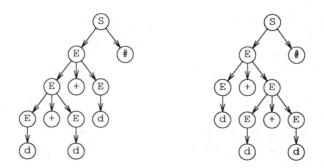

Figure 9.41 Parse trees in the accepting states of Figure 9.40

point (state ④) and extends up both stacks, comprising a different left-most E in both branches. To perform it properly, the stack combination is undone and the reduce is applied to both stacks (*h1*, *h2*). The reduce in (*h2*) results again in state ⑤, which necessitates another copy operation (*h2.1*, *h2.2*) and a reduce on one of the copies (*h2.1*).

Now the smoke has cleared and we have obtained five stacks (*h1*, *h2.1*, *h2.2* and a double *h3*) having four tops, two of which (*h1* and *h2.1*) carry the state ③, while the other two (*h2.2* and *h3*) carry a ⑤. These can be combined into two bundles (*h'* and *h"*). Next the shift of # obliterates all stacks with top state ⑤ (*i*). State ⑥, which is now on

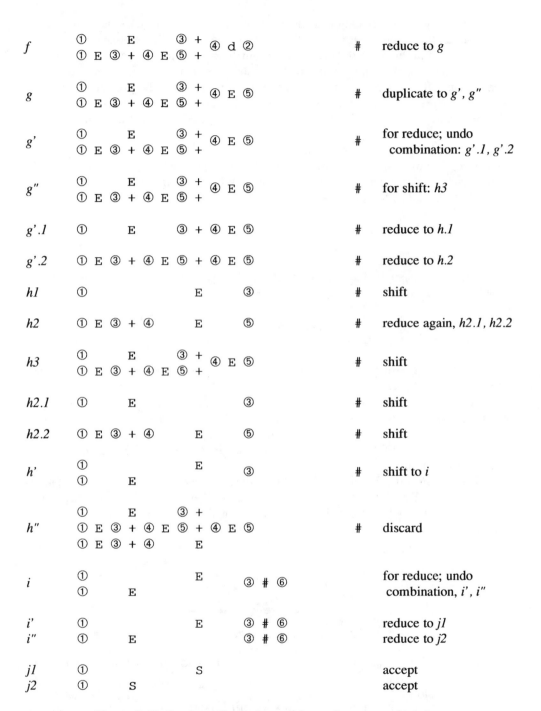

Figure 9.42 Stack configurations with equal-state combination

top, induces a reduce spanning a merge point, the combined stack is split and the reduce is applied to both stacks, resulting in the two parsings for d+d+d# ($j1$, $j2$).

Although in this example the stack combinations are undone almost as fast as they are performed, stack combination greatly contributes to the parsers efficiency in the general case. It is essential in preventing exponential growth wherever possible. Note, however, that, even though the state ⑤ in i is preceded by E in all branches, we cannot combine these E's since they differ in the partial parse trees attached to them.

9.8.3 Combining equal stack prefixes

When step 1 above calls for the stack to be copied, there is actually no need to copy the entire stack; just copying the top states suffices. When we duplicate the stack of Figure 9.40(d), we have one forked stack for (e):

e' ① E ③ + ④ E $\overset{⑤}{\underset{⑤}{}}$ +d#

Now the reduce is applied to one top state ⑤ and only so much of the stack is copied as is subject to the reduce:

e ①   E   ③   +d#   shift

           E ③ + ④ E ⑤   shift

In our example almost the entire stack gets copied, but if the stack is somewhat larger, considerable savings can result.

Note that the title of this section is in fact incorrect: in practice no equal stack prefixes are combined, they are never created in the first place. The pseudo-need for combination arises from our wish to explain first the simpler but impractical form of the algorithm in Section 9.8. A better name for the technique would be "common stack prefix preservation".

Both optimizations can combine to produce shuntyard-like stack constellations like the one in Figure 9.43; here Tomita's notation is used, in which ● represents a state and ■ a symbol. The reader may verify that the constellation represents seven stacks.

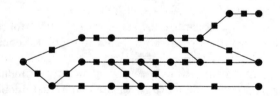

Figure 9.43 Stack constellation with combined heads and tails, in Tomita's notation

9.8.4 Discussion

We have explained Tomita's parser using an LR(0) table; in his book Tomita uses an SLR(1) table. In fact the method will work with any bottom-up table or even with no table at all. The weaker the table, the more non-determinism will have to be resolved by breadth-first search, and for the weakest of all tables, the absent table, the method degenerates into full breadth-first search. Since the latter is involved in principle in all variants of the method, the time requirements are in theory exponential; in practice they are very modest, generally linear or slightly more than linear and almost always less than those of Earley's parser or of the CYK parser, except for very ambiguous grammars.

9.9 NON-CANONICAL PARSERS

All parsers treated so far in this chapter are "canonical parsers", which means that they identify the productions in reverse right-most order. A "non-canonical parser" identifies the productions in arbitrary order, or rather in an unrestricted order. Removing the restriction on the identification order of the productions makes the parsing method stronger, as can be expected. Realistic examples are too complicated to be shown here (see Tai [LR 1979] for some), but the following example will demonstrate the principle.

$$
\begin{array}{rcl}
S_S & -> & P\ Q\ |\ R\ S \\
P & -> & a \\
Q & -> & b\ c \\
R & -> & a \\
S & -> & b\ d \\
\end{array}
$$

Figure 9.44 A short grammar for non-canonical parsing

The grammar of Figure 9.44 produces two sentences, abc and abd. Suppose the input is abc. The a can be a P or an R; for both, the look-ahead is a b, so an LR(1) parser cannot decide whether to reduce to P or to R and the grammar is not LR(1). Suppose, however, that we leave the undecidable undecided and search on for another reducible part (called a *phrase* in non-canonical parsing to distinguish it from the "handle"). Then we find the tokens bc, which can clearly be reduced to Q. Now, this Q provides the decisive look-ahead for the reduction of the a. Since P can be followed by a Q and R cannot, reduction to P is indicated based on look-ahead Q; the grammar is *NCLR(1)* (Non-Canonical LR(1)). We see that in non-canonical parsers the look-ahead sets contain non-terminals as well as terminals.

There are disadvantages too. After each reduce, one has to rescan possibly large parts of the stack. This may jeopardize the linear time requirement, although with some dexterity the problem can often be avoided. A second problem is that rules are recognized in essentially arbitrary order which makes it difficult to attach semantics to them. A third point is that although non-canonical parsers are more powerful than canonical ones, they are only marginally so: most grammars that are not LR(1) are not NCLR(1) either.

Overall the advantages do not seem to outweigh the disadvantages and non-canonical parsers are not used often. See, however, Salomon and Cormack [LR 1989].

Non-canonical precedence parsing has been described by Colmerauer [Precedence 1970].

9.10 LR(k) AS AN AMBIGUITY TEST

It is often important to be sure that a grammar is not ambiguous, but unfortunately it can be proved that there cannot be an algorithm that can, for every CF grammar, decide whether it is ambiguous or unambiguous. This is comparable to the situation described in 3.5.2, where the fundamental impossibility of a recognizer for Type 0 grammars was discussed. (See Hopcroft and Ullman [Books 1979, p. 200]). The most effective ambiguity test for a CF grammar we have at present is the construction of the corresponding LR(k) automaton, but it is of course not a perfect test: if the construction succeeds, the grammar is guaranteed to be unambiguous; if it fails, in principle nothing is known. In practice, however, the reported conflicts will often point to genuine ambiguities. Theoretically, the construction of an LL-regular parser (see 9.7.6) is an even stronger test, but the choice of the look-ahead automaton is problematic.

10

Error handling

Until now, we have discussed parsing techniques while largely ignoring what happens when the input contains errors. In practice, however, the input often contains errors, the most common being typing errors or misconceptions, but we could also be dealing with a grammar that only roughly, not precisely, describes the input, for instance in pattern matching. So, the question arises how to deal with errors. A considerable amount of research has been done on this subject, far too much to discuss in one chapter. We will therefore limit our discussion to some of the more well-known error handling methods, and not pretend to cover the field; see Section 13.11 for more in-depth information.

10.1 DETECTION VERSUS RECOVERY VERSUS CORRECTION

Usually, the least that is required of a parser is that it detects the occurrence of one or more errors in the input, that is, we require *error detection*. The least informative version of this is that the parser announces: "input contains syntax error(s)". We say that the input contains a *syntax error* when the input is not a sentence of the language described by the grammar. All parsers discussed in the previous chapters (except operator-precedence) are capable of detecting this situation without extensive modification. However, there are few circumstances in which this behaviour is acceptable: when we have just typed a long sentence, or a complete computer program, and the parser only tells us that there is a syntax error somewhere, we will not be pleased at all, not only about the syntax error, but also about the quality of the parser or lack thereof.

The question as to where the error occurs is much more difficult to answer; in fact it is almost impossible. Although some parsers have the *correct-prefix property*, which means that they detect an error at the first symbol in the input that results in a prefix that cannot start a sentence of the language, we cannot be sure that this indeed is the place in which the error occurs. It could very well be that there is an error somewhere before this symbol but that this is not a syntax error at that point. There is a difference in the perception of an error between the parser and the user. In the rest of this chapter, when we talk about errors, we mean syntax errors, as detected by the parser.

So, what happens when input containing errors is offered to a parser with a good error detection capability? The parser might say: "Look, there is a syntax error at position so-and-so in the input, so I give up". For some applications, especially highly interactive ones, this may be satisfactory. For many, though, it is not: often, one would like to know about all syntax errors in the input, not just about the first one. If the parser is to detect further syntax errors in the input, it must be able to continue parsing (or at least recognizing) after the first error. It is probably not good enough to just throw away the offending symbol and continue. Somehow, the internal state of the parser must be adapted so that the parser can process the rest of the input. This adaptation of the internal state is called *error recovery*.

The purpose of error recovery can be summarized as follows:

☐   an attempt must be made to detect all syntax errors in the input;
☐   equally important, an attempt must be made to avoid *spurious* error messages. These are messages about errors that are not real errors in the input, but result from the continuation of the parser after an error with improper adaptation of its internal state.

Usually, a parser with an error recovery method can no longer deliver a parse tree if the input contains errors. This is sometimes the cause of considerable trouble. In the presence of errors, the adaptation of the internal state can cause semantic actions associated with grammar rules to be executed in an order that is impossible for syntactically correct input, which sometimes leads to unexpected results. A simple solution to this problem is to ignore semantic actions as soon as a syntax error is detected, but this is not optimal and may not be acceptable. A better option is the use of a particular kind of error recovery method, an *error correction* method.

Error correction methods transform the input into syntactically correct input, usually by deleting, inserting, or changing symbols. It should be stressed that error correction methods cannot always change the input into the input actually intended by the user, nor do they pretend that they can. Therefore, some authors prefer to call these methods *error repair* methods rather than error correction methods. The main advantage of error correction over other types of error recovery is that the parser still can produce a parse tree and that the semantic actions associated with the grammar rules are executed in an order that could also occur for some syntactically correct input. In fact, the actions only see syntactically correct input, sometimes produced by the user and sometimes by the error corrector.

In summary, error detection, error recovery, and error correction require increasing levels of heuristics. Error detection itself requires no heuristics. A parser detects an error, or it does not. Determining the place where the error occurs may require heuristics, however. Error recovery requires heuristics to adapt the internal parser state so that it can continue, and error correction requires heuristics to repair the input.

10.2 PARSING TECHNIQUES AND ERROR DETECTION

Let us first examine how good the parsing techniques discussed in this book are at detecting an error. We will see that some parsing techniques have the correct-prefix property while other parsing techniques only detect that the input contains an error but give no indication where the error occurs.

10.2.1 Error detection in non-directional parsing methods

In Section 4.1 we saw that Unger's parsing method tries to find a partition of the input sentence that matches one of the right-hand sides of the start symbol. The only thing that we can be sure of in the case of one or more syntax errors is, that we will find no such partition. For example, suppose we have the grammar of Figure 4.1, repeated in Figure 10.1, and input ×+.

$$Expr_S \quad -> \quad Expr + Term \mid Term$$
$$Term \quad -> \quad Term \times Factor \mid Factor$$
$$Factor \quad -> \quad (\ Expr \ ) \mid i$$

Figure 10.1 A grammar describing simple arithmetic expressions

Fitting the first right-hand side of Expr with the input will not work, because the input only has two symbols. We will have to try the second right-hand side of Expr. Likewise, we will have to try the second right-hand side of Term, and then we will find that we cannot find an applicable right-hand side of Factor, because the first one requires at least three symbols, and the second one only one. So, we know that there are one or more errors, but we do not know how many errors there are, nor where they occur. In a way, Unger's method is too well prepared for dealing with failures, because it expects any partition to fail.

For the CYK parser, the situation is similar. We will find that if the input contains errors, the start symbol will not be a member of the top element of the recognition table.

So, the unmodified non-directional methods behave poorly on errors in the input.

10.2.2 Error detection in finite-state automata
Finite-state automata are very good at detecting errors. Consider for instance the deterministic automaton of Figure 5.10, repeated in Figure 10.2.

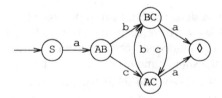

Figure 10.2 Deterministic automaton for the grammar of Figure 5.5

When this automaton is offered the input abcca, it will detect an error when it is in state AC, on the second c in the input.

Finite-state automata have the correct-prefix property. In fact, they have the *immediate error detection property*, which we discussed in Chapter 8 and which means that an error is detected as soon as the erroneous symbol is first examined.

10.2.3 Error detection in general directional top-down parsers
The breadth-first general directional top-down parser also has the correct-prefix property. It stops as soon as there are no predictions left to work with. Predictions are only dropped by failing match steps, and as long as there are predictions, the part of the input parsed so far is a prefix of some sentence of the language.

The depth-first general directional top-down parser does not have this property. It will backtrack until all right-hand sides of the start symbol have failed. However, it can easily be doctored so that it does have the correct-prefix property: the only thing that we must remember is the furthest point in the input that the parser has reached, a kind of high-water mark. The first error is found right after this point.

10.2.4 Error detection in general directional bottom-up parsers
The picture is quite different for the general directional bottom-up parsers. They will just find that they cannot reduce the input to the start symbol. This is only to be expected because, in contrast to the top-down parsers, there is no test before an input symbol is shifted.

As soon as a top-down component is added, such as in Earley's parser, the parser regains the correct-prefix property. For instance, if we use the Earley parser with the grammar from Figure 7.8 and input a→+a, we get the items sets of Figure 10.3 (compare this with Figure 7.11). Itemset$_3$ will be empty, and an error is detected.

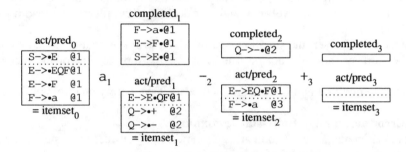

Figure 10.3 Items sets of the Earley parser working on a→+a

10.2.5 Error detection in deterministic top-down parsers
In Sections 8.2.3 and 8.2.4 we have seen that strong-LL(1) parsers have the correct-prefix property but not the immediate error detection property, because in some circumstances they may make some ε-moves before detecting an error, and that full LL(1) parsers have the immediate error detection property.

10.2.6 Error detection in deterministic bottom-up parsers
Let us first examine the error detection capabilities of precedence parsers. We saw in Section 9.2.1 that operator-precedence parsers fail to detect some errors. When they do detect an error, it is because there is no precedence relation between the symbol on top of the parse stack and the next input symbol. This is called a *character-pair error*.

The other precedence parsers (simple, weak, extended, and bounded-context) have three error situations:
□   there is no precedence relation between the symbol on top of the parse stack and the next input symbol (a *character-pair error*).
□   the precedence relations indicate that a handle is found and that a reduction must be applied, but there is no non-terminal with a right-hand side that matches the handle. This is called a *reduction error*.
□   after a reduction has been made, there is no precedence relation between the symbol at the top of the stack (the symbol that was underneath the <) and the left-hand side to be pushed. This is called a *stackability error*.

Reduction errors can be detected at an early stage by continuously checking that the symbols between the last < and the top of the stack form the prefix of some right-hand side. Graham and Rhodes [ErrHandl 1975] show that this can be done quite efficiently.

In Section 9.5.2 we saw that an LR(1) parser has the immediate error detection property. LALR(1) and SLR(1) parsers do not have this property, but they do have the correct prefix property. Error detection in Tomita's parser depends on the underlying parsing technique.

10.3 RECOVERING FROM ERRORS

Error handling methods fall in different classes, depending on what level they approach the error. The general parsers usually apply an error handling method that considers the complete input. These methods use global context, and are therefore called *global error handling* methods. The Unger and CYK parsers need such a method, because they have no idea where the error occurred. These methods are very effective, but the penalty for this effectivity is paid for in efficiency: they are very time consuming, requiring at least cubic time. As the general parsing methods already are time consuming anyway, this is usually deemed acceptable. We will discuss such a method in Section 10.4.

On the other hand, efficient parsers are used because they are efficient. For them, error handling methods are required that are less expensive. We will discuss the best known of these methods.

These methods have the following information at their disposal:

☐ in the case of a bottom-up parser: the parse stack; in the case of a top-down parser: the prediction;

☐ the input string, and the point where the error was detected.

There are four classes of these methods: the ad hoc methods, which do not really form a class; the *regional error handling* methods, which use some (regional) context around the point of error detection to determine how to proceed; the *local error handling* methods only use the parser state and the input symbol (local context) to determine what happens next; and the suffix methods, which use zero context. Examples of these methods will be discussed in Sections 10.5, 10.6, 10.7 and 10.8.

In our discussions, we will use the terms *error detection point*, indicating the point where the parser detects the error, and *error symbol*, which indicates the input symbol on which the error is detected.

10.4 GLOBAL ERROR HANDLING

The most well-known global error handling method is the *least-error correction* method. The purpose of this method is to derive a syntactically correct input from the supplied one using as few corrections as possible. Usually, a symbol deletion, a symbol insertion, and a symbol change all count as one correction (one edit operation).

It is important to realize that the number of corrections needed can easily be limited to a maximum: first, we compute the shortest sentence that can be generated from the grammar. Let us say it has length m. If the input has length n, we can change this input into the shortest sentence with a number of edit operations that is the maximum of m and n: change the first symbol of the input into the first symbol of the shortest sentence, etc. If the input is shorter than the shortest sentence, this results in a maximum of n changes, and we have to insert the last $m-n$ symbols of the shortest sentence. If the input is longer than the shortest sentence, we have to delete the last $n-m$ symbols of the input.

Another important point is that, when searching for a least-error correction, if we already know that we can do it with, say, k corrections, we do not have to investigate possibilities known to require more.

With this in mind, let us see how such an error correction method works when incorporated in an Unger parser. We will again use the grammar of Figure 10.1 as an example, again with input sentence ×+. This is a very short sentence indeed, to limit the amount of work. The shortest sentence that can be generated from the grammar is i, of length one. The observation above limits the number of corrections needed to a maximum of two.

Now, the first rule to be tried is Expr -> Expr + Term. This leads to the following partitions:

Expr		+		Term		
Expr		**+**		**Term**		max:2
	?		1	×+	?	
	?	×	1	+	?	
	?	×+	1		?	
×	?		1	+	?	
×	?	+	0		?	
×+	?		1		?	cut-off

Notice that we include the number of corrections needed for each part of a partition in the right of the column, a question mark indicating that the number of corrections is yet unknown. The total number of corrections needed for a certain partition is the sum of the number of corrections needed for each of the parts. The top of the table also contains the maximum number of corrections allowed for the rule. For the parts matching a terminal, we can decide how many corrections are needed, which results in the column below the +. Also notice that we have to consider empty parts, although the grammar does not have ε-rules. The empty parts stand for insertions. The cut-off comes from the Unger parser detecting that the same problem is already being examined.

Now, the Unger parser continues by trying to derive ε from Expr. The current partition already requires one correction, so the maximum number of corrections allowed is now one. The rule Expr -> Expr + Term has the following result:

Expr		+		Term		
Expr		**+**		**Term**		max:1
	?		1		?	cut-off

so we will have to try the other rule for Expr: Expr -> Term. Likewise, Term -> Term × Factor will result in a cut-off, so we will have to use Term -> Factor. The rule Factor -> (Expr) will again result in a cut-off, so Factor -> i will be used:

Expr	max:1
Term	max:1
Factor	max:1
i	max:1
	1

So, we find, not surprisingly, that input part ε can be corrected to i, requiring one correction (inserting i) to make it derivable from Expr (and Term and Factor). To complete our work on the first partition of ×+ over the right-hand side Expr + Term, we have to examine if, and how, Term derives ×+. We already need two corrections for this partition, so no more corrections are allowed because of the maximum of two. For the rule Term -> Term × Factor we get the following partitions (in which we cheated a bit: we used some information computed earlier):

	Term			max:0		
Term		×		Factor		
	1		1	×+	?	too many corrections
	1	×	0	+	?	too many corrections
	1	×+	1		1	too many corrections
×	?		1	+	?	too many corrections
×	?	+	1		1	too many corrections
×+	?		1		1	cut-off

So, we will have to try Term -> Factor. After that, Factor -> (Expr) results in the following partitions:

	Term			max:0		
	Factor			max:0		
(		Expr		)		
	1		1	×+	2	too many corrections
	1	×	?	+	1	too many corrections
	1	×+	?		1	cut-off
×	1		1	+	1	too many corrections
×	1	+	?		1	too many corrections
×+	2		1		1	too many corrections

This does not work either. The rule Factor -> i results in the following:

Term	max:0	
Factor	max:0	
i	max:0	
×+	2	too many corrections

So we get either a cut-off or too many corrections (or both). This means that the partition that we started with is the wrong one. The other partitions are tried in a similar way, resulting in the following partition table, with completed error correction counts:

Expr					max:2	
Expr		+		Term		
	1		1	x+	>0	too many corrections
	1	×	1	+		1	too many corrections
	1	×+	1		1	too many corrections
×	1		1	+		1	too many corrections
×	1	+	0		1	
×+	?		1		1	cut-off

So, provided that we do not find better corrections later on, using the rule Expr -> Expr + Term we find the corrected sentence i+i, by replacing the × with an i, and inserting an i at the end of the input. Now, the Unger parser proceeds by trying the rule Expr -> Term. Continuing this process, we will find two more possibilities using two corrections: the input can be corrected to ixi by inserting an i in front of the input and replacing the + with another i, or the input can be corrected by replacing × with an i and deleting + (or deleting × and replacing + with an i).

This results in three possible corrections for the input, all three requiring two edit operations. Choosing between these corrections is up to the parser writer. If the parser is written to handle ambiguous input anyway, the parser might deliver three parse trees for the three different corrections. If the parser must deliver only one parse tree, it could just pick the first one found. Even in this case, however, the parser has to continue searching until it has exhausted all possibilities or it has found a correct parsing, because it is not until then that the parser knows if the input in fact did contain any errors.

As is probably clear by now, least-errors correction does not come cheap, and it is therefore usually only applied in general parsers, because these do not come cheap anyway.

Lyon [ErrHandl 1974] has added least-errors correction to the CYK parser and the Earley parser, although his CYK parser only handles replacement errors. In his version of the CYK parser, the non-terminals in the recognition table have an error count associated with it. In the bottom row, which is the one for the non-terminals deriving a single terminal symbol, all entries contain all non-terminals that derive a single terminal symbol. If the non-terminal derives the corresponding terminal symbol it has error count 0, otherwise it has error count 1 (a replacement). Now, when we find that a non-terminal A with rule $A \rightarrow BC$ is applicable, it is entered in the recognition table with an error count equal to the sum of that of B and C, but only if it is not already a member of the same recognition table entry, but with a lower error count.

Aho and Peterson [ErrHandl 1972] also added least-errors correction to the Earley parser by extending the grammar with error productions, so that it produces any string of terminal symbols, with an error count. As in Lyon's method, the Earley items are extended with an error count indicating how many corrections were needed to create the item. An item is only added to an item set if it does not contain one like it which has a lower error count.

10.5 AD HOC METHODS

The *ad hoc error recovery* methods are called ad hoc because they cannot be automatically generated from the grammar. These methods are as good as the parser writer makes them, which in turn depends on how good the parser writer is in anticipating possible syntax errors. We will discuss three of these ad hoc methods: error productions, empty table slots and error tokens.

10.5.1 Error productions

Error productions are grammar rules, added by the grammar writer so that anticipated syntax errors become part of the language (and thus are no longer syntax errors). These error productions usually have a semantic action associated with them that reports the error; this action is triggered when the error production is used. An example where an error production could be useful is the Pascal if-statement. The latter has the following syntax:

```
       if-statement    ->    IF boolean-expression
                             THEN statement else-part
         else-part    ->    ELSE statement | ε
```

A common error is that an `if-statement` has an `else-part`, but the statement in front of the `else-part` is terminated by a semicolon. In Pascal, a semicolon is a statement separator rather than a statement terminator and is not allowed in front of an ELSE. This situation could be detected by changing the grammar rule for `else-part` into

```
     else-part    ->    ELSE statement | ε | ; ELSE statement
```

where the last right-hand side is the error production.

The most important disadvantages of error productions are:
☐   only anticipated errors can be handled;
☐   the modified grammar might (no longer) be suitable for the parsing method used, because conflicts could be introduced by the added rules.

The advantage is that a very adequate error message can be given. Error productions can be used profitably in conjunction with another error handling method, to handle some frequent errors on which the other method does not perform well.

10.5.2 Empty table slots

In most of the efficient parsing methods, the parser consults one or more parse tables and bases its next parsing decision on the result. These parsing tables have error entries (represented as the empty slots), and if one of these is consulted, an error is detected. In this error handling method, the empty table slots are used to refer to error handling routines. Each empty slot has its own error handling routine, which is called when the corresponding slot is consulted. The error handling routines themselves are written by the parser writer. By very careful design of these error handling routines, very good results can be obtained; see for instance Conway and Wilcox [ErrHandl 1973]. In order to achieve good results, however, the parser writer must invest considerable effort. Usually, this is not considered worth the gain, in particular because good error handling can be generated automatically.

10.5.3 Error tokens

Another popular error recovery method uses error tokens. An *error token* is a special token that is inserted in front of the error detection point. The parser will pop states from the parse stack until this token becomes valid, and then skip symbols from the input until an acceptable symbol is found. The parser writer extends the grammar with rules using this error token. An example of this is the following grammar:

```
        input     ->    input input_line | ε
   input_line     ->    ERROR_TOKEN NEWLINE | STRING NEWLINE
```

This kind of grammar is often seen in interactive applications, where the input is line by line. Here, ERROR_TOKEN denotes the error token, and NEWLINE denotes an end of line marker. When an error occurs, states are popped until ERROR_TOKEN becomes acceptable, and then symbols are skipped until a NEWLINE is encountered.

This method can be quite effective, provided that care is taken in designing the rules using the error token.

10.6 REGIONAL ERROR HANDLING

In regional error handling, most often applied in bottom-up parsers, recovery from errors is done by collecting some context around the error detection point, usually as a part of the parse stack around the error, and reducing that part (including the error) to a left-hand side. Therefore, this class of error handling methods is also often called *phrase level error handling*.

10.6.1 Backward/forward move

An error handling method that is applicable to bottom-up parsers is the backward/forward move error recovery method, presented by Graham and Rhodes [ErrHandl 1975]. It consists of two stages: the first stage condenses the context around the error as much as possible. This is called the *condensation phase*. Then the second stage, the *correction phase*, changes the parsing stack and/or the input so that parsing can continue. The method is best applicable to simple precedence parsers, and we will use such a parser as an example.

Our example comes from the grammar and precedence table of Figure 9.13. Suppose that we have input n×+n. The simple precedence parser has the following parse stacks at the end of each step, up to the error detection point:

$$
\begin{array}{ll}
\lessdot n \gtrdot & \text{shift n, next symbol is} \times \\
\lessdot F \gtrdot & \text{reduce n} \\
\lessdot T \doteq \times & \text{reduce F, shift} \times
\end{array}
$$

No precedence relation is found to exist between the × and the +, resulting in an error message that + is not expected.

Let us now examine the condensation phase in some detail. As said before, the purpose of this phase is to condense the context around the error as much as possible. The left-context is condensed by a so-called *backward move*: assuming a $\gtrdot$ relation between the top of the parse stack and the symbol on which the error is detected (that is, assuming that the parse stack built so far has the end of a handle as its top element),

perform all possible reductions. In our example, no reductions are possible. Now
assume a ≐ or a ⋖ between the top of the stack and the next symbol. This enables us to
continue parsing a bit. This step is the so-called *forward move*: first we shift the next
symbol, resulting in the following parse stack:

$$\lessdot T \doteq \times \doteq/\lessdot +   \quad \text{shift } +$$

Next, we disable the check that the top of the stack should represent a prefix of a right-
hand side. Then, we continue parsing until either another error occurs or a reduction is
called for that spans the error detection point. This gives us some right-context to work
with, which can be condensed by a second backward move, if needed. For our example, this results in the following steps:

$$\lessdot T \doteq \times \doteq/\lessdot + \lessdot n \gtrdot \qquad \text{shift n, next symbol is \#}$$
$$\lessdot T \doteq \times \doteq/\lessdot + \lessdot F \gtrdot \qquad \text{reduce n}$$
$$\lessdot T \doteq \times \doteq/\lessdot + \lessdot T \gtrdot \qquad \text{reduce F}$$
$$\lessdot T \doteq \times \doteq/\lessdot + \doteq T' \gtrdot \qquad \text{reduce T}$$

So now we have the situation depicted in Figure 10.4.

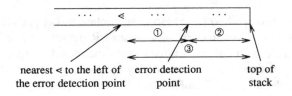

nearest ⋖ to the left of   error detection   top of
the error detection point   point   stack

Figure 10.4 Situation after the backward/forward moves

This is where the correction phase starts. The correction phase considers three parts of
the stack for replacement with some right-hand side. These parts are indicated with ①,
② and ③ in Figure 10.4. Part ① is considered because the precedence at the error
detection point could be ⋗, part ② is considered because the precedence at the error
detection point could be ⋖, and part ③ is considered because this precedence could be
≐. Another option is to just delete one of these parts. This results in a fairly large
number of possible changes, which now must be limited by making sure that the parser
can continue after reducing the right-hand side to its corresponding left-hand side.

In the example, we have the following situation:

$$\lessdot \quad T \quad \doteq \quad \times \quad ? \quad + \quad \doteq \quad T' \quad \gtrdot$$

The left-hand sides that could replace part ① are: E, T', T, and F. These are the non-
terminals that have a precedence relation with the next symbol: the +. The only left-
hand side that could replace part ② is F. Part ③ could be replaced by E, T', T, and F.

This still leaves a lot of choices, but some "corrections" are clearly better than others. Let us now see how we can discriminate between them.

Replacing part of the parse stack by a right-hand side can be seen as an edit operation on the stack. The cost of this edit operation can be assessed as follows. With every symbol, we can associate a certain insertion cost I and a certain deletion cost D. The cost for changing for instance T× to F would then be $D(\text{T})+D(\times)+I(\text{F})$. These costs are determined by the parser writer. The cheapest parse stack correction is then chosen. If there is more than one with the same lowest cost, we just pick one.

Assigning identical costs to all edit operations, in our example, we end up with two possibilities, both replacing part ①: T (deleting the ×), or T×F (inserting an F). Assigning higher costs to editing a non-terminal, which is not unreasonable, would only leave the first of these. Parsing then proceeds as follows:

$$
\begin{array}{ll}
< \text{T} \doteq \times\, ? + \doteq \text{T}' > & \text{error situation} \\
< \text{T} > + \doteq \text{T}' > & \text{error corrected by deleting} \times \\
< \text{T}' > + \doteq \text{T}' > & \text{reducing T} \\
< \text{E} \doteq + \doteq \text{T}' > & \text{reducing T}' \\
< \text{E} > & \text{reducing E+T}' \\
< \text{E}' > & \text{reducing E} \\
< \text{S} > & \text{reducing E}'
\end{array}
$$

The principles of this method have also been applied in LR parsers. There, however, the backward move is omitted, because in an LR parser the state on top of the stack, together with the next input symbol, determine the reduction that can be applied. If the input symbol is erroneous, we have no way of knowing which reductions can be applied. For further details, see Pennello and DeRemer [ErrHandl 1978] and also Mickunas and Modry [ErrHandl 1978].

10.7 LOCAL ERROR HANDLING

All local error recovery techniques are so-called *acceptable-set* error recovery techniques. These techniques work as follows: when a parser detects an error, a certain set called the *acceptable-set* is calculated from the parser state. Next, symbols from the input are skipped until a symbol is found that is a member of the acceptable-set. Then, the parser state is adapted so that the symbol that is not skipped becomes acceptable. There is a family of such techniques; the members of this family differ in the way they determine the acceptable-set, and in the way in which the parser state is adapted. We will now discuss several members of this family.

10.7.1 Panic mode
Panic mode is probably the simplest error recovery method that is still somewhat effective. In this method, the acceptable-set is determined by the parser writer, and is fixed for the whole parsing process. The symbols in this set usually indicate the end of a syntactic construct, for instance a statement in a programming language. For the programming language Pascal, this set could contain the symbols ; and end. When an error is detected, symbols are skipped until a symbol is found that is a member of this set. Then, the parser must be brought into a state that makes this symbol acceptable. In an LL parser, this might require deleting the first few symbols of the prediction, in an

LR parser this might involve popping states from the parse stack until a state is uncovered in which the symbol is acceptable.

The recovery capability of panic mode is often quite good, but many errors can go undetected, because sometimes large parts of the input are skipped. The method has the advantage that it is very easy to implement.

10.7.2 FOLLOW set error recovery

Another early acceptable-set recovery method is the *FOLLOW set error recovery* method. The idea is applicable in an LL parser, and works as follows: when we are parsing a part of the input, and the top of the prediction stack results most recently from a prediction for the non-terminal A, and we detect an error, we skip symbols until we find a symbol that is a member of FOLLOW(A). Next, we remove the unprocessed part of the current right-hand side of A from the prediction, and continue parsing. As we cannot be sure that the current input symbol can follow A in the present context and is thus acceptable, this is not such a good idea. A better idea is to use that part of FOLLOW(A) that can follow A in this particular context, making sure that the symbol that is not skipped will be accepted, but this is not trivial to do.

The existence of this method is probably the reason that the family of acceptable-set error recovery methods is often called *FOLLOW set error recovery*. However, for most members of this family this is a confusing name.

A variant of this method that has become very popular in recursive descent parsers is based on the observation that at any point during the parsing process, there are a number of active non-terminals (for which we are now trying to match a right-hand side), and in general this number is larger than one. Therefore, we should use the union of the FOLLOW sets of these non-terminals, rather than the FOLLOW set of just the most recent of them. A better variant uses the union of those parts of the FOLLOW sets that can follow the non-terminals in this particular context. An expansion of this idea is the following: suppose the parser is in the following state when it detects an error:

$$\begin{array}{|c|} \hline \cdots \quad a \cdots \\ \hline\hline \cdots \quad X_1 \cdots X_n \# \\ \hline \end{array}$$

We can then have the acceptable-set contain the symbols in FIRST(X_1), FIRST(X_2), $\cdots$, and #, and recover by skipping symbols until we meet a symbol of this acceptable-set, and then removing symbols from the prediction until the input symbol becomes acceptable.

Many variations of this technique exist; see for instance Pemberton [ErrHandl 1980] and Stirling [ErrHandl 1985].

10.7.3 Acceptable-sets derived from continuations

A very interesting and effective member of the acceptable-set recovery method family is the one discussed by Röhrich [ErrHandl 1980]. The idea is as follows. Suppose that a parser with the correct prefix property detects an error in the input after having processed a prefix u. Because of the correct prefix property, we know that this prefix u is the start of some sentence in the language. Therefore, there must be a *continuation*, which is a terminal string w, such that uw is a sentence of the language. Now suppose we can compute such a continuation. We can then correct the error as follows:

☐   Determine a continuation w of u.

☐   For all prefixes w' of w, compute the set of terminal symbols that would be accepted by the parser after it has parsed w', and take the union of these sets. If a is a member of this set, $uw'a$ is a prefix of some sentence in the language. This set is our acceptable-set. Note that it includes all symbols of w, including the end-marker.

☐   Skip symbols from the input until we find a symbol that is a member of this set. Note that as a result of this, everything up to the end-marker may be skipped.

☐   Insert the shortest prefix of w that makes this symbol acceptable in front of this symbol. If everything up to the end-marker was skipped, insert w itself.

☐   Produce an error message telling the user which symbols were skipped and which symbols were inserted.

☐   Restart the parser in the state where the error was detected and continue parsing, starting with the inserted symbols. Now, the error is corrected, and the parser continues as if nothing has happened.

10.7.3.1 Continuation grammars

There are two problems here, how to determine the continuation and how to calculate the acceptable-set without going through all possible parsings. Let us regard a grammar as a generating device. Suppose we are generating a sentence from a grammar, and have obtained a certain sentential form. Now, we want to produce a sentence from it as soon as possible, using the fewest possible production steps. We can do this if we know for each non-terminal which right-hand side is the quickest "exit", that is, which right-hand side leads to a terminal production in as few production steps as possible.

It turns out that we can compute these right-hand sides in advance. To this extent, we compute for each symbol the minimum number of production steps needed to obtain a terminal derivation from it. We call this number the step count. Terminal symbols have step count 0, non-terminal symbols have an as yet unknown step count, which we set to infinity. Next, we examine each right-hand side in turn. If we already have a step count for each of the members of a right-hand side, the right-hand side itself needs the sum of these step counts, and the left-hand side needs one more if it uses this right-hand side. If this is less than we had for this non-terminal, we update its step count.

We repeat this process until none of the step counts changes. If we had a proper grammar to begin with, all of the step counts will now be finite. Now, all we have to do is for each left-hand side to mark the right-hand side with the lowest step count. The grammar rules thus obtained are called a *continuation grammar*, although these rules together probably do not form a proper grammar.

Let us see how this works with an example. Consider the grammar of Figure 8.9, repeated in Figure 10.5 for reference.

```
Session   ->   Facts Question | ( Session ) Session
  Facts   ->   Fact Facts | ε
   Fact   ->   ! STRING
Question  ->   ? STRING
```

Figure 10.5 An example grammar

The first pass over the right-hand sides shows us that Facts, Fact, and Question each have step count 1. In the next pass, we find that Session has step count 3. The resulting continuation grammar is presented in Figure 10.6.

```
   Session   ->   Facts Question
     Facts   ->   ε
      Fact   ->   ! STRING
  Question   ->   ? STRING
```

Figure 10.6 The continuation grammar of the grammar of Figure 10.5

10.7.3.2 *Continuation in an LL parser*

In an LL parser, it now is easy to compute a continuation when an error occurs. We take the prediction, and derive a terminal string from it using only rules from the continuation grammar, processing the prediction from left to right. Each terminal that we meet ends up in the acceptable-set; in addition, every time a non-terminal is replaced by its right-hand side from the continuation grammar, we add to the acceptable-set the terminal symbols from the FIRST set of the current sentential form starting with this non-terminal.

Let us demonstrate this with an example. Suppose that we have the input (? STRING ? STRING for the LL(1) parser of Figure 8.10. When the parser detects an error, it is in the following state:

(? STRING	? STRING #
···	) Session #

Now, a continuation will be computed, starting with the sentential form) Session #, using the continuation grammar. During this computation, when the prediction starts with a non-terminal, the FIRST set of the prediction will be computed and the non-terminal will be replaced by its right-hand side in the continuation grammar. The FIRST set is shown in square brackets below the line:

```
) Session # ->

) [(!?] Facts Question # ->

) [(!?] [!?] ε Question # ->

) [(!?] [!?] [?] ? STRING #
```

Consequently, the continuation is) ? STRING # and the acceptable-set contains (,), !, ?, STRING and #. We see that we should keep the ? and insert the first symbol of the continuation,). So, the parser is restarted in the following state:

(	?	STRING	)	?	STRING	#
		$\cdots$	)	Session		#

and proceeds as usual.

10.7.3.3 Continuation in an LR parser

Unlike an LL parser, an LR parser does not feature a sentential form which represents the rest of the input. It is therefore more difficult to compute a continuation. Röhrich [ErrHandl 1980] demonstrates that an LR parser can be generated that has a terminal symbol associated with each state of the handle recognizer so that we can obtain a continuation by pretending that the parser has this symbol as input when it is in the corresponding state. The sequence of states that the parser goes through when these symbols are given as input then determines the continuation. The acceptable-set consists of the terminal symbols on which a shift or reduce can take place (i.e. which are acceptable) in any of these states.

10.7.4 Insertion-only error correction

Fischer, Milton and Quiring [ErrHandl 1980] propose an error correction method for LL(1) parsers using only insertions. This method has become known as the *FMQ* error correction method. In this method, the acceptable-set is the set of all terminal symbols. Fischer, Milton and Quiring argue that the advantage of using only insertions (and thus no deletions or replacements) is that a syntactically correct input is built around the input supplied by the user, so none of the symbols supplied by the user are deleted or changed. Of course, the question arises if every input can be corrected in this way, and in general the answer is no; for some languages it can however, and other languages are easily modified so that it can.

Let us investigate which properties a language must have for every error to be correctable by insertions only. Suppose we have an input $xa \cdots$ such that the start symbol does derive a sentence starting with x, but not a sentence starting with xa; so x is a correct prefix, but xa is not. Now, if this error is to be corrected by an insertion y, xya must again be a correct prefix. This leads to the notion of *insert-correctable* grammars: a grammar is said to be insert-correctable if for every prefix x of a sentence and every symbol a in the language there is a continuation of x that includes a (so an insertion can always be found). Fischer, Milton and Quiring demonstrate that it is decidable whether an LL(1) grammar is insert-correctable.

So, the FMQ error correction method is applicable in an LL(1) parser built from an insert-correctable grammar. In addition, the LL(1) parser must have the immediate error detection property. As we have seen in Section 8.2.4, the usual (strong-)LL(1) parser does not have this property, but the full LL(1) parser does. Fischer, Tai and Milton [ErrHandl 1979] show that for the class of LL(1) grammars in which every nonterminal that derives ε does so explicitly through an ε-rule, the immediate error detection property can be retained while using strong-LL(1) tables.

Now, how does the error corrector work? Suppose that an error is detected on input symbol a, and the current prediction is $X_1 \cdots X_n \#$. The state of the parser is then:

$\cdots$	$a \cdots$
$\cdots$	$X_1 \cdots X_n \#$

As a is an error, we know that it is not a member of FIRST($X_1 \cdots X_n \#$). We also know that the grammar is insert-correctable, so $X_1 \cdots X_n \#$ must derive a terminal string containing a. The error corrector now determines the cheapest insertion after which a is acceptable. Again, every symbol has associated with it a certain insertion cost, determined by the parser writer; the cost of an insertion is the sum of the costs of the symbols in the insertion.

To compute the cheapest insertion, the error corrector uses some tables that are precomputed for the grammar at hand (by the parser generator). First, there is a table that we will call cheapest_derivation, giving the cheapest terminal derivation for each symbol (for a terminal, this is of course the terminal itself). Second, there is a table that we will call cheapest_insertion giving for each symbol/terminal combination (X,a) the cheapest insertion y such that $X \xrightarrow{*} ya \cdots$, if it exists, or an indication that it does not exist. Note that in any prediction $X_1 \cdots X_n \#$ there must be at least one symbol X such that the (X,a) entry of the cheapest_insertion table contains an insertion (or else the grammar was not insert-correctable).

Going back to our parser, we can now compute the cheapest insertion z such that a becomes acceptable. Consulting cheapest_insertion(X_1, a), we can distinguish two cases:

☐ cheapest_insertion(X_1, a) contains an insertion y_1; in this case, we have found an insertion.

☐ cheapest_insertion(X_1, a) does not contains an insertion. In this case, we use cheapest_derivation(X_1) as the first part of the insertion, and continue with X_2 in exactly the same way as we did with X_1. In the end, this will result in an insertion $y_1 \cdots y_i$, where $y_1, \cdots, y_{i-1}$ come from the cheapest_derivation table, and y_i comes from the cheapest_insertion table.

In some LL(1) parsers, notably recursive descent ones, the prediction is not explicitly available, only the first part X_1 is. In this case, we can use this first part to compute an insertion y_1, either as cheapest_insertion(X_1, a) or as cheapest_derivation(X_1) (which may or may not make a acceptable), and we insert it:

$\cdots$	$y_1 a \cdots$
$\cdots$	$X_1 \cdots X_n \#$

If the insertion y_1 does not make a acceptable yet, after parsing y_1, the parser is in the following state:

$$\begin{array}{c|c} \cdots y_1 & a \cdots \\ \hline \cdots & X_2 \cdots X_n \# \end{array}$$

and the process is repeated (X_2 is now explicitly available).

The most serious disadvantage of the FMQ error corrector is that it behaves rather poorly on those errors that are better corrected by a deletion. Advantages are that it always works, can be generated automatically, and is simple.

Anderson and Backhouse [ErrHandl 1982] present a significant improvement of the implementation described above, which is based on the observation that it is suffi- cient to only compute the first symbol of the insertion: if we detect an error symbol a after having read prefix u, and $w = w_1 w_2 \cdots w_n$ is a cheapest insertion, then $w_2 \cdots w_n$ is a cheapest insertion for the error a after having read $u w_1$. So, the cheapest_derivation and cheapest_insertion tables are not needed. Instead, tables are needed that are indexed similarly, but only contain the first symbol of the insertion. The latter tables are much smaller, and easier to compute.

10.7.5 Locally least-cost error recovery

Like the FMQ error correction method, *locally least-cost error recovery* (see Back- house [Books 1979] and Anderson, Backhouse, Bugge and Stirling [ErrHandl 1983]) is a technique for recovering from syntax errors by editing the input string at the error detection point. The FMQ method corrects the error by inserting terminal symbols, the locally least-cost method corrects the error by either deleting the error symbol, or inserting a sequence of terminal or non-terminal symbols after which the error symbol becomes correct, or changing the error symbol. Unlike the least-errors analysis dis- cussed in Section 10.4, which considers the complete input string in determining the corrections to be made, the locally least-cost method only considers the error symbol itself and the symbol after that. The correction is determined by its cost: every symbol has a certain insertion cost, every terminal symbol has a certain deletion cost, and every replacement also has a certain cost. All these costs are determined by the parser writer. When considering if the error symbol is to be deleted, the cost of an insertion that would make the next input symbol acceptable is taken into account. The cheapest correction is chosen.

This principle does not rely on a particular parsing method, although the imple- mentation does. The method has successfully been implemented in LL, LR, and Earley parsers; see Backhouse [Books 1979], Anderson and Backhouse [ErrHandl 1981], Anderson, Backhouse, Bugge and Stirling [ErrHandl 1983], and Choe and Chang [ErrHandl 1986] for details.

10.8 SUFFIX PARSING

Although the error correction and error recovery methods discussed above have their good and bad points, they all have the following problems in common:

☐   On an error, they change the input and/or the parser state, using heuristics to choose one of the many possibilities. We can, however, never be sure that we picked the right change.

☐   Selecting the wrong change can cause an avalanche of spurious error messages.

Only the least-errors analysis of Section 10.4 does not have this problem.

A quite different approach to error recovery is that of Richter [ErrHandl 1985]. He proposes a method that does not have the problems mentioned above, but has some problems of its own. The author argues that we should not try to repair an error, because we cannot be sure that we get it right. Neither should we try to change parser state and/or input. The only thing that we can assume is that the rest of the input (the input that comes after the error symbol, excluding the error symbol itself) is a suffix (tail) of a sentence of the language. This is an assumption made in several error recovery methods, but the difference is that most error recovery methods assume more than that, in that they use (some of) the parser state information built so far.

The set of strings that are some suffix of some sentence of a language forms itself a language. This language of suffixes is called the *suffix-language* of the original language and, in fact, the suffix-language of a context-free language is again a context-free language, for which a grammar can be constructed given the grammar of the original language. Such a grammar is called a *suffix-grammar*, and one can be constructed in the following way: for every non-terminal A in the original grammar, we introduce a new non-terminal A' which derives a suffix of a sentence generated by the original non-terminal. If the original grammar contains a rule

$$A \quad \rightarrow \quad X_1 X_2 \cdots X_n$$

the suffix-grammar will also contain this rule and, in addition, it will contain the following rules deriving a suffix of what A can derive:

$$
\begin{aligned}
A' &\rightarrow X'_1 X_2 \cdots X_n \\
A' &\rightarrow X'_2 \cdots X_n \\
&\cdots \\
A' &\rightarrow X'_n
\end{aligned}
$$

If X_i is a terminal symbol, X'_i is the empty string.

All the new non-terminals (marked with a ′) derive the empty string, which is also a suffix, albeit a degenerate one. If S is the start symbol of the original grammar, the suffix-grammar has start symbol S^{suffix} with the following rules:

$$S^{suffix} \quad \rightarrow \quad S \mid S'$$

The error recovery method now works as follows: parsing starts with a parser for the original language, preferably one with the correct prefix property. When an error is detected, it is reported, the error symbol is skipped and a parser derived from the suffix-grammar, a so-called *suffix-parser*, is started on the rest of the input (which must be a suffix or else there is another error). When another error is detected, it is again reported, the error symbol is skipped, and the suffix-parser is reset to its starting state, ready to accept another suffix.

This method has several advantages:

□   Each error reported is guaranteed to be a different syntax error, and no error is reported more than once. This maintains a high level of user confidence in the error messages.

□   After each error, the parser is restarted in the proper state. There are no spurious

error messages.
☐   No input is skipped, apart from the error symbols.
This sounds just about perfect, so there must be a catch, and indeed there is one; it concerns the suffix-grammar. For the method to be practical, we need an efficient suffix-parser. However, the suffix-grammar may not be suitable for any of the deterministic parsing methods, such as LL or LR. In fact, the way we constructed the suffix-grammar almost certainly results in an ambiguous grammar. This, however, does not mean that the language is ambiguous. Richter conjectures that any kind of bounded-context property of the original grammar is sufficient for the existence of a deterministic suffix-grammar. This conjecture is confirmed by Cormack [ErrHandl 1989] for a subset of the bounded-context grammars.

Another, less important, disadvantage is that sometimes not all syntax errors are reported. This is not really a disadvantage in a highly interactive environment, where it is probably more important that all reported errors are real errors. Also, in the presence of errors, the parser is unable to deliver a meaningful parse tree, which may or may not be a disadvantage.

11

Comparative survey

Practical parsing is concerned almost exclusively with context-free (Type 2) and regular (Type 3) grammars. Unrestricted (Type 0) and context-sensitive (Type 1) grammars are hardly used since, first, they are user-unfriendly in that it is next to impossible to construct a clear and readable Type 0 or Type 1 grammar and, second, all known parsers for them have exponential time requirements. Van Wijngaarden grammars take a slightly different position: Van Wijngaarden grammars can be made very clear and informative, but we do not at present have any parsing technique for even a reasonable subset of them, regardless of time requirements; for some experimental results see Section 13.3.

Regular grammars are used mainly to describe patterns that have to be found in surrounding text. For this application a recognizer suffices. There is only one such recognizer: the finite-state automaton described in Section 5.3. Actual parsing with a regular grammar, when required, is generally done using techniques for CF grammars. For parsing with register-vector grammars, which are a special form of regular grammars, see Section 13.10.

In view of the above we shall restrict ourselves to CF grammars in the rest of this chapter.

11.1 CONSIDERATIONS

The initial demands on a CF parsing technique are obvious: it should be general (i.e., able to handle all CF grammars), it should be fast (i.e., have linear time requirements) and preferably it should be easy to program. There are two serious obstacles to this naive approach to choosing a parser. The first is that the automatic generation of a linear-time parser is possible only for a subset of the CF grammars. The second is that, although this subset is often described as "very large" (especially for LR(1) and LALR(1)), experience shows that a grammar that is designed to best describe the language without concern for parsing is virtually never in this set. What is true, though, is that for almost any arbitrary grammar a slightly different grammar can be found that generates the same language and that does allow linear-time parsing; finding such a grammar, however, almost always requires human intervention and cannot be automated. Using a modified grammar has the disadvantage that the resulting parse trees will differ to a certain extent from the ones implied by the original grammar.

Furthermore, it is important to notice that no linear-time method can handle ambiguous grammars.

An immediate consequence of the above observations is that the stability of the grammar is an important datum. If the grammar is subject to continual revision, it is impossible or at least highly inconvenient to adapt each version by hand to the requirements of a linear-time method, and we have no choice but to use a general method. Likewise, if the grammar is ambiguous, we are forced to use a general method.

11.2 GENERAL PARSERS

There are three general methods that should be considered: Unger's, Earley's and Tomita's.

11.2.1 Unger

An Unger parser (Section 4.1) is easy to program, especially the form given in Section 12.2, but its exponential time requirements limit its applicability to occasional use. The relatively small effort of adding a well-formed substring table (Section 12.3) can improve its efficiency dramatically, and in this form it can be very useful, especially if the average input string is limited to some tens of tokens. The thus modified Unger parser requires in principle a time proportional to n^{N+1}, where n is the number of tokens in the input and N is the maximum number of non-terminals in any right-hand side in the grammar, but in practice it is often much faster. An additional advantage of the Unger parser is that it can usually be readily understood by all participants in a project, which is something that can be said of almost no other parser.

11.2.2 Earley

A simple, robust and efficient version of the Earley parser has been presented by Graham, Harrison and Ruzzo [CF 1980]. It requires a time proportional to n^3 for ambiguous grammars (plus the time needed to enumerate the parse trees), at most n^2 for unambiguous grammars and at most n for grammars for which a linear-time method would work; in this sense the Earley parser is self-adapting. Since it does not require preprocessing on the grammar, it is possible to have one grammar-independent Earley parser and to supply it with the grammar and the input whenever a parsing is needed. If this is convenient, the Earley parser is preferable to Tomita's method.

11.2.3 Tomita

At the expense of considerably more programming and some loss of convenience in use, the Tomita parser (Section 9.8) will provide a parsing in slightly more than linear time for all but the most ambiguous grammars. Since it requires preprocessing on the grammar, it is convenient to generate a separate parser for each grammar (using a parser generator); if the grammar is, however, very unstable, the preprocessing can be done each time the parser is called. The Tomita parser is presently the parser of choice for serious parsing in situations where a linear-time method cannot be applied and the grammar is reasonably stable.

As explained in Section 9.8, the Tomita parser uses a table to restrict the breadth-first search and the question arises what type of table would be optimal. Experimental data on this are lacking. An LR(0) table is relatively easy to construct (9.4.1) and should give reasonable results but an SLR(1) table is still not difficult to construct

(9.6.4) and might be preferable. In view of the additional construction effort, an LALR(1) table may not have any advantage over the SLR(1) table in this case. An LR(1) table probably requires too much space.

11.2.4 Notes
It should be noted that if any of the general parsers performs in linear time, it may still be a factor of ten or so slower than a real linear-time method, due to the much heavier administration they need.

   None of the general parsers identifies with certainty a part of the parse tree before the whole parse tree is completed. Consequently, if semantic actions are connected to the grammar rules, none of these actions can be performed until the whole parse is finished. The actions certainly cannot influence the parsing process. They can, however, reject certain parse trees afterwards; this is useful to implement context conditions in a context-free parser.

11.3 LINEAR-TIME PARSERS
Among the grammars that allow linear-time parsing, the operator-precedence grammars (see Section 9.2.1) occupy a special place, in that they can be ambiguous. They escape the general rule that ambiguous grammars cannot be parsed in linear time by virtue of the fact that they do not provide a full parse tree but rather a parse skeleton. If every sentence in the generated language has only one parse skeleton, the grammar can be operator-precedence. Operator-precedence is by far the simplest practical method; if the parsing problem can be brought into a form that allows an operator-precedence grammar (and that is possible for almost all formula-like inputs), a parser can be constructed by hand in a very short time.

11.3.1 Requirements
Now we come to the full linear-time methods. As mentioned above, grammars are not normally in a form that allows linear-time parsing and have to be modified by hand to be so. This implies that for the use of a linear-time parser at least the following conditions must be fulfilled:
- the grammar must be relatively stable, so that the modification process will not have to be repeated too often;
- the user must be willing to accept a slightly different parse tree than would correspond to the original grammar.

It should again be pointed out that the transformation of the grammar cannot, in general, be performed by a program (if it could, we would have a stronger parsing method).

11.3.2 Strong-LL(1) versus LALR(1)
For two linear-time methods, strong-LL(1)[†] (Section 8.2.2) and LALR(1) (Section 9.6), parser generators are readily available, both as commercial products and in the public domain. Using one of them will in almost all cases be more practical and efficient than

---

[†] What is advertised as an "LL(1) parser generator" is almost always actually a strong-LL(1) parser generator.

writing your own; for one thing, writing a parser generator may be (is!) interesting, but doing a reasonable job on the error recovery is a protracted affair, not to be taken on lightly. So the choice is between (strong-)LL(1) and LALR(1); full LL(1) or LR(1) might occasionally be preferable, but parser generators for these are not (yet) easily available and their advantages will probably not provide enough ground to write one. The main differences between (strong-)LL(1) and LALR(1) can be summarized as follows:

☐   LL(1) generally requires larger modifications to be made to the grammar than LALR(1).

☐   LL(1) allows semantic actions to be performed even before the start of an alternative; LALR(1) performs semantic actions only at the end of an alternative.

☐   LL(1) parsers are often easier to understand and modify.

☐   If an LL(1) parser is implemented as a recursive-descent parser, the semantic actions can use named variables and attributes, much as in a programming language. No such use is possible in a table-driven parser.

☐   Both methods are roughly equivalent as to speed and memory requirements; a good implementation of either will outperform a mediocre implementation of the other.

People evaluate the difference in power between LL(1) and LALR(1) differently; for some the requirements made by LL(1) are totally unacceptable, others consider them a minor inconvenience, largely offset by the advantages of the method.

If one is in a position to design the grammar along with the parser, there is little doubt that LL(1) is to be preferred: not only will parsing and performing semantic actions be easier, text that conforms to an LL(1) grammar is also clearer to the human reader. A good example is the design of Modula-2 by Wirth (see *Programming in Modula-2 (Third, corrected edition)* by Niklaus Wirth, Springer-Verlag, Berlin, 1985).

11.3.3 Table size
The table size of a linear-time parser (in the order of 10K to 100K bytes) may be a serious problem to some applications. The strongest linear-time method with negligible table size is weak precedence with precedence functions.

12

A simple general context-free parser

Although LL(1) and LALR(1) parsers are easy to come by, they are of limited use outside the restricted field of programming language processing, and general parsers are not widely available. The general parser shown here in full detail will yield all parsings of a sentence according to a CF grammar, with no restriction imposed on the grammar. It can be typed in and made operational in a couple of hours, to enable the reader to experiment directly with a general CF parser. The parser, which is rather primitive, takes exponential time in the worst case; an extension to reduce the time requirement to polynomial time is discussed in Section 12.3. The interested reader who has access to a Prolog interpreter may wish to look into Definite Clause Grammars (Section 6.7). These are perhaps easier to use than the parser in this chapter, but cannot handle left-recursion.

12.1 PRINCIPLES OF THE PARSER
The parser, presented as a Pascal program in Figure 12.1, is the simplest we can think of that puts no restrictions on the grammar. Since it searches a forest of possible parse trees to find the applicable ones, it is not completely trivial, though. The parser is an Unger parser in that a top-down analysis is made, dividing the input into segments that are to be matched to symbols in the pertinent right-hand side. A depth-first search (using recursive-descent) is used to enumerate all possibilities. To keep the size of the parser reasonable, a number of oversimplifications have been made (for one thing, names of non-terminals can be one character long only). Once the parser is running, these can all be rectified.

```
program Unger(input, output);                   { Unger parser in Pascal }

const
    NoSymbol =          ' ';
    MaxRules =          10;
    MaxRhsLength =      10;
    MaxInputLength =    10;
    ArraySize =         1000;                   { for all stacks and lists }

type
```

```
      SymbolType = char;
      RuleNmbType = integer;

      RhsType = packed array [1..MaxRhsLength] of SymbolType;
      InputStringType = packed array [1..MaxInputLength] of SymbolType;

      RuleType = record LhsField: SymbolType; RhsField: RhsType; end;

      StackElemType =
      record
          NmbField: RuleNmbType; RhsUsedField: integer;      { the rule }
          PosField, LenField, InpUsedField: integer;   { the substring }
      end;

var
      InputString: InputStringType;
      InputLength: integer;

      Grammar: array [1..MaxRules] of RuleType;
      NRules: integer;
      Start: SymbolType;

      Stack: array [1..ArraySize] of StackElemType;
      NStackElems: integer;

      RuleStack: array [1..ArraySize] of RuleNmbType;
      NRulesStacked: integer;
      NDerivations: integer;

                                        { RULE ADMINISTRATION }
procedure StoreRule(lhs: SymbolType; rhs: RhsType);
    begin
        NRules:= NRules+1;
        with Grammar[NRules] do
        begin LhsField:= lhs; RhsField:= rhs; end;
    end { StoreRule };

procedure WriteRhs(rhs: RhsType);
    var n: integer;
    begin
        for n:= 1 to MaxRhsLength do
            if rhs[n] <> NoSymbol then write(rhs[n]);
    end { WriteRhs };

procedure WriteRule(nmb: RuleNmbType);
    begin
        with Grammar[nmb] do
        begin
            write(LhsField, ' -> "');
            WriteRhs(RhsField);
            write('"');
        end;
    end { WriteRule };

procedure PushRule(n: RuleNmbType);
    begin
```

```
        NRulesStacked:= NRulesStacked+1;
        RuleStack[NRulesStacked]:= n;
    end;

procedure PopRule;
    begin NRulesStacked:= NRulesStacked-1; end;

procedure ParsingFound;
    var r: integer;
    begin
        NDerivations:= NDerivations+1;
        for r:= 1 to NRulesStacked do
        begin WriteRule(RuleStack[r]); writeln; end;
        writeln;
    end { ParsingFound };

                                        { HANDLING OF KNOWN PARSINGS }
procedure StartNewKnownGoal(nmb: RuleNmbType; pos, len: integer);
    begin end;

procedure RecordKnownParsing;
    begin end;

                                            { PARSING STACK HANDLING }
procedure PushStack(nmb: RuleNmbType; pos, len: integer);
    begin
        NStackElems:= NStackElems+1;
        with Stack[NStackElems] do
        begin
            NmbField:= nmb; RhsUsedField:= 0;
            PosField:= pos; LenField:= len; InpUsedField:= 0;
        end;
    end { PushStack };

procedure PopStack;
    begin NStackElems:= NStackElems-1; end;

function IsToBeAvoided(nmb: RuleNmbType; pos, len: integer): Boolean;
    var i: integer;
    begin
        IsToBeAvoided:= false;
        for i:= 1 to NStackElems do
            with Stack[i] do
                if (NmbField=nmb)
                and (PosField=pos)
                and (LenField=len) then
                    IsToBeAvoided:= true;
    end { IsToBeAvoided };

procedure AdvanceTOS(len: integer);
    begin
        with Stack[NStackElems] do
        begin
            RhsUsedField:= RhsUsedField+1;
            InpUsedField:= InpUsedField+len;
        end;
```

```
        end { AdvanceTOS };

procedure RetractTOS(len: integer);
    begin
        with Stack[NStackElems] do
        begin
            RhsUsedField:= RhsUsedField-1;
            InpUsedField:=InpUsedField-len;
        end;
    end { RetractTOS };


                                              { THE AUTOMATON }
procedure TryAllRulesFor(lhs: SymbolType; pos, len: integer);
    var nmb: RuleNmbType;

    procedure DoTopOfStack;
        var tosSymb: SymbolType; { active symbol on top of Stack }

        procedure DoNextOnStack;
            var sv: StackElemType;
            begin { the non-terminal on top of Stack was recognized }
                RecordKnownParsing;
                { save top of Stack }
                sv:= Stack[NStackElems]; NStackElems:= NStackElems-1;
                if (NStackElems = 0) then ParsingFound else
                begin
                    AdvanceTOS(sv.LenField);
                    DoTopOfStack;
                    RetractTOS(sv.LenField);
                end;
                { restore top of Stack }
                NStackElems:= NStackElems+1; Stack[NStackElems]:= sv;
            end { DoNextOnStack };

        procedure TryAllLengthsFor
            (lhs: SymbolType; pos, maxlen: integer);
            var len: integer;
            begin
                for len:= 0 to maxlen do
                    TryAllRulesFor(lhs, pos, len);
            end { TryAllLengthsFor };

        begin { DoTopOfStack }
            with Stack[NStackElems] do
            begin
                tosSymb:= Grammar[NmbField].RhsField[RhsUsedField+1];

                if tosSymb = NoSymbol then
                begin
                    if (InpUsedField = LenField) then DoNextOnStack;
                end
                else if (InpUsedField < LenField) and
                        (tosSymb = InputString[PosField+InpUsedField])
                then
                begin { 1 symbol was recognized }
                    AdvanceTOS(1);
```

```
                    DoTopOfStack;
                    RetractTOS(1);
                end
            else TryAllLengthsFor(tosSymb, PosField+InpUsedField,
                        LenField-InpUsedField);
        end;
    end { DoTopOfStack };


    function KnownGoalSucceeds
        (nmb: RuleNmbType; pos, len: integer): Boolean;
        begin KnownGoalSucceeds:= false; end;

    procedure TryRule(nmb: RuleNmbType; pos, len: integer);
        begin
            if not IsToBeAvoided(nmb, pos, len) then
                if not KnownGoalSucceeds(nmb, pos, len) then
                begin
                    PushStack(nmb, pos, len);
                    StartNewKnownGoal(nmb, pos, len);
                    write('Trying rule '); WriteRule(nmb);
                    writeln(' at pos ', pos:0, ' for length ', len:0);
                    PushRule(nmb);
                    DoTopOfStack;
                    PopRule;
                    PopStack;
                end;
        end { TryRule };


    begin { TryAllRulesFor }
        for nmb:= 1 to NRules do
            if Grammar[nmb].LhsField = lhs then
                TryRule(nmb, pos, len);
    end { TryAllRulesFor };

procedure Parse(inp: InputStringType);
    var n: integer;
    begin
        NStackElems:= 0; NRulesStacked:= 0; NDerivations:= 0;
        InputLength:= 0;
        for n:= 1 to MaxInputLength do
        begin
            InputString[n]:= inp[n];
            if inp[n] <> NoSymbol then InputLength:= n;
        end;
        writeln('Parsing ', InputString);
        TryAllRulesFor(Start, 1, InputLength);
        writeln(NDerivations:0, ' derivation(s) found for string ',
            InputString);
        writeln;
    end { Parse };

procedure InitGrammar;                                    { Grammar 4 }
    begin
        Start:= 'S';
        StoreRule('S', 'LSR        ');
        StoreRule('S', '           ');
```

```
        StoreRule ('L', ' (        ');
        StoreRule ('L', '          ');
        StoreRule ('R', ')         ');
    end;

procedure DoParses;
    begin
        Parse (' ())        ');
        Parse (' ((()))))   ');
    end;

begin
    NRules:= 0;
    InitGrammar;
    DoParses;
end.
```

Figure 12.1 A full context-free parser

12.2 THE PROGRAM

As is usual with well-structured Pascal programs, the program of Figure 12.1 can most easily be read from the end backwards. The body of the program initializes the number of rules in the grammar NRules to zero, fills the array Grammar by calling InitGram—mar and then calls DoParses. The elements of Grammar are of the type RuleType and consist of a LhsField of the type SymbolType and a RhsField which is a packed array of SymbolType. Packed arrays of SymbolType use NoSymbol as a filler and are required to contain at leat one filler. InitGrammar sets the Start symbol and fills the array Grammar through successive calls of StoreRule, which also increases NRules.

In Figure 12.1, the grammar has been built into the program for simplicity; in practice InitGrammar would read the grammar and call StoreRule as needed. The same technique is used for DoParses: the input strings are part of the program text for simplicity, whereas they would normally be read in or obtained in some other fashion. DoParses calls Parse for each input string (which again uses NoSymbol as a filler). Parse initializes some variables of the parser, copies the input string to the global vari-able InputString[†] and then comes to its main task: calling TryAllRulesFor, to try all rules for the Start symbol to match InputString from 1 to InputLength.

Immediately above the declaration of Parse we find the body of TryAllRules—For, which is seen to scan the the grammar for the proper left-hand side and to call TryRule when it has found one.

To understand the workings of TryRule, we have to consider the parsing stack, implemented as the array Stack. Its elements correspond to the nodes just on the left of the dotted line in Figure 6.2 and together they form a list of goals to be achieved for the completion of the parse tree presently under consideration. Each element (of the

---

[†] If the parser is incorporated in a larger Pascal program, many of the globally defined names can be made local to the procedure Parse. Although this technique reduces the danger of con-fusion between names when there are many levels, we have not done so here since it is artificial to do so for the top level.

type StackElemType) describes a rule, given by its number (NmbField) and how much of its right-hand side has already been matched with the input (RhsUsedField); furthermore it records where the matched part in InputString starts (PosField), how much must be matched (LenField) and how much has already been matched (InpUsedField). An element is stacked by a call PushStack(nmb, pos, len), which records the number, position and length of the goal and sets both UsedFields to zero. An element is removed by calling PopStack.

Stack contains the active nodes in the parse tree, which is only a fraction of the nodes of the parse tree as already recognized (Figure 6.2). The left-most derivation of the parse tree as far as recognized can be found on the stack RuleStack, as an array of rule numbers. When the parse stack Stack becomes empty, a parsing has been found, recorded in RuleStack.

To prepare the way for a subsequent addition to the parser of a method to remember known parsings, three hooks have been placed, StartNewKnownGoal, RecordKnownParsing and KnownGoalSucceeds, each of which corresponds to a dummy procedure or function. We shall ignore them until Section 12.3.

We now return to TryRule. Ignoring for the moment the tests not IsTo-BeAvoided and not KnownGoalSucceeds, we see that a match of rule number nmb with the input from pos over len symbols is established as a goal by calling PushRule. The goal is then pursued by calling the local procedure DoTopOfStack. When this call returns, TryRule is careful to restore the original situation, to allow further parsings to be found.

DoTopOfStack is the most complicated of our system of (mutually recursive) procedures. It starts by examining the top element on the stack and establishes what the first symbol in the right-hand side is that has not yet been matched (tosSymb). If this is NoSymbol, the right-hand side is exhausted and cannot match anything any more. That is all right, however, if the input has been completely matched too, in which case we call DoNextOnStack; otherwise the goal has failed and DoTopOfStack returns. If the right-hand side is not exhausted, it is possible that we find a direct match of the terminal in the right-hand side (if there is one) to the terminal in the input. In that case we record the match in the top element on the stack through a call of AdvanceTOS(1) and call DoTopOfStack recursively to continue our search.

If there is no direct match, we assume that tosSymb is a non-terminal and use a call to the local procedure TryAllLengthsFor to try matches for all appropriate lengths of segments of the input starting at the first unmatched position. Since we do not visibly distinguish between a terminal and a non-terminal in our program (one of the oversimplifications), we cannot prevent TryAllLengthsFor from being called for a terminal symbol. Since there is no rule for that terminal, the calls of TryAllRules-For inside TryAllLengthsFor will find no match.

The local procedure TryAllLengthsFor selects increasingly longer segments of the input, and calls TryAllRulesFor for each of them; the latter procedure is already known.

DoNextOnStack is called when the goal on top of the stack has been attained. The top element of Stack is removed and set aside, to be restored later to allow further parsings to be found. If this removes the last element from the stack, a parsing has been found and the corresponding procedure is called. If not, there is more work to do on the present partial parsing. The successful match is recorded in the element presently on top of the stack (which ordered the just attained match) through a call of AdvanceTOS, and DoTopOfStack is called to continue the search. All procedures take care to restore the original situation.

The other procedures except IsToBeAvoided perform simple administrative tasks only.

Note that besides the parse stack and the rule stack, there is also a search stack. Whereas the former are explicit, the latter is implicit and is contained in the Pascal recursion stack and the variables sv in incarnations of DoNextOnStack.

12.2.1 Handling left recursion

It has been explained in Section 6.3.1 that a top-down parser will loop on a left-recursive grammar and that this problem can be avoided by making sure that no goal is accepted when that same goal is already being pursued. This is achieved by the test not IsToBeAvoided in TryRule. When a new goal is about to be put on the parse stack, the function IsToBeAvoided is called, which runs down the parse stack to see if the same goal is already active. If it is, IsToBeAvoided returns true and the goal is not tried for the second time.

The program in Figure 12.1 was optimized for brevity and, hopefully, for clarity. It contains many obvious inefficiencies, the removal of which will, however, make the program larger and less perspicuous. The reader will notice that the semicolon was used as a terminator rather than as a separator; the authors find that this leads to a clearer style.

12.3 PARSING IN POLYNOMIAL TIME

An effective and relatively simple way to avoid exponential time requirement in a context-free parser is to equip it with a *well-formed substring table*, often abbreviated to *WFST*. A WFST is a table that shows all partial parse trees for each substring (segment) of the input string; it is very similar to the table generated by the CYK algorithm. It is can be shown that the amount of work needed to construct the table cannot exceed $O(n^{k+1})$ where n is the length of the input string and k is the maximum number of non-terminals in any right-hand side. This takes the exponential sting out of the depth-first search.

The WFST can be constructed in advance (which is what the CYK algorithm does), or while parsing proceeds ("on the fly"). We shall do the latter here. Also, rather than using a WFST as defined above, we shall use a *known-parsing table*, which shows the partial parse trees for each combination of a grammar rule and a substring. These two design decisions have to do with the order in which the relevant information becomes available in the parser of Figure 12.1.

```
KnownParsingType = record StartField, EndField: integer; end;

KnownGoalType =
record
    NmbField: RuleNmbType; PosField, LenField: integer;{ the goal}
    StartParsingField: integer;                 { temporary variable }
    KnownParsingField: array [1..ArraySize] of KnownParsingType;
    NKnownParsingsField: integer;
end;
```

```
    KnownGoalList: array [1..ArraySize] of KnownGoalType;
    NKnownGoals: integer;
    KnownRuleList: array [1..ArraySize] of RuleNmbType;
    NKnownRules: integer;

function KnownGoalNumber(nmb: RuleNmbType; pos, len: integer):integer;
    var n: integer;
    begin
        KnownGoalNumber:= 0;
        for n:= 1 to NKnownGoals do
            with KnownGoalList[n] do
                if (nmb=NmbField)
                and (pos=PosField)
                and (len=LenField) then
                    KnownGoalNumber:= n;
    end { KnownGoalNumber };

procedure StartNewKnownGoal(nmb: RuleNmbType; pos, len: integer);
    begin
        NKnownGoals:= NKnownGoals+1;
        with KnownGoalList[NKnownGoals] do
        begin
            NmbField:= nmb; PosField:= pos; LenField:= len;
            StartParsingField:= NRulesStacked+1;
            NKnownParsingsField:= 0;
        end;
    end { StartNewKnownGoal };

procedure RecordKnownParsing;
    var n, i: integer;
    begin
        with Stack[NStackElems] do
        begin
            n:= KnownGoalNumber(NmbField, PosField, LenField);
            with KnownGoalList[n] do
            begin
                NKnownParsingsField:= NKnownParsingsField+1;
                with KnownParsingField[NKnownParsingsField] do
                begin
                    StartField:= NKnownRules+1;
                    for i:= StartParsingField to NRulesStacked do
                    begin
                        NKnownRules:= NKnownRules+1;
                        KnownRuleList[NKnownRules]:= RuleStack[i];
                    end;
                    EndField:= NKnownRules;
                end;
            end;
        end;
    end { RecordKnownParsing };

function KnownGoalSucceeds
    (nmb: RuleNmbType; pos, len: integer): Boolean;
    var n, oldNRulesStacked, i, j: integer;
    begin
        n:= KnownGoalNumber(nmb, pos, len);
```

```
if n = 0 then KnownGoalSucceeds:= false else
begin
    oldNRulesStacked:= NRulesStacked;
    with KnownGoalList[n] do
    begin
        for i:= 1 to NKnownParsingsField do
            with KnownParsingField[i] do
            begin
                for j:= StartField to EndField do
                begin
                    NRulesStacked:= NRulesStacked+1;
                    RuleStack[NRulesStacked]:=
                        KnownRuleList[j];
                end;
                AdvanceTOS(len);
                DoTopOfStack;
                RetractTOS(len);
                NRulesStacked:= oldNRulesStacked;
            end;
    end;
    KnownGoalSucceeds:= true;
end;
end { KnownGoalSucceeds };

NKnownGoals:= 0; NKnownRules:= 0;          { in procedure Parse }
```

Figure 12.2 Additions for the known-parsing table

Our parser can be equipped with the known-parsing table by incorporating the declarations of Figure 12.2 in it. StartNewKnownGoal, RecordKnownParsing and KnownGoalSucceeds replace the dummy declarations in Figure 12.1, the other declarations and the initialization statement are to be inserted in the appropriate places. The thus modified parser will no longer require exponential time (if sufficient memory is supplied; see the constant declarations).

Returning to the mechanism of the parser, we see that when a new goal is established in TryRule for which IsToBeAvoided yields false, a call is made to KnownGoalSucceeds. This function accesses the known-parsing table to find out if the goal has been pursued before. When called for the very first time, it will yield false since there are no known parsings yet and not KnownGoalSucceeds will succeed as in the unmodified parser. We enter the block that really tries the rule, preceded by a call to StartNewKnownGoal. This prepares the table for the recording of the zero or more parsings that will be found for this new goal.

Goals are recorded in a three-level data structure. The first level is the array KnownGoalList, whose elements are of type KnownGoalType. A known goal has three fields describing the rule number, position and length of the goal and a Known-ParsingField, which is an array of elements of type KnownParsingType and which forms the second level; it has also a field StartParsingField, which is only meaningful while the present table entry is being constructed. Each element in Known-ParsingField describes a partial parse tree for the described goal. The partial parse tree is represented as a list of rule numbers, just as the full parse tree. These lists are stored one after another in the array KnownRuleList, which is the third level; the beginning and end of each parsing are recorded in the StartField and EndField of the known parsing.

StartNewKnownGoal records the goal in a new element of KnownGoalList. It sets StartParsingField to NRulesStacked+1, since that is the position in RuleStack where the first rule number for the present goal will go. When the main mechanism of the parser has found a parsing for the goal (in DoNextOnStack) it calls RecordKnownParsing, which adds the parsing found in RuleStack between StartParsingField and NRulesStacked to the present known goal under construction. To this end, it finds the pertinent element in KnownGoalList, adds an element to the corresponding KnownParsingField and copies the parsing to the array KnownRuleList while recording the begin and end in the element in KnownParsing-Field. There is no need to signal the end of the construction of a known goal. Note that as long as the goal is under construction, it is also on the parse stack; this means that IsToBeAvoided will yield true which in turn guarantees that StartNewKnown-Goal will not be called again while the known goal is being constructed.

The next time the goal is tried by TryRule, KnownGoalSucceeds will indeed succeed: for each of the elements in the pertinent KnownParsingField, the corresponding segment of KnownRuleList, which contains one partial parse tree, is copied to the RuleStack as if the parsing had been performed normally. The advance in length is noted and DoTopOfStack is called, again just as in the normal parsing process. Upon its return, the original situation is restored, including the value of NRulesStacked.

It will be obvious that copying a ready-made solution is much faster than reconstructing that solution. That it makes the difference between exponential and polynomial behaviour is less obvious, but true nevertheless. The unmodified parser tries 41624 rules for the built-in example, the parser with the known-parsing table only 203. The new parser can be improved considerably in many points, with a corresponding increase in efficiency; the $O(n^{k+1})$ dependency remains, though.

13

Annotated bibliography

The purpose of this annotated bibliography is to supply the reader with more material and with more detail than was possible in the preceding chapters, rather than to just list the works referenced in the text. The annotations cover a considerable number of subjects that have not been treated in the rest of the book.

The articles and books presented here have been selected for two criteria: relevancy and accessibility. The notion of relevancy has been interpreted very widely; parsers are used in an increasing number of applications and relevancy to others is hard to judge. In practice, entries have only been rejected if they were either too theoretical or did not supply insight into or understanding of parsing. Accessibility has been taken to mean ready availability to a researcher who has access to a moderately well-equipped university or company research library. We expect such a library to hold most of the prominent computer science journals, but not all or even a major part of the proceedings of conferences on programming languages and compiler construction, let alone technical reports from various research institutes all over the world. We have often been forced to compromise this criterion, to include pertinent material not otherwise available; for instance, nothing seems to have been published on left-corner parsing in journals. Fortunately, relevant material that was first published in a technical report or as a PhD thesis was often published later in a prominent journal; in these cases a reference to the original publication can be found by consulting the journal paper referenced here. We have kept the references to technical reports to the absolute minimum. No non-English (that is, no non-English-language) material has been included. It is our intention that the present collection be complete under the above criteria, but we have no real hope that such perfection has been attained. We shall be grateful to be pointed to additional references.

The bibliography contains about 400 entries, almost all of them from the Western world. Some papers from the Soviet Union and Eastern Europe have been included, if available in translation. Much work on parsing has been done and is still being done in Japan; it has been sorely underrepresented in this collection, for reasons of accessibility. Only readily available full material in translation has been included, although much more is available in the form of abstracts in English.

This annotated bibliography differs in several respects from the habitual literature list.

☐   The entries have been grouped into fourteen categories:

13.1   miscellaneous literature (Misc);

13.2   unrestricted PS and CS grammars (PSCS);

13.3   van Wijngaarden grammars and affix grammars (VW);

13.4   general context-free parsers (CF);

13.5   LL parsing (LL);

13.6   LR parsing (LR);

13.7   left-corner parsing (LC);

13.8   precedence and bounded-context parsing (Precedence);

13.9   finite-state automata (FS);

13.10   natural language handling (NatLang);

13.11   error handling (ErrHandl);

13.12   transformations on grammars (Transform);

13.13   general books on parsing (Books);

13.14   some books on computer science (CSBooks).

The nature of publications in parsing is so that the large majority of them can easily be assigned a single category. Some that span two categories have been placed in one, with a reference in the other. Publications of a more general nature have found a place in "Miscellaneous Literature".

□   The entries are annotated. This annotation is not a copy of the abstract provided with the paper (which generally said something about the results obtained) but is rather the result of an attempt to summarize the technical content in terms of what has been explained elsewhere in this book.

□   The entries are ordered chronologically rather than alphabetically.

This arrangement has the advantage that it is much more meaningful than a single alphabetic list, ordered on author names. Each section can be read as the history of research on that particular aspect of parsing, related material is found closely together and recent material is easily separated from older publications. A disadvantage is that it is now difficult to locate entries by author; to remedy this, an author index has been supplied. Only a tiny fraction of the entries is referred to in the previous chapters; these occurrences are also included in the author index.

Terms from computer science have been used more freely in the annotations than in the rest of the book (an example is "transitive closure"). See, for instance, Sedgewick [CSBooks 1988] or Smith [CSBooks 1989] for an explanation.

Note that there is a journal called *Computer Languages (Elmsford, NY)* and one called *Computer Language (San Francisco, CA)*; both abbreviate to *Comput. Lang.*; the place name is essential to distinguish between them (although the first originates from Exeter, Devon, England).

13.1 MISCELLANEOUS LITERATURE

•   Noam **Chomsky**, "Three models for the description of language", *IEEE Trans. Inform. Theory*, vol. 2, no. 3, p. 113-124, 1956. In an attempt to delineate the set of correct English sentences, the author considers three mechanisms. Finite-state automata are rejected on the grounds that they cannot cope with arbitrary nesting. Phrase structure grammars are considered probably applicable but declared impractical due to their problems in expressing context conditions. Most of these problems can be solved if we augment PS grammars with *transformation rules*, which specify the rearrangement of parts of the derivation tree.

•   Noam **Chomsky**, "On certain formal properties of grammars", *Inform. Control*, vol. 2, p. 137-167, 1959. This article discusses what later became known as the Chomsky hierarchy. Chomsky defines type 1 grammars in the "context-sensitive" way. His motivation for this is that it permits the construction of a tree as a structural description. Type 2 grammars exclude ε-rules, so in Chomsky's system, type 2 grammars are a subset of type 1 grammars.

Next, the so called *counter languages* are discussed. A counter language is a language recognized by a finite automaton, extended with a finite number of counters, each of which can assume infinitely many values. $L_1=\{a^n b^n \mid n>0\}$ is a counter language, $L_2=\{xy \mid x,y \in \{a,b\}^*, y$ is the mirror image of $x\}$ is not, so there are type 2 languages that are not counter languages. The reverse is not investigated.

The Chomsky Normal Form is introduced, but not under that name, and a bit different: Chomsky calls a type 2 grammar *regular* if production rules have the form $A \rightarrow a$ or $A \rightarrow BC$, with $B \neq C$, and if $A \rightarrow \alpha A \beta$ and $A \rightarrow \gamma A \eta$ then $\alpha = \gamma$ and $\beta = \eta$. A grammar is *self-embedding* if there is a derivation $A \overset{*}{\rightarrow} \alpha A \beta$ with $\alpha \neq \varepsilon$ and $\beta \neq \varepsilon$. The bulk of the paper is dedicated to the theorem that the extra power of type 2 grammars over type 3 grammars lies in this self-embedding property.

- J.W. **Backus**, F.L. Bauer, J. Green, C. Katz, J. McCarthy, P. Naur (Ed.), A.J. Perlis, H. Rutishauser, K. Samelson, B. Vauquois, J.H. Wegstein, A. van Wijngaarden, M. Woodger, "Report on the algorithmic language ALGOL 60", *Commun. ACM*, vol. 3, no. 5, p. 299-314, May 1960. First application of a BNF grammar (for the definition of a programming language). Revised report by the same authors: *Commun. ACM*, vol. 6, no. 1, p. 1-17, Jan 1963.

- R.A. **Brooker**, I.R. MacCallum, D. Morris, J.S. Rohl, "The compiler-compiler", *Annual Review in Automatic Programming*, vol. 3, p. 229-275, 1960. One of the first extensive descriptions of a compiler-compiler. Parsing is done by a backtracking non-exhaustive top-down parser using a transduction-like grammar. This grammar is kept in an integrated form and modifications can be made to it while parsing.

- Robert W. **Floyd**, "A descriptive language for symbol manipulation", *J. ACM*, vol. 8, p. 579-584, Oct. 1961. Original paper describing Floyd productions. See Section 9.3.1.

- Robert S. **Ledley**, James B. Wilson, "Automatic-programming-language translation through syntactical analysis", *Commun. ACM*, vol. 5, no. 3, p. 145-155, March 1962. An English-to-Korean (!) translation system is described in detail, in which parts of the Korean translation are stored in attributes in the parse tree, to be reordered and interspersed with Korean syntactic markers on output. The parser is Irons' [CF 1961].

- Melvin E. **Conway**, "Design of a separable transition-diagram compiler", *Commun. ACM*, vol. 6, no. 7, p. 396-408, July 1963. The first to introduce *coroutines* and to apply them to structure a compiler. The parser is Irons' [CF 1961], made deterministic by a No-Loop Condition and a No-Backup Condition. It follows transition diagrams rather than grammar rules.

- Robert W. **Floyd**, "The syntax of programming languages–a survey", *IEEE Trans. Electronic Comput.*, vol. EC-13, p. 346-353, 1964. Early analysis of the advantages of and problems with the use of grammars for the specification of programming languages. Contains a bibliography of almost 100 entries.

- Jerome **Feldman**, David Gries, "Translator writing systems", *Commun. ACM*, vol. 11, no. 2, p. 77-113, Feb 1968. Grand summary of the work done on parsers (with semantic actions) before 1968.

- D.J. **Cohen**, C.C. Gotlieb, "A list structure form of grammars for syntactic analysis", *Computing Surveys*, vol. 2, no. 1, p. 65-82, 1970. CF rules are represented as linked lists of alternatives, which themselves are linked lists of members. The trick is that both lists end in different null pointers. This representation is very amenable to various backtracking and non-backtracking top-down and bottom-up parsing methods (by interpreting the grammar). Several practical parsers are given in flowchart form. An algorithm is given to "invert" a grammar, i.e. the linked lists, to create a data structure that will efficiently guide a bottom-up parser.

- A. **Birman**, J.D. Ullman, "Parsing algorithms with backtrack", *Inform. Control*, vol. 23, no. 1, p. 1-34, 1973. Models classes of recursive descent parsers, capable of recognizing all deterministic context-free languages and also some non-context-free languages.

- B.W. **Kernighan**, L.L. Cherry, "A system for typesetting mathematics", *Commun. ACM*, vol. 18, no. 3, p. 151-157, Mar 1975. A good example of the use of an ambiguous grammar to specify the preferred analysis of special cases.

- A.V. **Aho**, S.C. Johnson, J.D. Ullman, "Deterministic parsing of ambiguous grammars", *Commun. ACM*, vol. 18, no. 8, p. 441-452, 1975. Demonstrates how LL and LR parsers can be constructed for certain classes of ambiguous grammars, using simple disambiguating rules, such as operator-precedence.

- Jacques **Cohen**, "Experience with a conversational parser generation system", *Softw. Pract. Exper.*, vol. 5, p. 169-180, 1975. Realistic description of the construction of a professional interactive parser generator.

- Jay **Earley**, "Ambiguity and precedence in syntax description", *Acta Inform.*, vol. 4, p. 183-192, 1975. Informal description of how to use precedence information for disambiguation.

- Michael **Marcotty**, Henry F. Ledgard, Gregor V. Bochmann, "A sampler of formal definitions", *Computing Surveys*, vol. 8, no. 2, p. 191-276, June 1976. Describes and compares four semantic definition methods: VW grammars, production systems and the axiomatic approach, Vienna Definition Language, and attribute grammars. No clear winner emerges.

- R.M. **Wharton**, "Resolution of ambiguity in parsing", *Acta Inform.*, vol. 6, no. 4, p. 387-395, 1976. It is proposed that ambiguity be resolved in a bottom-up parser by 1) reducing upon a shift/reduce conflict, 2) reducing the shorter right-hand side upon a reduce/reduce conflict and 3) reducing the textual first right-hand side upon a reduce/reduce conflict with equal lengths. In a top-down parser, criteria similar to 2) and 3) are applied to each LL(1) conflict.

- R.B. **Hunter**, A.D. McGettrick, R. Patel, "LL versus LR parsing with illustrations from Algol 68", *ACM SIGPLAN Notices*, vol. 12, no. 6, p. 49-53, June 1977. Syntax-improved LL(1) (Foster [Transform 1968]) and LR(1) are equally unsuccessful in handling a CF version of the grammar of Algol 68. After hand adaptation LL(1) has the advantage.

- Niklaus **Wirth**, "What can we do about the unnecessary diversity of notation for syntactic definitions?", *Commun. ACM*, vol. 20, no. 11, p. 822-823, Nov 1977. Introduces Wirth's notation for extended CF grammars, using { . . . } for repetition, [. . .] for optionality, (. . .) for grouping and " . . . " for quoting.

- Jacques **Cohen**, Martin S. Roth, "Analyses of deterministic parsing algorithms", *Commun. ACM*, vol. 21, no. 6, p. 448-458, June 1978. Gives methods to calculate the average parsing times and their standard deviations from the input grammar, for several parsers. The resulting formulae are finite series, and are sometimes given in closed form.

- Kuo-Chung **Tai**, "On the implementation of parsing tables", *ACM SIGPLAN Notices*, vol. 14, no. 1, p. 100-101, Jan 1979. How to implement parsing tables using hashing.

- Peter **Deussen**, "One abstract accepting algorithm for all kinds of parsers". In *Automata, languages and programming; Lecture Notes in Computer Science #71*,

Hermann A. Maurer (eds.), Springer-Verlag, Berlin, p. 203-217, 1979. Parsing is viewed as an abstract search problem, for which a high-level algorithm is given. The selection predicate involved is narrowed down to give known linear parsing methods.

- Robert Endre **Tarjan**, Andrew Chi-Chih Yao, "Storing a sparse table", *Commun. ACM*, vol. 22, no. 11, p. 606-611, Nov 1979. Two methods of storing sparse tables are presented and analysed: trie structure and double displacement.

- Hanan **Samet**, "A coroutine approach to parsing", *ACM Trans. Prog. Lang. Syst.*, vol. 2, no. 3, p. 290-306, 1980. Some inputs consist of interleaved chunks of text conforming to different grammars. An example is programming text interrupted at unpredictable points by macroprocessor directives. This situation can be handled by having separate parsers for each grammar, cooperating in coroutine fashion.

- Anton **Nijholt**, "Parsing strategies: A concise survey". In *Mathematical Foundations of Computer Science; Lecture Notes in Computer Science #118*, J. Gruska & M. Chytil (eds.), Springer-Verlag, Berlin, p. 103-120, 1981. The context-free parser and language field is surveyed in terse prose. Highly informative to the connoisseur.

- Esko **Ukkonen**, "Lower bounds on the size of deterministic parsers", *J. Comput. Syst. Sci.*, vol. 26, p. 153-170, 1983. Worst-case lower bounds for the parser sizes are given for the various classes of LL(k) and LR(k) parsers for $k=0,1$ and $k \geq 2$. All LL(k) lower bounds are polynomial, except the one for full LL($k>1$), which is exponential; all LR(k) bounds are exponential.

- Fernando C.N. **Pereira**, David H.D. Warren, "Parsing as deduction". In *Proceedings of the 21st Annual Meeting of the Association for Computational Linguistics*, Cambridge, Mass., p. 137-144, 1983. The Prolog deduction mechanism is top-down depth-first. It can be exploited to do parsing, using Definite Clause grammars. Parsing can be done more efficiently with Earley's technique. The corresponding Earley deduction mechanism is derived and analysed.

- Anton **Nijholt**, *Deterministic top-down and bottom-up parsing: historical notes and bibliographies*, Mathematisch Centrum, Amsterdam, p. 118, 1983. Over a 1000 references about LL(k), LR(k) and precedence parsing, with short histories and surveys of the three methods.

- Peter **Dencker**, Karl Dürre, Johannes Heuft, "Optimization of parser tables for portable compilers", *ACM Trans. Prog. Lang. Syst.*, vol. 6, no. 4, p. 546-572, Oct 1984. Given an $n \times m$ parser table, an $n \times m$ bit table is used to indicate which entries are error entries; this table is significantly smaller than the original table and the remaining table is now sparse (typically 90-98% don't-care entries). The remaining table is compressed row-wise (column-wise) by setting up an interference graph in which each node corresponds to a row (column) and in which there is an edge between any two nodes the rows (columns) of which occupy an element in the same position. A (pseudo-)optimal partitioning is found by a minimal graph-colouring heuristic.

- W.M. **Waite**, L.R. Carter, "The cost of a generated parser", *Softw. Pract. Exper.*, vol. 15, no. 3, p. 221-237, 1985. Supports with measurements the common belief that compilers employing generated parsers suffer significant performance degradation with respect to recursive descent compilers. Reasons: interpretation of parse tables versus direct execution, attribute storage allocation and the mechanism to determine which action(s) to perform. Then, a parser interface is proposed that simplifies integration of the parser; implementation of this interface in assembly language results in generated parsers that cost the same as recursive descent ones. The paper does not consider generated recursive descent parsers.

- Gerard D. **Finn**, "Extended use of null productions in LR(1) parser applications", *Commun. ACM*, vol. 28, no. 9, p. 961-972, Sept 1985. Extensive account of how to use an LR parser for conversion purposes. Makes a strong case for the use of parsers for conversion. Contains a good introduction to parsing.

- Robert **Gerardy**, "Experimental comparison of some parsing methods", *ACM SIGPLAN Notices*, vol. 22, no. 8, p. 79-88, Aug 1987. Experimental time measurements for recursive descent, operator-precedence and SLR(1) parsing show a ratio of 1 : 4 : 10, in that order. All parsers were written in Pascal and parsed a mini-Pascal language.

- Michael **Share**, "Resolving ambiguities in the parsing of translation grammars", *ACM SIGPLAN Notices*, vol. 23, no. 8, p. 103-109, Aug 1988. The UNIX LALR parser generator *yacc* is extended to accept LALR conflicts and to produce a parser that requests an interactive user decision when a conflict occurs while parsing. The system is used in document conversion.

- Josef **Grosch**, "Generators for high-speed front-ends". In *Compiler Compilers and High-Speed Compilation; Lecture Notes in Computer Science #371*, D. Hammer (eds.), Springer-Verlag, Berlin, p. 81-92, 1989. A coherent system of lexical scanner generator, LALR(1) parser generator and LL(1) parser generator, using a uniform input syntax, is presented. The scanner beats UNIX *lex* by a factor of 5, the LALR parser beats *yacc* by a factor of 2.

- Vance E. **Waddle**, "Production trees: a compact representation of parsed programs", *ACM Trans. Prog. Lang. Syst.*, vol. 12, no. 1, p. 61-83, Jan 1990. Redundant items are removed from a traditional parse tree through a number of techniques: unit productions are contracted, terminals symbols are removed, structure information in links is replaced by a rule number, etc. Each node in the resulting parse tree corresponds to one right-hand side and contains the rule number and a list of pointer to the nodes for the non-terminals in the right-hand side. A space saving of a factor 20 is achieved on the average. A grammar form that corresponds more closely to this representation is defined.

- Frank G. **Pagan**, "Comparative efficiency of general and residual parsers", *ACM SIGPLAN Notices*, vol. 25, no. 4, p. 59-68, April 1990. The switch from table-driven LL(1) to recursive descent or from table-driven LR(1) to recursive ascent is viewed as an example of *partial computation*. Underlying theory and examples are given.

- Boris **Burshteyn**, "On the modification of the formal grammar at parse time", *ACM SIGPLAN Notices*, vol. 25, no. 5, p. 117-123, May 1990. Modifying the grammar under control of and utilizing information obtained by the parsing process is proposed as a means of handling context-sensitivity. For example, the recognition of the declaration of an array aaa could cause the introduction of a new grammar rule $expr \rightarrow$ aaa [*expr*], (generated from a template), thus allowing forms like aaa[3] to be used.

13.2 UNRESTRICTED PS AND CS GRAMMARS

This section also covers some other non-context-free grammar types, excluding VW (two-level) grammars and affix grammars, for which see Section 13.3.

- Alfred V. **Aho**, "Indexed grammars−an extension of context-free grammars", *J. ACM*, vol. 15, no. 4, p. 647-671, Oct 1968. In an *indexed grammar*, each non-terminal N in a sentential form is followed by zero or more "indices", which govern which of the alternatives for N are allowed for this occurrence of N. The indices propagate according to specific rules. $L(CF) \subset L(Indexed) \subset L(CS)$.

- William A. **Woods**, "Context-sensitive parsing", *Commun. ACM*, vol. 13, no. 7, p. 437-445, July 1970. The paper presents a canonical form for context-sensitive (ε-free) derivation trees. Parsing is then performed by an exhaustive guided search over these canonical forms exclusively. This guarantees that each possible parsing will be found exactly once.

- Jacques **Loeckx**, "The parsing for general phrase-structure grammars", *Inform. Control*, vol. 16, p. 443-464, 1970. The paper sketches two non-deterministic parsers for PS grammars, one top-down, which tries to mimic the production process and one bottom-up, which tries to find a handle. The instructions of the parsers are derived by listing all possible transitions in the grammar and weeding out by hand those that cannot occur. Trial-and-error methods are discussed to resolve the non-determinism, but no instruction selection mechanisms are given. Very readable, nice pictures.

- Daniel A. **Walters**, "Deterministic context-sensitive languages, Parts I & II", *Inform. Control*, vol. 17, no. 1, p. 14-61, 1970. The definition of LR(k) grammars is extended to context-sensitive grammars. Emphasis is more on theoretical properties than on obtaining a parser.

- Z.J. **Ghandour**, "Formal systems and analysis of context-sensitive languages", *Computer J.*, vol. 15, no. 3, p. 229-237, 1972. Ghandour describes a formal production system that is in some ways similar to but far from identical to a two-level grammar. A hierarchy of 4 classes is defined on these systems, with Class 1 $\supseteq$ Class 2 $\supset$ Class 3 $\supset$ Class 4, Class 1 $\supseteq$ CS and Class 4 = CF. A parsing algorithm for Class 1 systems is given in fairly great detail.

- N.A. **Khabbaz**, "Multipass precedence analysis", *Acta Inform.*, vol. 4, p. 77-85, 1974. A hierarchy of CS grammars is given that can be parsed using multipass precedence parsing. The parser and the table construction algorithm are given explicitly.

- Eberhard **Bertsch**, "Two thoughts on fast recognition of indexed languages", *Inform. Control*, vol. 29, p. 381-384, 1975. Proves that parsing with (tree-)unambiguous indexed grammars is possible in $O(n^2)$ steps.

- Robert W. **Sebesta**, Neil D. Jones, "Parsers for indexed grammars", *Intern. J. Comput. Inform. Sci.*, vol. 7, no. 4, p. 344-359, Dec 1978. Very good explanation of indexed grammars. Three classes of indexed grammars are defined, corresponding to strong-LL, LL and LR, respectively. It is shown that the flag sets generated by indexed grammars are regular sets.

- C.J.M. **Turnbull**, E.S. Lee, "Generalized deterministic left to right parsing", *Acta Inform.*, vol. 12, p. 187-207, 1979. The LR(k) parsing machine is modified so that the reduce instruction removes the reduced right-hand side from the stack and pushes an arbitrary number of symbols back into the input stream. (The traditional LR(k) reduce is a special case of this: it pushes the recognized non-terminal back into the input and immediately shifts it. The technique is similar to that put forward by Dömölki [CF 1968].) The new machine is capable of parsing efficiently a subset of the Type 0 grammars, *DRP grammars* (for Deterministic Regular Parsable). Membership of this subset is undecidable, but an approximate algorithm can be constructed by extending the LR(k) parse table algorithm. Details are not given, but can be found in a technical report by the first author.

- Kurt **Mehlhorn**, "Parsing macro grammars top down", *Inform. Control*, vol. 40, no. 2, p. 123-143, 1979. *Macro grammars* are defined as follows. The non-terminals in a CF grammar are given parameters, as if they were routines in a programming language. The values of these parameters are strings of terminals and non-terminals (the latter with the proper number of parameters). A parameter can be passed on, possibly concatenated with some terminals and non-terminals, or can be made part of the sentential form. An algorithm to construct a recursive-descent parser for a macro grammar (if possible) is given.

- G. **Barth**, "Fast recognition of context-sensitive structures", *Computing*, vol. 22, p. 243-256, 1979. A *recording grammar* (an RG) is a CF grammar in which each (numbered) production rule belongs to one of three classes: normal, recording and directed. During production, normal rules behave normally and a recording rule records its own occurrence by appending its number to a string called the π-element. When production leaves a "recording" stage, the entire π-element is added to a set called the Ω-component, which collects all contexts created so far. When production enters a "directed" stage, an element (a context) is retrieved from the Ω-component, transferred through a mapping I and used to direct the choice of production rules until the element is exhausted. The expressive power of RGs is equal to that of Type 0 grammars.

An LL(k) version of RGs can be defined, based on LL(k)-ness of the underlying CF grammar, plus a few simple restrictions on the mapping I; the resulting property is called *RLL(k)*.

For parsing, an LL(k) parse is performed; during "normal" parsing, nothing special is done, during "recording" parsing the rule numbers are recorded and subsequently added to the Ω-component; during "directed" parsing, which is actually "checking" parsing, the rule numbers are checked for consistency with the Ω-component, using a simple finite transducer. The parser (+ checker) works in linear time.

It is not clear how convenient RLL(k) RGs are; neither of the two examples provided to demonstrate the power of RGs is RLL(k).

*   G.Sh. **Vol'dman**, "A parsing algorithm for context-sensitive grammars", *Program. Comput. Softw.*, vol. 7, p. 302-307, 1981. Extends Earley's algorithm first to length-increasing phrase structure grammars and then to non-decreasing PS grammars (= CS grammars). The resulting algorithm has exponential time requirements but is often much better.

*   Lawrence A. **Harris**, "SLR(1) and LALR(1) parsing for unrestricted grammars", *Acta Inform.*, vol. 24, p. 191-209, 1987. The notion of an LR(0) item can easily be defined for unrestricted grammars: "For each item $\lambda \rightarrow \mu_1 \cdot X \mu_2$ there is a transition on X to the item $\lambda \rightarrow \mu_1 X \cdot \mu_2$ and an ε-transition to any item $X\delta \rightarrow \cdot \eta$", for any symbol X. These items are grouped by subset construction into the usual states, called here *preliminary states*, since some of them may actually be ineffective. A GOTO function is also defined. If we can, for a given grammar, calculate the FOLLOW sets of all left-hand sides (undecidable in the general case), we can apply a variant of the usual SLR(1) test and construct a parsing table for a parser as described by Turnbull and Lee [PSCS 1979].

To obtain the LALR(1) definition, a look-ahead grammar system is defined that will, for each item in each state, generate the (unrestricted) language of all continuations after that item. If we can, for a given grammar, calculate the FIRST sets of all these languages (undecidable in the general case), we can apply a variant of the usual LALR(1) test and construct a parsing table for a similar parser. If one of the above constructions succeeds, a linear-time parser is obtained.

The author gives many hand-calculated examples and explores error detection properties. More general definitions of SLR(1) and LALR(1) are possible, encompassing larger sets of grammars, at the cost of a still further reduced chance of decidability.

13.3 VAN WIJNGAARDEN GRAMMARS AND AFFIX GRAMMARS

Note that van Wijngaarden grammars and two-level grammars are synonyms; affix grammars are different.

*   M. **Sintzoff**, "Existence of a van Wijngaarden syntax for every recursively enumerable set", *Annales de la Société Scientifique de Bruxelles*, vol. 81, no. II, p. 115-118, 1967. A relatively simple proof of the theorem that for every semi-Thue system we can construct a VW grammar that produces the same set.

*   A. van **Wijngaarden**, B.J. Mailloux, J.E.L. Peck, C.H.A. Koster, M. Sintzoff, C.H. Lindsey, L.G.L.T. Meertens, R.G. Fisker, "Report on the algorithmic language ALGOL 68", *Numer. Math.*, vol. 14, p. 79-218, 1969. VW grammars found their widest application to date in the definition of ALGOL 68. Section 1.1.3 of the ALGOL 68 Revised Report contains a very carefully worded description of the two-level mechanism. The report contains many interesting applications.

*   C.H.A. **Koster**, "Affix grammars". In *ALGOL 68 Implementation*, J.E.L. Peck (eds.), North-Holland Publ. Co., Amsterdam, p. 95-109, 1971. Context conditions are expressed inside a context-free grammar by introducing *affixes*, which are divided in *derived* and

inherited and which have to fulfill user-defined *primitive predicates*. If the affix grammar is *well-formed*, a parser for it can be constructed.

- David **Crowe**, "Generating parsers for affix grammars", *Commun. ACM*, vol. 15, no. 8, p. 728-734, Aug 1972. A bounded-context (Floyd productions) parser is extended with affix manipulation.

- A. van **Wijngaarden**, "The generative power of two-level grammars". In *Automata, Languages and Programming; Lecture Notes in Computer Science #14*, J. Loeckx (eds.), Springer-Verlag, Berlin, p. 9-16, 1974. The generative power of VW grammars is illustrated by creating a VW grammar that simulates a Turing machine; the VW grammar uses only one metanotion, thus proving that one metanotion suffices.

- Sheila A. **Greibach**, "Some restrictions on *W*-grammars", *Intern. J. Comput. Inform. Sci.*, vol. 3, no. 4, p. 289-327, 1974. The consequences of two easily checkable restrictions on the form of the rules in a VW grammar are explored in great detail and are found to be surprising. Although this highly technical paper is not directly concerned with parsing, it is very instructive in that it shows methods of exploring the field.

- C.H.A. **Koster**, "Two-level grammars". In *Compiler Construction: An Advanced Course; Lecture Notes in Computer Science #21*, F.L. Bauer & J. Eickel (eds.), Springer-Verlag, Berlin, p. 146-156, 1974. Easy introduction to two-level (VW) grammars, starting from one-level VW grammars. Examples of practical handling of context in a VW grammar.

- P. **Deussen**, "A decidability criterion for van Wijngaarden grammars", *Acta Inform.*, vol. 5, p. 353-375, 1975. The criterion, which is given in detail, can be paraphrased very roughly as follows: the language generated by a VW grammar is decidable if (but not only if) there are no ε-rules and either there are no free metanotions (occurring on the right-hand side only) or there are no dummy metanotions (occurring on the left-hand side only).

- David A. **Watt**, "The parsing problem for affix grammars", *Acta Inform.*, vol. 8, p. 1-20, 1977. A technique is described to convert an affix grammar into a CF grammar called a *head grammar* which contains a special kind of non-terminal, *copy-symbols*. For the head grammar they are ε-rules, but for the affix grammar they effect affix manipulations on the affix stack. Primitive predicates are also ε-rules, but do checks on the affixes. Parsing is done by any CF parser, preferably LR(1). The affixes are not used to control the parsing but only to declare an input string erroneous: for the technique to work, the affix grammar must in effect be an attribute grammar.

- J. Craig **Cleaveland**, Robert C. Uzgalis, *Grammars for programming languages*, Elsevier, New York, p. 154, 1977. In spite of its title, the book is a highly readable explanation of two-level grammars, also known as van Wijngaarden grammars or VW grammars. After an introductory treatment of formal languages, the Chomsky hierarchy and parse trees, it is shown to what extent CF languages can be used to define a programming language. These are shown to fail to define a language completely and the inadequacy of CS grammars is demonstrated. VW grammars are then explained and the remainder of the book consists of increasingly complex and impressive examples of what a VW grammar can do. These examples include keeping a name list, doing type checking and handling block structure in the definition of a programming language. Recommended reading.

- R. **Meersman**, G. Rozenberg, "Two-level meta-controlled substitution grammars", *Acta Inform.*, vol. 10, p. 323-339, 1978. The authors prove that the uniform substitution rule is essential for two-level grammars; without it, they would just generate the CF languages. This highly technical paper examines a number of variants of the mechanisms involved.

- Lutz **Wegner**, "Bracketed two-level grammars – a decidable and practical approach to language definition". In *Automata, languages and programming;*

Lecture Notes in Computer Science #71, Hermann A. Maurer (eds.), Springer-Verlag, Berlin, p. 668-682, 1979. The metanotions of a VW grammar are partitioned into two blocks, "synthesized" and "derived"; they are separated in a hyperrule by special markers, "brackets", and are treated more or less as attributes. Under reasonable conditions parsability can be obtained. The thus restricted VW grammars are very readable.

- Lutz Michael **Wegner**, "On parsing two-level grammars", *Acta Inform.*, vol. 14, p. 175-193, 1980. The article starts by defining a number of properties a VW grammar may exhibit; among these are "left(right) bound", "free of hidden empty notions", "uniquely assignable" and "locally unambiguous". Most of these properties are undecidable, but sub-optimal tests can be devised. For each VW grammar G_{VW}, a CF *skeleton grammar* G_{SK} is defined by considering all hypernotions in the VW grammar as non-terminals of G_{SK} and adding the cross-references of the VW grammar as production rules to G_{SK}. G_{SK} generates a superset of G_{VW}. The cross-reference problem for VW grammars is unsolvable but again any sub-optimal algorithm (or manual intervention) will do. Parsing is now done by parsing with G_{SK} and then reconstructing and testing the metanotions. A long list of conditions necessary for the above to work are given; these conditions are in terms of the properties defined at the beginning.

- Dick **Grune**, "How to produce all sentences from a two-level grammar", *Inform. Process. Lett.*, vol. 19, p. 181-185, Nov 1984. All terminal productions are derived systematically in breadth-first order. The author identifies pitfalls in this process and describes remedies. A parser is used to identify the hyperrules involved in a given sentential form. This parser is a general CF recursive descent parser to which a consistency check for the metanotions has been added; it is not described in detail.

- A.J. **Fisher**, "Practical LL(1)-based parsing of van Wijngaarden grammars", *Acta Inform.*, vol. 21, p. 559-584, 1985. Fisher's parser is based on the idea that the input string was generated using only a small, finite, part of the infinite *strict grammar* that can be generated from the VW grammar. The parser tries to reconstruct this part of the strict grammar on the fly while parsing the input. The actual parsing is done by a top-down interpretative LL(1) parser, called the *terminal parser*. It is driven by a fragment of the strict grammar and any time the definition of a non-terminal is found missing by the terminal parser, the latter asks another module, the *strict syntax generator*, to try to construct it from the VW grammar. For this technique to work, the VW grammar has to satisfy three conditions: the defining CF grammar of each hyperrule is unambiguous, there are no free metanotions, and the skeleton grammar (as defined by Wegner [VW 1980]) is LL(1). The parser system is organized as a set of concurrent processes (written in occam), with both parsers, all hyperrule matchers and several other modules as separate processes. The author claims that "this concurrent organization ... is strictly a property of the algorithm, not of the implementation", but a sequential, albeit slower, implementation seems quite possible. The paper gives heuristics for the automatic generation of the cross-reference needed for the skeleton grammar; gives a method to handle *general hyperrules*, hyperrules that fit all hypernotions, efficiently; and pays much attention to the use of angle brackets in VW grammars.

- Jacques **Cohen**, Timothy J. Hickey, "Parsing and compiling using Prolog", *ACM Trans. Prog. Lang. Syst.*, vol. 9, no. 2, p. 125-164, April 1987. See same paper [CF 1987].

13.4 GENERAL CONTEXT-FREE PARSERS

- E.T. **Irons**, "A syntax-directed compiler for ALGOL 60", *Commun. ACM*, vol. 4, no. 1, p. 51-55, Jan 1961. The first to describe a full parser. It is essentially a full backtracking recursive descent left-corner parser. The published program is corrected in a Letter to the Editor by B.H. Mayoh, *Commun. ACM*, vol. 4, no. 6, p. 284, June 1961.

- Itiroo **Sakai**, "Syntax in universal translation". In *Proceedings 1961 International Conference on Machine Translation of Languages and Applied Language Analysis*, Her Majesty's Stationery Office, London, p. 593-608, 1962. Using a formalism that seems equivalent to a CF grammar in Chomsky Normal Form and a parser that is essentially a CYK parser, the author describes a translation mechanism in which the source language sentence is transformed into a binary tree (by the CYK parser). Each production rule carries a mark telling if the order of the two constituents should be reversed in the target language. The target language sentence is then produced by following this new order and by replacing words. A simple Japanese-to-English example is provided.

- E.T. **Irons**, "The structure and use of the syntax directed compiler", *Annual Review in Automatic Programming*, vol. 3, p. 207-228, 1962. Extended version of Irons [CF 1961].

- E.T. **Irons**, "An error-correcting parse algorithm", *Commun. ACM*, vol. 6, no. 11, p. 669-673, Nov 1963. Contrary to the title, the most interesting part of this paper is the parser it describes, which is essentially Earley's algorithm without look-ahead. The invention of this parser was prompted by the author's dissatisfaction with the error detection properties of backtracking parsers. This one does not backtrack, it keeps all possible parsings in parallel instead. When the set of possible parsings becomes exhausted due to an error in the input, the last non-empty set is analysed for continuations, both terminal and non-terminal, including all successors and alternatives. Then input symbols are discarded until one is found that is a terminal in the continuation set or the beginning of a non-terminal in that set. Symbols are then inserted to bridge any possible gap thus created, and parsing continues. Note that this is essentially Röhrich's algorithm. The author points out applications for this parser as a pattern matcher.

- Sheila A. **Greibach**, "Formal parsing systems", *Commun. ACM*, vol. 7, no. 8, p. 499-504, Aug 1964. "A formal parsing system $G=(V,\mu,T,R)$ consists of two finite disjoint vocabularies, V and T, a many-to-many map, μ, from V onto T, and a recursive set R of strings in T called syntactic sentence classes" (verbatim). This is intended to solve an additional problem in parsing, which occurs often in natural languages: a symbol found in the input does not always uniquely identify a terminal symbol from the language (for instance, *will* (verb) versus *will* (noun)). On this level, the language is given as the entire set R, but in practice it is given through a "context-free phrase structure generator", i.e. a grammar. To allow parsing, this grammar is brought into what is now known as Greibach Normal Form: each rule is of the form $Z \rightarrow aY_1 \cdots Y_m$. Now a *directed production analyser* is defined which consists of an unlimited set of pushdown stores and an input stream, the entries of which are sets of terminal symbols, derived through μ from the lexical symbols. For each consecutive input entry, the machine scans the stores for a top non-terminal Z for which there is a rule $Z \rightarrow aY_1 \cdots Y_m$ with a in the input set. A new store is filled with a copy of the old store and the top Z is replaced by $Y_1 \cdots Y_m$; if the resulting store is longer than the input, it is discarded. Stores will contain non-terminals only. For each store that is empty when the input is exhausted, a parsing has been found. This is in effect non-deterministic top-down parsing with a one-symbol look-ahead. This is probably the first description of a parser that will work for any CF grammar.
A large part of the paper is dedicated to undoing the damage done by converting to Greibach Normal Form.

- T.V. **Griffiths**, S.R. Petrick, "On the relative efficiencies of context-free grammar recognizers", *Commun. ACM*, vol. 8, no. 5, p. 289-300, May 1965. To achieve a unified view of the parsing techniques known at that time, the authors define a non-deterministic two-stack machine whose only type of instruction is the replacement of two given strings on the tops of both stacks by two other strings; the machine is started with the input on one stack and the start symbol on the other and it "recognizes" the input if both stacks get empty simultaneously. For each parsing technique considered, a simple mapping from the grammar to the machine instructions is given; the techniques covered are top-down (called top-down), left-corner (called bottom-up) and bottom-up (called direct-substitution). Next, look-ahead techniques are incorporated to attempt to make the machine deterministic. The authors identify left-recursion as a trouble-spot. All grammars are required to be ε-free. The procedures for the three parsing methods are given in a Letter to the Editor, *Commun. ACM*, vol. 8, no. 10, p. 594, Oct 1965.

- Susumu **Kuno**, "The predictive analyzer and a path elimination technique", *Commun. ACM*, vol. 8, no. 7, p. 453-462, July 1965. The author extends his *predictive analyser* (in modern terminology: an exhaustive top-down parser for grammars in Greibach Normal Form) (see Kuno and Oettinger, reprinted by Grosz, Sparck Jones and Webber [NatLang 1986]) with a table of well-formed substrings. Through ingenious bit manipulation the table is made to fit in a small memory. Time gains are considerable (as expected).

- Susumu **Kuno**, "An augmented predicative analyzer for context-free languages—its relative efficiency", *Commun. ACM*, vol. 9, no. 11, p. 810-823, Nov 1966. Converting a CF grammar to Greibach Normal Form often greatly distorts its structure. To keep track of the structure, the right-hand side of each rule in the CF grammar is prefixed with a marker, a special non-terminal which produces ε. A conversion algorithm is described that results in rules of the form $A \rightarrow M^+ aBC \cdots$, where M^+ is a non-empty sequence of markers. The Kuno predictive analyser (see Kuno [CF 1965]) is extended with a second stack on which the marker parts of the rules are kept. When a parsing is found, the marker stack allows easy reconstruction of the parsing according to the original CF grammar. The parser is compared to two other parsers, using a large number of criteria.

- D.H. **Younger**, "Recognition of context-free languages in time n^3", *Inform. Control*, vol. 10, no. 2, p. 189-208, Feb 1967. A Boolean recognition matrix R is constructed in a bottom-up fashion, in which $R[i,l,p]$ indicates that the segment of the input string starting at position i with length l is a production of non-terminal p. This matrix can be filled in $O(n^3)$ actions, where n is the length of the input string. If $R[0,n,0]$ is set, the whole string is a production of non-terminal 0. Many of the bits in the matrix can never be used in any actual parsing; these can be removed by doing a top-down scan starting from $R[0,n,0]$ and removing all bits not reached this way. If the matrix contains integer rather than Boolean elements, it is easy to fill it with the number of ways a given segment can be produced by a given non-terminal; this yields the ambiguity rate.

- S.H. **Unger**, "A global parser for context-free phrase structure grammars", *Commun. ACM*, vol. 11, no. 4, p. 240-247, Apr 1968. The Unger parser (as described in Section 4.1) is extended with a series of tests to avoid partitionings that could never lead to success. For instance, a section of the input is never matched against a non-terminal if it begins with a token no production of the non-terminal could begin with. Several such tests are described and ways are given to statically derive the necessary information (FIRST sets, LAST sets, EXCLUDE sets) from the grammar. Although none of this changes the exponential character of the algorithm, the tests do result in a considerable speed-up in practice. (There is an essential correction to one of the flowcharts given in *Commun. ACM*, vol. 11, no. 6, p. 427, June 1968.)

- B.A. **Chartres**, J.J. Florentin, "A universal syntax-directed top-down analyzer", *J. ACM*, vol. 15, no. 3, p. 447-464, July 1968. The non-deterministic two-stack top-down parser of Griffiths and Petrick [CF 1965] is extended with a third stack and a status variable. One stack holds the rest of the input, the second holds the prediction that should match that input and the third holds a tracing of the outline of the production tree constructed so far; when input and prediction stack are empty, the third stack holds the completed parse tree. This three-stack mechanism can be run both forward and backward; the status variable keeps track of the direction. By properly reacting to the values on the tops of the stacks and the direction variable, it is possible to make the mechanism perform a full backtracking exhaustive search. Much work is spent on handling left recursion and ε-rules.

- Bálint **Dömölki**, "A universal compiler system based on production rules", *BIT*, vol. 8, no. 4, p. 262-275, Oct 1968. The heart of the compiler system described here is a production system consisting of an ordered set of production rules, which are the inverses of the grammar rules; note that the notions "left-hand side" (lhs) and "right-hand side" (rhs) are reversed from their normal meanings in this abstract. The system attempts to derive the start symbol, by always applying the first applicable production rule (first in two respects: from the left in the string processed, and in the ordered set of production rules). This resolves shift/reduce conflicts in favour of reduce, and reduce/reduce conflicts by length and by the order of the production rules. When a reduction is found, the lhs of the reducing rule is offered for semantic processing and the rhs is pushed back into the input

stream, to be reread. Since the length of the rhs is not restricted, the method can handle non-CF grammars.
The so-called "Syntactic Filter" uses a bitvector technique to determine if, and if so which, production rule is applicable: for every symbol i in the alphabet, there is a bitvector $B[i]$, with one bit for each of the positions in each lhs; this bit set to 1 if this position contains symbol i. There is also a bitvector U marking the first symbol of each lhs, and a bitvector V marking the last symbol of each lhs. Now, a stack of bitvectors Q_t is maintained, with $Q_0 = 0$ and $Q_t = ((Q_{t-1} >> 1) \lor U) \land B[i_t]$, where i_t is the t-th input symbol. Q_t contains the answer to the question whether the last j symbols received are the first j symbols of some lhs, for any lhs and j. A 1 "walks" through an lhs part of the Q vector, as this lhs is recognized. An occurrence of a lhs is found if $Q^t \land V \neq 0$. After doing a replacement, t is set back k places, where k is the length of the applied lhs, so a stack of Q_t-s must be maintained. If some $Q_t = 0$, we have an error. An interesting implementation of the Dömölki algorithm is given by Hext and Roberts [CF 1970].

- T. **Kasami**, K. Torii, "A syntax-analysis procedure for unambiguous context-free grammars", *J. ACM*, vol. 16, no. 3, p. 423-431, July 1969. A rather complicated presentation of a variant of the CYK algorithm, including the derivation of a $O(n^2 \log n)$ time bound for unambiguous Chomsky Normal Form grammars.

- J. **Earley**, "An efficient context-free parsing algorithm", *Commun. ACM*, vol. 13, no. 2, p. 94-102, Feb 1970. This famous paper gives an informal description of the Earley algorithm. The algorithm is compared both theoretically and experimentally with some general search techniques and with the CYK algorithm. It easily beats the general search techniques. Although the CYK algorithm has the same worst-case efficiency as Earley's, it requires $O(n^3)$ on any grammar, whereas Earley's requires $O(n^2)$ on unambiguous grammars and $O(n)$ on bounded-state grammars. The algorithm is easily modified to handle Extended CF grammars. (Also reprinted by Grosz, Sparck Jones and Webber [NatLang 1986])

- J.B. **Hext**, P.S. Roberts, "Syntax analysis by Domölki's algorithm", *Computer J.*, vol. 13, no. 3, p. 263-271, Aug 1970. Dömölki's algorithm is a bottom-up parser in which the item sets are represented as bitvectors. A backtracking version is presented which can handle any grammar. To reduce the need for backtracking a 1-character look-ahead is introduced and an algorithm for determining the actions on the look-ahead is given. Since the internal state is recalculated by vector operations for each input character, the parse table is much smaller than usual and its entries are one bit each. This, and the fact that it is all bitvector operations, makes the algorithm suitable for implementation in hardware.

- Bernard **Lang**, "Parallel non-deterministic bottom-up parsing", *ACM SIGPLAN Notices*, vol. 6, no. 12, p. 56-57, Dec 1971. The full breadth-first search of an Earley parser is limited through the use of weak-precedence relations, in so far as these are unique. Abstract of a larger technical report.

- F.P. **Kaminger**, "Generation, recognition and parsing of context-free languages by means of recursive graphs", *Computing*, vol. 11, no. 1, p. 87-96, 1973. Formal description of the use of recursive graphs instead of CF grammars to describe, generate and parse context-free languages.

- Bernard **Lang**, "Deterministic techniques for efficient non-deterministic parsers". In *Automata, languages and programming; Lecture Notes in Computer Science #14*, J. Loeckx (eds.), Springer-Verlag, Berlin, p. 255-269, 1974. Explores the theoretical properties of doing breadth-first search to resolve the non-determinism in a bottom-up automaton with conflicts. See Tomita [CF 1986] for a practical realization.

- M. **Bouckaert**, A. Pirotte, M. Snelling, "Efficient parsing algorithms for general context-free parsers", *Inform. Sci.*, vol. 8, no. 1, p. 1-26, Jan 1975. The authors observe that the Predictor in an Earley parser will often predict items that start with symbols that can never match the first few symbols of the present input; such items will never bear fruit and could as well be left out. To accomplish this, they extend the k-symbol reduction look-ahead Earley parser with a t-symbol prediction mechanism; this results in very general M_k^t parsing machines, the properties of which are studied, in much formal detail. Three important conclusions can be drawn. Values of k or t larger than one lose much more on processing than they will normally gain on better prediction and sharper reduction; such parsers are better only for asymptotically long input strings. The Earley parser without look-ahead (M_0^0) performs better than the parser with 1 symbol look-ahead; Earley's recommendation to use always 1 symbol look-ahead is unsound. The best parser is M_0^1; i.e. use a one symbol predictive look-ahead and no reduction look-ahead.

- L. **Valiant**, "General context-free recognition in less than cubic time", *J. Comput. Syst. Sci.*, vol. 10, p. 308-315, 1975. Reduces CYK to bit matrix multiplication and then applies Strassen's[†] algorithm.

- C.H.A. **Koster**, "A technique for parsing ambiguous grammars". In *GI-4. Jahrestagung; Lecture Notes in Computer Science #26*, D. Siefkes (eds.), Springer-Verlag, New York, p. 233-246, 1975. Three recursive-descent parsing techniques are described: no backtrack, partial backtrack and full backtrack.

- B. **Sheil**, "Observations on context-free parsing", *Statistical Methods in Linguistics*, p. 71-109, 1976. The author proves that any CF backtracking parser will have polynomial time requirements if provided with a *well-formed substring table* (WFST), which holds the well-formed substrings recognized so far and which is consulted before each attempt to recognize a substring. The time requirements of the parser is $O(n^{c+1})$ where c is the maximum number of non-terminals in any right-hand side. A *2-form grammar* is a CF grammar such that no production rule in the grammar has more than two non-terminals on the right-hand side; nearly all practical grammars are already 2-form. 2-form grammars, of which Chomsky Normal Form grammars are a subset, can be parsed in $O(n^3)$. An algorithm for a dividing top-down parser with a WFST is supplied. Required reading for anybody who wants to write or use a general CF grammar. Many practical hints and opinions (controversial and otherwise) are given.

- Susan L. **Graham**, Michael A. Harrison, "Parsing of general context-free languages". In *Advances in Computing, Vol. 14*, Academic Press, New York, p. 77-185, 1976. The 109 page article describes three algorithms in a more or less unified manner: CYK, Earley's and Valiant's. The main body of the paper is concerned with bounds for time and space requirements. Sharper bounds than usual are derived for special grammars, for instance, for linear grammars.

- Jaroslav **Král**, "A top-down no backtracking parsing of general context-free languages". In *Mathematical Foundations of Computer Science; Lecture Notes in Computer Science #53*, J. Gruska (eds.), Springer-Verlag, Berlin, p. 333-341, 1977. The states of a top-down breadth-first general CF parser are combined whenever possible, resulting in an Earley-like parser without the bottom-up component.

- G.K. **Manacher**, "An improved version of the Cocke-Younger-Kasami algorithm", *Comput. Lang. (Elmsford, NY)*, vol. 3, p. 127-133, 1978. This paper discusses some modifications to the CYK algorithm that make it more efficient. First, the "length induction" iteration of CYK is replaced by an iteration that combines sets of non-terminals that derive strings of length $j-1$ with sets of non-terminals that derive strings of length $k \leq j-1$. Then, the recognition table of CYK is replaced by three tables of lists, where each table has a list for each non-terminal/number pair. The first table maps a non-terminal/length pair to a list of positions, indicating where substrings of this length start

---

[†] Volker Strassen, "Gaussian elimination is not optimal", *Numerische Mathematik*, vol. 13, p. 354-356, 1969. Shows how to multiply two 2×2 matrices using 7 multiplications rather than 8 and extends the principle to larger matrices.

that are derived by this non-terminal. The second table maps a non-terminal/position pair to a list of lengths, indicating the lengths of the substrings starting at this position that are derived by this non-terminal. The third table maps a non-terminal/position pair to a list of lengths, indicating the lengths of the substrings ending at this position that are derived by this non-terminal. With these modifications a time bound $O(s(n))$ is established for unambiguous grammars, where $s(n)$ is the number of triplets (A,i,j) for which the non-terminal A derives the substring starting at position i, with length j. This is at worst $O(n^2)$.

- W.L. **Ruzzo**, "On the complexity of general context-free language parsing and recognition". In *Automata, Languages and Programming; Lecture Notes in Computer Science #71*, Hermann A. Maurer (eds.), Springer-Verlag, Berlin, p. 489-497, 1979. This is an extended abstract, summarizing some time requirement results: it is shown that parsing strings of length n is only $O(\log n)$ harder than just recognizing them. Also, the time to multiply $\sqrt{n} * \sqrt{n}$ Boolean matrices is a lower bound on the time needed to recognize all prefixes of a string, and this, in turn, is a lower bound on the time needed to generate a convenient representation of all parses of a string (basically the CYK recognition table, but reduced so that a non-terminal only is present in the recognition table if it can be used to derive the sentence).

- S.L. **Graham**, M.A. Harrison, W.L. Ruzzo, "An improved context-free recognizer", *ACM Trans. Prog. Lang. Syst.*, vol. 2, no. 3, p. 415-462, July 1980. The well-formed substring table of the CYK parser is filled with dotted items as in an LR parser rather than with the usual non-terminals. This allows the number of objects in each table entry to be reduced considerably. Special operators are defined to handle ε- and unit rules.
The authors do not employ any look-ahead in their parser; they claim that constructing the recognition triangle is pretty fast already and that probably more time will be spent in enumerating and analysing the resulting parse trees. They speed up the latter process by removing all useless entries before starting to generate parse trees. To this end, a top-down sweep through the triangle is performed, similar to the scheme to find all parse trees, which just marks all reachable entries without following up any of them twice. The non-marked entries are then removed (p. 443).
Much attention is paid to efficient implementation, using ingenious data structures.

- A. **Bossi**, N. Cocco, L. Colussi, "A divide-and-conquer approach to general context-free parsing", *Inform. Process. Lett.*, vol. 16, no. 4, p. 203-208, May 1983.
The proposed parsing method yields for a string T two sets: a set of partial parse trees that may be incomplete at their left edge (which then coincides with the left end of T), called L, and a similar right-edge set called R. To parse a string, it is cut in two pieces, each is parsed and the R set of the left-hand piece is combined with the L set of the right-hand piece.

- Masaru **Tomita**, *Efficient parsing for natural language*, Kluwer Academic Publishers, Boston, p. 201, 1986. Tomita describes an efficient parsing algorithm to be used in a "natural-language setting": input strings of some tens of words and considerable but not pathological ambiguity. The algorithm is essentially LR, starting parallel parses when an ambiguity is found in the LR-table. Full examples are given of handling ambiguities, lexical elements with multiple meanings and unknown lexical elements.
The algorithm is compared extensively to Earley's algorithm by measurement and it is found to be consistently five to ten times faster than the latter, in the domain for which it is intended. Earley's algorithm is better in pathological cases; Tomita's fails on unbounded ambiguity. No time bounds are given explicitly, but graphs show a behaviour better than $O(n^3)$. Bouckaert's algorithm (Bouckaert, Pirotte and Snelling [CF 1975]) is shown to be between Earley's and Tomita's in speed.
MacLisp programs of the various algorithms are given and the application in the Nishida and Doshita Machine Translation System is described.

- Eiichi **Tanaka**, Mitsuru Ikeda, Kimio Ezure, "Direct parsing", *Patt. Recog.*, vol. 19, no. 4, p. 315-323, 1986. Variants of Unger's and Earley's parser are compared in a chromosome recognition situation. The possibility of stopping the Unger parser after the first parsing has been found is exploited.

- Jacques **Cohen**, Timothy J. Hickey, "Parsing and compiling using Prolog", *ACM Trans. Prog. Lang. Syst.*, vol. 9, no. 2, p. 125-164, April 1987. Several methods are given to convert grammar rules into Prolog clauses. In the bottom-up method, a rule $E \rightarrow E + T$ corresponds to a clause *reduce* $([n(t), t(+), n(e) | X], [n(e) | X])$ where the parameters represent the stack before and after the reduction. In the top-down method, a rule $T' \rightarrow *FT'$ corresponds to a clause *rule* $(n(tprime), [t(*), n(f), n(tprime)])$. A recursive descent parser is obtained by representing a rule $S \rightarrow aSb$ by the clause $s(ASB) :- append(A, SB, ASB), append(S, B, SB), a(A), s(S), b(B)$. which attempts to cut the input list *ASB* into three pieces *A*, *S* and *B*, which can each be recognized as an *a*, an *s* and a *b*, respectively. A fourth type of parser results if ranges in the input list are used as parameters: $s(X1, X4)$:- $link(X1, a, X2), s(X2, X3), link(X3, b, X4)$ in which $link(P, x, Q)$ describes that the input contains the token *x* between positions *P* and *Q*. For each of these methods, ways are given to limit non-determinism and backtracking, resulting among others in LL(1) parsers.
By supplying additional parameters to clauses, context conditions can be constructed and carried around, much as in a VW grammar (although this term is not used). It should be noted that the resulting Prolog programs are actually not parsers at all: they are just logic systems that connect input strings to parsings. Consequently they can be driven both ways: supply a string and it will produce the parsing; supply a parsing and it will produce the string; supply nothing and it will produce all strings with their parsings in the language.
As a separate topic, it is shown that Prolog is an effective language to do grammar manipulation in: calculation of FIRST and FOLLOW sets, etc. As an equally unrelated topic, examples of code generation in Prolog are shown.

- Masaru **Tomita**, "An efficient augmented-context-free parsing algorithm", *Am. J. Computational Linguistics*, vol. 13, no. 1-2, p. 31-46, Jan-June 1987. Tomita's parser [CF 1986] is extended with Boolean functions for the non-terminals that decide if a proposed reduce is applicable given the context. A method for deriving these functions in Lisp from more abstract specifications is given.

13.5 LL PARSING

- R. **Kurki-Suonio**, "On top-to-bottom recognition and left recursion", *Commun. ACM*, vol. 9, no. 7, p. 527-528, July 1966. Gives a good account of Greibach's algorithm for the removal of left-recursion from a grammar. The resulting distortion of the parsing process is countered by leaving (ϵ-producing) markers in the grammar at the original ends of the right-hand sides in a left-recursive rule. This 2-page paper also gives an algorithm for removing ϵ-rules. Again, these leave markers behind, which can interfere with the markers from a possibly subsequent removal of left-recursion. Rules for solving this interference are given.

- K. **Čulik II**, "Contribution to deterministic top-down analysis of context-free languages", *Kybernetica*, vol. 5, no. 4, p. 422-431, 1968. This paper introduces LL(*f*) grammars where *f* is a function mapping strings of terminals to an arbitrary range, always uniquely determining a right-hand side. *f* is called a *distinctive function*.

- P.M. **Lewis II**, R.E. Stearns, "Syntax-directed transduction", *J. ACM*, vol. 15, no. 3, p. 465-488, 1968. Although this article is about transduction, it is often given as a reference for LL(*k*), because it is one of the first articles discussing the LL(*k*) property, and it has an appendix on the recognition of LL(*k*) languages.

- D. **Wood**, "The theory of left factored languages, Part I", *Computer J.*, vol. 12, no. 4, p. 349-356, 1969. A description of a variant of LL(1) grammars and parsing.

- R. **Kurki-Suonio**, "Notes on top-down languages", *BIT*, vol. 9, p. 225-238, 1969. Gives several variants of the LL(*k*) condition. Also demonstrates the existence of an LL(*k*) language which is not LL(*k−1*).

- D. **Wood**, "The theory of left factored languages, Part II", *Computer J.*, vol. 13, no. 1, p. 55-62, 1970. More results about LL(1) and LL(k) grammars, including a recursive-descent parser in pseudo-Algol 60.

- D.J. **Rosenkrantz**, R.E. Stearns, "Properties of deterministic top-down grammars", *Inform. Control*, vol. 17, p. 226-256, 1970. Many formal properties of LL(k) grammars are derived and tests for LL(k) and strong-LL(k) are given.

- Donald E. **Knuth**, "Top-down syntax analysis", *Acta Inform.*, vol. 1, p. 79-110, 1971. A *Parsing Machine* (PM) is defined, which is effectively a set of mutually recursive Boolean functions which absorb input if they succeed and absorb nothing if they fail. Properties of the languages accepted by PMs are examined. This leads to CF grammars, dependency graphs, the null string problem, back-up, LL(k), follow-function, LL(1), s-languages and a comparison of top-down versus bottom-up parsing. The author is one of the few scientists who provide insight in their thinking process.

- Paul W. **Abrahams**, "A syntax-directed parser for recalcitrant grammars", *Intern. J. Comput. Math.*, vol. A3, p. 105-115, 1972. LL(1) parsing with conflict resolvers, called *oracles*.

- M. **Griffith**, "LL(1) grammars and analyzers". In *Compiler Construction: an advanced course; Lecture Notes in Computer Science #21*, F.L. Bauer & J. Eickel (eds.), Springer-Verlag, New York, p. 57-84, 1974. A discussion of the LL(1) property, including a decision algorithm and the production of an analyser in the form of executable text. These lecture notes also discuss some grammar transformations, including elimination of left-recursion, factorization, and substitution. Semantic insertions (or hooks for semantic actions) are also given some attention.

- T. **Komor**, "A note on left-factored languages", *Computer J.*, vol. 17, no. 3, p. 242-244, 1974. Points out an error in a paper by Wood on left-factored languages [LL 1970], and suggests an extension to Fosters SID [Transform 1968] involving ε-rules.

- S. **Jarzabek**, T. Krawczyk, "LL-regular grammars", *Inform. Process. Lett.*, vol. 4, no. 2, p. 31-37, 1975. Introduces LL-regular (LLR) grammars: for every rule $A \rightarrow \alpha_1 \mid \cdots \mid \alpha_n$, a partition $(R_1, \cdots, R_n)$ of disjoint regular sets must be given such that the rest of the input sentence is a member of exactly one of these sets. A parser can then be constructed by creating finite-state automata for these sets, and letting these finite state automata determine the next prediction.

- A. **Nijholt**, "On the parsing of LL-regular grammars". In *Mathematical Foundations of Computer Science; Lecture Notes in Computer Science #45*, A. Mazurkiewicz (eds.), Springer-Verlag, Berlin, p. 446-452, 1976. Derives a parsing algorithm for LL-regular grammars with a regular pre-scan from right to left that leaves markers, and a subsequent scan which consists of an LL(1)-like parser.

- D. **Wood**, "A bibliography of top-down parsing", *ACM SIGPLAN Notices*, vol. 13, no. 2, p. 71-76, Feb 1978. Contains some 90 literature references up to 1978 on deterministic top-down parsing and related issues.

- J. **Lewi**, K. de Vlaminck, J. Huens, M. Huybrechts, "The ELL(1) parser generator and the error-recovery mechanism", *Acta Inform.*, vol. 10, p. 209-228, 1978. See same paper [ErrHandl 1978].

- V.W. **Setzer**, "Non-recursive top-down syntax analysis", *Softw. Pract. Exper.*, vol. 9, no. 1, p. 237-245, 1979. Compares recursive and non-recursive implementations of table-driven top-down parsers. The introduction of actions is facilitated by implementing the driver and the tables as a loop over a case statement (on the states) over case statements (on the input token).

- Stephan **Heilbrunner**, "On the definition of ELR(k) and ELL(k) grammars", *Acta Inform.*, vol. 11, p. 169-176, 1979. Comparison and analysis of various definitions of extended LL(k) and extended LR(k), based on the transformations involved.

- D.R. **Milton**, L.W. Kirchhoff, B.R. Rowland, "An ALL(1) compiler generator", *ACM SIGPLAN Notices*, vol. 14, no. 8, p. 152-157, Aug 1979. Presents an LL(1) parser generator and attribute evaluator which allows LL(1) conflicts to be solved by examining attribute values; the generated parsers use the error correction algorithm of Fischer, Milton and Quiring [ErrHandl 1980].

- D.A. **Poplawski**, "On LL-regular grammars", *J. Comput. Syst. Sci.*, vol. 18, p. 218-227, 1979. Presents proof that, given a regular partition, it is decidable whether a grammar is LL-regular with respect to this partition; it is undecidable whether or not such a regular partition exists. The paper then discusses a two-pass parser; the first pass works from right to left, marking each terminal with an indication of the partition that the rest of the sentence belongs to. The second pass then uses these indications for its predictions.

- V.N. **Glushkova**, "Lexical analysis of LL(k) languages", *Program. Comput. Softw.*, vol. 5, p. 166-172, 1979. Examines the reduction of LL(k) grammars to simple-LL(1) grammars by combining terminal symbols into new terminal symbols.

- J. **Cohen**, R. Sitver, D. Auty, "Evaluating and improving recursive descent parsers", *IEEE Trans. Softw. Eng.*, vol. SE-5, no. 5, p. 472-480, Sept 1979. Derives formulas which express the execution time of systematically generated recursive descent parsers, and uses these formulas to estimate the gain of various optimizations, such as the elimination of some routine calls and merging of common code.

- S. **Sippu**, E. Soisalon-Soininen, "On constructing LL(k) parsers". In *Automata, Languages and Programming; Lecture Notes in Computer Science #71*, H.A. Maurer (eds.), Springer-Verlag, Berlin, p. 585-595, 1979. Presents a method for constructing canonical LL(k) parsers that can be regarded as the dual to the LR(k) technique of items and viable prefixes. In the LL(k) method we have LL(k) items and viable suffixes. Like in the LR case, the LL(k) method also has LA(p)LL(k) and SLL(k) variants; the SLL(k) variant coincides with the strong-LL(k) grammars. Note that, although the S of SLL stands for Simple, this is not the same Simple LL as the simple LL discussed in chapter 8.

- A. **Nijholt**, "LL-regular grammars", *Intern. J. Comput. Math.*, vol. A8, p. 303-318, 1980. This paper discusses strong-LL-regular grammars, which are a subset of the LL-regular grammars, exactly as the strong-LL(k) grammars are a subset of the LL(k) grammars, and derives some properties.

- Seppo **Sippu**, Eljas Soisalon-Soininen, "On LL(k) parsing", *Inform. Control*, vol. 53, no. 3, p. 141-164, June 1982. Theoretical background to Sippu and Soisalon-Soininen [LL 1979].

- K. John **Gough**, "A new method of generating LL(1) look-ahead sets", *ACM SIG-PLAN Notices*, vol. 20, no. 6, p. June 1985, 16-19. Presents an efficient method for computing the FIRST and FOLLOW sets, using "begun-by", "precedes", and "ends" relations.

- Thomas J. **Sager**, "A technique for creating small fast compiler front ends", *ACM SIGPLAN Notices*, vol. 20, no. 10, p. 87-94, Oct 1985. Presents a predictive parser that has its tables compacted through the use of a minimal perfect hash function, thus making them very small. An example is given for the Pascal language.

- Barry **Dwyer**, "Improving Gough's LL(1) look-ahead generator", *ACM SIGPLAN Notices*, vol. 20, no. 11, p. 27-29, Nov 1985. Refer to Gough [LL 1985]. Improves on

Gough's algorithm by not computing those FIRST and FOLLOW sets that are not needed for the LL(1) parser generation.

- David R. **Hanson**, "Compact recursive-descent parsing of expressions", *Softw. Pract. Exper.*, vol. 15, no. 12, p. 1205-1212, Dec 1985. Discusses recursive descent parsing of expressions by using a precedence table for the operators instead of a parsing routine for each precedence level. There is for instance only one routine for expressions involving binary operators; the precedence of the expression to be parsed is a parameter.

- Reinhold **Heckmann**, "An efficient ELL(1)-parser generator", *Acta Inform.*, vol. 23, p. 127-148, 1986. The problem of parsing with an ELL(1) grammar is reduced to finding various FIRST and FOLLOW sets. Theorems about these sets are derived and very efficient algorithms for their calculation are supplied.

- Dick **Grune**, Ceriel J.H. Jacobs, "A programmer-friendly LL(1) parser generator", *Softw. Pract. Exper.*, vol. 18, no. 1, p. 29-38, Jan 1988. Presents a practical ELL(1) parser generator, called *LLgen*, that generates fast error correcting recursive descent parsers. In addition to the error correction, *LLgen* features static as well as dynamic conflict resolvers and a separate compilation facility. The grammar can be viewed as a program, allowing for a natural positioning of semantic actions.

- Keiichi **Yoshida**, Yoshiko Takeuchi, "Some properties of an algorithm for constructing LL(1) parsing tables using production indices", *J. Inform. Process.*, vol. 11, no. 4, p. 258-262, 1988. Presents an LL(1) parse table algorithm that, rather than first computing FIRST and FOLLOW sets, computes a so-called FIRST-table and FOLLOW-table, which are indexed by a (non-terminal, symbol) pair, and deliver a grammar rule number.

- H. **Dobler**, K. Pirklbauer, "Coco-2, a new compiler compiler", *ACM SIGPLAN Notices*, vol. 25, no. 5, p. 82-90, May 1990. The authors present an integrated system consisting of a lexical phase using a heavily reduced FS automaton, and a syntactic phase which uses a table-driven LL(1) parser. Semantic actions are interspersed in the syntactic phase.

13.6 LR PARSING

- D.E. **Knuth**, "On the translation of languages from left to right", *Inform. Control*, vol. 8, p. 607-639, 1965. This is the original paper on LR(k). It defines the notion as an abstract property of a grammar and gives two tests for LR(k). The first works by constructing for the grammar a regular grammar which generates all possible already reduced parts (= stacks) plus their look-aheads; if this grammar has the property that none of its words is a prefix to another of its words, the original grammar was LR(k). The second consists of implicitly constructing all possible item sets (= states) and testing for conflicts. Since none of this is intended to yield a reasonable parsing algorithm, notation and terminology differs from that in later papers on the subject. Several theorems concerning LR(k) grammars are given and proved.

- A.J. **Korenjak**, "A practical method for constructing LR(k) processors", *Commun. ACM*, vol. 12, no. 11, p. 613-623, Nov 1969. The huge LR(1) parsing table is partitioned as follows. A non-terminal Z is chosen judiciously from the grammar, and two grammars are constructed, G_0, in which Z is considered to be a terminal symbol, and G_1, which is the grammar for Z (i.e. which has Z as the start symbol). If both grammars are LR(1) and moreover a master LR(1) parser can be constructed that controls the switching back and forth between G_0 and G_1, the parser construction succeeds (and the original grammar was LR(1) too). The three resulting tables together are much smaller than the LR(1) table for the original grammar. It is also possible to chose a set of non-terminals $Z_1 \cdots Z_n$ and apply a variant of the above technique.

- David **Pager**, "A solution to an open problem by Knuth", *Inform. Control*, vol. 17,

p. 462-473, 1970. Highly mathematical paper concerning the properties of certain partitions of the states of an LR(1) parser with a view to reducing the size of the LR automaton.

- H. **Langmaack**, "Application of regular canonical systems to grammars translatable from left to right", *Acta Inform.*, vol. 1, p. 111-114, 1971. Different proof of the decidability of LR(*k*).

- Franklin L. **DeRemer**, "Simple LR(*k*) grammars", *Commun. ACM*, vol. 14, no. 7, p. 453-460, July 1971. SLR(*k*) explained by its inventor. Several suggestions are made on how to modify the method; use a possibly different *k* for each state; use possibly different lengths for each look-ahead string. The relation to Korenjak's approach [LR 1969] is also discussed.

- A.V. **Aho**, J.D. Ullman, "Optimization of LR(*k*) parsers", *J. Comput. Syst. Sci.*, vol. 6, p. 573-602, 1972. An algorithm is given to determine which entries in an LR(*k*) table can never be accessed; the values of these entries are immaterial (so-called *don't-care entries*) and can be merged with other values. A second algorithm is given to determine which error entries could be merged with which reduce entry, with the only result that error detection is postponed. Both algorithms and a merging technique are used to reduce table size. It is proved that using these algorithms, one can produce SLR(1) and LALR(1) tables. It is also proved that SLR(1) is identical to Korenjak's method [LR 1969] with all non-terminals selected. See also Soisalon-Soininen [LR 1982].

- David S. **Wise**, "Generalized overlap resolvable grammars and their parsers", *J. Comput. Syst. Sci.*, vol. 6, p. 538-572, Dec 1972. See same paper [Precedence 1972].

- T. **Anderson**, J. Eve, J.J. Horning, "Efficient LR(1) parsers", *Acta Inform.*, vol. 2, p. 12-39, 1973. Coherent explanation of SLR(1), LALR(1), elimination of unit rules and table compression, with good advice.

- Karel **Čulik II**, Rina Cohen, "LR-regular grammars – an extension of LR(*k*) grammars", *J. Comput. Syst. Sci.*, vol. 7, p. 66-96, 1973. The input is scanned from right to left by a FS automaton which records its state at each position. Next this sequence of states is parsed from left to right using an LR(0) parser. If such a FS automaton and LR(0) parser exist, the grammar is LR-regular. The authors conjecture, however, that it is unsolvable to construct this automaton and parser. Examples are given of cases in which the problem can be solved.

- A.V. **Aho**, J.D. Ullman, "A technique for speeding up LR(*k*) parsers", *SIAM J. Computing*, vol. 2, no. 2, p. 106-127, June 1973. Describes two detailed techniques to eliminate unit rules, one by recognizing particular stack configurations and one by merging shifts on non-terminals (GOTO's).

- Shoji **Sekimoto**, Kuniaki Mukai, Masaru Sudo, "A method of minimizing LR(*k*) parsers", *Systems, Computers and Control*, vol. 4, no. 5, p. 73-80, 1973. The states of an LR(1) parser are grouped into classes by one of several equivalence relations. The parser records only in which class it is, not in which state. When a reduction is called for, additional computation is required to determine which reduction. The tables for the class transitions are much smaller than those for the state transitions.

- Jaroslav **Král**, Jiří Demner, "A note on the number of states of the DeRemer's recognizer", *Inform. Process. Lett.*, vol. 2, p. 22-23, 1973. Gives a formula for the number of states of an SLR(1) parser for an LL(1) grammar.

- A.V. **Aho**, S.C. Johnson, "LR parsing", *Computing Surveys*, vol. 6, no. 2, p. 99-124, 1974. LR parsing explained in a readable fashion, by the experts. Required reading.

- Matthew M. **Geller**, Susan L. Graham, Michael A. Harrison, "Production prefix parsing". In *Automata, languages and programming; Lecture Notes in Computer*

Science #14, J. Loeckx (eds.), Springer-Verlag, Berlin, p. 232-241, 1974. The items in a non-deterministic LR(0|1) automaton are simplified in that rather than $A \rightarrow \beta \cdot \gamma$ only β (the *production prefix*) is recorded. If the corresponding deterministic automaton is free of conflicts and has no compound states (that is, each state contains only one production prefix) the grammar is a *production prefix grammar*. Table size is proportional to grammar size. Production prefix(1) is between simple precedence and SLR(1) in power.

- David **Pager**, "On eliminating unit productions from LR(k) parsers". In *Automata, languages and programming; Lecture Notes in Computer Science #14*, J. Loeckx (eds.), Springer-Verlag, Berlin, p. 242-254, 1974. The unit rules (and only the unit rules) of the grammar are collected in a directed graph, which is a set of multi-rooted trees (no cycles allowed). For each leaf, the states of all its predecessors are contracted.

- J.J. **Horning**, "LR grammars and analyzers". In *Compiler Construction, an Advanced Course; Lecture Notes in Computer Science #21*, F.L. Bauer & J. Eickel (eds.), Springer-Verlag, New York, p. 85-108, 1974. These lecture notes present a concise discussion of LR(k) grammars and LR(0), SLR(1) (more restrictive adding of reduce entries by using FOLLOW sets), LALR(1) (using shift entries to determine state after reduce), and LR(1) (adding look-ahead to items) constructor algorithms. Also some attention is given to the representation of LR tables, including some compactification techniques.

- Paul **Purdom**, "The size of LALR(1) parsers", *BIT*, vol. 14, p. 326-337, 1974. Experimental size analysis for LALR(1) parsers. Although parser size can be exponential in the grammar size, it is found in practice to be linear in the grammar size.

- Hans H. **Kron**, Hans-Jürgen Hoffman, Gerhard Winkler, "On a SLR(k)-based parser system which accepts non-LR(k) grammars". In *GI-4. Jahrestagung; Lecture Notes in Computer Science #26*, D. Siefkes (eds.), Springer-Verlag, New York, p. 214-223, 1975. For each inadequate state in an LR(0) automaton, a resolution tree is constructed of maximum depth k. If this construction succeeds, the grammar is of type *FSLR(k)*. If it fails, a parser is generated that performs breadth-first search to resolve the remaining inadequacies. Detailed algorithms are given.

- A.J. **Demers**, "Elimination of single productions and merging of non-terminal symbols in LR(1) grammars", *Comput. Lang. (Elmsford, NY)*, vol. 1, no. 2, p. 105-119, April 1975. The unit rules are used to define subsets of the non-terminals, the members of which can be treated as equivalent, similar to Aho and Ullman [LR 1973]. Explicit proofs are given.

- Harry B. **Hunt III**, Thomas G. Szymanski, Jeffrey D. Ullman, "On the complexity of LR(k) testing", *Commun. ACM*, vol. 18, no. 12, p. 707-716, Dec 1975. Time bounds as a function of the grammar size are derived for testing many properties of grammars. A practical result is that both the LL(k) and the LR(k) properties can be tested in $O(n^{k+2})$. These and other bounds given in the paper are upper bounds, and actual testing is often much faster.

- O.L. **Madsen**, B.B. Kristensen, "LR-parsing of extended context-free grammars", *Acta Inform.*, vol. 7, no. 1, p. 61-73, 1976. The right parts are allowed to contain choices $\{\omega_1 | \cdots | \omega_n\}$ and repetitions $\{\omega\}^*$. In addition to the dotted items in the LR sets, there are also *marked* items, which have a # rather than a •. The # means one of three things: here starts a repetition, one element of a repetition has just been recognized or one member of a choice has just been recognized. Upon reduction, these marked items will tell how to unstack the entire right-hand side.

- R.C. **Backhouse**, "An alternative approach to the improvement of LR(k) parsers", *Acta Inform.*, vol. 6, no. 3, p. 277-296, 1976. Traditionally, the field of bottom-up parsing is described in terms of handle-finding automata. The author describes it in terms of left-contexts, in which a *left-context* is a set of stack configurations of the LR(k) parser. Other bottom-up techniques are explained as approximations to these sets.

• Thomas G. **Szymanski**, John H. Williams, "Non-canonical extensions of bottom-up parsing techniques", *SIAM J. Computing*, vol. 5, no. 2, p. 231-250, June 1976. Theory of non-canonical versions of several bottom-up parsing techniques, with good informal introduction.

• Marc L. **Joliat**, "A simple technique for partial elimination of unit productions from LR(k) parsers", *IEEE Trans. Comput.*, vol. C-25, no. 7, p. 763-764, July 1976. A very simple algorithm is given that alters some of the transitions in an LR parse table to bypass unit rules.

• M.M. **Geller**, M.A. Harrison, "Characteristic parsing: a framework for producing compact deterministic parsers", *J. Comput. Syst. Sci.*, vol. 14, no. 3, p. 265-317, June 1977. Given a deterministic LR(1) automaton, suppose we add some (arbitrary) items to some states. This will have two effects: the discriminatory power of the automaton will weaken and its minimum size will decrease (since now some states will coincide). For a large number of grammars there is a *characteristic* item addition technique that will minimize automaton size while preserving just enough power. This requires a heavy mathematical apparatus.

• Matthew M. **Geller**, Michael A. Harrison, "On LR(k) grammars and languages", *Theoret. Comput. Sci.*, vol. 4, p. 245-276, 1977. Theoretical groundwork for the "characteristic parsing technique" of Geller and Harrison [LR June 1977].

• D. **Pager**, "The lane-tracing algorithm for constructing LR(k) parsers and ways of enhancing its efficiency", *Inform. Sci.*, vol. 12, p. 19-42, 1977. An item $A{\rightarrow}\beta{\bullet}X\gamma$ in an LR parser (called a "configuration" here) has in general two kinds of successors: a set of "immediate successors" $X{\rightarrow}{\bullet}\xi_n$ and the "transition successor" $A{\rightarrow}\beta X{\bullet}\gamma$. An item together with a sequence of its successive successors is called a *lane*. Lanes are used 1) to collect enough look-ahead context to convert an LR(0) automaton to LALR(1); 2) to determine which LALR(1) states should be split to resolve remaining LALR(1) conflicts. The required algorithms are of considerable complexity.

• Wilf R. **LaLonde**, "Regular right part grammars and their parsers", *Commun. ACM*, vol. 20, no. 10, p. 731-741, Oct 1977. The notion of regular right part grammars and its advantages are described in detail. A parser is proposed that does LR(k) parsing to find the right end of the handle and then, using different parts of the same table, scans the stack backwards using a look-ahead (to the left!) of m symbols to find the left end; this is called *LR(m, k)*. The corresponding parse table construction algorithm is given by LaLonde [LR 1979].

• David **Pager**, "A practical general method for constructing LR(k) parsers", *Acta Inform.*, vol. 7, no. 3, p. 249-268, 1977. When during the construction of an LR(1) parser a state has to be added, one can consider merging it with an already existing state, if no conflict can arise from this. The problem is that it is not easy to tell whether conflicts may arise from a certain merge. To this end, the notions *weak compatibility* and *strong compatibility* are defined. Algorithms for the efficient construction of conflict-free small full LR(1) parse tables are given.

• D. **Pager**, "Eliminating unit productions from LR(k) parsers", *Acta Inform.*, vol. 9, p. 31-59, 1977. Very detailed description of a unit rule elimination algorithm.

• A. **Celentano**, "Incremental LR parsers", *Acta Inform.*, vol. 10, p. 307-321, 1978. Very clear exposition of how the Ghezzi and Mandrioli algorithm [LR 1979] can be made to work on parse sequences rather than on parse trees, thus improving efficiency.

• Stephen C. **Johnson**, *YACC: yet another compiler-compiler*, Bell Laboratories, Murray Hill, New Jersey 07974, p. 34, 1978. In spite of its title, *yacc* is one of the most widely used parser generators. It generates LALR(1) parsers from a grammar with embedded semantic actions and features a number of disambiguating and conflict-resolving mechanisms. The generated parser is in C.

*   Akifumi **Makinouchi**, "On single production elimination in simple LR(k) environment", *J. Inform. Process.*, vol. 1, no. 2, p. 76-80, 1978. An SLR(1) parser is extended with the possibility of specifying grammar rules of the form $\neg\{C_l\}A\neg\{C_r\}\rightarrow\cdots$, which can only be applied when the symbol before the A cannot produce a member of $\{C_l\}$ as its last token, and the token after A is not in $\{C_r\}$. Such rules allow some convenient ambiguities to be resolved without loosing the generative power of the system.

*   W.R **LaLonde**, "Constructing LR parsers for regular right part grammars", *Acta Inform.*, vol. 11, p. 177-193, 1979. Describes the algorithms for the regular right part parsing technique explained by LaLonde [LR 1977]. The back scan is performed using so-called *read-back tables*. Compression techniques for these tables are given.

*   Stephan **Heilbrunner**, "On the definition of ELR(k) and ELL(k) grammars", *Acta Inform.*, vol. 11, p. 169-176, 1979. See same paper [LL 1979].

*   Otto **Mayer**, "On deterministic canonical bottom-up parsing", *Inform. Control*, vol. 43, p. 280-303, 1979. A general framework is presented for deterministic canonical bottom-up parsers, from which well-known parsers arise as special cases.

*   Carlo **Ghezzi**, Dino Mandrioli, "Incremental parsing", *ACM Trans. Prog. Lang. Syst.*, vol. 1, no. 1, p. 58-70, July 1979. The authors observe that when a grammar allows bottom-up parsing using some technique T and is at the same time RL(k) for any k, then any modification to the input text can only affect nodes that produce the modified part. By keeping the entire parse tree in a both left-most and right-most threaded form, these nodes can be located and updated quickly. The case LR(1) $\wedge$ RL(1) is treated in full.

*   Kai **Koskimies**, Eljas Soisalon-Soininen, "On a method for optimizing LR parsers", *Intern. J. Comput. Math.*, vol. A7, p. 287-295, 1979. Defines criteria under which Pager's algorithm for the elimination of unit rules [LR 1977] can be safely applied to SLR(1) parsers.

*   Kuo-Chung **Tai**, "Noncanonical SLR(1) grammars", *ACM Trans. Prog. Lang. Syst.*, vol. 1, no. 2, p. 295-320, Oct 1979. A survey of non-canonical parsing methods is given and two non-canonical variants of SLR(1) parsing are described.

*   Gerald A. **Fisher Jr.**, Manfred Weber, "LALR(1) parsing for languages without reserved words", *ACM SIGPLAN Notices*, vol. 14, no. 11, p. 26-30, Nov 1979. A heuristic is given for designing an LALR(1) programming language without reserved words. First design the LALR(1) language *with* reserved words, using a non-terminal identifier for the identifiers. Now allow identifier to also produce all reserved words and modify the grammar (or the language) until the grammar is LALR(1) again, using feedback from an LALR(1) parser generator.

*   Eljas **Soisalon-Soininen**, "On the space-optimizing effect of eliminating single productions from LR parsers", *Acta Inform.*, vol. 14, p. 157-174, 1980. Improvement of Pager's unit rule elimination algorithm [LR 1977].

*   Carlo **Ghezzi**, Dino Madrioli, "Augmenting parsers to support incrementality", *J. ACM*, vol. 27, no. 3, p. 564-579, 1980. The algorithm of Ghezzi and Mandrioli [LR 1979] is extended to all LR(k) grammars.

*   Jacek **Witaszek**, "The LR/k/ parser". In *Mathematical Foundations of Computer Science; Lecture Notes in Computer Science #88*, P. Dembiński (eds.), Springer-

Verlag, New York, p. 686-697, 1980. Three size-reducing transformations on LR(k) tables are defined that leave the LR(k) property undisturbed. One is similar to minimising a FS automaton, one removes unused look-ahead and one allows delaying error detection. No full algorithms given, but see Witaszek [LR 1988].

• Bent Bruun **Kristensen**, Ole Lehrmann Madsen, "Methods for computing LALR(k) lookahead", *ACM Trans. Prog. Lang. Syst.*, vol. 3, no. 1, p. 60-82, Jan 1981. The LALR(k) look-ahead sets are seen as the solution to a set of equations, which are solved by recursive traversal of the LR(0) automaton. Full algorithms plus proofs are given.

• R. **Kemp**, "LR(0) grammars generated by LR(0) parsers", *Acta Inform.*, vol. 15, p. 265-280, 1981. Theoretical analysis of the set of LR(0) grammars that produce a given LR(0) parser.

• Theodore P. **Baker**, "Extending look-ahead for LR parsers", *J. Comput. Syst. Sci.*, vol. 22, no. 2, p. 243-259, 1981. A FS automaton is derived from the LR automaton as follows: upon a reduce to A the automaton moves to all states that have an incoming arc marked A. This automaton is used for analysing the look-ahead as in an LR-regular parser (Čulik and Cohen [LR 1973]).

• Stephan **Heilbrunner**, "A parsing automata approach to LR theory", *Theoret. Comput. Sci.*, vol. 15, p. 117-157, 1981. Parsing is explained in terms of *item grammars*, which describe the stack configurations of the parser. The theory is first developed for LR and then applied uniformly to LL and LC.

• Wilf R. **LaLonde**, "The construction of stack-controlling LR parsers for regular right part grammars", *ACM Trans. Prog. Lang. Syst.*, vol. 3, no. 2, p. 168-206, April 1981. Traditional LR parsers shift each input token onto the stack; often, this shift could be replaced by a state transition, indicating that the shift has taken place. Such a parser is called a *stack-controlling LR parser*, and will do finite-state recognition without stack manipulation whenever possible. Algorithms for the construction of stack-controlling LR parse tables are given. The paper is complicated by the fact that the new feature is introduced not in a traditional LR parser, but in an LR parser for regular right parts (for which see LaLonde [LR 1977]).

• Augusto **Celentano**, "An LR parsing technique for extended context-free grammars", *Comput. Lang. (Elmsford, NY)*, vol. 6, no. 2, p. 95-107, 1981. The results of repetitions or selections are popped off the parsing stack before the entire right-hand side has been recognized. Remarkably, this can be done for any extended LR(1) grammar. Explicit algorithms are given.

• Paul W. **Purdom**, Cynthia A. Brown, "Parsing extended LR(k) grammars", *Acta Inform.*, vol. 15, p. 115-127, 1981. An LR state is stacked only at the beginning of a right-hand side; all other work is done on a global state. At a reduce, the reduced non-terminal is already on the top of the stack and needs only to be unstacked. This does not work for all extended LR(k) grammars, but any extended LR(k) can be converted into one for which the method works.

• Takehiro **Tokuda**, "Eliminating unit reductions from LR(k) parsers using minimum contexts", *Acta Inform.*, vol. 15, p. 447-470, 1981. Very densely written analysis of algorithms for the elimination of unit rules from a special class of LR(k) parsers.

• C. **Burgess**, L. James, "An indexed bibliography for LR grammars and parsers", *ACM SIGPLAN Notices*, vol. 16, no. 8, p. 14-26, Aug 1981. Useful, detailed and structured bibliography containing around 115 entries.

• David **Spector**, "Full LR(1) parser generation", *ACM SIGPLAN Notices*, vol. 16, no. 8, p. 58-66, Aug 1981. A heuristic algorithm for enlarging an LR(0) table to full LR(1) is given and demonstrated on two examples. With discussion in subsequent months (vol. 16, no. 11, Nov 1981, p. 2). See also Ancona, Dodero and Gianuzzi [LR 1982] and Spector [LR 1988].

- Charles **Wetherell**, A. Shannon, "LR – automatic parser generator and LR(1) parser", *IEEE Trans. Softw. Eng.*, vol. SE-7, no. 3, p. 274-278, May 1981. This short paper discusses a full LR(1) parser generator and parser, written in ANSI 66 Fortran for portability, and using an algorithm by Pager [LR 1977].

- M. **Ancona**, V. Gianuzzi, "A new method for implementing LR(k) tables", *Inform. Process. Lett.*, vol. 13, no. 4/5, p. 171-176, 1981. For each inadequate state there is a separate automaton handling that inadequacy by doing a look-ahead of one token. If this automaton has inadequate states the process is repeated. A tables construction algorithm is given.

- Eljas **Soisalon-Soininen**, "Inessential error entries and their use in LR parser optimization", *ACM Trans. Prog. Lang. Syst.*, vol. 4, no. 2, p. 179-195, Apr 1982. More sophisticated and general algorithms are given for the techniques described by Aho and Ullman [LR 1972].

- M. **Ancona**, G. Dodero, V. Gianuzzi, "Building collections of LR(k) items with partial expansion of lookahead strings", *ACM SIGPLAN Notices*, vol. 17, no. 5, p. 24-28, May 1982. In addition to the usual terminals, non-terminals are allowed in the look-ahead sets, leading to very substantial savings in the number of states. Only if an inadequate state turns up the non-terminals are developed as far as needed to resolve the inadequacy. The algorithm will also work reasonably for $k > 1$.

- J.C.H. **Park**, "A new LALR formalism", *ACM SIGPLAN Notices*, vol. 17, no. 7, p. 47-61, July 1982. Simplified operators corresponding to Predict and Accept are defined precisely and applied to LR and LALR parser generation. Difficult to read.

- Frank **DeRemer**, Thomas J. Pennello, "Efficient computation of LALR(1) look-ahead sets", *ACM Trans. Prog. Lang. Syst.*, vol. 4, no. 4, p. 615-649, Oct 1982. 1. The LALR(1) look-ahead sets are calculated by four linear sweeps over the LR(0) automaton, calculating the sets Direct Read, Read, Follow and Look-Ahead, respectively. 2. An obvious simplification leads to "Not Quite LALR(1)", *NQLALR(1)*, and is shown to be inadequate. 3. The debugging of non-LALR(1) grammars is treated.

- Jorma **Tarhio**, "LR parsing of some ambiguous grammars", *Inform. Process. Lett.*, vol. 14, no. 3, p. 101-103, 1982. The reduction items in all inadequate states are collected. The rules in them are extended at the end with "synchronization symbols", to make the shift/reduce and reduce/reduce conflicts go away. These synchronization symbols are context-dependent; for instance each identifier could be followed by a token indicating its type. The synchronization symbols are inserted in the input stream by the lexical analyser while parsing.

- Rakesh **Agrawal**, Keith D. Detro, "An efficient incremental LR parser for grammars with epsilon productions", *Acta Inform.*, vol. 19, no. 4, p. 369-376, 1983. A linear time and space implementation of Celentano's algorithm [LR 1978] is described, which can also handle ε-rules.

- Takehiro **Tokuda**, "A fixed-length approach to the design and construction of bypassed LR(k) parsers", *J. Inform. Process.*, vol. 6, no. 1, p. 23-30, 1983. The idea of removing unit reductions is extended to removing *all* reductions that do not involve semantic actions; this leads to *bypassed LR(k) parsers*. Full algorithms are given. Some of the literature on removing unit rules is analysed critically.

- Dashing **Yeh**, "On incremental shift-reduce parsing", *BIT*, vol. 23, no. 1, p. 36-48, 1983. The input tokens to an LR parser are stored in a linked list; each node in this list also holds a pointer to a stack pertinent for the token in the node. These stacks can be merged and are in fact also stored in the nodes. This arrangement greatly simplifies incremental parsing. Very clear explanation.

- Kenzo **Inoue**, Fukumi Fujiwara, "On LLC(k) parsing method of LR(k) grammars", *J. Inform. Process.*, vol. 6, no. 4, p. 206-217, 1983. Assume an LR(k) grammar. Start parsing using the (full) LL(k) method, until an LL(k) conflict is encountered, say on non-terminal A. A is then parsed with the LR(k) method, using the proper predicted look-ahead set. If during the LR (sub)parsing the number of items narrows down to one, an LL(k) (sub-sub)parsing is started; etc. Full algorithms for all tables are given. LLC means "Least Left Corner".

- Lothar **Schmitz**, "On the correct elimination of chain productions from LR parsers", *Intern. J. Comput. Math.*, vol. 15, no. 2, p. 99-116, 1984. Rigorous proofs of some claims about unit-free LR(k) parsers.

- N.P. **Chapman**, "LALR(1,1) parser generation for regular right part grammars", *Acta Inform.*, vol. 21, p. 29-45, 1984. Efficient construction algorithm for LALR(1,1) parse tables, which find the right end of the handle by traditional LALR(1) parsing and then scan the stack backwards using a look-ahead of 1 symbol to find the left end.

- Joseph C.H. **Park**, K.M. Choe, C.H. Chang, "A new analysis of LALR formalisms", *ACM Trans. Prog. Lang. Syst.*, vol. 7, no. 1, p. 159-175, Jan 1985. The recursive closure operator *CLOSURE* of Kristensen and Madsen [LR 1981] is abstracted to an iterative δ-operator such that $CLOSURE \equiv \delta^*$. This operator allows the formal derivation of four algorithms for the construction of LALR look-ahead sets.

- Esko **Ukkonen**, "Upper bounds on the size of LR(k) parsers", *Inform. Process. Lett.*, vol. 20, no. 2, p. 99-105, Feb 1985. Upper bounds for the number of states of an LR(k) parser are given for several types of grammars.

- S. **Heilbrunner**, "Truly prefix-correct chain-free LR(1) parsers", *Acta Inform.*, vol. 22, no. 5, p. 499-536, 1985. A unit-free LR(1) parser generator algorithm, rigorously proven correct.

- Fred **Ives**, "Unifying view of recent LALR(1) lookahead set algorithms", *ACM SIGPLAN Notices*, vol. 21, no. 7, p. 131-135, July 1986. A common formalism is given in which the LALR(1) look-ahead set construction algorithms of DeRemer and Pennello [LR 1982], Park, Choe and Chang [LR 1985] and the author can be expressed. See also Park and Choe [LR 1987].

- Manuel E. **Bermudez**, Karl M. Schimpf, "A practical arbitrary look-ahead LR parsing technique", *ACM SIGPLAN Notices*, vol. 21, no. 7, p. 136-144, July 1986. To resolve LR(0) conflicts at run time, for each conflict state a FS automaton is developed that will do arbitrary look-ahead. Grammars for which parsers can be constructed by this technique are called *LAM(m)* where m in some way limits the size of the look-ahead FS automata. It can handle some non-LR(k) grammars. See also Baker [LR 1981].

- Thomas J. **Pennello**, "Very fast LR parsing", *ACM SIGPLAN Notices*, vol. 21, no. 7, p. 145-151, July 1986. The tables and driver of a traditional LALR(1) parser are replaced by assembler code performing linear search for small fan-out, binary search for medium and a calculated jump for large fan-out. This modification gained a factor of 6 in speed at the expense of a factor 2 in size.

- Ikuo **Nakata**, Masataka Sassa, "Generation of efficient LALR parsers for regular right part grammars", *Acta Inform.*, vol. 23, p. 149-162, 1986. The stack of an LALR(1) parser is augmented with a set of special markers that indicate the start of a right-hand side; adding such a marker during the shift is called a *stack-shift*. Consequently there can now be a shift/stack-shift conflict, abbreviated to *stacking conflict*. The stack-shift is given preference and any superfluous markers are eliminated during the reduction. Full algorithms are given.

- A.M.M. **Al-Hussainin**, R.G. Stone, "Yet another storage technique for LR parsing tables", *Softw. Pract. Exper.*, vol. 16, no. 4, p. 389-401, 1986. Excellent introduction to LR table compression in general. The *submatrix technique* introduced in this paper partitions the rows into a number of submatrices, the rows of each of which are similar enough to allow drastic compressing. The access cost is $O(1)$. A heuristic partitioning algorithm is given.

- Masataka **Sassa**, Ikuo Nakata, "A simple realization of LR-parsers for regular right part grammars", *Inform. Process. Lett.*, vol. 24, no. 2, p. 113-120, Jan 1987. For each item in each state on the parse stack of an LR parser, a counter is kept indicating how many preceding symbols on the stack are covered by the recognized part in the item. Upon reduction, the counter of the reducing item tells us how many symbols to unstack. The manipulation rules for the counters are simple. The counters are stored in short arrays, one array for each state on the stack.

- Joseph C.H. **Park**, Kwang-Moo Choe, "Remarks on recent algorithms for LALR lookahead sets", *ACM SIGPLAN Notices*, vol. 22, no. 4, p. 30-32, April 1987. Careful analysis of the differences between the algorithms of Park, Choe and Chang [LR 1985] and Ives [LR 1986]. See also Ives [LR 1987].

- Fred **Ives**, "Response to remarks on recent algorithms for LALR lookahead sets", *ACM SIGPLAN Notices*, vol. 22, no. 8, p. 99-104, 1987. Remarks by Park and Choe [LR 1987] are refuted and a new algorithm is presented that is significantly better than that of Park, Choe and Chang [LR 1985] and that previously presented by Ives [LR 1986].

- Nigel P. **Chapman**, *LR Parsing: Theory and Practice*, Cambridge University Press, New York, NY, p. 228, 1987. Detailed treatment of the title subject. Highly recommended for anybody who wants to acquire in-depth knowledge about LR parsing. Good on size of parse tables and attribute grammars.

- Eljas **Soisalon-Soininen**, Jorma Tarhio, "Looping LR parsers", *Inform. Process. Lett.*, vol. 26, no. 5, p. 251-253, Jan 1988. For some (non-LR) grammars it is true that there are ways to resolve the conflicts in an LR parser for them that will make the parser loop on some inputs (executing an endless sequence of reduces). A test is given to detect such grammars.

- Jacek **Witaszek**, "A practical method for finding the optimum postponement transformation for LR(k) parsers", *Inform. Process. Lett.*, vol. 27, no. 2, p. 63-67, Feb 1988. By allowing the LR(k) automaton to postpone error checking, the size of the automaton can be reduced dramatically. Finding the optimum postponement transformation is, however, a large combinatorial problem. A good heuristic algorithm for finding a (sub)optimal transformation is given.

- Dashing **Yeh**, Uwe Karstens, "Automatic construction of incremental LR(1) parsers", *ACM SIGPLAN Notices*, vol. 23, no. 3, p. 33-42, March 1988. Detailed algorithms for an incremental LR(1) parser that allows multiple modifications and ε-rules.

- Manuel E. **Bermudez**, Karl M. Schimpf, "On the (non-)relationship between SLR(1) and NQLALR(1) grammars", *ACM Trans. Prog. Lang. Syst.*, vol. 10, no. 2, p. 338-342, April 1988. Shows a grammar that is SLR(1) but not NQLALR(1).

- Pierpaolo **Degano**, Stefano Mannucci, Bruno Mojana, "Efficient incremental LR parsing for syntax-directed editors", *ACM Trans. Prog. Lang. Syst.*, vol. 10, no. 3, p. 345-373, July 1988. The non-terminals of a grammar are partitioned by hand into sets of "incrementally compatible" non-terminals, meaning that replacement of one non-terminal by an incrementally compatible one is considered a minor structural change. Like in Korenjak's method [LR 1969], for a partitioning in n sets $n+1$ parse tables are constructed, one for each set and one for the grammar that represents the connection between the sets. The parser user is allowed interactively to move or copy the string produced by a given non-terminal to a position where an incrementally compatible one is required. This approach keeps the text (i.e. the program text) reasonably correct most of the time and uses rather small tables.

- George H. **Roberts**, "Recursive ascent: an LR analog to recursive descent", *ACM SIGPLAN Notices*, vol. 23, no. 8, p. 23-29, Aug 1988. Each LR state is represented by a subroutine. The shift is implemented as a subroutine call, the reduction is followed by a subroutine return possibly preceded by a return stack adjustment. The latter prevents the generation of genuine subroutines since it requires explicit return stack manipulation. A small and more or less readable LR(0) parser is shown, in which conflicts are resolved by means of the order in which certain tests are done, like in a recursive descent parser.

- F.E.J. **Kruseman Aretz**, "On a recursive ascent parser", *Inform. Process. Lett.*, vol. 29, no. 4, p. 201-206, Nov 1988. Each state in an LR automaton is implemented as a subroutine. A shift calls that subroutine. A reduce to X is effected as follows. X and its length n are stored in global variables; all subroutines are rigged to decrement n and return as long as $n>0$, and to call the proper GOTO state of X when n hits 0. This avoids the explicit stack manipulation of Roberts [LR 1988].

- David **Spector**, "Efficient full LR(1) parser generation", *ACM SIGPLAN Notices*, vol. 23, no. 12, p. 143-150, Dec 1988. A relatively simple method is given for extending an LR(0) table to full LR(1). The method isolates the inadequate states, constructs the full look-ahead sets for them and then splits them (and possible predecessor states). The algorithm is described informally.

- Manuel E. **Bermudez**, George Logothetis, "Simple computation of LALR(1) look-ahead sets", *Inform. Process. Lett.*, vol. 31, no. 5, p. 233-238, 1989. The original LALR(1) grammar is replaced by a not much bigger grammar that has been made to incorporate the necessary state splitting through a simple transformation. The SLR(1) automaton of this grammar is the LALR(1) automaton of the original grammar.

- George H. **Roberts**, "Another note on recursive ascent", *Inform. Process. Lett.*, vol. 32, no. 5, p. 263-266, 1989. The fast parsing methods of Pennello [LR 1986], Kruseman Aretz [LR 1988] and Roberts are compared. A special-purpose optimizing compiler can select the appropriate technique for each state.

- James **Kanze**, "Handling ambiguous tokens in LR parsers", *ACM SIGPLAN Notices*, vol. 24, no. 6, p. 49-58, June 1989. It may not always be possible to infer from the appearance of an input symbol the terminal symbol it corresponds to in the parser. In that case a default assumption can be made and the error recovery mechanism of the parser can be rigged to try alternatives. A disadvantage is that an LALR parser may already have made reductions (or a strong-LL parser may have made ε-moves) that have ruined the context. An implementation in UNIX's *yacc* is given.

- Daniel J. **Salomon**, Gordon V. Cormack, "Scannerless NSLR(1) parsing of programming languages", *ACM SIGPLAN Notices*, vol. 24, no. 7, p. 170-178, July 1989. The traditional CF syntax is extended with two rule types: $A \nrightarrow B$, which means that any sentential form in which A generates a terminal production of B (with B regular) is illegal, and $A \dashv B$, which means that any sentential form in which terminal productions of A and B are adjacent, is illegal. The authors show that the addition of these two types of rules allow one to incorporate the lexical phase of a compiler into the parser. The system uses a non-canonical SLR(1) parser.

- J. **Heering**, P. Klint, J. Rekers, "Incremental generation of parsers", *ACM SIGPLAN Notices*, vol. 24, no. 7, p. 179-191, July 1989. In a very unconventional approach to parser generation, the initial information for an LR(0) parser consists of the grammar only. As parsing progresses, more and more entries of the LR(0) table (actually a graph) become required and are constructed on the fly. LR(0) inadequacies are resolved using Tomita's method. All this greatly facilitates handling (dynamic) changes to the grammar.

- R. Nigel **Horspool**, "ILALR: an incremental generator of LALR(1) parsers". In *Compiler Compilers and High-Speed Compilation; Lecture Notes in Computer Science #371*, D. Hammer (eds.), Springer-Verlag, Berlin, p. 128-136, 1989.

Grammar rules are checked as they are typed in. To this end, LALR(1) parse tables are kept and continually updated. When the user interactively adds a new rule, the sets FIRST and NULLABLE are recalculated and algorithms are given to distribute the consequences of possible changes over the LR(0) and look-ahead sets. Some serious problems are reported and practical solutions are given.

- Daniel J. **Salomon**, Gordon V. Cormack, "Corrections to the paper: Scannerless NSLR(1) parsing of programming languages", *ACM SIGPLAN Notices*, vol. 24, no. 11, p. 80-83, Nov 1989. More accurate time measurements and corrections to the algorithms are supplied. See same authors [LR July 1989].

- Stylianos D. **Pezaris**, "Shift-reduce conflicts in LR parsers", *ACM SIGPLAN Notices*, vol. 24, no. 11, p. 94-95, Nov 1989. It is shown that if an LR(1) parser either has no shift/reduce conflicts or has shift/reduce conflicts that have been decided to be solved by shifting, the same parsing behaviour can be obtained from the corresponding LR(0) parser (which will have no reduce/reduce conflicts) in which all shift/reduce conflicts are resolved in favour of the shift. With this resolution principle, for instance the programming language C can be parsed with an LR(0) parser.

- Gregor **Snelting**, "How to build LR parsers which accept incomplete input", *ACM SIGPLAN Notices*, vol. 25, no. 4, p. 51-58, April 1990. When an LR parser finds a premature end-of-file, the incomplete parse tree is completed using some heuristics on the top state of the stack. The heuristics mainly favour reduction over shift and their application is repeated until the parse tree is complete or further completion would involve too much guessing. The technique is explained in the setting of a language-based editor.

- George H. **Roberts**, "From recursive ascent to recursive descent: via compiler optimizations", *ACM SIGPLAN Notices*, vol. 25, no. 4, p. 83-89, April 1990. Shows a number of code transformations that will turn an LR(1) recursive ascent parser (see Roberts [LR 1988] and [LR 1989]) for an LL(1) grammar into a recursive descent parser.

13.7 LEFT-CORNER PARSING

This section also covers a number of related techniques: production-chain, LLP(k), PLR(k), etc.

- D.J. **Rosenkrantz**, P.M. Lewis II, "Deterministic left-corner parsing". In *IEEE Conference Record 11th Annual Symposium on Switching and Automata Theory*, p. 139-152, 1970. An LC(k) parser decides the applicability of a rule when it has seen the initial non-terminal of the rule if it has one, plus a look-ahead of k symbols. Identifying the initial non-terminal is done by bottom-up parsing, the rest of the rule is recognized top-down. A canonical LC pushdown machine can be constructed in which the essential entries on the pushdown stack are pairs of non-terminals, one telling what non-terminal has been recognized bottom-up and the other what non-terminal is predicted top-down. As with LL, there is a difference between LC and strong-LC. There is a simple algorithm to convert an LC(k) grammar into LL(k) form; the resulting grammar may be large, though.

- Y. Eric **Cho**, "Simple left-corner grammars". In *Proc. Seventh Princeton Conference on Information Sciences and Systems*, Princeton, p. 557, 1973. LC parsing is simplified by requiring that each right-hand side be recognizable (after LC reduction) by its first two symbols and by handling left recursion as a special case. The required tables are extremely small.

- David B. **Lomet**, "Automatic generation of multiple exit parsing subroutines". In *Automata, languages and programming; Lecture Notes in Computer Science #14*, J. Loeckx (eds.), Springer-Verlag, Berlin, p. 214-231, 1974. A *production chain* is a chain of production steps $X_0 \rightarrow X_1 \alpha_1, X_1 \rightarrow X_2 \alpha_2, \cdots X_{n-1} \rightarrow t \alpha_n$, with $X_0, \cdots, X_{n-1}$ non-terminals and t a terminal. If the input is known to derive from X_0 and starts with t, each production chain from X_0 to t is a possible explanation of how t was produced. The set of all production chains connecting X_0 to t

is called a *production expression*. An efficient algorithm for the construction and compression of production expressions is given. Each production expression is then implemented as a subroutine which contains the production expression as a FS automaton.

- Michael **Hammer**, "A new grammatical transformation into LL(k) form". In *Proceedings Sixth Annual ACM Symposium on Theory of Computing*, p. 266-275, 1974. Each left corner in a left-corner parser is described as a FS automaton and implemented as a subroutine. Parsing is then performed by recursive descent using these subroutines. The FS automata can be incorporated into the grammar to yield an LL(k) grammar.

- J. **Král**, J. Demner, "Parsing as a subtask of compiling". In *Mathematical Foundations of Computer Science; Lecture Notes in Computer Science #32*, J. Bečvář (eds.), Springer-Verlag, Berlin, p. 61-74, 1975. Various considerations that went into the design of a variant of left-corner parsing, called *semi-top-down*.

- E. **Soisalon-Soininen**, E. Ukkonen, "A characterization of LL(k) grammars". In *Automata, Languages and Programming*, S. Michaelson & R. Milner (eds.), Edinburgh University Press, Edinburgh, p. 20-30, 1976. Introduces a subclass of the LR(k) grammars called predictive LR(k) (PLR(k)). The deterministic LC(k) grammars are strictly included in this class, and a grammatical transformation is presented to transform a PLR(k) into an LL(k) grammar. PLR(k) grammars can therefore be parsed with the LL(k) parser of the transformed grammar. A consequence is that the classes of LL(k), LC(k), and PLR(k) languages are identical.

- A. **Nijholt**, "Simple chain grammars". In *Automata, Languages and Programming; Lecture Notes in Computer Science #52*, A. Salomaa & M. Steinby (eds.), Springer-Verlag, Berlin, p. 352-364, 1977. A non-terminal X is said to be *chain-independent* if all production chains (see Lomet [LC 1974]) of X end in a different terminal symbol. Two symbols X and Y are "mutually chain-independent" if different chains, one starting with X and the other with Y, end with different symbols. A CF grammar is a *simple chain grammar* if it satisfies the following conditions: (1) all its symbols are chain-independent, (2) if $A \rightarrow \alpha X \beta$ and $A \rightarrow \alpha Y \gamma$, then X and Y are mutually chain-independent, and (3) if $A \rightarrow \alpha$ and $A \rightarrow \alpha \beta$ then $\beta = \varepsilon$. This class of grammars contains the LL(1) grammars without ε-rules, and is a subset of the LR(0) grammars. A simple parser for these grammars is presented.

- Jaroslav **Král**, "Almost top-down analysis for generalized LR(k) grammars". In *Methods of algorithmic language implementation; Lecture Notes in Computer Science #47*, A.P. Ershov and C.H.A. Koster (eds.), Springer-Verlag, Berlin, p. 149-172, 1977. Very well-argued introduction to semi-top-down parsing; see Král [LC 1975].

- Jan **Pittl**, "Exponential optimization for the LLP(k) parsing method". In *Mathematical Foundations of Computer Science; Lecture Notes in Computer Science #53*, J. Gruska (eds.), Springer-Verlag, Berlin, p. 435-442, 1977. The automata by Lomet [LC 1974] are reduced using the "characteristic parsing" technique of Geller and Harrison [LR 1977].

- Alan J. **Demers**, "Generalized left corner parsing". In *Fourth ACM Symposium on Principles of Programming Languages*, p. 170-182, 1977. The right-hand side of each rule is required to contain a marker. The part on the left of the marker is the left corner; it is recognized by SLR(1) techniques, the rest by LL(1) techniques. An algorithm is given to determine the first admissible position in each right-hand side for the marker.

- Eljas **Soisalon-Soininen**, Esko Ukkonen, "A method for transforming grammars into LL(k) form", *Acta Inform.*, vol. 12, p. 339-369, 1979. A restricted class of LR(k) grammars is defined, the predictive LR(k) or PLR(k) grammars, which can be handled by left-corner techniques. Like LC(k) grammars, they can be transformed into LL(k) grammars.

- Esko **Ukkonen**, "A modification of the LR(k) method for constructing compact bottom-up parsers". In *Automata, Languages and Programming; Lecture Notes in Computer Science #71*, Hermann A. Maurer (eds.), Springer-Verlag, Berlin, p. 646-658, 1979. An LR(k) parser is extended to do left-corner parsing simultaneously by compounding the states on the stack. This can be done for *weak-PLR(k) grammars* only, which, however, include almost all LR(k) grammars. The resulting table is gigantic but highly structured, and can be condensed considerably.

- Daniel **Chester**, "A parsing algorithm that extends phrases", *Am. J. Comput. Linguist.*, vol. 6, no. 2, p. 87-96, April-June 1980. See same paper [NatLang 1980].

- Jan **Pittl**, "On LLP(k) grammars and languages", *Theoret. Comput. Sci.*, vol. 16, p. 149-175, 1981. See Pittl [LC 1982]. All LR(k) languages have an LLP(k) grammar. LLP(k) lies somewhere between LL(k) and LR(k).

- Jan **Pittl**, "On LLP(k) parsers", *J. Comput. Syst. Sci.*, vol. 24, p. 36-68, 1982. This paper first presents a non-deterministic parser using a mixed top-down-bottom-up strategy, and then examines the circumstances under which these parsers are deterministic, resulting in the class of LLP(k) grammars. The parser does not have the correct-prefix property, as the LL(k) and LR(k) parsers have.

- Yuji **Matsumoto**, Hozumi Tanaka, Hideki Hirakawa, Hideo Miyoshi, Hideki Yasukawa, "BUP: a bottom-up parser embedded in Prolog", *New Generation Computing*, vol. 1, p. 145-158, 1983. A bottom-up parser for natural language text embedded in Prolog is described, in which each grammar rule corresponds to a Prolog clause. The parser, which is fact left-corner, can deal with any cycle-free grammar with no ε-rules. The dictionary is handled separately. Explicit rules are given how to convert a grammar into Prolog clauses. A facility for remembering previous successes and failures is included. A tracing facility is also described.

- Kenzo **Inoue**, Fukumi Fujiwara, "On LLC(k) parsing method of LR(k) grammars", *J. Inform. Process.*, vol. 6, no. 4, p. 206-217, 1983. See same paper [LR 1983].

- Susan **Hirsh**, "P-PATR: a compiler for unification-based grammars". In *Natural Language Understanding and Logic Programming, II*, V. Dahl & P. Saint-Dizier (eds.), Elsevier Science Publ., Amsterdam, p. 63-78, 1988. Left-corner parsing in Prolog. How to handle ε-rules that hide left recursion (remove them by duplicating the rule).

13.8 PRECEDENCE AND BOUNDED-CONTEXT PARSING

- Harold **Wolpe**, "Algorithm for analyzing logical statements to produce a truth function table", *Commun. ACM*, vol. 1, no. 3, p. 4-13, March 1958. The paper describes an algorithm to convert a Boolean expression into a decision table. The expression is first fully parenthesized through a number of substitution rules that represent the priorities of the operators. Parsing is then done by counting parentheses. Further steps construct a decision table.

- J.H. **Wegstein**, "From formulas to computer-oriented language", *Commun. ACM*, vol. 2, no. 3, p. 6-8, March 1959. A program that converts from arithmetic expressions to three-address code is given as a one-page flowchart. The parser is basically operator-precedence, with built-in precedences.

- Robert W. **Floyd**, "Syntactic analysis and operator precedence", *J. ACM*, vol. 10, no. 3, p. 316-333, July 1963. Operator-precedence explained and applied to an Algol 60 compiler.

- J. **Eickel**, M. Paul, F.L. Bauer, K. Samelson, "A syntax-controlled generator of

formal language processors", *Commun. ACM*, vol. 6, no. 8, p. 451-455, Aug 1963.
In this early paper, the authors develop and describe what is basically a (2,1) bounded-context parser. Reduction rules have to have the form $U \leftarrow V$ or $R \leftarrow ST$. Such a grammar is called an *R-language*; it is "unique" if the parse tables can be constructed without conflict. The terminology in the paper differs considerably from today's.

- Robert W. **Floyd**, "Bounded context syntax analysis", *Commun. ACM*, vol. 7, no. 2, p. 62-67, Feb 1964. For each right-hand side R in the grammar, enough context is constructed (by hand) so that when R is found in a sentential form in the right context in a bottom-up parser, it can safely be assumed to be the handle.

- Niklaus **Wirth**, Helmut Weber, "EULER – A generalization of ALGOL and its formal definition, Part 1/2", *Commun. ACM*, vol. 9, no. 1/2, p. 13-25/89-99, Jan/Feb 1966. Detailed description of simple and extended precedence. A table generation algorithm is given. Part 2 contains the complete precedence table plus functions for the language EULER.

- David F. **Martin**, "Boolean matrix methods for the detection of simple precedence grammars", *Commun. ACM*, vol. 11, no. 10, p. 685-687, Oct 1968. Finding the simple-precedence relations is explained as matrix operations on matrices derived trivially from the grammar.

- James R. **Bell**, "A new method for determining linear precedence functions for precedence grammars", *Commun. ACM*, vol. 12, no. 10, p. 567-569, Oct 1969. The precedence relations are used to set up a connectivity matrix. Take the transitive closure and count 1's in each row. Check for correctness of the result.

- Alain **Colmerauer**, "Total precedence relations", *J. ACM*, vol. 17, no. 1, p. 14-30, Jan 1970. The non-terminal resulting from a reduction is not put on the stack but pushed back into the input stream; this leaves room for more reductions on the stack. This causes precedence relations that differ considerably from simple precedence.

- A. **Learner**, A.L. Lim, "A note on transforming grammars to Wirth-Weber precedence form", *Computer J.*, vol. 13, p. 142-144, 1970. An algorithm is given to transform any CF grammar to simple precedence form (with possible duplicate right-hand sides).

- Jacques **Loeckx**, "An algorithm for the construction of bounded-context parsers", *Commun. ACM*, vol. 13, no. 5, p. 297-307, May 1970. By systematically generating all BC states the parser may encounter.

- J. **Ichbiah**, S. Morse, "A technique for generating almost optimal Floyd-Evans productions of precedence grammars", *Commun. ACM*, vol. 13, no. 8, p. 501-508, Aug 1970. The notion of "weak precedence" is defined in the introduction. The body of the article is concerned with efficiently producing good Floyd-Evans productions from a given weak precedence grammar.

- A.V. **Aho**, P.J. Denning, J.D. Ullman, "Weak and mixed strategy precedence parsing", *J. ACM*, vol. 19, no. 2, p. 225-243, Apr 1972. The theory behind and a comparison of various bottom-up (shift/reduce) parsing algorithms.

- Shoji **Sekimoto**, "Extended right precedence grammars and analyzing technique for them", *Inform. Process. Japan*, vol. 12, p. 21-25, 1972. In the presence of two rules $A \rightarrow \alpha X \beta$ and $B \rightarrow \beta$, weak precedence requires that there be no precedence relation between X and B. This requirement is replaced by a more lenient (but more complicated) one, resulting in *right precedence* and is further relaxed to *extended right precedence*.

- David F. **Martin**, "A Boolean matrix method for the computation of linear precedence functions", *Commun. ACM*, vol. 15, no. 6, p. 448-454, June 1972. Detailed description of a variant of Bell's method [Precedence 1969].

- A.V. **Aho**, J.D. Ullman, "Linear precedence functions for weak precedence grammars", *Intern. J. Comput. Math.*, vol. A3, p. 149-155, 1972. The entries in a precedence table have four values: <, ≐, > and blank. Since precedence functions can only represent three relations: <, = and >, the blank is sacrificed, to the detriment of error detection. A weak precedence table holds only three kinds of entries: ≤, > and blank, which can be mapped onto <, > and =. The resulting matrix will normally not allow precedence functions, but it will if a number of the ='s are sacrificed. An algorithm is given to (heuristically) determine the minimal set of ='s to sacrifice; unfortunately this is done by calling upon a heuristic algorithm for partitioning graphs.

- J. **McAfee**, L. Presser, "An algorithm for the design of simple precedence grammars", *J. ACM*, vol. 19, no. 3, p. 385-395, July 1972. An algorithm to construct for any CF grammar a grammar with conflict-free simple-precedence relations that generates the same language (with possible duplicate right-hand sides, though).

- David **Crowe**, "Generating parsers for affix grammars", *Commun. ACM*, vol. 15, no. 8, p. 728-734, Aug 1972. See same paper [VW 1972].

- David S. **Wise**, "Generalized overlap resolvable grammars and their parsers", *J. Comput. Syst. Sci.*, vol. 6, p. 538-572, Dec 1972. A CF grammar is *Generalized Overlap-Resolvable* (GOR) if the handle in a bottom-up parser can be found deterministically by identifying the right-hand side on the top of the stack, preceded on the stack by a token from a set of admissible left-context tokens and by requiring that the next input token belong to a set of admissible right-context tokens. A grammar is *Overlap-Resolvable* (OR) if it is GOR and ε-free. These grammars are between mixed-strategy precedence and SLR(1) in power. A very efficient and flexible implementation using Dömölki's technique is described.

- Rainer **Zimmer**, "Soft precedence", *Inform. Process. Lett.*, vol. 1, p. 108-110, 1972. A grammar with a conflict-free precedence table in which not all right-hand sides are different, causes reduce conflicts. For each reduce conflict a simple pattern is constructed which resolves the conflict by checking the parse stack. If for each reduce conflict such a pattern exists, the grammar is *soft precedence*. A matrix algorithm to find the patterns if they exist is given.

- A.V. **Aho**, J.D. Ullman, "Error detection in precedence parsers", *Math. Syst. Theory*, vol. 7, no. 2, p. 97-113, 1973. The full precedence matrix is split into two copies, one used to decide between shifts and reduces, which contains ≤, > and blank, and the other to determine the left end of the handle which contains <, ≐ and blank. The techniques of Aho and Ullman [Precedence 1972] are now applied to both matrices.

- James N. **Gray**, Michael A. Harrison, "Canonical precedence schemes", *J. ACM*, vol. 20, no. 2, p. 214-234, April 1973. The theory behind precedence parsing.

- G. **Terrine**, "Coordinate grammars and parsers", *Computer J.*, vol. 16, p. 232-244, 1973. A bounded-context parser is made to stack dotted items rather than terminals and non-terminals. This makes it stronger than bounded-context but still weaker than LR.

- M.D. **Mickunas**, V.B. Schneider, "A parser-generating system for constructing compressed compilers", *Commun. ACM*, vol. 16, no. 11, p. 669-676, Nov 1973. Describes a bounded-context parser with transduction facilities. Includes a compression algorithm for BC tables.

- Susan L. **Graham**, "On bounded right context languages and grammars", *SIAM J. Computing*, vol. 3, no. 3, p. 224-254, Sept 1974. Theory of same.

- J.H. **Williams**, "Bounded-context parsable grammars", *Inform. Control*, vol. 28, no. 4, p. 314-334, Aug 1975. A more general non-canonical form of bounded-context, called *bounded-context parsable*, is defined which allows, among others, the parsing in linear time of some non-deterministic languages. Although a parser could be constructed, it would not be practical.

- M.R. **Levy**, "Complete operator precedence", *Inform. Process. Lett.*, vol. 4, no. 2, p. 38-40, Nov 1975. Establishes conditions under which operator-precedence works properly.

- D.S. **Henderson**, M.R. Levy, "An extended operator precedence parsing algorithm", *Computer J.*, vol. 19, no. 3, p. 229-233, 1976. The relation $<$ is split into $<_1$ and $<_2$. $a <_1 b$ means that a may occur next to b, $a <_2 b$ means that a non-terminal has to occur between them. Likewise for $\doteq$ and $>$. This is *extended operator-precedence*.

- M.S. **Krishnamurthy**, H.R. Ramesha Chandra, "A note on precedence functions", *Inform. Process. Lett.*, vol. 4, no. 4, p. 99-100, Jan 1976. Proves for some simple-precedence tables that no grammars for them exist.

- R.K. **Shyamasundar**, "A note on linear precedence functions", *Inform. Process. Lett.*, vol. 5, no. 3, p. 81, 1976. Comments on Krishnamurthy and Ramesha Chandra [Precedence 1976].

- M.H. **Williams**, "Complete operator precedence conditions", *Inform. Process. Lett.*, vol. 6, no. 2, p. 60-62, April 1977. Revision of the criteria of Levy [Precedence 1975].

- Eberhard **Bertsch**, "The storage requirement in precedence parsing", *Commun. ACM*, vol. 20, no. 3, p. 192-194, March 1977. Suppose for a given grammar there exists a precedence matrix but the precedence functions f and g do not exists. There always exist sets of precedence functions f_i and g_j such that for two symbols a and b, comparison of $f_{c(b)}(a)$ and $g_{d(a)}(b)$ yields the precedence relation between a and b, where c and d are selection functions which select the f_i and g_j to be compared. An algorithm is given to construct such a system of functions.

- R.K. **Shyamasundar**, "Precedence parsing using Dömölki's algorithm", *Intern. J. Comput. Math.*, vol. A6, p. 105-114, 1977. Dömölki's algorithm can find a reducible right-hand-side efficiently but cannot know if it is a handle. Precedence parsing can find the handle easily but has trouble determining which right-hand side it is. Together they are a perfect match.

- I.H. **Sudborough**, "A note on weak operator precedence grammars", *Inform. Process. Lett.*, vol. 7, no. 5, p. 213-218, 1978. Introduces *weak operator-precedence* and states that $L(SP)=L(WP)$ and $L(SP) \supset L(WOP) \supset L(OP)$, where SP is simple precedence, WP is weak precedence, WOP is weak operator-precedence and OP is operator-precedence, and $L(X)$ is the set of languages generatable by X grammars.

- R.K. **Shyamasundar**, "Precedence-regular grammars", *Intern. J. Comput. Math.*, vol. A7, p. 173-186, 1979. Characterization of the class of grammars for which the Shyamasundar/Dömölki technique (Shyamasundar [Precedence 1977]) works. Note that whereas in LL- and LR-regular it is the rest of the input that is analysed by a FS automaton to resolve a conflict, in precedence-regular it is the stack that is analysed by a Dömölki-like automaton.

- Peter **Ružička**, "Validity test for Floyd's operator precedence parsing algorithms". In *Mathematical Foundations of Computer Science; Lecture Notes in Computer Science #74*, J. Bečvář (eds.), Springer-Verlag, Berlin, p. 415-424, 1979. Additions to the criteria by Levy [Precedence 1975].

- M.H. **Williams**, "Conditions for extended operator precedence parsing", *Computer J.*, vol. 22, no. 2, p. 164-168, 1979. Tighter analysis of extended operator-precedence than Henderson and Levy [Precedence 1976].

- Amiram **Yehudai**, "A new definition for simple precedence grammars", *BIT*, vol. 19, p. 282-284, 1979. A weaker definition of simple precedence is given, which is then shown to define the same class.

- K.R. **Moll**, "Left context precedence grammars", *Acta Inform.*, vol. 14, p. 317-335, 1980. Elaborate and definitely non-trivial refinement of the notion of precedence, to achieve the viable-prefix property.

- Wilf R. **LaLonde**, Jim des Rivieres, "Handling operator precedence in arithmetic expressions with tree transformations", *ACM Trans. Prog. Lang. Syst.*, vol. 3, no. 1, p. Jan 1981, 83-103. Algorithms that will restructure the parse tree when the operator precedences are modified. The algorithm is also used to do parsing: first produce a parse tree in standard form and then add the precedence information.

- David A. **Workman**, "SR(s,k) parsers: A class of shift-reduce bounded-context parsers", *J. Comput. Syst. Sci.*, vol. 22, no. 1, p. 178-197, 1981. The look-back over all combinations of m symbols on the stack in BC(m,n) parsers is replaced by an LR(m)-like automaton, resulting in an SR(m,n) parser, if possible. The paper is mainly concerned with theoretical properties of SR grammars and parsers.

- M.H. **Williams**, "A systematic test for extended operator precedence", *Inform. Process. Lett.*, vol. 13, no. 4,5, p. 187-190, End 1981. The criteria of Williams [Precedence 1979] in algorithmic form.

- M.C. **Er**, "A note on computing precedence functions", *Computer J.*, vol. 25, no. 3, p. 397-398, 1982. By determining longest paths in a digraph.

- Junichi **Aoe**, Yoneo Yamamoto, Ryosaku Shimada, "A practical method for reducing weak precedence parsers", *IEEE Trans. Softw. Eng.*, vol. SE-9, no. 1, p. 25-30, Jan 1983. When a weak-precedence parser finds a > relation and starts a reduce sequence, the sequence stops when a ≤ is met; all intermediate relations are required to be >, to continue the sequence. The authors modify the parser to continue the sequence anyway, until a ≤ is found; the intermediate relations are never tested and their values are immaterial. This is exploited to reduce the parse table.

- Piotr **Wyrostek**, "On the 'correct prefix property' in precedence parsers", *Inform. Process. Lett.*, vol. 17, no. 3, p. 161-165, Oct 1983. Extremely complicated transformation of precedence grammars to mixed-strategy grammars which have, for some parsers, the correct-prefix property. With an erratum in *Inform. Process. Lett.*, vol. 19, no. 2, p. 111, Aug 1984.

- Piotr **Wyrostek**, "Precedence technique is not worse than SLR(1)", *Acta Inform.*, vol. 23, p. 361-392, 1986. The thesis in the title is proved by giving an algorithm that transforms an SLR(1) grammar into a (1,1)-mixed-strategy precedence grammar with the viable-prefix property (see also Graham [Precedence 1974]). The resulting precedence table is often smaller than the SLR(1) table.

- R. Nigel **Horspool**, Michael R. Levy, "Correctness of an extended operator-precedence parsing algorithm", *Inform. Process. Lett.*, vol. 24, no. 4, p. 265-273, March 1987. Establishes conditions under which extended operator-precedence (see Henderson and Levy [Precedence 1976]) works properly.

13.9 FINITE-STATE AUTOMATA

• M.O. **Rabin**, D. Scott, "Finite automata and their decision problems", *IBM J. Research and Development*, vol. 3, p. 114-125, Apr 1959. A finite-state automaton is considered as the definition of the set of strings it accepts. Many fundamental properties of FS automata are exposed and proved. The very useful subset construction algorithm can be found in Definition 11.

• Ken **Thompson**, "Regular expression search algorithm", *Commun. ACM*, vol. 11, no. 6, p. 419-422, June 1968. The regular expression is turned into a transition diagram, which is then interpreted in parallel. Remarkably, each step generates (IBM 7094) machine code to execute the next step.

• Walter L. **Johnson**, James S. Porter, Stephanie I. Ackley, Douglas T. Ross, "Automatic generation of efficient lexical processors using finite state techniques", *Commun. ACM*, vol. 11, no. 12, p. 805-813, Dec 1968. Semantic actions are attached to some rules of a FS grammar. A variant of the subset construction is described that requires the unique determination of the states in which a semantic action is required.

• Franklin L. **DeRemer**, "Lexical analysis". In *Compiler Construction: An Advanced Course; Lecture Notes in Computer Science #21*, F.L. Bauer & J. Eickel (eds.), Springer-Verlag, Berlin, p. 109-120, 1974. 1. General introduction to lexical analysers, hand-written and generated. 2. Simplification of the LR parser generator algorithm for the case of non-self-embedding CF grammars (which is possible since the latter in fact generate a regular language).

• Alfred V. **Aho**, Margaret J. Corasick, "Efficient string matching: an aid to bibliographic search", *Commun. ACM*, vol. 18, no. 6, p. 333-340, June 1975. A given string embedded in a longer text is found by a very efficient FS automaton derived from that string.

• M.E. **Lesk**, E. Schmidt, "Lex – a lexical analyzer generator". In *UNIX Manuals*, Bell Laboratories, Murray Hill, New Jersey, p. 13, 1975. The regular grammar is specified as a list of regular expressions, each associated with a semantic action, which can access the segment of the input that matches the expression. Substantial look-ahead is performed if necessary. *lex* is a well-known and often-used lexical-analyser generator.

• D. **Langendoen**, "Finite-state parsing of phrase-structure languages", *Linguistic Inquiry*, vol. 6, no. 4, p. 533-554, 1975. See same author [NatLang 1975].

• Roman **Krzemień**, Andrzej Łukasiewicz, "Automatic generation of lexical analyzers in a compiler-compiler", *Inform. Process. Lett.*, vol. 4, no. 6, p. 165-168, Mar. 1976. A grammar is *quasi-regular* if it does not feature nested recursion; consequently it generates a regular language. An algorithm is given that identifies all quasi-regular subgrammars in a CF grammar, thus identifying the "lexical part" of the grammar.

• Thomas J. **Ostrand**, Marvin C. Paull, Elaine J. Weyuker, "Parsing regular grammars with finite lookahead", *Acta Inform.*, vol. 16, p. 125-138, 1981. Every regular (Type 3) language can be recognized by a finite-state automaton without look-ahead, but such a device is not sufficient to do parsing. For parsing, look-ahead is needed; if a regular grammar needs a look-ahead of k tokens, it is called *FL(k)*. FS grammars are either FL(k), FL(∞) or ambiguous; a decision algorithm is described, which also determines the value of k, if appropriate.
A simple parsing algorithm is a FS automaton gouverned by a look-up table for each state, mapping look-aheads to new states. A second algorithm avoids these large tables by constructing the relevant look-ahead sets on the fly.

• V.P. **Heuring**, "The automatic generation of fast lexical analysers", *Softw. Pract. Exper.*, vol. 16, no. 9, p. 801-808, 1986. The lexical analyser is not based directly on a FS automaton but has a number of built-in analysers for, e.g., *identifier*, *integer*, *string*, which can be parametrized. The lexical analyser is about 6 times faster than UNIX *lex*.

- Douglas W. **Jones**, "How (not) to code a finite-state machine", *ACM SIGPLAN Notices*, vol. 23, no. 8, p. 19-22, Aug 1988. Small, well-structured and efficient code can be generated for a FS machine by deriving a single deterministic regular expression from the FS machine and implementing this expression directly using **while** and **repeat** constructions.

- Duane **Szafron**, Randy Ng, "LexAGen: an interactive incremental scanner generator", *Softw. Pract. Exper.*, vol. 20, no. 5, p. 459-483, May 1990. Extensive description of an interactive generator for lexical analysers, in Smalltalk-80.

13.10 NATURAL LANGUAGE HANDLING

- Hamish P. **Dewar**, Paul Bratley, James P. Thorne, "A program for the syntactic analysis of English sentences", *Commun. ACM*, vol. 12, no. 8, p. 476-479, 1969. The authors argue that the English language can be described by a regular grammar: most rules are regular already and the others describe concatenations of regular sublanguages. The finite-state parser used constructs the state subsets on the fly, to avoid large tables. Features (attributes) are used to check consistency and to weed out the state subsets.

- W.A **Woods**, "Transition networks for natural languages", *Commun. ACM*, vol. 13, no. 10, p. 591-606, Oct 1970. A recursive-descent parser guided by transition networks rather than by grammar rules.

- D. **Langendoen**, "Finite-state parsing of phrase-structure languages", *Linguistic Inquiry*, vol. 6, no. 4, p. 533-554, 1975. A subset of the CF grammars that produces regular (FS) languages is analysed and an algorithm is given to produce a FS parser for any grammar belonging to this subset. Much attention is paid to the linguistic applicability of such grammars. We advice the reader of this paper to make a list of the abbreviations used in it, to assist in reading.

- William A. **Woods**, "Cascaded ATN grammars", *Am. J. Computational Linguistics*, vol. 6, no. 1, p. 1-12, Jan-March 1980. The grammar (of a natural language) is decomposed into a number of grammars, which are then *cascaded*, that is, the parser for grammar G_n obtains as input the linearized parse tree produced by the parser for G_{n-1}. Each grammar can then represent a linguistic hypothesis. An efficient implementation is given.

- Daniel **Chester**, "A parsing algorithm that extends phrases", *Am. J. Comput. Linguist.*, vol. 6, no. 2, p. 87-96, April-June 1980. A variant of a backtracking left-corner parser is described that is particularly convenient for handling continuing phrases like: "the cat that caught the rat that stole the cheese".

- Harry **Tennant**, *Natural language processing*, Petrocelli Books, Inc., Princeton, N.J., p. 276, 1981. Easy-going introduction to natural language processing; covers syntax, semantics, knowledge representation and dialog with many amusing examples. With glossary.

- Philips J. **Hayes**, George V. Mouradian, "Flexible parsing", *Am. J. Comput. Linguist.*, vol. 7, no. 4, p. 232-242, Oct-Dec 1981. A directional breadth-first bottom-up parser yields some sets of partial parse trees for segments of the input text. Then several heuristics are used to combine these into a "top-level hypothesis". The purpose is to be able to parse fragmented or ungrammatical natural language input.

- Ursula **Klenk**, "Microcomputers in linguistic data processing: Context-free parsing", *Microprocess. Microprogram.*, vol. 9, no. 5, p. 281-284, May 1982. Shows the feasibility of the implementation of four general CF parsers on a very small (48 kbytes) PC: breadth-first top-down, backtracking top-down, bottom-up and Earley's algorithm.

- K. **Sparck Jones**, Y. Wilks, *Automatic natural language parsing*, Ellis Horwood
  Ltd., Chicester, p. 208, 1983. Eighteen short chapters on the application of parsing in NL
  processing, using CF grammars, Augmented Transition Networks, transducers, Generalized Phrase
  Structure Grammars and otherwise. Many literature references.

- Margaret **King** (Ed.), *Parsing Natural Language*, Academic Press, London/New
  York, p. 308, 1983. A compilation of twelve tutorials on aspects of parsing in a linguistic
  setting. Very readable.

- Stuart M. **Shieber**, "Direct parsing of ID/LP grammars", *Linguistics and Philoso-
  phy*, vol. 7, p. 135-154, 1984. In this very readable paper, the Earley parsing technique is
  extended in a straightforward way to ID/LP grammars (Gazdar et al. [NatLang 1985]). Practical algorithms are given.

- Gerald **Gazdar**, Ewan Klein, Geoffrey Pullum, Ivan Sag, *Generalized phrase
  structure grammar*, Basil Blackwell Publisher, Ltd., Oxford, UK, p. 276, 1985.
  The phrase structure of natural languages is more easily and compactly described using *Generalized
  Phrase Structure Grammars* (GPSGs) or *Immediate Dominance/Linear Precedence grammars* (ID/LP
  grammars) than using conventional CF grammars. Theoretical foundations of these grammars are given
  and the results are used extensively in linguistic syntactic theory. GPSGs are not to be confused with
  general phrase structure grammars, aka Chomsky Type 0 grammars, which are called "unrestricted"
  phrase structure grammars in this book.
  The difference between GPSGs, ID/LP grammars and CF grammars is explained clearly. A GPSG is a
  CF grammar, the non-terminals of which are not unstructured names but sets of *features* with their
  values; such compound non-terminals are called *categories*. An example of a feature is NOUN, which can
  have the values + or −; <NOUN, +> will be a constituent of the categories "noun phrase", "noun", "noun
  subject", etc.
  ID/LP grammars differ from GPSGs in that the right-hand sides of production rules consist of multisets
  of categories rather than of ordered sequences. Thus, production rules (Immediate Dominance rules)
  define vertical order in the production tree only. Horizontal order in each node is restricted through (but
  not necessarily completely defined by) Linear Precedence rules. Each LP rule is considered to apply to
  every node; this is called the *Exhaustive Constant Partial Ordering property*.

- Mary Dee **Harris**, *Natural Language Processing*, Reston Publ. Comp, Prentice
  Hall, Reston, Virg., p. 368, 1985. A good and slow-paced introduction to natural language
  processing, with a clear algorithmic view. Lexical analysis including look-up algorithms, phrase structure grammars (actually context-free) and semantic networks are explained and much attention is paid to
  attaching semantics to the structures obtained.

- Veronica **Dahl**, Patrick Saint-Dizier, *Natural language understanding and logic
  programming*, Elsevier Science Publ., Amsterdam, p. 243, 1985. Seventeen papers on
  the application of various grammar types to natural languages.

- Glenn **Blank**, "A new kind of finite-state automaton: Register vector grammar".
  In *Proceedings Ninth International Conference on Artificial Intelligence*, UCLA,
  p. 749-756, Aug 1985. In FS grammars, emphasis is on the states: for each state it is specified
  which tokens it accepts and to which new state each token leads. In *Register-Vector grammars* (RV
  grammars) emphasis is on the tokens: for each token it is specified which state it maps onto which new
  state(s). The mapping is done through a special kind of function, as follows. The state is a (global) vector
  (array) of registers (features, attributes). Each register can be *on* or *off*. For each token there is a condition vector with elements which can be *on*, *off* or *mask* (= *ignore*); if the condition matches the state, the
  token is allowed. For each token there is a result vector with elements which can be *on*, *off* or *mask* (=
  copy); if the token is applied, the result-vector elements specify how to construct the new state. ε-moves
  are incorporated by having tokens (called *labels*) which have ε for their representation. Termination has

to be programmed as a separate register.
RV grammars are claimed to be compact and efficient for describing the FS component of natural languages. Examples are given. Embedding is handled by having a finite number of levels inside the state.

* Barbara J. **Grosz**, Karen Sparck Jones, Bonnie Lynn Webber, *Readings in natural language processing*, Morgan Kaufmann Publishers, Inc., Los Altos, Ca. 94022, p. 664, 1986. Selected papers on NL processing, covering syntactic models, semantic interpretation, discourse interpretation, language action and intention, NL generation and actual systems.

* Walter **Goshawke**, Ian D.K. Kelly, J. David Wigg, *Computer Translation of Natural Language*, Sigma Press, Wilslow, UK, p. 275, 1987. The book consists of three parts. 1) Overview of progress in Machine Translation. 2) Description of the intermediate code SLUNT (Spoken Languages Universal Numeric Translation), a stylized numeric language-independent vehicle for semantics. 3) The International Communicator System, a set of programs to manipulate SLUNT structures.

* Leonard **Bolc** (Ed.), *Natural language parsing systems*, Springer-Verlag, Berlin, p. 367, 1987. A collection of recent papers on parsing in a natural language environment. Among the subjects are Earley and CYK parsers, assigning probabilities to ambiguous parsings, error recovery and, of course, attaching semantics to parsings.

* Jonathan H. **Reed**, "An efficient context-free parsing algorithm based on register vector grammars". In *Proceedings Third Annual IEEE Conference on Expert Systems in Government*, p. 34-40, 1987. The principles of RV grammars (Blank [NatLang 1985]) are applied to CF grammars by having a separate RV grammar for each syntactic category, each allowing the names of syntactic categories as tokens. The Earley parsing algorithm is then adapted to handle these grammars. Measurements indicate that the parser is 1 to 3 times faster on small grammars and 5 to 10 times on large grammars.

* V. **Dahl**, P. Saint-Dizier, *Natural language understanding and logic programming, II*, Elsevier Science Publ., Amsterdam, p. 345, 1988. Eighteen papers and two panel sessions on programs for natural language understanding, mostly in Prolog.

* Glenn D. **Blank**, "A finite and real-time processor for natural language", *Commun. ACM*, vol. 32, no. 10, p. 1174-1189, Oct 1989. Several aspects of the register-vector grammars of Blank [NatLang 1985] are treated and extended: notation, center-embedding (3 levels), non-determinism through boundary-backtracking, efficient implementation.

13.11 ERROR HANDLING

* W.B. **Smith**, "Error detection in formal languages", *J. Comput. Syst. Sci.*, vol. 4, p. 385-405, Oct 1970. A formal paper that examines properties of recognizers that determine whether the number of substitution errors that has occurred is bounded by some function. Different language classes and different levels of numbers of errors are examined. It appears that there is little difference between languages under a constant maximum number of errors and under a constant maximum number of errors per block.

* J.E. **LaFrance**, "Optimization of error-recovery in syntax-directed parsing algorithms", *ACM SIGPLAN Notices*, vol. 5, no. 12, p. 2-17, Dec 1970. Floyd productions are divided into groups, and each production in a group is tried in order. If all productions of a group fail, error recovery takes place, depending on the type(s) of the rules in the group. Apart from local corrections, in some cases all possible productions are traced three symbols ahead. The result is compared with the next four input symbols, using a set of twenty patterns, each pattern modeling a particular kind of error. If this fails, a FOLLOW-set recovery technique is applied. The implications of

implementing this error recovery technique in a backtracking recursive descent parser are discussed.

- A.V. **Aho**, T.G. Peterson, "A minimum-distance error-correcting parser for context-free languages", *SIAM J. Computing*, vol. 1, no. 4, p. 305-312, 1972. A CF grammar is extended with error productions so that it will produce Σ^*; this is effected by replacing each occurrence of a terminal in a rule by a non-terminal that produces said terminal "with 0 errors" and any amount of garbage, including ε, "with 1 or more errors". The items in an Earley parser are extended with a count, indicating how many errors were needed to create the item. An item with error count k is added only if no similar item with a lower error count is present already.

- C.J. **Burgess**, "Compile-time error diagnostics in syntax-directed compilers", *Computer J.*, vol. 15, no. 4, p. 302-307, 1972. This paper attempts to define error diagnostics formally by incorporating them as error productions in the grammar, and examines the extent to which the positioning of these productions and messages in the grammar can be done automatically. For left-factored grammars it appears to be easy.

- E.G. **James**, D.P. Partridge, "Adaptive correction of program statements", *Commun. ACM*, vol. 16, no. 1, p. 27-37, Jan 1973. Discusses an error correction technique that uses artificial intelligence and approximate pattern matching techniques, basing corrections on built-in statistics, which are adapted continuously.

- R.W. **Conway**, T.R. Wilcox, "Design and implementation of a diagnostic compiler for PL/I", *Commun. ACM*, vol. 16, no. 3, p. 169-179, 1973. Describes a diagnostic PL/C compiler, using a systematic method for finding places where repair is required, but the repair strategy for each of these places is chosen by the implementor. The parser uses a separable transition diagram technique (see Conway [Misc 1963]). The error messages detail the error found and the repair chosen.

- G. **Lyon**, "Syntax-directed least-errors analysis for context-free languages: a practical approach", *Commun. ACM*, vol. 17, no. 1, p. 3-14, Jan 1974. Discusses a least-errors analyser, based on Earley's parser without look-ahead. The Earley items are extended with an error count, and the parser is started with items for the start of each rule, in each state set. Earley's scanner is extended as follows: for all items with the dot in front of a terminal, the item is added to the same state set with an incremented error count and the dot after the terminal (this represents an insertion of the terminal); if the terminal is not equal to the input symbol associated with the state set, add the item to the next state set with an incremented error count and the dot after the terminal (this represents a replacement); add the item as it is to the next state set, with an incremented error count (this represents a deletion). The completer does its work as in the Earley parser, but also updates error counts. Items with the lowest error counts are processed first, and when a state set contains an item, the same item is only added if it has a lower error count.

- R.A. **Wagner**, "Order-n correction for regular languages", *Commun. ACM*, vol. 17, no. 5, p. 265-268, May 1974. Presents an $O(n)$ algorithm which, given a string and a finite-state automaton, can correct the string to an acceptable one with a minimum number of edit operations.

- C. **Ghezzi**, "LL(1) grammars supporting an efficient error handling", *Inform. Process. Lett.*, vol. 3, no. 6, p. 174-176, July 1975. Faced with an erroneous token in an environment where empty productions can occur, a strong-LL(1) parser will often do some ε-moves before reporting the error; this makes subsequent error recovery more difficult. This undesirable behaviour can be avoided by splitting each rule into a number of copies, one for each set of tokens it may be followed by. An efficient algorithm for this transformation on the grammar is supplied. The resulting grammar is of type *CRLL(1)*.

- Susan L. **Graham**, Steven P. Rhodes, "Practical syntactic error recovery", *Commun. ACM*, vol. 18, no. 11, p. 639-650, Nov 1975. See Section 10.6.1 for a discussion of this error recovery method.

- **J.-P. Lévy**, "Automatic correction of syntax errors in programming languages", *Acta Inform.*, vol. 4, p. 271-292, 1975. When a bottom-up parser encounters an error, part of the stack is pushed back into the input stream (for instance, until a *beacon token* is on the top of the stack). Starting from the new state now uncovered on the stack, all possible parsings of the input allowing at most n errors are constructed, using breadth-first search and Lyon's scheme [ErrHandl 1974], until all parsers are in the same state or all parsers need to assume an $n+1$-st error. In the latter case the input is rejected, otherwise one parse is chosen and parsing continues.

- **S. Feyock**, P. Lazarus, "Syntax-directed correction of syntax errors", *Softw. Pract. Exper.*, vol. 6, p. 207-219, 1976. When an error is detected, the following error correction strategy is applied:
1. A set of correction strings is generated (delete current symbol, insert symbol, replace symbol, interchange with next symbol).
2. This set is filtered (correction syntactically and semantically acceptable?).
3. If there is more than one element left, use a heuristic to determine the "best" one. If only one is left, this is the one. If none are left, back-up one input symbol, and go back to step 1.

- David **Gries**, "Error recovery and correction". In *Compiler Construction, an Advanced Course, Second Edition*, F.L. Bauer & J. Eickel (eds.), Springer-Verlag, New York, p. 627-638, 1976. Mostly an annotated bibliography containing some 35 entries, not all on error handling.

- J. **Ciesinger**, "Generating error recovery in a compiler generating system". In *GI-4 Fachtagung über Programmiersprachen; Lecture Notes in Computer Science #34*, H.-J. Schneider & M. Nagl (eds.), Springer-Verlag, New York, p. 185-193, 1976. Proposes an error recovery method using pairs of elements of the alphabet, called "braces", which are used to select part of the input that contains the error and select a goal (non-terminal) to which this part must be reduced. Some conditions are derived which must be fulfilled by the braces, and it is shown that the braces can be computed automatically, at parser generation time.

- K.S. **Fu**, "Error-correcting parsing for syntactic pattern recognition". In *Data Structure, Computer Graphics and Pattern Recognition*, A. Klinger et al. (eds.), Academic Press, New York, p. 449-492, 1977. Discusses the least-errors analyser of Aho and Peterson [ErrHandl 1972] in the context of stochastic grammars. Least-errors then becomes maximum likelihood. Many examples are given.

- S.Y. **Lu**, K.S. Fu, "Stochastic error-correcting syntax analysis for recognition of noisy patterns", *IEEE Trans. Comput.*, vol. 26, no. 12, p. 1268-1276, 1977. This paper models deletion, insertion, and replacement errors into a stochastic disformation model: each error has a probability associated with it. Then, the model is incorporated into the stochastic context-free grammar, and an Earley parser is modified to look for the most likely error correction. This proves to be inefficient, so a sequential classification algorithm (SCA) is used. This SCA uses a stopping rule that tells when it has seen enough terminals to make a decision. The authors are interested in pattern recognition rather than in parse trees.

- George **Poonen**, "Error recovery for LR(k) parsers". In *Inf. Process. 77*, Bruce Gilchrist (eds.), IFIP, North Holland Publ. Co., Amsterdam, p. 529-533, Aug 1977. A special token, ERRORMARK, is added to the grammar, to represent any incorrect stretch of input. When encountering an error in an LR(1) parser, scan the stack for states having a shift on ERRORMARK, collect all shift tokens of these states into an acceptable-set, skip the input until an acceptable token is found and unstack until the corresponding accepting state is uncovered.

- Jean E. **Musinski**, "Lookahead recall error recovery for LALR parsers", *ACM SIGPLAN Notices*, vol. 12, no. 10, p. 48-60, Oct 1977. Shows how the error recovery of a specific LALR(1) parser can be improved by what amounts to the restricted decomposition of symbols on the stack, to increase the acceptable set.

- E.-W **Dieterich**, "Parsing and syntactic error recovery for context-free grammars by means of coarse structures". In *Automata, Languages and Programming; Lecture Notes in Computer Science #52*, A. Salomaa & M. Steinby (eds.), Springer-Verlag, Berlin, p. 492-503, 1977. Proposes a two-level parsing process that separates the coarse structures from the rest of the grammar. These coarse structures consist of characteristic brackets, for instance **begin** and **end**. Error recovery can then also be applied to these two levels.

- S. **Sippu**, E. Soisalon-Soininen, "On defining error recovery in context-free parsing". In *Automata, Languages and Programming; Lecture Notes in Computer Science #52*, A. Salomaa & M. Steinby (eds.), Springer-Verlag, Berlin, p. 492-503, 1977. Uses a grammatical transformation that leads to an LR grammar that incorporate certain replacement, deletion, or insertion errors.

- Charles **Wetherell**, "Why automatic error correctors fail", *Comput. Lang. (Elmsford, NY)*, vol. 2, p. 179-186, 1977. Shows that there is no hope of building efficient automatic syntactic error correctors which can handle large classes of errors perfectly. The author argues that parser writers should instead study the error patterns and work for efficient correction of common errors. Language designers must concentrate on ways to make languages less susceptible to common errors.

- D.A. **Turner**, "Error diagnosis and recovery in one pass compilers", *Inform. Process. Lett.*, vol. 6, p. 113-115, 1977. Proposes an extremely simple(minded) error recovery method for recursive descent parsers: when an error occurs, the parser enters a recovering state. While in this recovering state, error messages are inhibited. Apart from that, the parser proceeds until it requires a definite symbol. Then, symbols are skipped until this symbol is found or the end of the input is reached. Because this method can result in a lot of skipping, some fine-tuning can be applied.

- Thomas J. **Pennello**, Frank DeRemer, "A forward move algorithm for LR error recovery". In *Fifth Annual ACM Symposium on Principles of Programming Languages*, p. 241-254, Jan 1978. Refer to Graham and Rhodes [ErrHandl 1975]. Backward moves are found to be detrimental to error recovery. The extent of the forward move is determined as follows. At the error, an LALR(1) parser is started in a state including *all* possible items. The thus extended automaton is run until it wants to reduce past the error detection point. The resulting right context is used in error correction. An algorithm for the construction of a reasonably sized extended LALR(1) table is given.

- Kuo-Chung **Tai**, "Syntactic error correction in programming languages", *IEEE Trans. Softw. Eng.*, vol. SE-4, no. 5, p. 414-425, 1978. Presents a technique for syntactic error correction called *pattern mapping*. Patterns model the editing of the input string at the error detection point. These patterns are constructed by the parser developer. The patterns are sorted by a criterion called the *minimum distance correction with k correct look-ahead symbols*, and whenever correction is required, the first matching pattern is used. If no such pattern is found, error correction fails and another error recovery method must be applied.

- M. Dennis **Mickunas**, John A. Modry, "Automatic error recovery for LR parsers", *Commun. ACM*, vol. 21, no. 6, p. 459-465, June 1978. When an error is encountered, a set of provisional parsings of the beginning of the rest of the input (so-called *condensations*) are constructed: for each state a parsing is attempted and those that survive according to certain criteria are accepted. This yields a set of target states. Now the stack is "frayed" by partly or completely undoing any reduces; this yields a set of source states. Attempts are made to connect a source state to a target state by inserting or deleting tokens. Careful rules are given.

- J. **Lewi**, K. de Vlaminck, J. Huens, M. Huybrechts, "The ELL(1) parser generator and the error-recovery mechanism", *Acta Inform.*, vol. 10, p. 209-228, 1978. Presents a detailed recursive descent parser generation scheme for ELL(1) grammars, and also presents an error recovery method based on so-called *synchronization triplets* (*a,b,A*). *a* is a terminal from FIRST(*A*), *b* is a terminal from LAST(*A*). The parser operates either in parsing mode or in error mode. It starts in parsing mode, and proceeds until an error occurs. Then, in error mode, symbols are skipped until either an end-marker *b* is found where *a* is the last encountered corresponding begin-marker, in which case parsing mode resumes, or a begin-marker *a* is found, in which case *A* is invoked in parsing mode. As soon as *A* is accepted, error-mode is resumed. The success of the method depends on careful selection of synchronization triplets.

- G. David **Ripley**, "A simple recovery-only procedure for simple precedence parsers", *Commun. ACM*, vol. 21, no. 11, p. 928-930, Nov 1978. When an error (character-pair, reduction or stackability) is encountered, the error is reported and the contents of the stack are replaced by the one error symbol ??, which has the relation ⋖ to all other symbols. Then the parser is restarted. Subsequent attempts to reduce across the error symbol just result in a reduction to the error symbol; no semantic routine is called.

- Joachim **Ciesinger**, "A bibliography of error-handling", *ACM SIGPLAN Notices*, vol. 14, no. 1, p. 16-26, Jan 1979. Around 90 literature references from 1963-1978.

- C.N. **Fischer**, K.-C. Tai, D.R. Milton, "Immediate error correction in strong LL(1) parsers", *Inform. Process. Lett.*, vol. 8, no. 5, p. 261-266, June 1979. A strong-LL(1) parser will sometimes perform some incorrect parsing actions, connected with ε-matches, when confronted with an erroneous input symbol, before signalling an error; this impedes subsequent error correction. A subset of the LL(1) grammars is defined, the *nullable LL(1) grammars*, in which rules can only produce ε directly, not indirectly. A special routine, called before an ε-match is done, hunts down the stack to see if the input symbol will be matched or predicted by something deeper on the stack; if not, an error is signalled immediately. An algorithm to convert any strong-LL(1) grammar into a non-nullable strong-LL(1) grammar is given. (See also Mauney and Fischer [ErrHandl 1981]).

- Susan L. **Graham**, Charles B. Haley, William N. Joy, "Practical LR error recovery", *ACM SIGPLAN Notices*, vol. 14, no. 8, p. 168-175, Aug 1979. A considerable number of techniques is integrated. First-level error recovery does forward-move, restricting the possibilities to one correction only, using a cost function. The backward move is controlled by error tokens in the grammar. The second level does panic mode error recovery using "beacon tokens"; disaster is prevented by dividing the grammar into sections (like "declarations" or "statement"), which the error recovery will not leave.

- T. **Krawczyk**, "Error correction by mutational grammars", *Inform. Process. Lett.*, vol. 11, no. 1, p. 9-15, 1980. Discusses an error correction method that automatically extends a grammar by adding certain mutations of grammar rules, so that input with separator and parenthesis errors can be corrected, while retaining the LR(*k*) grammar class. The parser delivers the parsing in the form of a list of grammar rules used; the mutated rules in this list are replaced by their originals.

- Ajit B. **Pai**, Richard B. Kieburtz, "Global context recovery: a new strategy for syntactic error recovery by table-driven parsers", *ACM Trans. Prog. Lang. Syst.*, vol. 2, no. 1, p. 18-41, Jan 1980. A *fiducial* symbol is a terminal symbol that has the property that if it occurs on the top of the stack of an LL(1) parser, it will to a large degree determine the rest of the stack. Two more explicit definitions are given, the most practical being: a terminal symbol that occurs only once in the grammar, in a rule for a non-terminal that occurs only once in the grammar, etc. Now, if an error occurs that cannot be repaired locally, the input is discarded until a fiducial symbol *z* appears. Then the stack is popped until *z*, or a non-terminal *N* that produces *z*, appears. In the latter case *n* is "developed" until *z* appears. Parsing can now continue. If the stack gets empty in this process, the start symbol is pushed anew; it will produce *z*.

The paper starts with a very readable introduction to error recovery and a good local error correction algorithm.

• Steven **Pemberton**, "Comments on an error-recovery scheme by Hartmann", *Softw. Pract. Exper.*, vol. 10, no. 3, p. 231-240, 1980. Error recovery in a recursive descent parser is done by passing to each parsing routine a set of "acceptable" symbols. Upon encountering an error, the parsing routine will insert any directly required terminals and then skip input until an acceptable symbol is found. Rules are given and refined on what should be in the acceptable set for certain constructs in the grammar.

• Johannes **Röhrich**, "Methods for the automatic construction of error correcting parsers", *Acta Inform.*, vol. 13, no. 2, p. 115-139, Feb 1980. See Section 10.7.3 for a discussion of this error recovery method. The paper also discusses implementation of this method in LL(k) and LR(k) parsers, using so-called *deterministic continuable stack automata*.

• Seppo **Sippu**, Eljas Soisalon-Soininen, "A scheme for LR(k) parsing with error recovery, Part I: LR(k) parsing/Part II: Error recovery/Part III: Error correction", *Intern. J. Comput. Math.*, vol. A8, p. 27-42/107-119/189-206, 1980. A thorough mathematical theory of non-deterministic and deterministic LR(k)-like parsers (which subsumes SLR(k) and LALR(k)) is given. These parsers are then extended with error productions such that all errors that are at least k tokens apart are corrected. It should be noted that the resulting parsers are almost certainly non-deterministic.

• C.N. **Fischer**, D.R. Milton, S.B. Quiring, "Efficient LL(1) error correction and recovery using only insertions", *Acta Inform.*, vol. 13, no. 2, p. 141-154, 1980. See Section 10.7.4 for a discussion of this error recovery method.

• Kuo-Chung **Tai**, "Predictors of context-free grammars", *SIAM J. Computing*, vol. 9, no. 3, p. 653-664, Aug 1980. Author's abstract: "A *predictor* of a context-free grammar G is a substring of a sentence in $L(G)$ which determines unambiguously the contents of the parse stack immediately before (in top-down parsing) or after (in bottom-up parsing) symbols of the predictor are processed. Two types of predictors are defined, one for bottom-up parsers, one for top-down parsers. Algorithms for finding predictors are given and the possible applications of predictors are discussed." Predictors are a great help in error recovery.

• C.N. **Fischer**, J. Mauney, "On the role of error productions in syntactic error correction", *Comput. Lang. (Elmsford, NY)*, vol. 5, p. 131-139, 1980. Presents a number of examples in a Pascal parser illustrating the use of error productions in cases where an automatic error corrector would not find the right continuation. Error productions can be added to the grammar regardless of the error corrector.

• Jon **Mauney**, Charles N. Fischer, "An improvement to immediate error detection in strong LL(1) parsers", *Inform. Process. Lett.*, vol. 12, no. 5, p. 211-212, 1981. The technique of Fischer, Tai and Milton [ErrHandl 1979] is extended to all LL(1) grammars by having the special routine which is called before an ε-match is done do conversion to non-nullable on the fly. Linear time dependency is preserved by setting a flag when the test succeeds, clearing it when a symbol is matched and by not performing the test if the flag is set: this way the test will be done at most once for each symbol.

• Stuart O. **Anderson**, Roland C. Backhouse, "Locally least-cost error recovery in Earley's algorithm", *ACM Trans. Prog. Lang. Syst.*, vol. 3, no. 3, p. 318-347, July 1981. Parsing and error recovery are unified so that error-free parsing is zero-cost error recovery. The information already present in the Earley items is utilized cleverly to determine possible continuations. From these and from the input, the locally least-cost error recovery can be calculated, albeit at considerable expense. Detailed algorithms are given.

• Rodney W. **Topor**, "A note on error recovery in recursive descent parsers", *ACM SIGPLAN Notices*, vol. 17, no. 2, p. 37-40, Feb 1982. Followset error recovery is implemented in a recursive-descent parser by having one parse-and-error-recovery routine which is passed the actual routine for a rule, its FIRST set and its FOLLOWS set. This reduces the size of the parser considerably and prevents clerical errors in hand-written parsers.

- Michael G. **Burke**, Gerald A. Fisher, "A practical method for syntactic error diagnosis and repair", *ACM SIGPLAN Notices*, vol. 17, no. 6, p. 67-78, June 1982. See Burke and Fisher [ErrHandl 1987].

- Jon **Mauney**, Charles N. Fischer, "A forward-move algorithm for LL and LR parsers", *ACM SIGPLAN Notices*, vol. 17, no. 6, p. 79-87, June 1982. Upon finding an error, a Graham, Harrison and Ruzzo general CF parser [CF 1980] is started to do a forward move analysis using cost functions. The general CF parser is run over a restricted piece of the input, allowing *regional least-cost error correction*.

- F. **Jalili**, J.H. Gallier, "Building friendly parsers". In *9th Annual ACM Symposium on Principles of Programming Languages*, ACM, New York, p. 196-206, 1982. An interactive LALR(1) parser is described that uses forward move error recovery to better prompt the user with possible corrections. The interactions of the interactive parsing and the forward move algorithm are described in fairly great detail.

- S.O. **Anderson**, R.C. Backhouse, "An alternative implementation of an insertion-only recovery technique", *Acta Inform.*, vol. 18, p. 289-298, 1982. Argues that the FMQ error corrector of Fischer, Milton and Quiring [ErrHandl 1980] does not have to compute a complete insertion. It is sufficient to compute the first symbol. If $w = w_1w_2 \cdots w_n$ is an optimal insertion for the error a following prefix u, then $w_2 \cdots w_n$ is an optimal insertion for the error a following prefix uw_1. Also, immediate error detection is not necessary. Instead, the error corrector is called for every symbol, and returns an empty insertion if the symbol is correct.

- S.O. **Anderson**, R.C. Backhouse, E.H. Bugge, C.P. Stirling, "An assessment of locally least-cost error recovery", *Computer J.*, vol. 26, no. 1, p. 15-24, 1983. Locally least-cost error recovery consists of a mechanism for editing the next input symbol at least cost, where the cost of each edit operation is determined by the parser developer. The method is compared to Wirth's followset method (see Stirling [ErrHandl 1985]) and compares favorably.

- Seppo **Sippu**, Eljas Soisalon-Soininen, "A syntax-error-handling technique and its experimental analysis", *ACM Trans. Prog. Lang. Syst.*, vol. 5, no. 4, p. 656-679, Oct 1983. Phrase level error recovery replaces the top m elements from the stack and the next n input tokens by a single non-terminal such that parsing can continue. The authors explore various search sequences to determine the values of m and n. Local error recovery can be incorporated by introducing for each terminal t a new production rule Term_t -> Empty t, and having a production rule Empty -> ε. This allows both the correction of a phrase (n=0,m=0) to Term_t (i.e. insertion of t) and of a phrase (n,m) to Empty (i.e. deletion of (n,m)). Experimental results are given.

- K. **Hammond**, V.J. Rayward-Smith, "A survey on syntactic error recovery and repair", *Comput. Lang.*, vol. 9, no. 1, p. 51-68, 1984. Divides the error recovery schemes into three classes:
1. local recovery schemes, such as "panic mode", the followset method, the FMQ method (see Fischer, Milton and Quiring [ErrHandl 1980]), LaFrance's pattern matching method (see LaFrance [ErrHandl 1970]), and Backhouse's locally least-cost method (see Backhouse et al. [ErrHandl 1983]);
2. regional error recovery schemes, such as forward/backward move (see for instance Graham and Rodhes [ErrHandl 1975]); and
3. global error recovery schemes, such as global minimum distance error recovery (see for instance Aho and Peterson [ErrHandl 1972] and Lyon [ErrHandl 1974]), and mutational grammars (see for instance Krawczyk [ErrHandl 1980]).

The paper summarizes the advantages and disadvantages of each method.

- Michael **Spenke**, Heinz Mühlenbein, Monika Mevenkamp, Friedemann Mattern, Christian Beilken, "A language-independent error recovery method for LL(1) parsers", *Softw. Pract. Exper.*, vol. 14, no. 11, p. 1095-1107, Nov 1984. Presents an error recovery method using deletions and insertions. The choice between different possible corrections is made by comparing the cost of the insertion with the reliability of the symbol. A correction is plausible if the reliability of the first non-skipped symbol is larger than the insert-cost of the insertion. The correction is selected among the plausible corrections, such that the fewest symbols are skipped. Reliability and insert-cost of each symbol are tunable.

- Colin P. **Stirling**, "Follow set error recovery", *Softw. Pract. Exper.*, vol. 15, no. 3, p. 239-257, March 1985. Describes the followset technique for error recovery: at all times there is a set of symbols that depends on the parse stack and that will not be skipped, called the *followset*. When an error occurs, symbols are skipped until one is found that is a member of this set. Then, symbols are inserted and/or the parser state is adapted until this symbol is legal. In fact there is a family of error recovery (correction) methods that differ in the way the followset is determined. The paper compares several of these methods.

- Pyda **Srisuresh**, Michael J. Eager, "A portable syntactic error recovery scheme for LR(1) parsers". In *Proc. 1985 ACM Comput. Sc. Conf.*, W.D. Dominick (eds.), ACM, New Orleans, p. 390-399, Mar 1985. Presents a detailed account of the implementation of an error recovery scheme that works at four levels, each one of a more global nature. The first and the second level are local, attempting to recover from the error by editing the symbol in front of the error detection point and the error symbol itself. The third level uses error tokens, and the last level is panic mode.

- Helmut **Richter**, "Noncorrecting syntax error recovery", *ACM Trans. Prog. Lang. Syst.*, vol. 7, no. 3, p. 478-489, July 1985. See Section 10.8 for a discussion of this method. The errors can be pinpointed better by parsing backwards from the error detection point, using a reverse grammar until again an error is found. The actual error must be in the indicated interval. Bounded-context grammars are conjectured to yield deterministic suffix-grammars.

- Kwang-Moo **Choe**, Chun-Hyon Chang, "Efficient computation of the locally least-cost insertion string for the LR error repair", *Inform. Process. Lett.*, vol. 23, no. 6, p. 311-316, 1986. Refer to Anderson, Backhouse, Bugge and Stirling [ErrHandl 1983] for locally least-cost error correction. The paper presents an efficient implementation in LR parsers, using a formalism described by Park, Choe and Chang [LR 1985].

- Tudor **Bălănescu**, Serban Gavrilă, Marian Gheorghe, Radu Nicolescu, Liviu Sofonea, "On Hartman's error recovery scheme", *ACM SIGPLAN Notices*, vol. 21, no. 12, p. 80-86, Dec 1986. More and tighter acceptable-sets for more grammar constructions; see Pemberton [ErrHandl 1980].

- Michael G. **Burke**, Gerald A. Fisher, "A practical method for LL and LR syntactic error diagnosis and recovery", *ACM Trans. Prog. Lang. Syst.*, vol. 9, no. 2, p. 164-197, April 1987. Traditional error recovery assumes that all tokens up to the error symbol are correct. The article investigates the option of allowing earlier tokens to be modified. To this end, parsing is done with two parsers, one of which is a number of tokens ahead of the other. The first parser does no actions and keeps enough administration to be rolled back, and the second performs the semantic actions; the first parser will modify the input stream or stack so that the second parser will never see an error. This device is combined with three error repair strategies: single token recovery, scope recovery and secondary recovery. In single token recovery, the parser is rolled back and single tokens are deleted, inserted or replaced by tokens specified by the parser writer. In scope recovery, closers as specified by the parser writer are inserted before the error symbol. In secondary recovery, sequences of tokens around the error symbol are discarded. In each case, a recovery is accepted if it allows the parser to advance a specified number of tokens beyond the error symbol. It is reported that this techniques corrects three quarters of the normal errors in Pascal programs in the same way as a knowledgeable human would. The effects of fine-tuning are discussed.

- Jon **Mauney**, Charles N. Fischer, "Determining the extent of lookahead in syntactic error repair", *ACM Trans. Prog. Lang. Syst.*, vol. 10, no. 3, p. 456-469, July 1988. A correction of an error can be validated by trying it and parsing on until a symbol is found with the so-called Moderate Phrase Level Uniqueness. Once such a symbol is found, all minimal corrections of the error are equivalent in the sense that after this MPLU symbol, the acceptable suffixes will be identical. Measurements indicate that in Pascal the distance between two such symbols is fairly short, for the most part.

- Gordon V. **Cormack**, "An LR substring parser for noncorrecting syntax error recovery", *ACM SIGPLAN Notices*, vol. 24, no. 7, p. 161-169, July 1989. Presents a method to produce an LR parser for the substrings of a language described by a bounded-context(1,1) grammar, thereby confirming Richter's [ErrHandl 1985] conjecture that this can be done for BC grammars. The resulting parser is about twice as large as an ordinary LR parser.

13.12 TRANSFORMATIONS ON GRAMMARS

- J.M. **Foster**, "A syntax-improving program", *Computer J.*, vol. 11, no. 1, p. 31-34, May 1968. The parser generator SID (Syntax Improving Device) attempts to remove LL(1) conflicts by eliminating left-recursion, and then left-factoring, combined with inline substitution. If this succeeds, SID generates a parser in machine language.

- Kenichi **Taniguchi**, Tadao Kasami, "Reduction of context-free grammars", *Inform. Control*, vol. 17, p. 92-108, 1970. Considers algorithms to reduce or minimize the number of non-terminals in a grammar.

- M.D. **Mickunas**, R.L. Lancaster, V.B. Schneider, "Transforming LR(k) grammars to LR(1), SLR(1) and (1,1) bounded right-context grammars", *J. ACM*, vol. 23, no. 3, p. 511-533, July 1976. The required look-ahead of k tokens is reduced to $k-1$ by incorporating the first token of the look-ahead into the non-terminal; this requires considerable care. The process can be repeated until $k=1$ for all LR(k) grammars and even until $k=0$ for some grammars.

- D.J. **Rosenkrantz**, H.B. Hunt, "Efficient algorithms for automatic construction and compactification of parsing grammars", *ACM Trans. Prog. Lang. Syst.*, vol. 9, no. 4, p. 543-566, Oct 1987. Many grammar types are defined by the absence of certain conflicts: LL(1), LR(1), operator-precedence, etc. A simple algorithm is given to modify a given grammar to avoid such conflicts. Modification is restricted to the merging of non-terminals and possibly the merging of terminals; semantic ambiguity thus introduced will have to be cleared up by later inspection. Proofs of correctness and applicability of the algorithm are given. The maximal merging of terminals while avoiding conflicts is also used to reduce grammar size.

13.13 GENERAL BOOKS ON PARSING

- Peter Zilany **Ingerman**, *A Syntax-Oriented Translator*, Academic Press, New York, p. 132, 1966. Readable and realistic (for that time) advice for DIY compiler construction, in archaic terminology. Uses a backtracking LC parser improved by FIRST sets.

- William M. **McKeeman**, James J. Horning, David B. Wortman, *A compiler generator*, Prentice Hall, Englewood Cliffs, N.J., p. 527, 1970. Good explanation of precedence and mixed-strategy parsing. Full application to the XPL compiler.

- Alfred V. **Aho**, Jeffrey D. Ullman, *The theory of parsing, translation and*

compiling, Volume I: Parsing, Prentice Hall, Englewood Cliffs, N.J., p. 542, 1972.
The book describes the parts of formal languages and automata theory relevant to parsing in a strict
mathematical fashion. Since much of the pertinent theory of parsing had already been developed in 1972,
the book is still reasonably up to date and is a veritable trove of definitions, theorems, lemmata and
proofs.
The required mathematical apparatus is first introduced, followed by a survey of compiler construction
and by properties of formal languages. The rest of the book confines itself to CF and regular languages.
General parsing methods are treated in full: backtracking top-down and bottom-up, CYK and Earley.
Directional non-backtracking methods are explained in detail, including general LL(k), LC(k) and LR(k),
precedence parsing and various other approaches. A last chapter treats several non-grammatical methods
for language specification and parsing.
Very little attention is paid to practical matters. Implementation of LL(k) and LR(k) parsers is covered in
one nine-line paragraph. Error correction is hardly touched upon, LALR and recursive descent are not
mentioned.

- Frederick W. **Weingarten**, *Translation of computer languages*, Holden-Day, San
  Francisco, Calif., p. 180, 1973. Describes some parsing techniques in an clear and easy style.
The coverage of subjects is rather eclectic. A full backtracking top-down parser for ε-free non-left-
recursive grammars and a full backtracking bottom-up parser for ε-free grammars are described. The
author does not explicitly forbid ε-rules, but his internal representation of grammar rules cannot represent
them. The Earley parser is described well, with an elaborate example. For linear-time parsers, bounded-
context and precedence are treated; a table-construction algorithm is given for precedence but not for
bounded-context. LR(k) is vaguely mentioned, LL(k) not at all. Good additional reading. Contains many
algorithms and flowcharts similar to Cohen and Gotlieb [Misc 1970].

- P.M. **Lewis II**, D.J. Rosenkrantz, R.E. Stearns, *Compiler design theory*, Systems
  Programming Series, Addison-Wesley, Reading, Mass, p. 647, 1976. The book
covers the theory of formal languages and parsers in a slow-paced fashion. Grammars are treated
separately from parsers, which gives the book an odd structure. Precedence parsing is explained without
mentioning the word "precedence".
It has a valuable appendix on grammar transformations and an extensive bibliography.

- R.C. **Gonzales**, M.G. Thomason, *Syntactic Pattern Recognition*, Addison-Wesley,
  Reading, Mass., p. 283, 1978. This book provides numerous examples of syntactic
descriptions of objects not normally considered subject to a syntax. Examples range from simple seg-
mented closed curves, trees and shapes of letters, via bubble chamber events, electronic networks, and
structural formulas of rubber molecules to snow flakes, ECGs, and fingerprints. Special attention is paid
to grammars for non-linear objects, for instance web grammars, plex grammars and shape grammars. A
considerable amount of formal language theory is covered. All serious parsing is done using the CYK
algorithm; Earley, LL(k) and LR(k) are not mentioned. Operator-precedence, simple precedence and finite automata are occasionally used. The authors are wrong in claiming that an all-empty row in the CYK
recognition matrix signals an error in the input.
Interesting chapters about *stochastic grammars*, i.e. grammars with probabilities attached to the production rules, and about *grammatical inference*, i.e. methods to derive a reasonable grammar that will produce all sentences in a representative set R^+ and will not produce the sentences in a counterexample set
R^-.

- John E. **Hopcroft**, Jeffrey D. Ullman, *Introduction to automata theory, languages,
  and computation*, Addison-Wesley, Reading, Massachussetts, p. 418, 1979. A must
for readers interested in formal language theory and computational (im)possibilities.

- Roland C. **Backhouse**, *Syntax of programming languages*, Prentice Hall, London,
  p. 290, 1979. Grammars are considered in depth, as far as they are relevant to programming
languages. FS automata and the parsing techniques LL and LR are treated in detail, and supported by lots
of well-explained math. Often complete and efficient algorithms are given in Pascal. Much attention is
paid to error recovery and repair, especially to least-cost repairs and locally optimal repairs. Definitely

recommended for further reading.

- A.J.T. **Davie**, R. Morisson, *Recursive descent compiling*, Ellis Horwood Ltd., Chichester, p. 195, 1981. Well-balanced description of the design considerations that go into a recursive descent compiler; uses the St. Andrews University S-algol compiler as a running example.

- V.J. **Rayward-Smith**, *A first course in formal languages*, Blackwell Scientific, Oxford, p. 123, 1983. Very useful intermediate between Révész [Books 1985] and Hopcroft and Ullman [Books 1979]. Quite readable (the subject permitting); simple examples; broad coverage. No treatment of LALR, no bibliography.

- György E. **Révész**, *Introduction to formal languages*, McGraw-Hill, Singapore, p. 199, 1985. This nifty little book contains many results and elementary proofs of formal languages, without being "difficult". It gives a description of the ins and outs of the Chomsky hierarchy, automata, decidability and complexity of context-free language recognition, including the *hardest CF language*. Parsing is discussed, with descriptions of the Earley, LL(k) and LR(k) algorithms, each in a few pages.

- William A. **Barrett**, Rodney M. Bates, David A. Gustafson, John D. Couch, *Compiler construction: theory and practice*, Science Research Associates, Chicago, p. 504, 1986. A considerable part (about 50%) of the book is concerned with parsing; formal language theory, finite-state automata, top-down en bottom-up parsing and error recovery are covered in very readable chapters. Only those theorems are treated that relate directly to actual parsing; proofs are quite understandable. The book ends with an annotated bibliography of almost 200 entries, on parsing and other aspects of compiler construction.

- A.V. **Aho**, R. Sethi, J.D. Ullman, *Compilers: principles, techniques and tools*, Addison-Wesley, Reading, Mass., p. 796, 1986. The "Red Dragon Book". Excellent, UNIX-oriented treatment of compiler construction. Even treatment of the various aspects.

- Anton **Nijholt**, *Computers and Languages: Theory and Practice*, Studies in Computer Science and Artificial Intelligence, 4, North-Holland, Amsterdam, p. 482, 1988. Treats in narrative form computers, natural and computer languages, and artificial intelligence, their essentials, history and interrelationships; for the sophisticated layperson. The account is interspersed with highly critical assessments of the influence of the military on computers and artificial intelligence. Much global information, little technical detail; treats parsing in breadth but not in depth.

13.14 SOME BOOKS ON COMPUTER SCIENCE

- David **Harel**, *Algorithms: The Spirit of Computing*, Addison-Wesley, Reading, Mass, p. 425, 1987. Excellent introduction to the fundamentals of computer science for the sophisticated reader.

- Robert **Sedgewick**, *Algorithms*, Addison-Wesley, Reading, Mass., p. 657, 1988. Comprehensive, understandable treatment of many algorithms, beautifully done.

- Jeffrey D. **Smith**, *Design and Analysis of Algorithms*, PWS-Kent Publ. Comp., Boston, p. 447, 1989. Good introductory book, treating list handling, searching, breadth-first and depth-first search, dynamic programming, etc., etc.

Author index

Page numbers in roman indicate pages referring to the author; page numbers in *italic* refer to annotations of works by the author.

Abrahams, P.W., *280*
Ackley, S.I., *299*
Agrawal, R., *288*
Aho, A.V., 42, 118, 214, 219, 236, *267*, *269*, *283*, 284, 288, *295*, 296, 296, *299*, *303*, 304, 308, *310*, *312*
Al-Hussainin, A.M.M., 204, 289
Ancona, M., 287, 288
Anderson, S.O., 246, *307*, *308*, 309
Anderson, T., 214, *283*
Aoe, J., *298*
Auty, D., *281*

Backhouse, R.C., 246, *284*, *307*, *308*, 308, 309, *311*
Backus, J.W., *266*
Baker, T.P., 287, 289
Barrett, W.A., *312*
Barth, G., 42, 270
Bates, R.M., *312*
Bauer, F.L., *266*, 294
Beilken, C., *309*
Bell, J.R., 192, *295*, 296
Bermudez, M.E., 221, *289*, 290, *291*
Bertsch, E., 194, 270, 297
Birman, A., *267*
Blank, G.D., 108, *301*, *302*, 302
Bochmann, G.V., *267*
Bolc, L., *302*

Bossi, A., *278*
Bouckaert, M., 161, *276*, 278
Bratley, P., 108, *300*
Brooker, R.A., *266*
Brown, C.A., 287
Bălănescu, T., *309*
Bugge, E.H., 246, *308*, 309
Burgess, C.J., 287, *303*
Burke, M.G., *308*, 308, *309*
Burshteyn, B., 269

Carter, L.R., 181, *268*
Celentano, A., *285*, 287, 288
Chang, C.-H., 221, 246, *289*, 289, 290, *309*, 309
Chapman, N.P., 220, *289*, 290
Chartres, B.A., *275*
Cherry, L.L., 219, *267*
Chester, D., *294*, *300*
Cho, Y.E., *292*
Choe, K.-M., 214, 221, 246, *289*, 289, 290, 290, *309*, 309
Chomsky, N., 24, 51, *265*
Ciesinger, J., *304*, *306*
Cleaveland, J.C., 45, *272*
Cocco, N., *278*
Cohen, D.J., *266*, 311
Cohen, J., 143, *267*, *273*, *279*, 281
Cohen, R., 221, *283*
Colmerauer, A., 227, *295*
Colussi, L., *278*
Conway, M.E., *266*, 303

Conway, R.W., 237, *303*
Corasick, M.J., 118, *299*
Cormack, G.V., 227, 248, *291*, 292, *310*
Couch, J.D., *312*
Crowe, D., 272, *296*
Čulik, K., 221, *279*, *283*

Dahl, V., *301*, *302*
Davie, A.J.T., *312*
Degano, P., 221, *290*
Demers, A.J., *284*, *293*
Demner, J., *283*, *293*
Dencker, P., 112, 204, *268*
Denning, P.J., *295*
DeRemer, F.L., 218, 221, 240, *283*, 288, 289, *299*, *305*
Detro, K.D., 288
Deussen, P., 79, *267*, 272
Dewar, H.P., 108, *300*
Dieterich, E.-W., *305*
Dobler, H., *282*
Dodero, G., 287, *288*
Dömölki, B., 270, *275*
Dürre, K., 112, 204, *268*
Dwyer, B., *281*

Eager, M.J., *309*
Earley, J., 15, 149, 206, *267*, 276
Eickel, J., *294*
Er, M.C., *298*
Eve, J., 214, *283*
Ezure, K., *278*

Feldman, J., *266*
Feyock, S., *304*
Finn, G.D., *268*
Fischer, C.N., 244, 281, *306*, 306, *307*, 307, *308*, 308, *310*
Fisher, A.J., 72, *273*
Fisher, G.A., *286*, *308*, 308, *309*
Fisker, R.G., *271*
Florentin, J.J., *275*
Floyd, R.W., *266*, *294*, 295
Foster, J.M., 179, 267, 280, *310*
Fu, K.S., *304*
Fujiwara, F., *289*, *294*

Gallier, J.H., *308*
Gavrilă, S., *309*
Gazdar, G., *301*, 301
Geller, M.M., *283*, *285*, 293
Gerardy, R., *269*
Ghandour, Z.J., *270*
Gheorghe, M., *309*
Ghezzi, C., 285, *286*, 286, *303*
Gianuzzi, V., *287*, 288
Glushkova, V.N., *281*
Gonzales, R.C., *311*
Goshawke, W., *302*
Gotlieb, C.C., *266*, 311
Gough, K.J., *281*, 281
Graham, S.L., 156, 159, 163, 233, 238, 250, *277*, *278*, *283*, *296*, 298, *303*, 305, *306*, 308
Gray, J.N., *296*
Green, J., *266*
Greibach, S.A., 45, 127, *272*, *274*
Gries, D., *266*, *304*
Griffith, M., *280*
Griffiths, T.V., 79, *274*, 275
Grosch, J., *269*
Grosz, B.J., 275, 276, *302*
Grune, D., 49, 179, 183, *273*, *282*
Gustafson, D.A., *312*

Haley, C.B., *306*
Hammer, M., *293*
Hammond, K., *308*
Hanson, D.R., *282*
Harel, D., *312*
Harris, L.A., *271*
Harris, M.D., *301*

Harrison, M.A., 156, 159, 163, 250, *277*, *278*, *283*, *285*, 293, *296*, 308
Hayes, P.J., *300*
Heckmann, R., 183, *282*
Heering, J., 221, *291*
Heilbrunner, S., 220, *281*, *286*, *287*, *289*
Henderson, D.S., *297*, 298
Heuft, J., 112, 204, *268*
Heuring, V.P., *299*
Hext, J.B., 148, *276*, 276
Hickey, T.J., 143, *273*, *279*
Hirakawa, H., *294*
Hirsh, S., *294*
Hoffman, H.-J., *284*
Hopcroft, J.E., 22, 30, 71, 95, 122, 228, *311*, 312
Horning, J.J., 214, *283*, *284*, *310*
Horspool, R.N., 221, *291*, 298
Huens, J., *280*, 305
Hunt, H.B., 179, *284*, *310*
Hunter, R.B., *267*
Huybrechts, M., *280*, 305

Ichbiah, J., 197, *295*
Ikeda, M., *278*
Ingerman, P.Z., *310*
Inoue, K., *289*, 294
Irons, E.T., *266*, *273*, *274*, 274
Ives, F., 221, *289*, *290*, 290

Jacobs, C.J.H., 179, 183, *282*
Jalili, F., *308*
James, E.G., *303*
James, L., *287*
Jarzabek, S., *280*
Johnson, S.C., 214, 219, *267*, *283*, 285
Johnson, W.L., *299*
Joliat, M.L., *285*
Jones, D.W., *300*
Jones, N.D., *270*
Joy, W.N., *306*

Kaminger, F.P., *276*
Kanze, J., *291*
Karstens, U., *290*
Kasami, T., 75, *276*, *310*
Katz, C., *266*
Kelly, I.D.K., *302*
Kemp, R., *287*
Kernighan, B.W., 219, *267*
Khabbaz, N.A., *270*

Kieburtz, R.B., *306*
King, M., *301*
Kirchhoff, L.W., 179, *281*
Klein, E., *301*
Klenk, U., *300*
Klint, P., 221, *291*
Knuth, D.E., 206, 213, *280*, *282*
Komor, T., *280*
Korenjak, A.J., 213, *282*, 283, 290
Koskimies, K., *286*
Koster, C.H.A., 42, *271*, *272*, 277
Král, J., *277*, *283*, *293*, 293
Krawczyk, T., *280*, *306*, 308
Krishnamurthy, M.S., *297*, 297
Kristensen, B.B., *284*, *287*, 289
Kron, H.H., *284*
Kruseman Aretz, F.E.J., 221, *291*, 291
Krzemień, R., 107, *299*
Kuno, S., *275*, 275
Kurki-Suonio, R., 181, *279*

LaFrance, J.E., *302*, 308
LaLonde, W.R., 220, *285*, 285, *286*, *287*, 287, 298
Lancaster, R.L., 212, *310*
Lang, B., *276*
Langendoen, D., *299*, 300
Langmaack, H., *283*
Lazarus, P., *304*
Learner, A., *295*
Ledgard, H.F., *267*
Ledley, R.S., *266*
Lee, E.S., *270*, 271
Lesk, M.E., 39, *299*
Lévy, J.-P., *304*
Levy, M.R., 191, *297*, 297, *298*, 298
Lewi, J., 183, *280*, 305
Lewis II, P.M., *279*, *292*, *311*
Lim, A.L., *295*
Lindsey, C.H., *271*
Loeckx, J., 198, *270*, 295
Logothetis, G., 221, *291*
Lomet, D.B., *292*, 293
Lu, S.Y., *304*
Łukasiewicz, A., 107, *299*
Lyon, G., 236, *303*, 304, 308

MacCallum, I.R., *266*

Madrioli, D., 286
Madsen, O.L., 284, 287, 289
Mailloux, B.J., 271
Makinouchi, A., 286
Manacher, G.K., 277
Mandrioli, D., 285, 286, 286
Mannucci, S., 221, 290
Marcotty, M., 267
Martin, D.F., 295, 296
Matsumoto, Y., 294
Mattern, F., 309
Mauney, J., 306, 307, 308, 310
Mayer, O., 286
McAfee, J., 296
McCarthy, J., 266
McGettrick, A.D., 267
McKeeman, W.M., 198, 310
Meersman, R., 45, 272
Meertens, L.G.L.T., 271
Mehlhorn, K., 270
Mevenkamp, M., 309
Mickunas, M.D., 212, 240, 296, 305, 310
Milton, D.R., 179, 244, 281, 281, 306, 307, 307, 308
Miyoshi, H., 294
Modry, J.A., 240, 305
Mojana, B., 221, 290
Moll, K.R., 298
Morisson, R., 312
Morris, D., 266
Morse, S., 197, 295
Mouradian, G.V., 300
Mühlenbein, H., 309
Mukai, K., 283
Musinski, J.E., 304

Nakata, I., 220, 289, 290
Naur, P., 266
Ng, R., 300
Nicolescu, R., 309
Nijholt, A., 79, 268, 280, 281, 293, 312

Ostrand, T.J., 113, 299

Pagan, F.G., 269
Pager, D., 282, 284, 285, 286, 288
Pai, A.B., 306
Park, J.C.H., 214, 221, 288, 289, 289, 290, 290, 309
Partridge, D.P., 303
Patel, R., 267
Paul, M., 294

Paull, M.C., 113, 299
Peck, J.E.L., 271
Pemberton, S., 241, 307, 309
Pennello, T.J., 218, 221, 240, 288, 289, 289, 291, 305
Pereira, F.C.N., 268
Perlis, A.J., 266
Peterson, T.G., 236, 303, 304, 308
Petrick, S.R., 79, 274, 275
Pezaris, S.D., 292
Pirklbauer, K., 282
Pirotte, A., 161, 276, 278
Pittl, J., 293, 294, 294
Poonen, G., 304
Poplawski, D.A., 281
Porter, J.S., 299
Presser, L., 296
Pullum, G., 301
Purdom, P.W., 284, 287

Quiring, S.B., 244, 281, 307, 308

Rabin, M.O., 299
Ramesha Chandra, H.R., 297, 297
Rayward-Smith, V.J., 22, 308, 312
Reed, J.H., 302
Rekers, J., 221, 291
Révész, G.E., 25, 27, 30, 71, 312, 312
Rhodes, S.P., 233, 238, 303, 305, 308
Richter, H., 247, 309, 310
Ripley, G.D., 306
Rivieres, J. des, 298
Roberts, G.H., 221, 291, 291, 292, 292
Roberts, P.S., 148, 276, 276
Rohl, J.S., 266
Röhrich, J., 241, 244, 307
Rosenkrantz, D.J., 179, 280, 292, 310, 311
Ross, D.T., 299
Roth, M.S., 267
Rowland, B.R., 179, 281
Rozenberg, G., 45, 272
Rutishauser, H., 266
Ružička, P., 297
Ruzzo, W.L., 156, 159, 163, 250, 278, 308

Sag, I., 301

Sager, T.J., 281
Saint-Dizier, P., 301, 302
Sakai, I., 75, 88, 273
Salomon, D.J., 227, 291, 292
Samelson, K., 266, 294
Samet, H., 268
Sassa, M., 220, 289, 290
Schimpf, K.M., 289, 290
Schmidt, E., 39, 299
Schmitz, L., 289
Schneider, V.B., 212, 296, 310
Scott, D., 299
Sebesta, R.W., 270
Sedgewick, R., 75, 118, 265, 312
Sekimoto, S., 197, 283, 295
Sethi, R., 214, 312
Setzer, V.W., 280
Shannon, A., 288
Share, M., 219, 269
Sheil, B., 75, 88, 104, 277
Shieber, S.M., 301
Shimada, R., 298
Shyamasundar, R.K., 297, 297
Sintzoff, M., 45, 271
Sippu, S., 281, 281, 305, 307, 308
Sitver, R., 281
Smith, J.D., 74, 265, 312
Smith, W.B., 302
Snelling, M., 161, 276, 278
Snelting, G., 292
Sofonea, L., 309
Soisalon-Soininen, E., 281, 281, 283, 286, 288, 290, 293, 305, 307, 308
Sparck Jones, K., 275, 276, 301, 302
Spector, D., 287, 287, 291
Spenke, M., 309
Srisuresh, P., 309
Stearns, R.E., 279, 280, 311
Stirling, C.P., 241, 246, 308, 308, 309, 309
Stone, R.G., 204, 289
Sudborough, I.H., 297
Sudo, M., 283
Szafron, D., 300
Szymanski, T.G., 284, 285

Tai, K.-C., 227, 244, 267, 286, 305, 306, 307, 307
Takeuchi, Y., 282
Tanaka, E., 278
Tanaka, H., 294

Taniguchi, K., *310*
Tarhio, J., *288, 290*
Tarjan, R.E., *268*
Tennant, H., *300*
Terrine, G., *296*
Thomason, M.G., *311*
Thompson, K., 115, *299*
Thorne, J.P., 108, *300*
Tokuda, T., *287, 288*
Tomita, M., 79, 153, 157, 222, 276, *278, 279, 279*
Topor, R.W., *307*
Torii, K., *276*
Turnbull, C.J.M., *270,* 271
Turner, D.A., *305*

Ukkonen, E., 211, *268, 289, 293, 294*
Ullman, J.D., 22, 30, 71, 95, 122, 214, 219, 228, *267, 283, 284,* 284, 288, *295, 296,* 296, *310, 311, 312,* 312
Unger, S.H., 75, 82, 85, *275*
Uzgalis, R.C., 45, *272*

Valiant, L., 76, *277*
Vauquois, B., *266*
Vlaminck, K. de, *280, 305*
Vol'dman, G.Sh., *271*

Waddle, V.E., *269*
Wagner, R.A., *303*
Waite, W.M., 181, *268*
Walters, D.A., *270*
Warren, D.H.D., *268*
Watt, D.A., *272*
Webber, B.L., 275, 276, *302*
Weber, H., *295*
Weber, M., *286*
Wegner, L.M., *272, 273,* 273
Wegstein, J.H., *266, 294*
Weingarten, F.W., *311*
Wetherell, C., *288, 305*
Weyuker, E.J., 113, *299*
Wharton, R.M., *267*
Wigg, J.D., *302*
Wijngaarden, A. van, 42, 45, *266, 271, 272*
Wilcox, T.R., 237, *303*
Wilks, Y., *301*
Williams, J.H., *285, 297*
Williams, M.H., 191, *297, 298,* 298
Wilson, J.B., *266*

Winkler, G., *284*
Wirth, N., *267, 295*
Wise, D.S., *283, 296*
Witaszek, J., *286,* 287, *290*
Wolpe, H., *294*
Wood, D., *279, 280,* 280
Woodger, M., *266*
Woods, W.A., *269, 300*
Workman, D.A., *298*
Wortman, D.B., *310*
Wyrostek, P., *298*

Yamamoto, Y., *298*
Yao, A.C.-C., *268*
Yasukawa, H., *294*
Yeh, D., *288, 290*
Yehudai, A., *298*
Yoshida, K., *282*
Younger, D.H., 75, 88, *275*

Zimmer, R., *296*

Index

Page numbers in **bold** refer to pages where a definition of the indicated term can be found. Two page numbers separated by a dash describe a range of pages on each of which the term is used; page numbers separated by two dots indicate intermittent use of the term over the range.

acceptable-set, **240**, 241-244, 304, 309
accepting state, 110..113, 117-118, 122,
  200..205, 210, 223, 304
accessible non-terminal, **97**
ad hoc error recovery, **237**
affix, **46**, 271-272
affix grammar, 42, **46**, 265, 269..272
Aho and Corasick bibliographic search algorithm, **118**, 299
Algol 60, 35, 266, 273, 280, 294-295
Algol 68, 136, 267, 271
alphabet, **17**, 20-21, 45, 276, 304
alternative, **25**
ambiguity, **62**, 63-64, 93, 110, 113, 136, 153,
  156-157, 219, 222, 227-228, 236,
  248..251, 267, 277-278, 288, 291, 299,
  302, 310
ambiguity rate, 275
ambiguity test, 62, 228
analysis stack, **123**, 125, 130-131
angle brackets, 35, 45, 273
attribute, **58**, 59, 180, 252, 266, 268, 273, 281
attribute grammar, 46, 58-59, 179, 267, 272, 290

backtracking, **75**, 76, 79, 130..147, 180, 232,
  266-267, 273..279, 300-302, 311
Backus-Naur Form, **35**, 45, 266
backward move, **238**, 239-240, 305..308
beacon token, **304**, 306
bitvector, 276
blind alley, **26**, 48, 56

BNF, *see* Backus-Naur Form
bottom-up parsing, **65**
bounded-context, 79, **198**, 199, 204-205, 232,
  248, 272, 294..298, 309-311
bounded-context parsable, **297**
Boyer-Moore algorithm, 118
bracketed grammar, 273
breadth-first production, **48**, 273
breadth-first search, **75**, 76, 79, 124, 148, 164,
  200, 222-223, 226, 250, 276, 284, 304,
  312
bypassed LR(k) parser, **288**

C, 137, 286, 292
Cantor, 22
cascaded grammar, **300**
category (GPSG), **301**
chain rule, **89**, 220
chain-independent, **293**
channel algorithm, **214**, 220
characteristic parsing, 285, 293
character-pair error, **232**, 306
chart, **105**
chart parsing, **105**
Chomsky hierarchy, **28**, 40, 51, 53, 266, 272,
  312
Chomsky Normal Form, **92**, 94, 98..104, 266,
  274..277
chromosome recognition, 11, 278
closure, 289, 295
CNF, *see* Chomsky Normal Form

Cocke-Younger-Kasami, *see* CYK parser
condensation phase, **238**, 305
conflict resolver, **179**, 180..182, 219, 280, 282
context-free grammar, **32**
context-sensitive grammar, 29, **32**, 53, 60, 72, 249, 266, 270-271
continuation, **241**, 242-244, 307
continuation grammar, **242**, 243
control mechanism, 68..71, 77-79, 186
copy-symbol, **272**
coroutine, 266, 268
correction phase, **238**, 239
correct-prefix property, **175**, 229-232, 241, 294, 298
counter language, **266**
CRLL(1), **303**
cubic time dependency, **70**, 76-77, 149, 155, 157, 200, 233, 250, 275-278
CYK parser, 15, 57, 69, 75, 79, 81, **88**, 89..92, 99, 102, 104, 153..157, 227, 231, 233, 236, 260, 274..278, 302, 311

definite clause, 15, 79, 139, **141**, 143, 253, 268
depth-first search, **75**, 79, 83, 124, 142, 164, 253, 260, 312
derived affix, 271
derived attribute, 58
derived information, **58**
derived metanotion, 273
deterministic automaton, **77**, 78, 111, 122, 203, 205, 208, 210, 216, 219, 231, 284-285
deterministic language, **212**, 267, 270, 297
deterministic parser, 15, 57, **164**, 167-168, 172, 174, 213, 232, 268, 276, 294, 307
Deterministic Regular Parsable, 270
directed production analyser, **274**
directional parsing method, **74**
disambiguating rule, **179**, 267, 286
document conversion, 11, 219, 269
don't-care entry, 268, **283**
dot, 134, 151, 201, 284-285, 303
DRP grammar, **270**

Earley deduction, 268
Earley item, **151**, 152, 201, 236, 303, 307
Earley parser, 15, 69, 76, 79, 149..161, 200-201, 206, 227, 232, 236, 246, 250, 268..278, 301..307, 311-312
Earley set, 155, 162
eliminating ε-rules, 94-95, 101, 128
eliminating left recursion, 128-129, 178, 280, 310
eliminating unit rules, 94, 96, 102, 128, 220
empty word, **20**

end-marker, 23, 29, **125**, 130, 137, 165, 172, 181, 187, 205, 242
error correction, **230**, 234, 244, 246, 281-282, 303..311
error detection, 173, 175, 192, 197, 212, 220, **229**, 230-233, 237..242, 247, 271, 274, 283, 287, 296, 304
error detection point, **233**, 238-239, 246, 305, 309
error production, 236, **237**, 303, 307
error recovery, 176-177, 199, 213, 229, **230**, 233, 238..241, 246-247, 252, 291, 302..311
error repair, 13, **230**, 309, 311
error symbol, **233**, 246-248, 306, 309
error token, 237, **238**, 304, 306, 309
essential ambiguity, **62**, 63
EULER, 295
EXCLUDE set, 275
Exhaustive Constant Partial Ordering property, **301**
exponential explosion, 149
exponential time dependency, **70**, 71..79, 88, 94, 110, 148, 227, 249-250, 253, 260, 262, 271
extended context-free grammar, **35**, 36, 183, 267, 276
extended LL(1), 183, 282, 306
extended LL(k), 281
extended LR(k), 281, 287
extended operator-precedence, **297**, 298
extended precedence, **197**, 198, 232, 295
extended right precedence, **295**
extended weak precedence, **197**

fast string search, 116, 299
feature (GPSG), **301**
fiducial symbol, **306**
FILO list, *see* stack
finite-choice grammar, **40**, 53
finite-state automaton, 15, 106, **110**, 112, 116, 118, 122, 200-201, 220-222, 231, 249, 265, 280..283, 287, 289, 293, 297..303, 311
finite-state grammar, **38**, 41
FIRST set, 160-162, **168**, 169..183, 195, 207, 211, 215-216, 241, 243, 245, 271, 275, 279..282, 292, 306, 308, 310
$FIRST_{ALL}$ set, **195**
$FIRST_k$ set, 168, **181**, 182
$FIRST_{OP}$ set, **190**, 191
FL(k), **299**
Floyd production, **199**, 266, 272, 295, 302
FMQ error correction, **244**, 246, 308
FOLLOW set, 162, **173**, 172-177, 181, 218, 241, 271, 279..284

FOLLOW set error recovery, **241**
FOLLOW$_k$ set, **181**, 182
formal definition, 24
forward move, 238, **239**, 306, 308
free of hidden empty notions, 273
FSLR(k), **284**
full LL(1), 175-176, 182, 232, 244, 252
full LL(k), 182, 268, 289
fully parenthesized expression, **187**, 294

gap, 144, 146, 151, 199
general hyperrule, 273
Generalized Overlap-Resolvable, **296**
Generalized Phrase Structure Grammar, **301**
generative grammar, **18**, 24, 272
global error handling, **233**, 306, 308
GNF, *see* Greibach Normal Form
GOR, *see* Generalized Overlap-Resolvable
GOTO-action, **204**, 271, 283, 291
GPSG, *see* Generalized Phrase Structure Grammar
grammar, **17**
grammatical inference, **311**
Greibach Normal Form, **121**, 122-123, 127, 274-275

handle, **73**, 113, 184..206, 220, 222, 227, 232, 238, 244, 284-285, 289, 295-297
hardest CF language, **312**
head grammar, **272**
hypernotion, **44**, 273
hyper-rule, **44**

ID/LP grammar, *see* Immediate Dominance/Linear Precedence grammar
Immediate Dominance/Linear Precedence grammar, **301**
immediate error detection property, **175**, 176, 212, 231-233, 244, 306-308
immediate left-recursion, **128**
immediate successor, *see* successor
inadequate state, **205**, 208, 221-223, 284, 288, 291
incremental parser generation, 221, 291
incremental parsing, 221, 285..290, 300
indexed grammar, 42, **269**, 270
indirect left-recursion, **128**, 129, 168
infinite ambiguity, **57**, 96, 157
infinite symbol set, 45
infix notation, **64**, 68
inherited affix, 272
inherited attribute, 58
inherited information, **58**
insert-correctable, **244**
instantaneous description, **124**

item, **151**, 206
item grammar, **287**

keyword, *see* reserved word
Kleene star, **36**
known-parsing table, **260**

LALR(1), 79, 199, 233, 249..253, 269, 271, 283..292, 305, 308
LALR(1) automaton, **213**, 216, 218, 291
LALR(1,1), 289
LALR(k), **213**, 287, 307
LAM(m), **289**
lane, **285**
LAST set, 275
LAST$_{ALL}$ set, **195**
LAST$_{OP}$ set, **190**
LC(k), 292-293, 311
Least Left Corner, 289
least-error correction, **233**, 234..236, 246-247, 303-304
left bound, 273
left priority, **192**
left-context, 179, 238, **285**, 296
left-corner derivation, **64**
left-corner parsing, 68-69, **79**, 264-265, 273-274, 292-294, 300
left-factoring, **179**, 303, 310
left-hand side, **23**
left-most derivation, **50**, 51, 64, 101, 106, 120, 125, 127, 134-135, 167, 259
left-recursion, 79, 127, **128**, 135, 149, 168, 178, 253, 260, 274, 279, 294
lex, 39, 269, 299-300
lineage, **54**
linear grammar, **38**, 277
linear time dependency, **70**, 73, 76-77, 155, 191, 205, 213, 227, 249-252, 271, 297, 307, 311
linearized parse tree, **64**, 300
LL(1), 78, **170**, 167..183, 211, 243-245, 252-253, 267, 269, 273, 279-283, 292-293, 306-307
LL(1) conflict, **178**, 179, 183, 267, 289, 310
LL(2), 182
LLC, 289
LL(f), **279**
LL(k), 79, **181**, 182, 268, 271, 279-281, 284, 292-294, 307, 311-312
LL(k) item, 281
LLP(k), 292-294
LLR, *see* LL-regular
LL-regular, 228, 280-281, 297
local error handling, **233**, 240, 306, 308
locally least-cost error recovery, **246**, 307..311

locally unambiguous, 273
loop, **57**, 82-83, 86, 103, 128, 222
LR(0), 201, **205**, 204-206, 209, 212-214, 218,
    222, 226, 250, 283..293
LR(0) automaton, **203**, 204..222, 284..288
LR(1), 78, 197, 205..227, 233, 249..252, 267-
    269, 272, 282..292, 304, 309-310
LR(1) automaton, 206..217, 285
LR(2), 211-212
LR(k), 79, 211-213, 228, 268, 270, 281..294,
    304..312
LR(m, k), **285**
LR-regular, **221**, 283, 287, 297

macro grammar, **270**
Manhattan turtle, **27**
match, **72**
maze, 75-77, 110
metagrammar, 45
metanotion, **44**, 45-46, 272-273
metarule, **44**
minimum distance error handling, 303, 305, 308
mixed-strategy precedence, 197, **198**, 295..298,
    310
modifying a grammar, 77, 123, 196, 237, 249-
    252, 267, 310
Modula-2, 131, 137, 252

NCLR(1), **227**
NDA, *see* non-deterministic automaton
non-canonical parsing, 184, 227, 285-286, 291,
    297
non-deterministic automaton, **68**, 69..71, 75, 77,
    110-111, 118, 145, 201..218, 284
non-directional parsing method, 15, **74**, 75-76,
    79, 81, 230-231
non-productive non-terminal, 57, **96**, 94-98, 104
non-reachable non-terminal, **97**, 94..102
non-terminal, **23**
NQLALR(1), **288**, 290
nullable, 211, 216, 292, **306**
nullable grammar, 307

occam, 273
operator grammar, **190**, 191, 195
operator-precedence, **191**, 188..196, 232, 251,
    267, 269, 294, 297-298, 310-311
OR, *see* Overlap-Resolvable
original symbol, **54**
Overlap-Resolvable, **296**

panic mode, **240**, 241, 306..309
parse table, **165**, 166..183, 214, 220, 237, 252,
    268, 270, 276..298

parser generator, 37, 39, **69**, 78, 179-180, 183,
    204, 208, 214..221, 245, 250-252, 267,
    269, 281-282, 286..289, 299-300, 310
partial computation, 269
Pascal, 12, 15, 21, 60-61, 131, 133, 136-137,
    237, 240, 253, 258, 260, 269, 281, 307,
    310-311
pattern mapping, **305**
PDA, *see* pushdown automaton
phrase, **227**
phrase level error handling, **238**, 308, 310
phrase structure grammar, **25**, 26..28, 34, 41, 53,
    55, 60-61, 71, 76, 265, 271, 274, 301
PL/C, 303
PLR(k), 292-293
polynomial time dependency, **70**, 88, 253, 260,
    263, 277
postfix notation, **64**
precedence functions, **192**, 194, 252, 295-298
precedence relation, **187**, 188..190, 195..198,
    232, 238-239, 276, 295-298, 306
precedence table, **187**, 188, 196, 282, 311
predict, **72**
prediction stack, **121**, 122..131, 241, 275
predictive analyser, **275**
predictor, **307**
prefix notation, **64**
prefix-free, **136**
preliminary state, **271**
primitive predicate, **46**, 272
production chain, 38, **292**, 293
production expression, **293**
production graph, **25**, 28, 32, 51
production prefix, **284**
production rule, **25**
production step, **25**, 66, 73, 168, 242, 292
production tree, **32**, 38, 50..74, 120, 148, 269,
    275, 301
Prolog, 139-143, 253, 268, 279, 294, 302
Prolog clause, 141, 279, 294
propagated input, 215-216
proper grammar, 97, 242
pumping lemma for context-free languages, **55**
pumping lemma for regular languages, **56**
pushdown automaton, **121**, 122-123, 127, 292

quadratic time dependency, **70**, 155, 270, 276,
    278
quasi-regular grammar, 107-108, **299**

Rabin-Karp algorithm, 118
reachable non-terminal, **97**, 98, 102, 114
read-back tables, **286**
real-time parser, **70**, 302

recognition table, **93**, 94, 99-105, 231, 236, 277-278

recording grammar, 42, **270**

recursive ascent, **221**, 269, 291-292

recursive descent, 15, 76..79, **135**, 131..137, 180..183, 221, 241, 245, 252-253, 267..273, 277..282, 291-293, 300..307, 312

reduce, **73**

reduce/reduce conflict, **205**, 210, 217, 219, 288, 292

reduction error, **232**, 233, 306

reduction look-ahead, **161**, 162-163, 277

regional error handling, **233**, 238, 308

regional least-cost error correction, **308**

register-vector grammar, **301**, 302

regular expression, **36**, 40, 53, 113-116, 189, 299-300

regular grammar, **38**

regular language, 56, 107, 114, 299-300, 303, 311

regular right part grammar, **36**, 220, 285..290

reserved word, 40, 74, 286

RG, *see* recording grammar

right bound, 273

right precedence, **295**

right priority, **192**

right-hand side, **23**

right-most derivation, **51**, 64, 101, 106, 144, 184

RL(1), **78**, 286

R-language, **295**

RLL(*k*), **271**

RR(1), **78**

RRP grammar, *see* regular right part grammar

RV grammar, *see* register-vector grammar

RV grammar, 302

self-embedding, **266**, 299

semantic action, 180, 185, 204, 220, 230, 237, 251-252, 266, 280, 282, 286, 288, 299, 309

semantic clause, **57**, 58-59

semi-top-down, **293**

sentence, **25**

sentential form, **25**

sequence, **17**

set, **17**

SGML, **33**

s-grammar, **167**

shift, **73**

shift/reduce conflict, **205**, 206, 210, 219, 288, 292

simple chain grammar, **293**

simple LL(1), 281

simple LR(1), 218

simple precedence, **195**, 194-196, 232, 238, 284, 295..298, 306, 311

single rule, **89**, 220

skeleton grammar, **273**

SLL(1) (simple LL(1)), **167**, 170

SLL(1) (Simple LL(1)), 281

SLR(1), 79, **218**, 219, 222, 226, 233, 250-251, 269, 271, 283..298, 310

SLR(*k*), 283-284, 307

SLUNT, 302

soft precedence, **296**

space requirements, 155, 204, 213, 251-252, 269, 277, 288

spontaneous input, 215-216

spurious ambiguity, **62**

spurious error message, **230**, 246, 248

stack, **121**

stack alphabet, **121**

stack duplication, 223

stackability error, **232**, 306

stack-controlling LR parser, **287**

stacking conflict, **289**

stacking error, *see* stackability error

stack-shift, **289**

start symbol, **23**

state, **109**

state transition, **109**, 220, 283, 287

station, **201**, 203, 207, 210-211, 215-216

stochastic grammar, 304, **311**

strict grammar, **273**

strict syntax generator, **273**

strong compatibility, **285**

strong-LL(1), **174**, 175, 178, 181, 232, 244, 251-252, 270, 291, 303, 306-307

strong-LL(*k*), **181**, 182, 270, 280-281, 291

Subject-Verb-Object language, 107

submatrix technique, **290**

subset algorithm, 216

subset construction, **111**, 203..206, 271, 299

successor, 285

suffix-grammar, **247**, 248, 309

suffix-language, **247**

suffix-parser, **247**, 246-248

synchronization triplet, **306**

syntactic graph, *see* production graph

syntax, **17**, 34, 58, 266-267, 271, 273, 291, 300, 310-311

syntax error, 198, **229**, 230, 237, 246-248, 304, 308-310

syntaxis, *see* syntax

synthesized attribute, 58

synthesized metanotion, 273

table compaction, *see* table compression

table compression, 112, 204, 213, 268, 281..286, 290, 293, 296

table-driven, **69**, 180-181, 252, 269, 280, 282, 306

terminal, **23**, 41, 45, 49

terminal parser, **273**

terminal symbol, **23**

time complexity, **70**

time requirements, **70**, 251-252, 277-278, 284

token, *see* terminal symbol

Tomita notation, 226

Tomita parser, 15, 69, 79, 153, 157, 222, 226, 233, 250, 276..279, 291

top-down parsing, **64**

transduction grammar, 58, **59**, 266, 279

transformation rule, **265**

transformations on grammars, 53, 92..104, 115-116, 122, 127-128, 167, 170, 212, 251, 265, 267, 280, 291, 293, 295, 298, 303, 305, 310-311

transition diagram, **109**, 110-111, 266, 299, 303

transition successor, *see* successor

Type 1 context-sensitive, **29**, 51, 53

Type 1 monotonic, **29**, 31

typesetting, 11, 219, 267

Unger parser, 15, 75..92, 101, 103, 153, 156, 230..236, 250, 253, 275, 278

uniquely assignable, 273

unit rule, **89**, 90..92, 96, 98, 104, 113, 128, 191, 220, 283-288

unreduce, **145**, 147

unshift, **145**, 146-147

useless non-terminal, **57**

Valiant parser, 76, 277

viable suffix, 281

weak compatibility, **285**

weak operator-precedence, **297**

weak precedence, 196, **197**, 232, 252, 276, 295-298

weak-PLR(k), **294**

well-formed affix grammar, 272

well-formed substring table, *see* recognition table

well-formed substring table, 250, 260, 275..278

well-tuned Earley/CYK parser, 163

word, **17**

yacc, 214, 269, 285, 291

2-form grammar, **277**

$\aleph_0$, 22

$\aleph_1$, 22

ε-closure, **114**

ε-free, **34**, 52-53, 96, 122, 269, 274, 296, 311

ε-move, 113-114, **173**, 175, 202, 207, 232, 291, 301, 303

ε-rule, **34**, 52-53, 57, 73, 82, 85, 90..98, 104, 113, 123, 128, 136, 149, 157, 161, 168, 170, 173, 210-211, 216, 234, 244, 266, 272, 275, 279-280, 288, 290, 294, 311

ε-transition, 113, 201, 271

$\xrightarrow{}$, 51

$\xrightarrow{+}$, 51

$\xrightarrow{*}$, 51

$\nleftrightarrow$, 291

$\nvdash$, 291

$\lessdot$, **187**

$\lessgtr$, **197**

$\gtrdot$, **187**

$\doteq$, **187**

ELLIS HORWOOD SERIES IN COMPUTERS AND THEIR APPLICATIONS

Series Editor: IAN CHIVERS, Senior Analyst, The Computer Centre, King's College, London, and formerly Senior Programmer and Analyst, Imperial College of Science and Technology, University of London

Rahtz, S.P.Q.	INFORMATION TECHNOLOGY IN THE HUMANITIES
Ramsden, E.	MICROCOMPUTERS IN EDUCATION 2
Rubin, T.	USER INTERFACE DESIGN FOR COMPUTER SYSTEMS
Rudd, A.S.	PRACTICAL USAGE OF ISPF DIALOG MANAGER
Rudd, A.S.	PRACTICAL USAGE OF REXX
Rudd, A.S.	IMPLEMENTING PRACTICAL DB2 APPLICATIONS
de Saram, H.	PROGRAMMING IN MICRO-PROLOG
Savic, D.	OBJECT-ORIENTED PROGRAMMING WITH SMALLTALK/V
Schirmer, C.	PROGRAMMING IN C FOR UNIX
Schofield, C.F.	OPTIMIZING FORTRAN PROGRAMS
Sharp, J.A.	DATA FLOW COMPUTING
Sherif, M.A.	DATABASE PROJECTS
Smith & Sage	EDUCATION AND THE INFORMATION SOCIETY
Smith, J.M & Stutely, R.	SGML
Späth, H.	CLUSTER ANALYSIS ALGORITHMS
Späth, H.	CLUSTER DISSECTION AND ANALYSIS
Stratford-Collins, P.	ADA
Teunissen, W.J. & van den Bos, J.	3D INTERACTIVE COMPUTER GRAPHICS
Tizzard, K.	C FOR PROFESSIONAL PROGRAMMERS
Turner, S.J.	AN INTRODUCTION TO COMPILER DESIGN
Tsuji, T.	OPTIMIZING SCHEMES FOR STRUCTURED PROGRAMMING LANGUAGE PROCESSORS
Wexler, J.	CONCURRENT PROGRAMMING IN OCCAM 2
Whiddett, R.J.	CONCURRENT PROGRAMMING FOR SOFTWARE ENGINEERS
Whiddett, R.J., Berry, R.E., Blair, G.S., Hurley, P.N., Nicol, P.J. & Muir, S.J.	UNIX
Xu, Duan-Zheng	COMPUTER ANALYSIS OF SEQUENTIAL MEDICAL TRIALS
Yannakoudakis, E.J. & Hutton, P.J.	SPEECH SYNTHESIS AND RECOGNITION SYSTEMS
Zech, R.	FORTH FOR THE PROFESSIONAL

Computer Communications and Networking

Currie, W.S.	LANS EXPLAINED
Deasington, R.J.	A PRACTICAL GUIDE TO COMPUTER COMMUNICATIONS AND NETWORKING, 2nd Edition
Deasington, R.J.	X.25 EXPLAINED, 2nd Edition
Henshall, J. & Shaw, S.	OSI EXPLAINED, 2nd Edition
Kauffels, F.-J.	PRACTICAL LANS ANALYSED
Kauffels, F.-J.	PRACTICAL NETWORKS ANALYSED
Kauffels, F.-J.	UNDERSTANDING DATA COMMUNICATIONS
Muftic, S.	SECURITY MECHANISMS FOR COMPUTER NETWORKS